Stealing Games

A Call to Arms: Mobilizing America for World War II

The Power Makers: Steam, Electricity, and the
Men Who Invented Modern America

The Change Makers: From Carnegie to Gates, How the Great
Entrepreneurs Transformed Ideas into Industries

Days of Defiance: Sumter, Secession, and the Coming of the Civil War

The Genesis of Industrial America, 1870–1920

Unfinished Business: The Railroad in American Life

Union Pacific: Volume I, 1862–1893

Union Pacific: Volume II, 1894–1969

Union Pacific: The Reconfiguration: America's Greatest Railroad
from 1969 to the Present

The Great Richmond Terminal: A Study in Businessmen and
Business Strategy

The Life and Legend of E. H. Harriman

The Life and Legend of Jay Gould

Rainbow's End: The Crash of 1929

Prisoners of Progress: American Industrial Cities 1850–1920
(with Harvey A. Kantor)

History of the Louisville & Nashville Railroad

The Flowering of the Third America

Edward Porter Alexander

STEALING GAMES

*How John McGraw
Transformed Baseball
with the 1911
New York Giants*

MAURY KLEIN

BLOOMSBURY PRESS

NEW YORK · LONDON · OXFORD · NEW DELHI · SYDNEY

Bloomsbury Press
An imprint of Bloomsbury Publishing Plc

1385 Broadway	50 Bedford Square
New York	London
NY 10018	WC1B 3DP
USA	UK

www.bloomsbury.com

BLOOMSBURY and the Diana logo are trademarks of Bloomsbury Publishing Plc

First published 2016

ISBN: HB: 978-1-63286-024-8
       ePub: 978-1-63286-026-2

Library of Congress Cataloging-in-Publication Data
Names: Klein, Maury, 1939– author.
Title: Stealing games: the amazing 1911 New York Giants and their world /
Maury Klein.
Description: New York: Bloomsbury USA, 2016.
Identifiers: LCCN 2015036717 | ISBN 9781632860248 (Hardcover: alk. paper) |
ISBN 9781632860262 (ePub)
Subjects: LCSH: New York Giants (Baseball team)—History—20th century.
Classification: LCC GV875.N42 K56 2016 | DDC 796.357/6409747109041—dc23
LC record available at http://lccn.loc.gov/2015036717

2 4 6 8 10 9 7 5 3 1

Typeset by RefineCatch Limited. Bungay, Suffolk, UK
Printed and bound in the U.S.A. by Berryville Graphics Inc., Berryville, Virginia

To find out more about our authors and books visit www.bloomsbury.com. Here you will
find extracts, author interviews, details of forthcoming events and the option to sign up for
our newsletters.

For Kim, the guiding light, with love

Contents

CONTENTS

Introduction

FOR MANY DECADES BASEBALL RULED AS THE unchallenged national pastime of the United States. No other sport or activity had yet risen to the same prominence. Between 1900 and 1914 the game as we know it evolved through changes in the rules. The National League finally stabilized, a second major league emerged in 1901 and proved enduring, and within a few years the playing of a postseason series between the two pennant winners became a much-anticipated annual ritual. This book portrays this evolving process through the story of one National League team that was instrumental in changing the game, the 1911 New York Giants.

Then as now, baseball reflected in many ways the larger world around it. America in 1900 was a nation in transition with all the strains that come with accelerating change. The business of America was fast becoming big business. Two major forces, the industrial revolution and the organizational revolution, created a new society based on large, integrated organizations using the latest technology as well as cheap labor to increase productivity. A maturing industrial system displayed all its benefits in the form of a spectacular output of goods and all its liabilities in the host of social and economic problems that accompanied it.

The first generation of Americans born into an industrial society was coming of age and confronting these problems. Their efforts and the confusion surrounding them gave rise to a powerful but amorphous movement called Progressivism, which at its best looked to harness the forces of change to create a more orderly, stable, and humane nation. But that task grew ever more difficult because change came to American life at an ever-quickening pace. Everything seemed to be going faster, especially in the cities, those hotbeds of change. Then, between 1914 and 1918, a global cataclysm put an abrupt and unexpected end to the prewar world.

Baseball reflected these changes as it did so much else of American life. Managers increasingly referred to their teams as a machine, the parts of which had to be integrated as perfectly as possible to function effectively. Every player, however great his talent, was considered a single part of that machine. To win, a team had to perform as smoothly as a well-run production line. Maximum output depended not only on smooth coordination but speed as well, the ability to play the game at a faster and more alert pace than rival teams.

The two most obvious symbols of that faster pace in society were the automobile and the airplane. Baseball embodied it in the form of a new approach to the game that emerged in the 1890s with the Baltimore Orioles. Where teams had always preferred large, burly players who could hit the ball with authority, the Orioles built their team around speed, deception, clever play, and, above all, aggressiveness. Like the titans of industry they gave no quarter and asked none. Like George Washington Plunkitt, the fabled Tammany ward leader, they saw their opportunities and did whatever was necessary to win, sharpening both their spikes and their wits. Umpires no less than rival players became the targets of their belligerence. In the process they introduced or refined new tactics such as the hit-and-run, Baltimore chop, and delayed steal, and paid close attention to the smallest details of the contest.

Along with several championships the Orioles produced a crop of outstanding major league managers, such as Hughie Jennings, Wilbert Robinson, and Kid Gleason, who had imbibed the new style thoroughly. Foremost among them was John J. McGraw, who managed the Orioles briefly before leaving to oversee the New York Giants in 1902. He remained in that post for thirty-one years and compiled a record never equaled. During his reign the Giants won ten pennants and three World Series while finishing lower than fourth only twice. Even his worst enemies acknowledged his genius at every aspect of the game. "The little Napoleon," as the sportswriters dubbed him, was a man of startling contradictions, as fiercely combative on the field as he was generous and giving off of it. The style of play he introduced lasted for more than two decades before giving way grudgingly to the era of the long ball.

A word about statistics and box scores of the era. While the figures given in modern record books are doubtless the best we have, in 1911 scorekeepers were still trying to standardize their methods. My study leans heavily on contemporary newspaper accounts because baseball was followed so closely in the dailies by then. However, the sportswriters often did not agree either on the details of their scoring of a game or even on what actually happened, let alone the mood or attitude of the players involved. New York in 1911 had thirteen major daily newspapers; I have examined six or seven of them closely, as well as one Chicago and one St. Louis paper, and gleaned material from some of the others too. I also consulted the full set of box scores in *Sporting Life*, which billed itself as the "official record" of the National League. Comparing different accounts of any given game can be a frustrating experience, and at many points of disagreement among them I tended to rely on majority opinion.

In writing this book several people proved invaluable in the help they rendered. Emily Greene has been my go-to person at the University of Rhode Island's Carothers Library for many years. As with so many other books, she somehow managed to find for me nearly every source I asked for. At the National Hall of Fame Cassidy Lent expedited my research in many ways, not least of which was making available a wide range of source materials. My longtime agent, Marian Young, encouraged the project from the beginning, for which I am grateful as always. The book began its life under the aegis of Peter Ginna, my editor on other projects at Bloomsbury USA, but he left the house shortly after I started work. George Gibson stepped in as reliever and provided continual encouragement and enthusiasm throughout the writing process. I am grateful for his support. Once again my wife, Kim, endured my daily retreats to my basement office. Her support helped immensely to bring the book into being.

Maury Klein
Saunderstown, Rhode Island

Prologue: The Rite of Spring

*"When you train under most managers, you
merely get yourself in good physical condition.
When you train under McGraw, you learn
baseball."*

—ROGERS HORNSBY

*"He treats his players fairly, gives each one the
same deal, is the absolute boss, and plans his
games and executes his moves with the
precision of an expert chess player maneuvering
his pieces. McGraw will not brook
insubordination, and has a tongue which will
cut any man who crosses him in his judgment.
He never gives up, and this spirit of his has
been soaked up by the players on the Giants . . .
He drives unmercifully, and forgets everything
about the battle when it is over."*

—LITERARY DIGEST

IGOR STRAVINSKY'S REVOLUTIONARY BALLET, *Le Sacre du printemps*, would not appear for another two years, but in the United States most men, along with a surprising number of women, knew well and awaited eagerly our own version of the rite of spring built around the undisputed national pastime, baseball. In December the hot stove league heated up, fueled by rumors and fantasies of trades, acquisitions, and retirements. Within only a few weeks that sometimes seemed as long as geological eras the scattered practitioners of the game would leave their mundane off-season lives and occupations to congregate in camps designed to whip them into competitive shape and sharpen their instincts for the game they were fortunate enough to play for pay, however tough the toll on their minds and bodies.

In January 1911 the New York Giants looked to some to be the team to beat. "The way the bugs [fans] view things," reported *Sporting Life*, "the Cubs have gone and the Pirates are going, while the Giants are coming, and coming fast. The New York team made more runs than any club in the National League in 1910 and also hit harder. The Polo Grounds, unfortunately, had an erratic set of pitchers and also possessed the unhappy facility of making costly errors at the right time—for their opponents." The *New York Herald* agreed that the Giants would be stronger but cautioned that "the team is built around one man—a pitcher. Mathewson is his name . . . If Mathewson is as good this season as he was last, if he approaches his normal standard, the Giants should have an excellent chance. He has truly been called the god of the Polo Ground."[1]

Late in February the small town of Marlin, Texas, about thirty miles southeast of Waco, awoke from the silence of its usual obscurity to prepare eagerly for the coming of the Giants. The Chicago White Sox had trained there in 1904, followed by the St. Louis Cardinals in 1905 and the Cincinnati Reds in 1907, but none of them had returned after one season. This was the fourth seasonal visit of the Giants, who prior to 1908 had held their camps in such cities as Savannah, Birmingham, Memphis, and Los Angeles until manager John J. McGraw decided that he wanted the boys secluded in more isolated surroundings free from other distractions.[2]

"Marlin is a typical Texas town in appearance," reported Sam Crane of the *New York Evening Journal*, "with low, one-story stores and one main street. Saddle horses and mules are tied in front of the offices and stores." The team would headquarter at the Arlington Hotel, located at Marlin Springs, a spa about two miles east of town, noted for mineral waters that had drawn tourists since their discovery in 1892. The hotel's bathhouse was a magnet for players with sore and aching muscles.[3]

Early in December John Murphy, who along with his brother Tom had been McGraw's groundskeeper with the old Baltimore Orioles in the 1890s, arrived in Marlin to work his magic on the neglected surface of Emerson Park, named for the town's postmaster. The sons of Irish immigrants who had wound up in Indianapolis, the Murphy brothers had somehow found their way into an arcane business. In 1888, John had jumped at an opportunity to become the groundskeeper for an Indianapolis department store owner, John T. Brush, who had just acquired a National League franchise. Brush later became owner of the New York Giants. In 1904, after a nomadic career with other teams, John Murphy rejoined the Giants and remained with them until his death.[4]

Three years earlier, on his first sojourn to Marlin, Murphy found that "the grounds had been given up to steers, stray pigs and horses, so I had my work laid out to fix things right." Since then the field had remained in decent shape, and Murphy had mostly to groom it for the players, the first batch of whom boarded ship for the trip to Texas on February 11. Another group gathered in St. Louis two days later to make the journey by train under the eye of coach Wilbert Robinson, a fine former catcher and team-mate of McGraw on the old Baltimore Orioles and his longtime close friend. McGraw himself left early for Texas to visit with team owner John Brush, who had wintered in San Antonio to ease the pain of a crippling disease.[5]

Veteran players seldom looked forward to the ritual. As one Pittsburgh writer put it, "Men are loud in their protest against being dragged from their homes and in many cases their business and forced to drill for over a month and a half without pay." Salaries started only with the season, and many players needed the winter months to earn a living. However, their contracts obliged them to participate or pay a severe fine. They could try to skirt the requirement by holding out until camp had finished; Honus Wagner of the Pirates was not alone in playing this game. But McGraw made it clear that any Giant who had not signed his contract would have to pay his own way to camp as well as his hotel expenses. Once camp broke up, the team had twenty-two exhibition games on its schedule before opening day on April 12.[6]

"Spring training was the worst," declared outfielder Edd Roush. "Some of those parks they'd want you to play exhibition games in had outfields like sand dunes, and others were hard as a cement sidewalk. The hell with that! I wouldn't go to spring training, that's all. I used to hold out every year until the week before the season opened . . . Why should I go down there and fuss around in spring training? Twist an ankle, or break a leg."[7]

For the "yannigans," or rookies, spring training offered not ordeal but opportunity to show what they could do in hopes of catching on with a big-league club. It was an audition, possibly the only one they would ever get, and like most auditions it would disappoint far more hopefuls than it rewarded. "A young ball-player looks on his first spring training trip as a stage-struck young woman regards the theatre," said Christy Mathewson. "She cannot wait for her first rehearsal, and she thinks only of the lobster suppers and the applause and the lights and the life, but nowhere in her dream is there a place for the raucous voice of the stage manager and the long jumps of 'one night stands' with the loss of sleep and the poor meals and the cold dressing rooms. As actors begin to dread the drudgery of rehearsing, so do baseball men detest the drill of the spring training."[8]

The first arrivals were all rookies except for one special-case veteran, pitcher Bugs Raymond, who was on trial for quite another reason, and Beals Becker, a reserve outfielder trying to crack the starting lineup. Their ranks also included an umpire, Charles A. Hansel, hired by McGraw to work the intrasquad and exhibition games. One eager newcomer, Cy Forsythe, left his job in a coal mine to come to Marlin in January because McGraw wanted him to boil off some weight in the hot mineral waters before camp started.[9]

The group that assembled in Marlin on February 19 was the usual mix of highly touted and invited wannabes. A pair of Texans, first baseman Hank Gowdy and pitcher Walter Shontz, attracted attention because McGraw had outbid two other clubs to acquire them from Dallas of the Texas League. Gowdy had played in a few games for the Giants in 1910; so had two pitchers, Dick Rudolph and Ed Hendricks. They would be watched closely along with another strapping right-hander, Jeff Tesreau. Other promising newcomers included catcher Grover Cleveland Hartley, infielders Forsythe, Clyde Fullerton, and Frank Manush, and outfielders Jack Johnston, Maurice McKnight, and Ernie Lush. At Marlin they were greeted by cold, hard rain that forced Murphy to spend the afternoon draining the field as best he could.[10]

Along with the rookies Marlin welcomed the first contingent of New York reporters sent to cover spring training. Baseball had become a big business, and its presence in the papers had grown steadily. New York had no less than seven morning and six afternoon dailies, each with its own writers covering the Giants, the top team in town. Several specialized publications also concentrated on baseball, most notably *Sporting News*, *Sporting Life*, and *Baseball* magazine. Most of those who sent someone to spring training accepted the hospitality of the Giants, who paid their expenses because the coverage amounted to valuable free publicity.[11]

Getting to the field, two miles from the hotel, was itself a workout. On February 20, everyone, including McGraw, donned whatever uniform they had along with their sweaters and set out walking or running—depending on the manager's decree—along the railroad tracks near the hotel that ran by the field. A cold wind hurried them along and kept them moving once at the park. Raymond and Hendricks both had pounds to shed and were told to run around the field eight times. Robinson took charge of the pitchers, getting them to loosen up easily before throwing nothing balls to the hitters in batting practice. Little fielding was done because McGraw didn't want to risk injuries to cold fingers. After a two-hour workout the team trotted back to the hotel for lunch, then returned to the field for an afternoon workout followed by relief in the baths and a massage by trainer Ed Mackall.[12]

On day two the workouts began in earnest despite a cold north wind. McGraw had decided to convert Gowdy into a catcher, and he spent considerable time drilling the men on proper bunting techniques. McKnight, who was small and fast, tried to leave the plate too quickly while Gowdy, big and slow, swung late and got away late. "Get on your toes so that you can run at the crack of the bat," McGraw told him. "The only way to keep from being slow is to start quickly. McKnight starts too quickly and you start too late." After practice ended, an impressed Johnston told a *New York World* reporter, "I've learned more about the little things at the plate than I had in the two whole years that I have played in the minor league." While the team toiled, Murphy put together a sliding box of loose earth and sand so that the players could practice the fadeaway slide that McGraw insisted was the best method.[13]

Spring training was a special time for McGraw. Although he had played his last regular season game in 1902 and made only token appearances since then, he worked out with the men in uniform, directed their practices, and played in most of the exhibition games at whatever position he was needed, including pitcher. When not playing he often umpired. So, too, with Arlie Latham, the clown prince of the Giants and the man outfielder Fred Snodgrass called "a fine fellow, but . . . probably the worst third-base coach who ever lived." E. H. Simmons of *Sporting Life* agreed that Latham had "undoubtedly lost a lot of games by bad coaching. He got so unreliable that in a tight pinch McGraw would shift him from third to first and take the third line himself." Latham had been a good third baseman in his day but his last full season was 1895; even so, he filled in during intrasquad and exhibition games as needed. So did Wilbert Robinson.[14]

In the first intrasquad game between Robinson's "Marbleheads" and Latham's "Lignum Vitaes," McGraw gave an artful demonstration by dropping a perfect bunt toward first base to score the winning run. "Half the battle in training players in spring practice is to be able to do the thing that you want them to grasp," he declared. "Nothing so impresses your pupils, old or young, with the correctness of your ideas and system as personal demonstration." He let the pitchers go only two innings and forbade them to throw curveballs so soon in camp. After the six-inning contest he kept the men on the field another half hour for batting and fielding practice.[15]

At midnight on the twenty-fourth most of the team boarded a train for Dallas, where they pounded that city's minor-league club, 8–0 and 11–1. Before their departure, Marlin citizens at the intrasquad game presented John Murphy with an Elks emblem in thanks for his beautiful work on Emerson Park. "Murphy has allowed his love of landscape gardening to have free rein," marveled one reporter. The *New York Times* man said that "Murphy can make grass grow on the bald spots of a baseball diamond faster than any groundkeeper in captivity." Not content to create a fine playing field, he adorned it all around with plantings. An eight-foot fence, paid for by the locals, enclosed the field. Shortly afterward, Murphy left for New York to ply his craft on the Polo Grounds in preparation for opening day on April 12.[16]

Warm weather finally arrived, and every day McGraw put the yannigans through their ritual of practice, running, instruction, and games. "My pitchers are always my first study," he explained. "There are so many boxmen and some so green that to size them up intelligently and fairly is a long and difficult task." Christy Mathewson believed that pitchers had "the hardest time of any of the specialists who go into camp." Over the years he had seen many young pitchers ruin their careers by trying too hard too early to make the team. One of the youngsters, named Nagle, tried to impress by throwing at full speed from the very first. Within three days his arm was so sore that he needed a sling and did little pitching the rest of camp. Much of the time McGraw pitched batting practice at a time when no screens or other protection were used.[17]

For the last week in February the rookies had him all to themselves and worked hard to impress as well as learn. The work of the two veterans in camp pleased McGraw even more. Beals Becker, the diminutive outfielder with surprising power, hit well from the start, while Bugs Raymond dutifully shed excess poundage, rounded into shape, and, most important of all, stayed sober and out of trouble. A chronic alcoholic, Raymond had spent much of the fall in an Illinois sanitarium taking the Keeley or Gold Cure to dry out, which accounted for his excess weight. On the mound he was an amazing maestro of the spitball; off it he was a clown with an insatiable thirst and an unmatched gift for getting into trouble. On the eve of his third season with the Giants, he had been told in no uncertain terms by McGraw that this was his last chance to stay clean.

Raymond had not finished his term at the Keeley Institute. In fact, he had been expelled for scaring his roommate, an older businessman, half to death with some rugged horseplay. But he came to camp proud of his time there, wearing a class button and proudly showing an album containing photographs and other souvenirs of his fellow inmates. "He really had quit drinking," McGraw said later. "I never saw him look better." The question, as always with Bugs, was how long the good behavior would last.[18]

Rain wiped out practice on the twenty-eighth, the day the regulars were due in town. Billy Gray, the Giants secretary, arrived on a morning train, as did pitcher Louis Drucke. The only unsigned player, Drucke greeted McGraw by handing him his contract, saying it was easier to carry than to mail. The big, fireballing, right-handed Texan had been hailed as "the Pitching Find of 1910" when he compiled a record of 12–10 for the Giants. Sam Crane hailed him as "a coming Mathewson . . . He is crude of course, but . . . he is one of the most promising pitchers that has ever broken into the business." Mathewson was reputed to have worked with him even to the point of teaching him the famous fadeaway pitch that he alone used. Like many young hurlers, Drucke suffered from control problems, but he had come along fast. McGraw hoped that 1911 would be the year he emerged as the strong starter desperately needed to reinforce Mathewson.[19]

That afternoon a crowd of citizens along with the rookies gathered at the depot to welcome the 4:20 train from St. Louis bearing most of the Giants regulars. Catcher John Tortes "Chief" Meyers was the first to disembark amid the crowd's applause. Behind him came pitchers Red Ames, George "Hooks" Wiltse, Doc Crandall, Rube Marquard, and the crowd favorite, Christy Mathewson, infielders Fred Merkle, Larry Doyle, Al Bridwell, Art Devlin, and Art Fletcher, and outfielders Red Murray and Josh Devore. Catchers Art Wilson and Admiral Schlei came to Marlin on their own, as did Fred Snodgrass, who arrived the next day from Los Angeles. Mathewson brought along his wife and young son, Wiltse his wife, and Devlin his brother-in-law "to show him the beauties of Texas and a real baseball team." Their arrival filled the Arlington with players who had nothing to do as the rain continued. Becker, Raymond, and Hendricks tried to go for a run but got bogged down in the mud and soon returned.[20]

Cloistered in the hotel with little to do but play checkers or dominos— strict Texas law forbade poker for money in public—the two groups sized each other up: the regulars with jobs they were determined to keep against all comers, and the rookies equally determined to win a place on the team, hopefully as a starter. Raymond and Becker alone moved easily among the regulars. Mathewson had put on fourteen pounds, which he said he needed, while Meyers needed to sweat off some extra weight. Marquard, the southpaw who had greatly disappointed expectations for two and a half years, towered over the others at nearly six-four. Wilbert Robinson was assigned the vital task of turning Marquard into a productive asset for the Giants.[21]

Robinson, nicknamed Robbie, had been out of baseball since 1904 and was managing a meat market in Maryland when McGraw summoned him. In 1908 the Giants had paid a record price for Marquard, who had flopped dismally since then. Both Robinson and McGraw still thought he had great stuff, and that what he needed most was a massive dose of self-confidence. To help in that department, McGraw shrewdly assigned Marquard to room with Mathewson, who willingly tutored him in the fine arts of control, proper mechanics, and when to throw what pitch to which batter. Matty even taught him the fadeaway and helped him master the changeup, what Marquard liked to call his "turkey trot" pitch. If Marquard could overcome his wildness, his fear of crowds, and his sensitivity to criticism, McGraw thought, he might finally realize the potential the Giants had seen in him.[22]

Writers were free in their assessments of what the Giants needed to take home the pennant. Simmons thought the infield had "lost more games by bad fielding than by any other method." He singled out Larry Doyle as the main culprit and suggested shifting him to the outfield and finding a better second baseman. Hartley was "touted as the best young catcher of the year," and the Giants urgently needed a backup to Meyers, whose "catching is not up to what the fielding of a World's Champion catcher ought to be." However, he applauded McGraw's grit in sticking with Fred Merkle after the fiasco of 1908 when everyone cried for his head. McGraw was impressed by young Hartley but he already had a good candidate for backup catcher in Art Wilson, who had been sick for most of 1910 and got into only twenty-six games. "He is not only a good man behind the plate," he told Simmons, "but he can peg fast and accurate, and can also slam the ball." Gowdy was learning the position very quickly. Simmons pronounced him as "good a catcher right now as Chief Meyers was two years ago." And what of Admiral Schlei, who had served as backup since 1909?[23]

Relations between the veterans and the newcomers could be touchy. "It was practically impossible for a youngster, a rookie, to get up to the plate in batting practice," claimed Snodgrass. "Those old veterans weren't about to make it easy for him to take away one of their jobs." Art Devlin was one regular who might well have been looking over his shoulder. Long regarded by many as the best third baseman in the league, he had endured sneers from veterans who called him "McGraw's college boy" when he first joined the team in 1904. He had more than proven his worth over the years, but he was thirty-one years old on a team built around youth, and one of the hottest prospects among the yannigans was third baseman Frank Manush, fresh from the New Orleans club. Simmons called him "by far the best fielding and throwing third baseman ... since Arthur Devlin ... made good several years ago."[24]

Mathewson thought the old-timers were often more helpful to the rookies than most people supposed. "When a young player really seems to want to know something, any of the older men will gladly help him, but the trouble with most of them is that they think they are wonders when they arrive." When a rookie wanted to see how he held his curveball, Mathewson willingly showed him. When the kid asked him if he thought Honus Wagner was as good as Ty Cobb, however, Matty said curtly, "Listen! Did you come down here to learn to play ball or with the idea that you are attending some sort of conversational soiree?" Even Charles Hansel, the umpire, was there to gain experience in hopes of landing a major-league job. Already the rookies had practiced the art of giving him a hard time. McGraw had brought him along, quipped one reporter, "as a sort of bone for the players to gnaw on." Hansel took a philosophical approach to his rude treatment. "If I fail to get back to New York," he said, "just tell the boys that I died game."[25]

On the morning of March 1 the rain finally gave way to a chilly wind. After lunch McGraw ordered the troops to assemble on the hotel lawn. Bundled in their heavy sweaters, they played catch gingerly before retreating to the bathhouse. Mathewson was the lone absentee, having gone duck hunting with Billy Gray and Wilbert Robinson; his exercise consisted of wading through marshes. He knew what lay ahead. "Nothing looms on the horizon," he sighed, "but the hardest five weeks' grind in the world." It began the next morning promptly at nine. After leading them to the park, McGraw instructed the rookies for an hour before the regulars arrived for their first workout before an audience of locals black and white. The sun shone brightly, summer-like warmth had returned, and the players finally got limber for the first time. After a lap around the field they trotted down the tracks to the hotel for lunch. Then it was back to Emerson Park, where McGraw had a pleasant surprise for them: Even though it was the first day for the regulars, he decided to play a six-inning game between them and the yannigans after some practice.[26]

The regulars expected to lose these early games and they did, but only by 3–2. The regular pitchers did some warming up but none of them pitched. Next day McGraw split the players into two mixed squads of rookies and veterans, an innovation he had come up with the previous year. One team went to Dallas to play over the weekend while the other traveled to Waco for games there. This arrangement gave all the players more time on the field. McGraw took charge of the Waco squad, team captain Larry Doyle the Dallas group. Before leaving, the rookies handed the regulars a 10–1 thumping in a five-inning game. McGraw pitched the final inning for both sides.[27]

Only a few regulars joined the traveling squads. Most stayed behind to continue their workouts. To everyone's surprise Raymond continued on the straight and narrow path of sobriety. He ran hard to shed poundage and accompanied McGraw's team to Waco. The traveling teams both split their weekend games and returned to Marlin late at night. On the morning of the sixth, after a pair of laps around the field, McGraw let the pitchers snap off their first curveballs. The sliding box came into use for the first time and saw heavy duty every day with McGraw supervising. That afternoon the rookies beat the regulars again 7–4 in what Arlie Latham called the "great moving picture" game. All day long a motion picture man filmed practice and the game from as many angles as possible.[28]

On Tuesday the seventh the temperature climbed into the high eighties. McGraw had the men break out the giant pushball and shove it around for an hour or so. The afternoon featured a ceremony at the park in which Mayor F. S. Hafner and Postmaster Emerson of Marlin presented McGraw with a deed to Emerson Park, good for as long as the Giants continued to train there. The mayor lobbed a ball to Chief Meyers, then retreated to his automobile to watch what McGraw arranged to be the "boob" championship between the two teams that had gone to Dallas and Waco, with five quarts of ice cream at stake. After an intense struggle the Waco squad prevailed 5–3 with the motion picture camera again capturing all the day's festivities.[29]

A year earlier George Carter, the president of Marlin's Commercial Club, had broached to McGraw the novel idea of a club owning its training facilities. The team had become the town's claim to fame along with its hot springs, and Carter was eager to keep the Giants coming as an attraction. There was talk of piping hot mineral water to a bathhouse on the grounds for next season, and plans had been made to spend half a million dollars on a new hotel in town. The goal was to promote Marlin as a first-class health resort with the Giants as an annual attraction. To that end, the deed was made out in McGraw's name and embraced not only the field but several surrounding acres on the edge of town. No other major-league team owned its own spring training grounds.[30]

The next day grew so hot that McGraw skipped the intrasquad game and simply held practice. Bunting, batting, and sliding took priority, followed by races around the bases between players of equal speed. McGraw got the idea after racing Chief Meyers around the bases, finishing in a dead heat and collapsing from exhaustion in the heat. He then paired off the players for races and even included one between Hansel and the portly Robinson. Both men claimed victory and agreed to run again the next day for a side bet. After the inevitable lap around the field, some of the players muscled the pushball all the way back to the bathhouse. Mathewson ducked practice altogether, staying at the hotel to play checkers, a game at which he was expert. No one objected to his absence; he had long been in the habit of setting his own training regimen.[31]

Everyone was into the routine now, even the club secretary, Billy Gray, whose vigorous workouts with the team enabled him to shed fifteen pounds in only a few days. Some veterans had their own peculiar routines. Mathewson marveled at Wiltse's preparation. "He is a tireless worker," he said, "and when he is not pitching he is doing hand springs and other acrobatic acts to limber up all his muscles. It is torture then, but it pays in the end." Some of the rookie pitchers complained of sore arms, and Rube Marquard made himself the first real casualty by horsing around on the six-foot pushball and toppling off, knocking himself out and injuring his jaw. Asked if his head was okay, he replied sheepishly, "You can't hurt wood." That night he ate soup instead of steak for dinner.[32]

For the next two weeks every day featured similar rounds of batting, fielding, and sliding practice with McGraw personally overseeing the fade-aways until they were to his liking. Intrasquad games followed practice except on days when teams were put together to play exhibitions against

Texas teams. As the regulars regained their legs and timing, the clashes with the rookies grew more feisty. Neither group wanted to lose, and McGraw loved their competitive spirit. When Red Ames unleashed his vaunted curveball, it baffled the yannigans.[33]

On occasion the team charged admission for the practice games, donating the proceeds to local organizations such as the Marlin chapter of the Daughters of the Confederacy. McGraw allowed the teams to play nine innings instead of six, and in that game the spectators got their money's worth. No less than six home runs were hit, and Devore again provided comic relief. Having forgotten his sunglasses, he lost a fly ball in the sun that bounced off his head for a triple. It was good experience, left being the sun field at the Polo Grounds. In that same game Mathewson made his debut on the mound, hurling three innings to a roar of approval. Only after his departure, and that of Ames, did the game turn into a slugfest with a final score of 9–6.[34]

Afterward twenty-five of the players hurried to change and catch an early train to Fort Worth, where Marquard made his spring debut in a win over Dallas. With Bridwell sidelined by a sore heel, McGraw played shortstop. Showing old-time form, he handled four chances, started a double play, and knocked in two runs with a perfect day at the plate that included a single, two walks, a sacrifice fly, and a stolen base. Behind Crandall and Marquard the regulars blanked Dallas 6–0 while the rookies lost 1–0 to Fort Worth. Switching places the next day, the regulars crushed Fort Worth 13–0 as the rookies pounded out twenty hits in a 10–8 win over Dallas. Both teams took a sleeper back to Marlin and spent the night on a siding so as not to disembark in the middle of the night.[35]

The routine was fast turning into a grind, especially for the rookies wondering if and when their day of departure might soon be coming. To their surprise the first defector was umpire Hansel. The regulars had tested him severely since their arrival in camp, kicking about calls in true McGraw fashion. During the intrasquad game on a chilly first day back in Marlin, Hansel had to endure a disputed call from Fred Merkle in the third inning. As tempers heated, Hansel walked off the field and handed his baseballs to McGraw, saying, "Go in and umpire yourself; you're the only man who can get away with it." McGraw tried in vain to get Latham to umpire, then took up the job himself. The next day Hansel declared that he would umpire no more intrasquad games. When rain canceled the game that afternoon, McGraw talked to reporters about potential changes in the roster. Already

Maurice McKnight, who had been recommended to McGraw by Cubs catcher Johnny Kling, had gone home to Kansas City on his own even though McGraw liked his style of play.[36]

McGraw had the men playing two games a day along with their regular workouts. In one game Red Murray wowed everyone by becoming the first Giant to hit a ball over the fence at Emerson Park. A right-handed batter, he smacked it over the right-field fence. On St. Patrick's Day, Doyle and Murray presented every player with a green bow to tie around his left arm. That afternoon the Giants agreed reluctantly to play the Marlin high school team in a benefit for the local Catholic church. "Watching the slaughter was punishment," noted a reporter. Although McGraw used a total of thirty players, the Giants won the massacre 23–4. In the evening the team was treated first to a smoker at the Elks Lodge and then to "the biggest ball of Marlin's social season" at the hotel. They danced until midnight, when the men, divided among three teams, boarded trains for Galveston, Houston, and San Antonio.[37]

The San Antonio group, mostly regulars headed by McGraw, were especially pleased. They wanted to see not only the local sights but evidence of the big troop buildup splashed all over the newspapers. A long-smoldering revolution had broken out in Mexico against President Porfirio Díaz, prompting President William Howard Taft to dispatch twenty thousand American troops to the border. Owner John Brush greeted the players at the station, disappointed that a severe rainstorm canceled all baseball activities for the day. While Brush and McGraw conferred, some of the players went by automobile to visit the Alamo and the military encampment at Fort Sam Houston. "San Antonio is jammed full of soldiers," observed a *New York Press* reporter, "and there is as much talk of war as there is in the major league newspapers in the winter time when the American and National leagues have one of their little disagreements." Later McGraw and Chief Meyers called on General W. H. Carter, commander of the fort, who showed them the sea of tents spread across the prairie.[38]

The following day several hundred of the soldiers braved a sea of mud to watch the Giants win a sloppy squeaker from the San Antonio Broncos, 2–1. Brush watched the game from his automobile parked behind center field. Next day the team moved to Austin, where a large crowd gathered on advance notice that Mathewson would pitch. He did not disappoint, blanking the local team for five innings. Hooks Wiltse, playing right field because Murray had gone to join the Galveston team, switched places with

Mathewson in the sixth and completed the shutout, thanks in part to a sweet play by Matty, who made a fine catch and turned it into a double play. Austin's starting pitcher, a deaf-mute named Jenkins, got a pleasant surprise in discovering that Mathewson and other Giant veterans could converse with him in sign language. They had picked it up some years earlier from a deaf-mute teammate named Luther "Dummy" Taylor.[39]

When all the teams returned to Marlin late on the night of March 20, they had only four more days of training before heading out on the exhibition trail that would lead them to New York. Next afternoon McGraw put the regulars at their usual positions and drilled them hard on fast infield work and signals before the usual six-inning intrasquad game. The regulars took this one 5–0, the first shutout in what both sides considered to be the Championship of Emerson Park. Raymond, still working hard, had shed more than twenty-five pounds from his frame and mowed the rookies down, striking out six in three innings; Wiltse finished the job. A pleased McGraw told Raymond to cut loose and he did, leaving observers even more convinced that he could be a major factor for the Giants in the pennant race. For his part Raymond informed his teammates that thereafter he preferred being called Arthur.[40]

Another hour of fielding and sliding practice after the game left the players tired and eager for the warm baths. One writer wondered aloud why "men who play on a ball club as much as three years find it much more difficult to get in condition than the youngsters who have never reached the big league." McGraw thought it was because veterans were worked so hard during the season that their muscles grew more set in the off season. The cerebral Johnny Evers of the Chicago Cubs offered another explanation. "Conditioning for baseball," he observed, "is unlike training for any other sport . . . The ball player must begin March 1 to work for the maximum of speed, agility and strength, yet store up enough reserve power to carry him to October 15." No other sport had so long a season with so many games making constant demands on speed, stamina, strength, and flexibility. And always there loomed the threat of injuries large and small, which many of the Giants had already discovered anew.[41]

"Massage, baths, and the use of every conceivable device," added Evers, "goes on steadily fourteen hours a day . . . The players are working for individual condition and effectiveness in their own way." Some considered the charley horse an injury peculiar to baseball. In the battle to stay fit the players relied heavily on the overworked trainer. Ed Mackall of the Giants put in a longer day than any of the players. Bert Simmons, the Cubs' trainer, actually kept a log of his work one season and found that between March 1 and October 16 he massaged an average of eleven men every day along with treating 181 cuts, wounds, abrasions, sprains, broken bones, spike cuts, and sliders (skin torn off while sliding). In the process he used nearly forty quarts of antiseptic lotion. On most teams the trainer served, in Evers's words, as "expert masseur, something of a medical practitioner, surgeon, nurse, osteopath, bat boy, assistant ticket taker, general all-around man, and the object of the wrath of every player who happens to have a grievance."[42]

On the twenty-second the Giants again got to combine business with pleasure. After practice, a procession of automobiles and carriages led by Mayor Hefner appeared at the hotel to carry the players off to the falls of the Brazos River, about five miles away, for the annual fish fry. A large number of citizens welcomed them at a country club by the river, where the players gorged themselves on gaspergou fresh caught from the river and fried before their eyes. The meal gave way to songs by a black quartet and a few brief speeches before the players returned to the hotel around six thirty.[43]

The next day a large crowd turned out to watch an intrasquad game played for the benefit of Marlin's Ladies Social Club. This time Raymond pitched for the rookies and stifled the regulars for five innings with Hendricks completing the 3–0 whitewash. Cy Forsythe, who had hit well all along, outdid himself with a single, double, triple, and walk in five trips to the plate. That evening the Giants repaid the hospitality of the locals by hosting a "dress suit and low neck" ball at the hotel. Some two hundred invitations were sent out. Art Devlin took charge of all the arrangements, hired a Waco orchestra to provide the music, and proudly led the grand march. On this occasion McGraw allowed the punch to be spiked with champagne, taking care to keep Raymond away from it. The dancing lasted well into the morning hours.[44]

If the players thought McGraw would let them sleep in the next morning, they got a rude awakening when he sent porters to haul those out of bed who failed to respond to the morning call. Devlin alone was left undisturbed because of the time and energy he put into organizing the ball. Practice began at eleven and lasted only an hour, after which the men hurried back to pack their trunks and have lunch. Mackall kept busy stowing gear into a large hamper and packing other equipment. News came of the death of M. Stanley Robison, owner of the St. Louis Cardinals. He had become the team's president two years earlier when his brother died; now no one knew what the team's fate would be.[45]

At two o'clock the team trotted back to Emerson Park for one last practice. McGraw had reluctantly agreed to play a short exhibition game with the town team to raise money for uniforms for them. The Giants brushed them aside 10–2, after which Mackall stuffed the last of the equipment into the hamper and clamped a padlock on the gate to the field. Spring training in Marlin was over for another year. Several town notables went to the depot to bid the team farewell; the scribes, as they liked to call themselves, had already departed. McGraw divided the team into three units, two of which went to Dallas and Fort Worth; the third, nearly all of them rookies, was sent to San Antonio under the charge of Latham and would not join the others until later. Robinson was supposed to oversee the yannigans but he asked to keep working with Marquard.[46]

Marquard and Raymond remained McGraw's best bets for reliable seconds to Mathewson. The sagas of both pitchers had gone on long enough to turn into a soap opera. Both had pitched well in the spring, reviving hopes that had been dashed in previous seasons. "If Marquard could only realize some of these brilliant hopes upon his return that he inspires every spring in the training camp," wrote E. H. Simmons, "it would, of course, mean a vast deal for the Giants, but he has disappointed us all so many times in this way that we don't dare hope too much for fear of being once more disappointed."[47]

Ahead lay two weeks of meandering travel and exhibition games. On the road, and especially on the train, the rule of seniority prevailed. Rookies never received a lower berth until all the regulars had been provided one or elected to sleep in an upper. The camaraderie among the players often sorted itself into the close circle of regulars and the looser collection of newcomers. On these early trips most of the yannigans traveled elsewhere to play under McGraw's system of splitting the squad into separate teams.[48]

All three teams met with rainouts on their first day. McGraw surprised everyone with his first cut, selling Cy Forsythe to the Dallas club. Before his departure, the other rookies presented him with a silver watch fob. The Dallas and Fort Worth Giants reached Birmingham on the morning of the twenty-eighth and played a game with the Birmingham Barons, which they barely won 7–6 despite having Mathewson and Wiltse on the mound. "It has been some time since a minor-league team lit on Mathewson with so much vigor," commented one New York scribe.[49]

From Birmingham the team pushed on to Atlanta, where the weather was so cold and windy that McGraw called off morning practice but decided to play the afternoon game against the Atlanta Crackers. Before a crowd that barely outnumbered the players, the Giants prevailed 10–3. Throughout the game an oversized fan named King Brewster spewed invective at the Giants until the umpire told him to shut up. When the Giants reported at one o'clock the next afternoon for practice before the game, Brewster was there again, this time on the field mingling with the Atlanta players. He started insulting Meyers; the Chief moved to silence him until McGraw restrained him. Al Bridwell, "the quietest ball player in the business," happened by and Brewster transferred his insults to him. Although much smaller and lighter, Bridwell lit into Brewster with punches to his generous stomach until his arms grew tired.[50]

Brewster then turned his abuse to Mathewson, who told him to get off the field. He dared Mathewson to make him leave, and Christy went at it with him. The Atlanta manager waded into the melee to break it up, but Murray thought he was going after Mathewson and put him on the ground. Finally Brewster left the field and the two managers calmed the players down. By the time the game started, both teams were laughing at the whole affair. Devore led off with a single and stole second, Doyle followed with a long home run, and the Giants romped to an 11–0 victory. Reporters lapped it all up. "This series with the Atlanta Crackers," chortled the *New York Press*, "is getting to be more fun than an old-fashioned circus, a dog fight and a battle royal, all under one tent."[51]

The third day of what another reporter called "the battle of Atlanta" produced more fisticuffs and a farce of a game, this time on a bright, warm day. As both teams were warming up beforehand, the Crackers third baseman made slurring remarks about the Giants being "yellow dogs for jumping on one man yesterday." Devlin challenged him to fight. The players formed a ring and Devlin handed him a good thrashing before he quit. Fans had not yet arrived at the game, but the reporters were there to record the fun. The verbal sniping continued during the game, in which the umpire caught the spirit of the day by missing one call after another. By the fifth inning he had ejected Marquard, Merkle, and Devlin. McGraw took Merkle's place on first, then moved to the mound because he had no other pitcher warmed up when Marquard departed. Robinson became his catcher, and Latham played third. With this jumbled lineup the Giants batted freely out of turn and won 11–1 as McGraw baffled the Crackers with slow stuff.[52]

A decent crowd of about four hundred fans turned out the next day in hopes of more combat, but all they saw was a ball game in which the Giants fumbled their way to a 6–5 loss in ten innings. Fittingly, the winning run scored on an error by Doyle, one of five committed by the Giants along with a wild pitch. McGraw vowed not to come back to Atlanta because of the weather, poor attendance, and lack of a place to hold morning practices. April 2 was the first ideal day for a baseball game, but it was Sunday and Atlanta, like New York City, prohibited games on the Sabbath. Instead the players loafed in the sunshine before moving on to Greensboro, North Carolina, and then Richmond, where cold and rain greeted them.[53]

McGraw was pleased with the shape of the team. Everyone came through spring camp in good shape, and none of the pitchers had sore arms. The final stop on the exhibition tour was Baltimore, where McGraw first won fame as a major leaguer and found a wife. Baltimore pitcher Jimmy Dygert, a former Philadelphia Athletics spitballer, held the Giants to two runs in seven innings only to weaken in the eighth, when the Giants poured seven runs across the plate to win 9–4.[54]

"Well, here they are, Mr. Fan," blared the *World* beneath a team picture when the Giants finally reached New York on April 8. "Look 'em all over and then tell your next door neighbor that 'there's the bunch that'll cop the pennant.'" Pundits believed that for all the hoopla about some of the rookies, McGraw would start the season with the same lineup that finished the 1910 race. The team was young, fast, quick, and gaining experience. The pitching staff looked improved, especially if Marquard and Raymond performed well. For once, McGraw did not look to make other acquisitions but seemed content with what he had.[55]

It had become a tradition for the Giants to play an exhibition double-header against Yale at the Polo Grounds after their return to New York, giving New Yorkers their first look at the team. On a frigid afternoon braved by about three thousand fans, the Giants, playing in their heavy sweaters, blanked the collegians in two five-inning games with the regulars playing one and the rookies the other. "The athletes limbered up delicately," wrote one reporter, "giving the impression that they were tossing eggs instead of baseballs." Three final exhibition games remained. On a cold, windy day a large contingent of fans followed the Giants to Jersey City, where the team bested the Skeeters 6–3 on a muddy field that, quipped one writer, "had 'Josh' Devore howling for rubber boots."[56]

Next day Jersey City returned the visit and was walloped 16–5 at the

Polo Grounds with Mathewson pitching seven innings followed by Raymond. The team scored twice in the first inning and ten times in the third on twenty-one hits. "When the game is sifted down to the sediment," observed the *Herald*, "just one thing impressive remains, and that is the speed shown by the Giants. Their ability to make the most of a little batting capital was striking—not that they hadn't copious capital."[57]

In their final tune-up at the Polo Grounds on April 11 the Giants downed the Newark Indians, a team managed by former Giant pitching great Joe McGinnity, 5–1. McGraw pronounced the team ready for opening day against the Phillies. John Murphy had the field in fine shape, the Polo Grounds had been refurbished, and the usual wave of preseason excitement had begun to mount. Owner John Brush, whose illness had worsened during the previous summer, returned from his exile in Texas for the opening of the campaign. The owners were no less eager than the players for the season to begin. Even without yet paying salaries they had shelled out a total of more than half a million dollars, according to the *New-York Tribune*. About $300,000 had gone to acquire young players and another $200,000 for spring training expenses to get their teams in shape and find out whether any of the new players were worth the money spent on them.[58]

"The test of the major league player is brains and quick thinking," said the *Tribune*. The reporter thought that two men "stand head and shoulders above all others in being able to pick out the brainy men and in knowing a ball player when they see one. These are John J. McGraw ... and Connie Mack, manager of the Philadelphia Athletics." Mack's team had won the World Series in 1910 and looked to be even stronger this year. The reporter recalled a day in Marlin Springs when McGraw pointed to Cy Forsythe and said simply, "That man won't do." Why not? asked the reporter. Forsythe had both hit and fielded well, and looked to be a sure thing. McGraw stood silently for a while, watching Forsythe pull down some high and wide throws to first.[59]

"Did you see him make that last play?" he said at last. "There was a runner on first base, and a fast grounder came his way. He ran back to touch the bag while the man on first got to second safely. The play was to throw the ball to second first, forcing out the runner, and then to cover the bag. There would have been lots of time for a double play. That sort of work will do in the minors, but it won't do here. I've tried to teach him, but it's no use. He won't learn. It's too bad, too, because if he had a head he would be a good ball player." Larry Doyle offered the perfect contrast. He was a poor fielder in many ways with a gift for making hard plays look easy and easy plays look hard, but he was quick and clever and knew what to do with the ball. And he could hit as well as run.[60]

Predictions on who would prevail in 1911 varied within the usual range. Francis Richter of *Sporting Life* declared that "the Chicago team is still the favorite in the race, notwithstanding its signal defeat in the World Series." Others believed the Giants would make a strong run for the pennant. The team had finished strong in 1910 and was as ready as any team McGraw had ever had. In his own mind he was convinced that, after too long a wait, his time had come again. He had not won a pennant since 1905, although the team had come agonizingly close in 1908. The road to this and every other opening day had begun long before spring training. This team had in fact been a rugged five years in the making. Now he was anxious to see what they could do when the games counted.[61]

THE GROUNDWORK

CHAPTER 1

The Mastermind

*"When I broke into the game roughly thirty
years ago I was considered a freak. Ball-players
at that time were selected much as football-
players are now, for their size . . . Size and
weight were supposed to be necessary, because a
ball-player in those days was primarily a batter,
and the bigger a man was the harder he could
hit . . . Willie Keeler and some of the rest of us
on the old Baltimore Orioles were rather short
and light. The big mastodons of pitchers
laughed at us . . . But they presently began to
laugh out of the other corner of their mouths.
For we bunted the ball, and they were so big
and cumbrous they couldn't field well. . . . The
old type of ball-player died out pretty largely in
those years when the Orioles were the pick of
the circuit. I was one of those who drove them
out of the game. The managers came to realize
that speed was quite as important as bulk."*
—JOHN J. MCGRAW (1919)

HE HAD COME A LONG WAY FROM Truxton, the small town in
upstate New York where he had been born on April 7, 1873, to
Ellen and John McGraw, the eldest of eight children who kept the
couple scrambling to support them. A widower before his marriage to
Ellen, John already had a daughter. Dirt-poor, hardworking, and devoutly
Catholic, the McGraws scraped by like most families until the disastrous
winter of 1884–85, when a diphtheria epidemic swept through Tioughnioga

Valley, closing schools and churches and sending people into virtual hiding. Within days after giving birth to her eighth child, a girl, Ellen McGraw developed a high fever and was dead forty-eight hours later. By the end of January four more McGraw children, including Johnny's stepsister, had died from the disease, leaving the survivors in a dazed confusion from which the father never fully recovered.[1]

As an already tough life grew even harsher, young Johnny, or "Jack," assumed greater responsibilities and found solace in his passion for base-ball. At an early age he acquired a new Spalding baseball for a hard-earned dollar and carried it everywhere in his hip pocket. "He looked like a person afflicted with permanent tumor of the buttock," recalled one resident. In his spare time he played with other boys on the school grounds or pitched the ball against a shed behind the Methodist church until darkness fell, or gathered stones from the railroad bed to smack with a stick. More than once his hits crashed into a nearby windowpane, obliging his father to pay fifteen cents to replace it. Father and son argued constantly over his time wasted on the game and the money it drained from the family's meager resources. But Jack would not let go of the game he had come to love.[2]

One night in the autumn of 1885, after another broken pane, John McGraw exploded in rage and began beating his son. Jack scrambled free, hastily crammed some possessions into a sack, and managed to slip by his father into the rain outside. Wet and frightened, he found his way to the kitchen of the nearby Truxton House, a small two-story hotel run by Mary Goddard, a widow in her late thirties. A kindly woman who was raising two sons of her own, she took the boy in. When John McGraw appeared at her door to claim his son, she talked him into letting the boy stay with her. Jack's defection set in motion the end of a family his father could not hold together while working ten-hour days as a section hand on the railroad. Over the next few years his brothers and sisters also moved into other people's homes. When they were gone, his father also left, and Jack seldom saw him afterward.

At Mary Goddard's the boy willingly took on new responsibilities. He went to school, handled a variety of jobs, and earned enough to feed his love of baseball. He used some of his money to buy new baseballs and the annual baseball guides; earlier he had spent precious dimes on the small, paperback DeWitt's annual guides and the Spalding company's *Constitution and Playing Rules of the National League of Professional Base Ball Clubs*. From them he memorized the rules and their changes for both the National League and the American Association until he knew them better than most diehards. He became the best player on the school team and began playing for the town team. By the age of sixteen he was a fast runner, a good left-handed batter, and a right-handed pitcher with a sharp curveball. Along the way he learned that no one else would look out for him, and that he had to make his own way in life.

Baseball offered escape from the humdrum life of a routine job in a small town, but the road to success was crowded and fiercely competitive. Legions of boys from farms, mill towns, and big-city slums played the game in the fervent hope of beating the odds and becoming one of the lucky few to make a living at it, latching onto any team that would have them, hoping to earn a few dollars and encounter someone who might recognize their ability and advance their career.

The well-thumbed rule books Jack McGraw studied confirmed that over the years the game was changing rapidly. In 1886 the pitcher's box was lengthened to seven feet and moved back five feet to fifty feet from home plate. The pitcher was also allowed to raise his arm above his shoulder and throw overhand. A year later the pitcher's box shrank to five and a half feet, and the pitcher could no longer take more than one step toward the batter or lift his rear foot. At the same time the batter had to swing at a "fair" pitch over home plate between his knees and shoulders; if he declined to swing four times, the umpire called him out. Seven pitches outside the fair zone entitled him to first base. The new rules enhanced the power of the umpire by allowing him to decide whether pitches were fair or not.

As a boy McGraw had already learned to shorten his swing and place his hits. He grew skilled at bat control, running the bases, and finding different ways to win games. He used his knowledge of the latest rules to figure out how to take advantage of them before many players even knew they existed. Managers could afford to pay players like McGraw thanks to the time-honored practice of betting on games or with money gleaned from grateful spectators who had won bets on a game. In 1889 the rules underwent another round of major changes. Substitutes could enter the game at any time. The catcher could use a padded mitt and wear a mask so that he could set up closer to the batter and cut down on bases taken on muffed pitches. The four-strike rule was reduced to three and the seven-ball count to four. Fielders could use padded, fingerless gloves for catching the ball. By 1893 a flat bat could no longer be used for bunting.

McGraw absorbed these rules as he had others before them. In 1890, just before his seventeenth birthday, he wheedled his way onto a team in the newly created New York–Pennsylvania League, signing his first professional contract on April 1. He didn't stick; in his first game, playing third base, he had ten chances and committed eight errors. The team lost its first six games and released McGraw as its first step to an overhaul. Like his father, Mary Goddard urged him to forget baseball and find a regular job at home, but Jack couldn't bear the thought of returning to Truxton and the dead-end future it offered. He caught on with a team in Wellsville, New York, where he managed to finish out the season with a weak team in a weaker league. Afterward he returned to Truxton and worked for his room and board until after the New Year, when an unexpected opportunity beckoned.

A chance encounter got him a place on a team traveling to Cuba to play local nines that winter. Dressed in brilliant yellow uniforms, McGraw and his teammates, including three major leaguers, split ten games with the locals in baseball-mad Havana. The Cubans admired the diminutive, hustling shortstop and bestowed on him the nickname "El Mono Amarillo" or "the Yellow Monkey." For his part McGraw was enchanted by Cuba, still under Spanish rule, and returned there many times in later years. On the way back through Florida, the team played a few exhibition games, including one against the Cleveland Spiders of the National League. McGraw gained some recognition by collecting three doubles in five times at bat and playing errorless ball.

In the spring of 1891, McGraw hooked on with the Cedar Rapids Canaries in Iowa for a salary of $125. There he earned a reputation as a tough, scrappy shortstop. By mid-August the Iowa-Illinois League was floundering, but McGraw got the lucky break every young player prayed for but seldom saw. A favorable report got him recruited by the Baltimore Orioles of the American Association. Arriving at Camden Station on August 24, 1891, he stepped into the biggest city he had ever seen in his life. At the Eutaw Hotel he hunted up Bill Barnie, the Baltimore manager. Barnie stared at the five-foot-six-and-a-half-inch, 121-pound specimen before him and growled, "You don't mean to say that this is the ballplayer I've been writing to Billy Gleason about! Why, you're just a kid—can you play ball?"

"If you don't think so," retorted McGraw, "get me out there and watch my smoke. I'm bigger than I look."[3]

Barnie had little choice. In nine seasons the Orioles had never finished higher than fifth place. Union Park held about eight thousand people but was rarely even close to crowded after opening day. It soon became clear that McGraw was in over his head. His erratic fielding forced Barnie to shift him from one position to another; then the manager quit a week before the season ended. McGraw hit a paltry .245 and made eighteen errors in eighty-six chances. His odds of sticking looked anything but bright. However, two momentous changes were about to transform the future of the Orioles as well as that of McGraw.[4]

In December 1891, after a bitter fight that had weakened both leagues, the National League and American Association agreed to merge into a twelve-team league. Only four of the American Association's nine franchises moved to the National League, but Baltimore was one of them. Then, early in the 1892 season, the Orioles brought in Edward "Ned" Hanlon as manager. Nothing in his résumé promised a sudden uplift for the Orioles. In his first season under Hanlon, McGraw did only slightly better, batting .269 while playing four positions in seventy-nine games for a team that finished dead last in the twelve-team league with a record of 48 wins and 105 losses.

In 1893 the team managed only a modest climb to eighth place. During that year, however, Hanlon launched a turnover of personnel and attitude that over the next five years produced an astounding three straight pennants and two second-place finishes. He also bought a 30 percent share in the club and got elected president, giving him full authority over player transactions. Beginning in 1894, the reborn Orioles emerged as the most exciting, colorful, and notorious team in baseball.[5]

That year only three of the players Hanlon inherited still remained on the team: pitcher John "Sadie" McMahon, McGraw, and catcher Wilbert Robinson. Hanlon revealed an impressive talent for organization and handling of personnel. Shrewd trades soon earned him the nickname of "Foxy Ned." The newly arrived talent included a diminutive outfielder named Willie Keeler, outfielders Walter "Steve" Brodie and Joe Kelley, infielders Dan Brouthers, Hughie Jennings, and Heinie Reitz, and several new pitchers. Brouthers was an overweight first baseman who, at thirty-six, seemed washed-up; Keeler was a pint-sized untried rookie of twenty-two whose size alone seemed to doom his career. Somehow Hanlon got one more outstanding year from Brouthers, and Keeler blossomed into one of the greatest hitters of all time.[6]

Despite McGraw's poor statistics, Hanlon installed him at shortstop until Jennings arrived, and then at third base. He also imposed on a team known best for its drinking ability a sense of discipline and an aggressive style of play that demanded hard work and full commitment. In practice and after games in Hanlon's hotel room, the players kept going over tactics and plays designed to give them an edge. As he did with other players, Hanlon saw in McGraw qualities and potential not obvious to other baseball men.[7]

MCGRAW THRIVED UNDER Hanlon's regimen. Already the hardest worker on the team, he improved himself off the field as well. While playing for Olean, New York, he had struck up a friendship with the Reverend Joseph F. Dolan, who taught and oversaw athletics at tiny Allegany College, soon to be St. Bonaventure. Convinced by Dolan that a college education was worthwhile even for a ballplayer, McGraw offered to form and coach the school's baseball team that winter if the college would let him enroll, waive tuition for some courses, and provide him room and board. When the offer was accepted, he plunged into first-year courses with the same energy he displayed on the ball field.

During the off season the rules underwent another significant change. The pitcher was moved back another ten feet to sixty feet six inches and he could no longer take a skip step in the pitching box before releasing the ball. Instead he had to throw with his rear foot anchored to a rubber slab. The intent was to spice the game up with more hitting, and it succeeded. In 1892, Dan Brouthers had led the National League hitters with a .335 average; a year later Billy Hamilton of Philadelphia took the honors by hitting .380. In 1894 he upped his average to .399 but finished only fifth, topped by four men batting over .400 led by the Boston Beaneaters' Hugh Duffy at .441, a mark that has never since been equaled.[8]

The new emphasis on hitting fit Hanlon's plans beautifully. In 1894 every regular on the Orioles hit above .300, topped by Joe Kelley's .393. McGraw emerged as a sparkplug for the team, batting .340 and stealing seventy-eight bases, second in the league. He developed a keen eye at the plate and a knack for fouling off pitches until he got one to his liking or took a walk. This proved a handy talent, especially prior to 1901 when foul balls did not count as strikes. Even more, he was a disruptive presence on the field, not only harassing umpires and rival players but shoving, bumping, and holding runners on the base paths. All the Orioles were belligerent but none outdid McGraw, whose behavior on and off the field revealed a Jekyll-and-Hyde personality. His antics in an exhibition game led one New Orleans reporter to complain that "he has the vilest tongue of any ball-player . . . While he is a fine ball-player, yet he adopts every low and contemptible method that his erratic brain can conceive to win a play by a dirty trick."⁹

In an age that prized big, beefy sluggers, Hanlon filled his roster with whippets who could play his brand of ball. The Orioles hit to all fields and ran the bases with reckless abandon. Keeler was hardly alone in his ability, as he famously said, to "hit 'em where they ain't." He perfected the art of the "Baltimore chop," a ball smacked into the ground so hard that he reached first before it came down. Hanlon recognized early that he had the ideal personnel for the hit-and-run play, which McGraw and Keeler elevated into an art form. Off the field the team lived and breathed baseball. McGraw and Hughie Jennings became fast friends. Like McGraw, Jennings was a refugee from a small town, a "hungry boy in a poor coal-mining family" that took a dim view of his ball playing. They roomed together and shared their mutual obsession with the game.¹⁰

"No two people ever talked more baseball than Hughie and I," McGraw said later. "No two people ever had so much unexpressed baseball packed away in their craws, so many experiments and untried ideas. We had dreamed and schemed for so long we couldn't wait until one was finished with a new play before the other had a new one to tell . . . We would talk all night. We would forget sleep entirely, there was so much baseball to talk. I never thought I'd ever meet anyone so baseball-minded as Hughie. And I never thought I'd ever meet anyone so gentle and patient and understanding."¹¹

They did more than talk. On their own they measured leads off first base and each other's running speed from first to second against throws by Robinson. Before practice they hit endless fungoes to each other and tested running speed to first base against different speeds of a ball rolling down the third base line. To protect their feet against blisters, they bought thick steaks to put in their shoes.

At a time when individual efforts dominated games, Hanlon's team approach was a revelation to the rest of the league. Prior to the 1894 season he surprised and amused other teams by taking the Orioles to Macon, Georgia, for what became known as spring training to drill them in practices he wanted to become second nature for them. On a ball hit to the outfield, the nearest outfielder was expected to back up the one chasing the ball. The ball was thrown in not just to the nearest base but to a "cutoff" man who went to meet it while other infielders backed up the throw or a base. Hanlon taught his catchers to fake a throw to one base and heave it to another. On an attempted steal of second with men on base, the throw might go to a cutoff man, who would immediately try to get one of the other runners moving on the throw.[12]

Hanlon expedited the Baltimore chop by having groundskeeper Tom Murphy keep the infield hard and dry. He let the grass along the foul lines grow slightly higher and gave the ground a slight slope to keep bunts fair. When the pitcher was moved back to sixty feet six inches, Hanlon saw at once that bunting would be easier because of the extra distance he would have to cover. Writer Hugh Fullerton noted that "the edges of the base lines were banked up like billiard cushions to keep bunts from rolling foul . . . The runways were down hill to first base, down hill to second, up a steep grade to third, and down hill to home."[13]

On the bases the Orioles used their own rule book. If the lone umpire's back was turned, a base runner might cut across part of the infield instead of touching second base. Enemy runners got bumped, tripped, and kicked to slow them down. McGraw perfected the ruse of hooking his fingers over the belt of a man on third base so that he got off to a halting start; it worked until one clever runner undid his belt and left it dangling in McGraw's hand. Sliding runners got tagged hard in the mouth to lessen their resolve. This take-no-prisoners style of play endeared the Orioles to the hometown fans and drew the wrath of hostile crowds, who protested their approach as dirty baseball. No other team matched their ability to work as a unit. So close did the players become that long afterward they held annual reunions.[14]

The hard work McGraw put in during these years did more than elevate him into an excellent player. It shaped an approach to the game that he carried into his managerial years, one that asked no quarter and gave none, that made a shrine of winning and settled for nothing less than maximum effort. The Orioles became his classroom and he absorbed its lessons well. From Hanlon he learned the importance of good organization and the need to foresee what kind of players the team needed. Running would always be at the center of his philosophy: hustling on defense, taking the extra base, stealing instead of sacrificing, using the hit-and-run to keep the other team on its heels, doing whatever the opponent least expected of them. Other teams took the same approach, looking for any way to gain an edge; the Orioles simply did it better. To McGraw's eyes the game was a thing of beauty when played the right way, and he was certain at an early age what that was.

The next two seasons saw the Orioles repeat as champions but often without McGraw. In 1895 he suffered some hand injuries along with a lingering illness that was finally diagnosed as malaria. Still he managed to get into ninety-six games and hit .369 before a relapse put him out again in September. The following year, after overworking himself at St. Bonaventure, he looked forward eagerly to spring training only to fall ill again, this time with a serious bout of typhoid fever. Hovering near death for a time, he did not get into an Oriole game until August 25 and played in only twenty-three games, batting .325. By then he had regained his health and taken his first steps toward fashioning a life outside of baseball.

No one knows just when or where McGraw first met Minnie Doyle, the dark-haired daughter of a retired Baltimore court clerk. After a courtship that must have been relatively brief, McGraw married her in February 1897 and settled into what he hoped would be the domestic life he had never had. That same month, thinking of his future after baseball, he went partners with Wilbert Robinson in buying a saloon and restaurant they named the Diamond Café. They upgraded the place by installing bowling alleys at the street level and a billiard parlor upstairs. By the time spring training opened, the Diamond had gained a large clientele and was making good money for its owners.

Despite his newfound stability, McGraw's 1897 season got off to a rocky start. He missed three weeks after spraining an ankle in the opening game, then lost another two weeks with a hurt arm. A plague of injuries and illnesses beset the Orioles all season. McGraw got into 106 games and again hit .325, but the Orioles lost the pennant to the Boston Beaneaters despite a career season by Keeler, who hit .424 with a record 239 hits. Rumors of discord on the team surfaced, and at least one finger pointed at McGraw. A teammate said later that McGraw "had a mean way of nagging a man that worked against the success of the team." He also claimed that McGraw was insubordinate to Hanlon. "I often wonder," he said, "how McGraw got away with some of the plays he made on and off the field."[15]

McGraw's dual personality grew even more pronounced that winter. With the Diamond Café netting them three times their baseball income, he and Robinson bought adjoining row houses. McGraw brought his brother Mike down from Truxton and put him in business school. Hanlon improved the team with another trade, but the Orioles again fell short of Boston. Restored to health, McGraw had a good season, batting .342 and leading the league in walks and runs scored.

For all their talent and determination, the Orioles had slipped behind the Boston Beaneaters and their talented manager, Frank Selee. Unlike Hanlon, he paid little attention to strategy or game tactics, but he was uncanny at building a team through shrewd evaluation of talent. He acquired a great pitcher in Kid Nichols, who *averaged* more than thirty wins a season over a nine-year period. His outfield featured Hugh Duffy and speedster Billy Hamilton, who stole ninety-three bases in 1896. The infield included second baseman Bobby Lowe, the first man to hit four homers in one game, and Jimmy Collins, who McGraw among others considered the greatest third baseman he had ever seen.[16]

The following year brought a startling change to the league. Public excitement over the Spanish-American War had seriously hurt attendance, as had the unbroken domination of the league by Boston and Baltimore. Despite their run at the pennant, the Orioles drew only 123,416 fans, less than half their earlier efforts, while the Brooklyn Superbas drew 300,000 customers with a tenth-place team. To counter the domination of Boston and Baltimore, the Robison brothers, Frank and Stanley, hit upon what became known as the syndicate plan. Already owners of the Cleveland Spiders, they bought control of the hapless St. Louis franchise and proceeded to strengthen it by stripping Cleveland of its best players. Hanlon took the same approach, going in with the owners of the Brooklyn team for joint control of the two franchises.[17]

Disillusioned with Baltimore and convinced that Brooklyn would prosper with a winning team, Hanlon began shuttling the best Oriole players to the Superbas. Brooklyn not only had a new ballpark, it had in 1898 become part of Greater New York. Keeler, Kelley, Jennings, first baseman Dan McGann, and three quality pitchers went to Brooklyn, which unloaded on Baltimore seven players of little value except for young outfielder Jimmy Sheckard and an untried pitcher the Orioles managed to slip by Hanlon, Joe McGinnity. McGraw and Robinson, their roots firmly set in Baltimore, flatly refused to go to Brooklyn. Hanlon then surprised McGraw by offering to make him the manager of the Orioles at the tender age of twenty-five.[18]

Despite his youth, he was well equipped for the job. He knew the game inside and out, had seemingly inexhaustible energy, knew how to get good work even from mediocre players, and quickly gained the respect of his men. He joked with the players, enjoyed their company, but held them to strict account for his style of play with its emphasis on speed and alertness. The stripped Orioles played solid ball under McGraw, who hit .391 in 1899 and again led the league in walks and runs scored. He also stole seventy-three bases, second only to Sheckard's seventy-seven. McGinnity, dubbed the Iron Man because of his early years working in his father's foundry, proved to be an iron horse, pitching a staggering 380 innings with a record of 28-17. Under their kid manager, the Orioles gave Boston and Brooklyn a run for the pennant.

The Orioles finished in fourth place and might have climbed higher had not a tragedy deprived them of McGraw late in August. During a double-header at Louisville, McGraw received a telegram that Minnie had fallen desperately ill at home. He hurried back to Baltimore to find that she had suffered a ruptured appendix. On August 31, with McGraw at her side, Minnie died; she was only twenty-two years old. Nothing so devastating had happened to McGraw since his mother's death. For a time he isolated himself in his row house, explaining to well-wishers that "I feel exhausted physically and mentally, and am in no condition to play ball . . . It seems to me just now as if the last thing I could interest myself in would be baseball."[19]

McGRAW DID NOT REJOIN THE TEAM UNTIL September 11 and did not put himself in the lineup until the twenty-third. Hanlon's Superbas took the pennant by eight games but the Orioles outdrew them slightly. Rumors started that the National League would eliminate its weak sisters and keep only eight teams. In March 1900 the National League officially dumped four franchises: Washington, Cleveland, Louisville, and Baltimore. The new arrangement meant that McGraw, Robinson, and others belonged to Brooklyn.[20]

Hanlon promptly sold the contracts of McGraw and Robinson to St. Louis. They tried doggedly to get traded to another team closer to Baltimore but failed. Thanks to the notorious reserve clause that gave owners absolute power over their players, McGraw and Robinson had to play for St. Louis or no one. Grudgingly, they reported on May 5 and played out the season. Under tough conditions McGraw hit .344 and drew eighty-five walks in ninety-eight games, his presence limited by two injuries. When the season ended, Cincinnati owner John Brush tried for the second year in a row to lure McGraw to the Reds as manager only to be turned down again. McGraw still thought a better future awaited him, hopefully with a new team to be installed in Baltimore.

Despite his lack of bargaining power and a generous salary offered to him, McGraw had refused to sign his contract with St. Louis unless the reserve clause was struck. Robinson did likewise, making them both free agents at the end of the 1900 season. "My reason should have been quite obvious to anybody," he said later. "Baltimore, Cleveland and Washington had been dropped from the National League, and it was evident that Ban Johnson and his associates would grab that territory to expand the rapidly forming American League. Everybody in baseball felt nervous. Players all over the country sat on the anxious seat, worried as to where they might land, undecided which way to move. I saw many opportunities for myself and wanted to be in position to seize the one that I liked best."[21]

Another league was in the process of being formed, this one by a former newspaperman named Byron Bancroft "Ban" Johnson, who had presided over the well-run and profitable Western League. His ambition was to create a second major league, one operated more efficiently and with no tolerance for the rowdiness and abuse of umpires typical of the National League. "My determination," he said later, "was to pattern baseball in this new league along the lines of scholastic contests, to make ability and brains and clean, honorable play, not the swinging of clenched fists, coarse oaths, riots or assaults upon the umpires, decide the issue."[22]

That the National League owners underestimated his ability and had a gift for antagonizing the public helped his cause. In 1900, Johnson changed his league's name from the Western to the American League and expanded into Chicago and Cleveland, adding them to existing franchises in Detroit, Minneapolis, Milwaukee, Kansas City, and Indianapolis. That same year delegates from each National League team showed their displeasure with management by forming the Protective Association of Professional Baseball Players. Earlier they had gone so far as to create not only a union but a league of their own, the Players' National League, only to have it end in a debacle during the summer of 1890 that left all sides drained and damaged.[23]

The prospect of another uprising by the players helped distract the owners from the threat posed by Johnson. After a successful 1900 season Johnson and his supporters looked to another round of expansion that would transform the American League from a sectional to a major national league. That meant invading the East, in particular Philadelphia, Washington, Boston, and Baltimore. The National League aided his cause by outraging the players' union, thereby prompting scores of players to defect to the new league.[24]

Into this murky mess waded a hopeful John McGraw and Wilbert Robinson. In November 1900 they acquired the franchise for Baltimore, capitalized it at $40,000, and recruited several associates as stockholders. It is difficult to imagine an odder couple than McGraw and Johnson, given the fact that the former represented everything that the latter wanted to eliminate from the game, but McGraw wanted desperately to get back to Baltimore, and Johnson impressed him. That winter he scoured the East in search of players for his new team and came up with two prize catches: Joe McGinnity and a talented young outfielder named Mike Donlin.[25]

McGraw hit .349 for the Orioles but got into only seventy-nine games because of injuries to his right knee. Two weeks into the season witnessed what proved to be the first of several clashes with Johnson. At one point Johnson accused McGraw of trying to persuade two other clubs to join him in deserting to the National League. McGraw denounced the charge as "mean, cruel, malicious lies." By season's end the Orioles had finished fifth and drawn only 142,000 patrons, third worst in the league, and McGraw's future as a player was in doubt.[26]

Amid this turmoil of change McGraw happened to meet a small, dark-eyed nineteen-year-old student at Mount Saint Agnes College, a women's school, who knew absolutely nothing about baseball. Blanche Sindall, her older sister Jeannette, their three younger brothers, and their mother liked to host Sunday evening gatherings for young people at their row house on York Road in the fashionable Waverly section of north Baltimore. Blanche's father, James Sindall, was a self-made contractor who tolerated the influx of potential suitors but made his feelings clear by hanging a sign on the hall coat tree that read: THIS ESTABLISHMENT CLOSES AT 11 P.M.[27]

One Sunday evening in the fall of 1900, McGraw was invited to the gathering along with Hughie Jennings, who had lost his wife shortly after the death of Minnie McGraw, by Charles Schryver, a chance acquaintance who loved baseball and was thrilled to know the players. Schryver fancied himself a suitor to his cousin Blanche, but McGraw caught her eye that evening as they stood around the piano singing. McGraw admitted he couldn't sing a lick; she knew so little about baseball that, asking him what position he played, added, "I'll bet you're one of the batters." It was the one position she had heard her baseball-mad brothers talk about.[28]

Her unimpressed father had never heard of McGraw but soon got to know him from visits that became more frequent and lasted longer. McGraw did not then smoke or drink, dressed well—he had his shirts and shoes made in Havana—and was soft-spoken, considerate, and Catholic to boot. By the time he left in the spring to get ready for the inaugural American League season, he and Blanche had become a couple. On opening day in 1901 he provided a large box for the entire family to attend the game, which finally took place after two rainouts. McGraw ignored them during the game but afterward surprised Blanche by sending over a wagonload of flowers given him and the team for opening day.

Nothing revealed the Jekyll-and-Hyde personality of John McGraw more starkly than his courtship of Blanche Sindall. He was quiet, attentive, and affectionate but never demonstrative. Simple pleasures pleased him as much as they did Blanche. On summer evenings when the Orioles were in town, he took her for long drives through Baltimore, using the time to wind down from the day's game, or joined the family in their parlor. When not fielding baseball questions from the brothers, he was content to sit in silence and enjoy what Blanche called "the family warmth and the air of peace," something he had never known in his own fractured family. Later Blanche described it as "a sort of gnawing hunger." It was a new and wondrous experience for him, and he found Blanche a good companion. The ogre of the diamond and newspaper accounts never appeared in the Sindall parlor or in the quiet hours spent on the porch in the evenings.

Sometimes on the way home they stopped at Fouch's drugstore on North Charles for ice cream sodas. On other nights they went downtown to see a musical or vaudeville. McGraw preferred something light, saying he had to deal with enough problems at the ballpark. The leisurely pace of their court- ship suited McGraw perfectly as counterpoint to his hectic days on the playing field. On Sunday mornings when in town he joined the family for mass at Saint Ann Catholic Church, bringing Blanche a bunch of Parma violets. When he was on a road trip, the violets still arrived every Sunday morning. Marriage was a foregone conclusion, but McGraw tried and failed three times to summon the nerve to ask James Sindall for his daughter's hand before leaving on a road trip. After his return he still hesitated to approach Sindall.

"In baseball," he explained to Blanche, "you have to fight all the time for survival. And if your father was an umpire for one minute, I'd have it all over in half a minute. But he's not an umpire, and this is different." Finally he screwed up his courage and the engagement was sealed. On January 8, 1902, they were married at Saint Ann's in an elaborate ceremony with an overflow crowd that included John's younger brother James, Hughie

Jennings, Willie Keeler, Joe Kelley, Wilbert Robinson, Steve Brodie, and other Orioles.

After a lavish reception McGraw took his bride first to Washington, and then to Savannah, where the Orioles were to train in six weeks. They stayed at the seedy Pulaski Hotel because, he explained to Blanche, it had given the team a good deal, and he couldn't "accept their generosity for the team, and then take my personal business elsewhere. It wouldn't be fair." They moved on to the Breakers Hotel in Palm Beach, Florida, where they chuckled at the idea of bringing a baseball team to so dignified a place. After a few days in St. Augustine they returned to Baltimore and moved into the Northampton Hotel. On her honeymoon Blanche received not only her introduction to the Deep South but her first taste of the itinerant life of a baseball player.

More lessons were soon forthcoming. McGraw began making secret trips to New York and Philadelphia, leaving Blanche mystified. "It concerns New York baseball," he said cryptically, "but we can't even talk about it out loud. If anyone asks, you can't even say where I've gone, or when I'm coming back. Something may come of it, and maybe not. I've just got to visit and meet people and listen and wait."

Within only a few weeks Blanche came to understand her role and duty as the wife of John McGraw. "I learned that John's business was indeed highly competitive," she wrote later. "I also learned not to talk about him or what he did or said. Trusting him was part of my love, and I was certain that whatever he was doing or would do was the right thing. It was not in my province or my mind to ask for facts or explanations. He needed understanding and silence, and obedience to his needs was a sacred mission in itself."

As she soon discovered, that sacred mission posed some formidable challenges, which she proved eminently capable of meeting. Blanche made herself into the ideal helpmate for one of baseball's most brilliant and controversial masterminds. But the price came high. Early in the 1902 season she sat behind third base watching the Orioles entertain the Detroit Tigers. In the first inning two Tigers outfielders, Dick Harley and Jimmy Barrett, hit singles and then tried to pull a double steal. Roger Bresnahan, the Orioles catcher, anticipated their move and fired the ball to McGraw at third base. Out by twenty feet, Harley slid into McGraw with spikes flashing and ripped his left leg below the kneecap. As the umpire called Harley out, McGraw went after Harley with a fury that shocked Blanche. "It was the first outburst of his rage that I had seen," she said later, "and it wasn't easy to watch."

For the first time she saw the other McGraw that never appeared at home. Later McGraw apologized for his outburst. "It's usually the outfielders," he explained to her. "They're always the bravest ones with the spikes. That's because they don't have to stay on the bases and take it from the ones they cut." As she was beginning to see, there was more to the game than she had suspected, and to the man she had married. "In six months of marriage I had discovered many things about John McGraw, his character and personality," she admitted. "Somewhat smugly I had gauged the extent of his fame, popularity, and importance to the baseball. But the splash of accusations, vilification, and insinuation in the headlines made me wonder if I knew anything at all."

CHAPTER 2

The Business of Baseball

"Baseball is a business, not simply a sport."
—JOHN MONTGOMERY WARD

T HE SECOND YEAR OF THE NEW CENTURY also brought McGraw an unexpected new opportunity, thanks to the near chaos into which the leadership of the National League had plunged. Ever since the league was founded in 1876 the club owners had bickered among themselves almost as vigorously as they fought other leagues for supremacy in what was from the first a business rather than a sport. Along with show business in its many guises, horse racing, and boxing, baseball helped usher in an entire new industry that became known as entertainment.

After its creation in 1876 the National League drifted along a bumpy course, searching for credibility as well as a viable business plan. From the first owners realized that salaries were the single most important factor in their expenses, and that competition for players was the main factor in driving them upward. In seeking ways to restrain the cost of players, they groped their way toward an ingenious solution that became known as the "reserve clause." First introduced in September 1879 and refined over the years, it bound a player to his original team year after year by reserving his services for the original contract year and the following season as well. He could move to another team only by having his contract traded or sold or by sitting out the next season. Prior to its introduction players had been free to sign with any team after completion of their current season.[1]

Within a short time the reserve clause emerged as an enduring pillar for the entire business of baseball. By itself, however, it could not solve the salary riddle, especially in the face of growing competition from other leagues. As a sport the goal of baseball teams was to be as competitive on the field as possible; as a business, the key to success lay in stifling any competitive threat posed by rival teams or leagues. This could be done either through open warfare or collusion to eliminate competition. The owners regarded monopoly, or something near it, as the most desirable state if they could get away with it.

Between 1892 and 1900 the National League enjoyed a monopoly and did not hesitate to exploit it. A severe national depression between 1893 and 1897 dampened its efforts while also giving the owners another rationale for squeezing player salaries. During the decade only three teams—Baltimore, Boston, and Brooklyn—won pennants, all of them under two managers, Frank Selee of Boston and Ned Hanlon of Baltimore and Brooklyn. Players bore the brunt of the inevitable financial retrenchment. Rosters were cut from fifteen to thirteen and salaries slashed 30 to 40 percent. The few players who tried to hold out got little or nothing for their efforts.[2]

After 1895 overall attendance dropped as the depression finally caught up with baseball. A number of factors accounted for the decline, including the unwieldy imbalance of a twelve-team league in which the bottom feeders dropped out of contention early and aroused little fan enthusiasm. Monopoly by itself, it seemed, could not guarantee success, especially when the owners continued to wrangle and scheme among themselves over any issue that faced them. Unable to get past the opportunistic, short-sighted policies that had long characterized their behavior, they eroded public confidence even more when hard times hit again.[3]

The lack of competitive balance especially plagued the league. While three teams dominated for the entire decade, Louisville, St. Louis, and Washington nearly always brought up the rear. The New York Giants, occupying the largest market, managed a second- and third-place finish but more often bounced between seventh and eleventh. Critics and even some owners recognized the shortcomings of a twelve-team league but could not agree on how best to solve its defects. Instead the magnates continued to squabble over such issues as the division of gate receipts and the fifty-cent admission charge.[4]

Their mistrust of each other was inflamed by the fact that several of them owned pieces of more than one team. Frank Robison owned both the St. Louis and Cleveland franchises; Arthur Soden owned a third of the Boston team and was the principal minority holder of the Giants. John Brush owned Cincinnati and also held stock in the Giants, while Albert G. Spalding held a large block of Chicago stock and some shares in the Giants. Harry

Von der Horst owned 40 percent of the stock in both Baltimore and Brooklyn, while Ned Hanlon and Charles Ebbets each had 10 percent of the stock in the same two teams. These interlocking syndicates, and the shuffling of players that resulted, reduced competition to little more than a farce and convinced many fans that the league was a fraud.[5]

Although Arthur Soden was considered the "Dean of the National League," two other personalities dominated its activities. John Brush was deemed "the ablest man in baseball" by some and a damned nuisance by others. More clearheaded and purposeful than most of his peers, he took strong positions on issues and stood by them. "I never pretended that every-thing which I suggested to the National League was right," he told a writer. "I have made it clear that several things which have been suggested by me were right, in spite of the fact that they were rejected at the time, and taken up afterward, when it was seen that they could not be avoided."[6]

As controversial as Brush could be, he paled before the odium generated by Andrew Freedman, who bought control of the Giants in 1895. A lawyer by training, Freedman had made a fortune in real estate and grown close to Tammany Hall boss Richard Croker. Although he could be charming, he had a quick temper, an aggressive personality, was easily offended, and did not hesitate to tell his fellow owners how they should go about their busi-ness. The *New York World* marveled at his "astonishing faculty for making enemies." While amassing an impressive list of vendettas with his peers, sportswriters, and players, he went so far as to weaken his own team to show the other magnates how the league and its revenue stream suffered from a poor-performing New York team.[7]

As sensitive to criticism as he was generous in dispensing it, Freedman took on everyone—owners, managers, players, reporters, umpires, even actors. By 1900 he had no less than twenty-two libel suits pending against the *New York Sun*. He clashed repeatedly with Brush, whose ideas about the business were as determined as his own. In 1899 he put forth a plan to reorganize the league into an actual trust consisting of the "most powerful and wealthy franchises" in the most lucrative cities with the best players even if it meant redistributing them every year. A few owners thought his proposal made sense as a way to curb the self-defeating individualism that kept the owners at each other's throats. Most regarded "Freedmanism" as anathema.[8]

By 1899, however, everyone conceded that something had to be done with the awkward twelve-team monopoly that one writer called "the melancholy wreck." The syndicate approach of interlocking ownerships flopped because it worsened competition and killed public interest in the weaker teams. At the December owners' meeting, Brush, Freedman, and Soden surprised the other owners by joining forces to urge that the Baltimore, Cleveland, Louisville, and Washington franchises be eliminated for the 1900 season. In a spirit of diplomatic compromise thought to be impossible among the owners, Brush and Freedman put aside past grudges and agreed to work together to bring about changes in the league. This wholly unexpected alliance was to have a profound effect on the league's future as well as that of the Giants and John McGraw.[9]

In March the four designated clubs were dumped, leaving the National League with eight teams—Boston, Brooklyn, New York, and Philadelphia in the East and Chicago, Cincinnati, Pittsburgh, and St. Louis in the West—a lineup that would endure until 1953. At the same time, its monopoly was about to be challenged by the upstart American League and a new players' union. Ban Johnson cheerfully used the latest player revolt as a wedge for luring more National Leaguers to the new league. As players defected in droves, the league found itself in even greater disarray than usual. During the 1900 season every team except Pittsburgh and Brooklyn lost money; Brooklyn, which won the pennant, barely managed to break even.[10]

National League attendance dropped below two million, a level four hundred thousand below the crisis year of 1898. Freedman did nothing to improve the Giants, whose floundering performance kept fans away and hurt the other clubs counting on revenues from their games in New York. Both the press and fans continued to rail against the cynicism and dishonesty of syndicate baseball, the faults of which became even more glaring when compared to the newborn American League. The new circuit seemed to have honest, capable leadership free of corrupt or scandalous bargaining and deals.[11]

In November, New York City voters swept Tammany Hall from power and elected reformer Seth Low as mayor. The change encouraged the magnates to stand up to Freedman and evidently altered Freedman's own thinking. Prior to the December owners' meeting, Freedman invited Soden and two of his erstwhile antagonists, Brush and Robison, to a secret meeting at his mansion in Red Bank, New Jersey. Brush arrived with a bold plan to convert the league into a trust that would pool franchises, players, and profits in a single organization. The proposed baseball trust would issue stock to each franchise; Freedman's Giants would control 30 percent, the other conferees 12 percent each, and the absent four owners amounts ranging from 6 to 10 percent.[12]

A precedent already existed in the form of a theater trust organized in 1896. Baseball could easily be viewed as just another form of show business. If the trust worked as envisioned, the governing board would make all major decisions, reducing the individual clubs to mere administrators. It also offered complete control over the players at a time when the American League and players' union threatened it. Above all, it promised financial security and a guarantee of profits to the hungrier owners. However, it ignored the deepening public resentment of trusts in general and the importance of fan attachment to their teams. By 1900 baseball was already a game of traditions and customs that even the rapid changes of the past decade had not eroded. Fans rooted for their local team and its players; their loyalties could vanish if the whole apparatus was dissolved into something more flexible and alien.[13]

Although the Red Bank conference was secret, details of the scheme leaked into the *New York Sun* of December 11, 1901, amid the annual meeting. Led by Barney Dreyfuss, the other four owners united behind Spalding to be the new league president. The Red Bank faction procured an injunction barring him from acting as president, leaving the league paralyzed for leadership in the midst of its fight with the American League and players' union. Finally, after more delays, Nick Young, the incumbent, gratefully accepted a pension and the league's affairs were put in the hands of a stopgap three-man executive committee consisting of Brush as head, Soden, and Jim Hart of Chicago, who had bought the team from Spalding.[14]

As the 1902 season got under way, the war between the leagues grew more bitter and the intrigues within the National League more complex. Ban Johnson had shifted the American League's Milwaukee franchise to St. Louis, the largest city next to Chicago that allowed Sunday baseball. The league stepped up its raids on National League players and under Johnson's leadership seemed to be winning on the field, at the gate, and in the management offices. The portly president had his eye on one other prize. His league needed a team in New York, the nation's largest market, to compete with the hapless Giants. That desire ran afoul of Johnson's already strained relationship with John McGraw.[15]

THE ONE AREA NOT GOING WELL FOR Johnson was his campaign to rid the game of rowdyism. The major obstacle was McGraw and his unending clashes with umpires. Johnson and McGraw had crossed swords several times during the 1901 season, the collision of two strong egos and relentless personalities driven by ambition. Although they corresponded amicably during the off season, McGraw suspected that Johnson wanted to move the Baltimore franchise to New York and didn't want him to come with it. By the end of 1901 McGraw thought he knew why: "To me it was quite obvious now that Johnson intended to drop the Baltimore club and to put a team in New York." If he did so, McGraw concluded, "someone would be left holding the bag, and I made up my mind it wouldn't be me."[16]

McGraw did not know that matters in New York had grown much more complicated for reasons that had nothing to do with him. Most of the National League owners had long wanted to get rid of Freedman but dared not try because of his political connections. However, having failed to conquer the baseball business, Freedman had grown more interested in his real estate and transit investments, especially the new IRT subway project. His volatile, unpredictable style had, by one estimate, run through no less than sixteen managers between 1895 and 1902. During his ownership the team managed a lone third-place finish but nothing else higher than seventh; in the eight-team seasons of 1900 and 1901 the club came in last and next to last.[17]

Freedman's interest in baseball waned as the complex subway negotiations demanded more of his attention. "Baseball affairs in New York have been going on just as I wished and expected them to go," he said bluntly at one point. "I have given the club little attention and I would not now give five cents for the best ball-player in the world to strengthen it."[18]

During the spring and summer of 1902 these disparate threads came together in a complex and improbable tapestry. In January and February, after returning from his wedding trip, McGraw slipped into New York for mysterious secret meetings that ended when he took the Orioles to Savannah for spring training. John J. Mahon, a contractor and politico, bought a large enough block of Orioles stock to get himself elected president. On April 28, McGraw put himself in the Orioles lineup for the first time; two days later he got into a ruckus with an umpire that drew a five-day suspension from Johnson.[19]

On May 24, with the Orioles playing Detroit at Oriole Park, Blanche McGraw witnessed the severe spiking of her husband and his explosive temper for the first time. In those days a bad spiking could lead to anything from blood poisoning to gangrene, and McGraw's knee became badly infected. For two weeks he could not leave his hotel room; the team left for its first western swing with Wilbert Robinson in charge. In June, McGraw began meeting with Freedman, who wanted him to manage the Giants. While the events that followed seem clear in retrospect, the question of who devised which parts of the outcome remains an intriguing mystery. It is not that the parts do not add up to a whole but rather that they can be made to add up to several differing wholes.[20]

The murkiest part of the story concerns McGraw's secret meeting—or meetings—with John Brush. Blanche McGraw mentioned a "supposedly secret meeting" between them in June 1901 at which Brush floated the idea of a return to the National League under the "most ideal conditions." McGraw dutifully reported the meeting to Johnson, but within a short time some reporters pounced on it to accuse McGraw of "startling crimes and treason to the American League." McGraw was quick to deny the charges. But were there other meetings between Brush and McGraw, and if so, what kind of plans were laid?[21]

Writer Joseph Durso, relying on an account given him by the son of Brush's son-in-law, claims that McGraw was summoned to a secret meeting with Brush at the latter's home in Indianapolis. McGraw arrived before dawn and was picked up in a carriage by Mrs. Brush and carried to the meeting. Brush motioned him into the dining room, where, after some earnest discussion, a contract was signed. No date was given for the meeting, which raises the question of whether it took place in 1901 or 1902; nor were its contents revealed. Given the events that followed, it is plausible that McGraw was acting as an emissary between Brush and Freedman, which he eventually did, or as agent for one or the other.[22]

Brush was not the only prominent person McGraw visited. Early in June 1902, ignoring doctor's orders, he limped his way to the Gravesend Race Track at Coney Island to meet with Frank Farrell, a Tammany figure known as the "Pool Room King" for his billiards establishments, which were little more than fronts for wagering on the ponies. McGraw loved going to the track and betting on the horses; one of the inducements of St. Louis was that the ballpark was located conveniently near the local racetrack. What they discussed is not known, but Blanche McGraw observed later that "action on the New York deal accelerated from this meeting at Gravesend."[23]

Blanche insisted that through the months that followed, her husband kept Johnson informed of developments. According to her version, the matter had by the spring of 1902 gone far beyond McGraw's defecting to the Giants to include the sale of the Giants, the financing and sale of the Cincinnati Reds, and the creation of an American League franchise for New York. Did the scheme involve a grand collusion among Freedman, Brush, Johnson, and McGraw, or did its components evolve piecemeal? If the former, then what followed amounted to an impressive piece of theater; if not, then events happened to unfold in a way that suited the needs of all of them perfectly.[24]

On June 28, McGraw finally returned to the Orioles lineup. In his first game he seemed to go out of his way to provoke both umpires. Predictably he was ejected but refused to leave the field. Umpire Tom Connolly, no stranger to McGraw's antics, forfeited the game to Boston, and Johnson slapped indefinite suspensions on both McGraw and outfielder Joe Kelley, who happened to be John Mahon's son-in-law. Barred from appearing on the field or even the bench, McGraw was free to strike a deal with Freedman. He agreed to manage the Giants for four years at an annual salary of $11,000, making him the highest paid manager or player at that time.[25]

Why would Freedman, whose interest in the team had waned and who was reluctant to spend any money on talent, lavish so rich a contract on McGraw to manage the club? Partly it was to eliminate the threat of McGraw heading an American League New York team. McGraw was careful to extract from Freedman absolute authority over every aspect of baseball operations, including trades or releases. The willingness of Freedman to go along in both cases had to do with several more layers of intrigue. First, McGraw had to wind up his affairs with the Orioles, disposing of his shares and obtaining his release. Once signed with the Giants, he became an emissary in some of the remaining components, which fell into place over the next several weeks.[26]

On July 5, McGraw secretly signed a contract with the Giants. Two nights later he met with Mahon and the other Orioles directors and reminded them that the club owed him $7,000 for funds he had advanced for salaries and other expenses. He wanted either his money back or his release. To bolster his stock holdings, he had earlier swapped his half interest in the Diamond Café to Wilbert Robinson for the latter's shares in the Orioles. The directors agreed to release McGraw in exchange for his stock holdings, which McGraw agreed to sell to Mahon for $6,500. A day later McGraw publicly signed a contract to manage the Giants. That seemed to settle the matter, but in fact it marked only the first step. Late on the evening of July 16, Brush and McGraw met with Mahon, Freedman's attorney Joseph

France, and Joe Kelley. From several sources, including McGraw, Mahon had accumulated 201 of the 400 shares in the Orioles; these were transferred to Freedman via France.[27]

Freedman now owned both the Giants and the Orioles, enabling him to give McGraw whatever players he wished from the Orioles. Six of the fourteen Orioles departed, leaving the club without enough players even to field a team. Pitchers Joe McGinnity and Jack Cronin, first baseman Dan McGann, and utility man Roger Bresnahan joined McGraw on the Giants. Outfielders Joe Kelley and Cy Seymour went to the Cincinnati Reds, where Kelley became manager. The Cincinnati transfer looked to be a payoff to Brush, but it had more to do with a favor for Kelley. While befuddled onlookers struggled to keep pace with events, Brush arranged to sell the Reds to an Ohio group headed by the Fleischmann brothers of yeast and gin fame, Republican boss George B. Cox, and his close ally August "Garry" Herrmann. The proceeds from that sale enabled him to buy the Giants from Freedman, who then moved the now moribund Baltimore franchise to New York for the 1903 season, giving the American League its long-awaited team in the nation's biggest market.[28]

On July 12, Freedman announced, "I will turn the inside affairs of the business over to Mr. Brush, as I have little or no time to give to baseball, while Mr. Brush will be able to devote practically all his time to the game." During the following winter of 1903, Brush finally completed his purchase of the Giants from Freedman, who in turn acquired full ownership of the Baltimore franchise and moved it to New York. Brush and McGraw had already come to terms, with Brush pledging to provide whatever resources McGraw needed to build a strong team. McGraw in turn acted as intermediary for the negotiations leading to the sale of the Giants. When the series of meetings finally drew to a close, McGraw told his wife that four shares of Giants stock still remained. Blanche bought them with $1,000 of her own money, saying, "I'll invest in John McGraw's future," and kept them for the rest of her life.[29]

Freedman was not quite finished. Instead of keeping the New York team, he sold it to a syndicate of seven stockholders—all Tammany men—that included Frank Farrell, former police commissioner William Devery, and Joseph Gordon, the city's deputy inspector of buildings, after which he retired from baseball. Gordon, who happened to be the brother-in-law of former Giants owner John B. Day, became club president. Farrell co-owned some racehorses with the Fleischmann brothers and was reputed to be the

intermediary who brought them into the Cincinnati Reds deal. After a dili-
gent search that Brush did everything in his power to block, the new regime
located a rocky site in the area around 168th Street and Broadway, blasted it
level, and threw up what became Hilltop Park in time to open on April 30,
1903. It became the home of the New York Highlanders (later Yankees) and
in 1911 would prove crucial to the Giants.[30]

The business of baseball took these momentous and tortuous turns
amid the National League's ongoing war with the American League and
the players' union. By the fall of 1902 the National League owners were
desperate for peace and stability, and Johnson was willing to talk. Negotiations
produced a new national agreement in January 1903 that restored the house
of organized baseball. The owners again agreed to respect their reserve
rights and contracts. The old sticking point of territorial rights was resolved
by agreeing to share New York, Philadelphia, Boston, Chicago, and St. Louis,
giving exclusive rights for Brooklyn, Pittsburgh, and Cincinnati to the
National League and Cleveland, Detroit, and Washington to the American
League.[31]

A new three-man National Commission composed of the two league presidents and a third man chosen by them would preside over the agreement as
its supreme court. The third member turned out to be Garry Herrmann,
president of the Cincinnati Reds, who served as chairman. After some floundering around, the National League owners elected Harry Pulliam, the thirty-
three-year-old secretary of the Pirates, as their new president.[32]

The son of a tobacco farmer in Scottsburg, Kentucky, Pulliam was something of a prodigy in baseball. He graduated from the University of
Virginia law school, then took a job as reporter for the *Louisville Commercial*.
While on the paper he also won a seat in the state legislature. After rising
through the ranks to city editor, he left to become secretary for the Louisville
Colonels owned by Barney Dreyfuss. For a time he served as the club president, then relinquished the office to Dreyfuss and returned to his old position. His supreme gift to the Colonels and later the Pirates was scouting
and eventually acquiring an awkward-looking infielder named Honus
Wagner.[33]

Bright and high-strung, Pulliam was not likely to challenge the hard-
driving Johnson on the new commission. Neither was the convivial
Herrmann, a newcomer to baseball and part of the syndicate that bought
the Reds from Brush. Although Herrmann proved to be a decent diplomat,
the energetic Johnson quickly emerged as the dominant figure on the new

commission, which ruled organized baseball until 1920. Once again the players found themselves dealing with a de facto monopoly even as the two major leagues' owners continued to squabble over players and related issues.[34]

CHAPTER 3

The Master Builder

*"All successful endeavors in life are based on
that idea of being able to find faults and of
being just as quick to correct them."*
——JOHN MCGRAW

*"That was Mac all the time, all our years.
What was worth doing was worth doing well.
That was the secret of his preparation. That's
been the secret of his success."*
——HUGHIE JENNINGS

ON JULY 17, 1902, JOHN AND BLANCHE MCGRAW arrived in New York to take up their new lives. They moved into the Victoria Hotel at Fifth Avenue and Twenty-seventh Street, where the manager obligingly gave them a parlor on an upper floor to escape the incessant noise of horses' hooves on the busy avenue. The Giants had their offices in the St. James Building at Broadway and Twenty-sixth, only two blocks from the Victoria. McGraw soon got into the habit of stopping by the office before catching a hack or the elevated train uptown to the Polo Grounds, where he liked to be by ten o'clock. On one of his first visits to the office, he stunned Andrew Freedman by scratching nine names off the list of twenty-three players reserved by the Giants. "You can begin by releasing these," McGraw said. "We've got to build for next season," he said. "I will center on that and do what we can with what we've got."[1]

Purging the roster and adding the former Orioles gave New Yorkers their first hint that McGraw might actually give them a team worth watching. On July 19 a large crowd turned out to watch the new-look Giants in their first game at the Polo Grounds under McGraw, who played shortstop. Although they lost 4–3, their hustle impressed most of the spectators. "That the people of New York want to see good baseball and will liberally patronize the same was proved by the crowds that went to the Polo Grounds to see what their team would do under the new regime," observed the *New York Times*.[2]

When McGraw arrived, the Giants were in last place by thirty-three and a half games and showing few signs of life. The papers paid little attention to the team except to mock its pitiful style of play. Freedman had compounded his lack of credibility at the start of the season by announcing Ned Hanlon as the team's new manager. Hanlon, still in charge of Brooklyn, promptly denied agreeing to any contract. Forced to backtrack the next day, Freedman then came up with the improbable Horace Fogel, a Philadelphia sports-writer who had once managed a team in 1887.[3]

In true Freedman fashion, the owner abruptly sacked Fogel after only forty-three games and put second baseman Heinie Smith in charge. McGraw became the third Giants manager that season. The players he brought with him from Baltimore helped, but the club had little to work with beyond a talented young pitcher named Christy Mathewson; outfielder Steve Brodie, McGraw's former Orioles teammate; and catcher Frank Bowerman. Shortly after his arrival McGraw picked up outfielder George Browne and pitcher Roscoe Miller. Under his management the team did better but still finished dead last, a whopping fifty-three and a half games behind the triumphant Pirates.[4]

"More than the mere lack of skill had put the Giants in last place," said Blanche McGraw. "Key players simply were not interested in anything except their salary checks ... All were known as knockers, shirkers, and loafers in the sports pages. Ringleaders were openly accused and named."[5]

Well might McGraw have cringed at the challenge before him. One writer scorned the Giants as "positively the rankest apology for a first class ball club that was ever imposed upon any major city." Blanche recalled a sense of uneasiness, "almost holding our breath and secretly wondering if we had made any kind of mistake by leaving Baltimore." Yet she was serene in her belief that her husband could conquer any obstacle. "I knew that men in baseball were tugging in different directions," she added, "but it was still John's business and none of mine. My job was faith. He would succeed, because of his unquenchable fire and desire to succeed." She marveled at "how he could find the answer, the solution, to all of his troubles through victory or merely hard play on the baseball field."[6]

McGraw took the business of baseball with utmost seriousness and expected his players to do the same. Apart from his knowledge of the game and its rules, imbibed since boyhood, he had a memory that retained what every pitcher he saw threw best and what pitch every batter liked most to hit. Over the years he compiled a mental scrapbook of styles, idiosyncrasies, and weaknesses that he could recall on the spot. His wife claimed that he "could reconstruct a full ball game, pitch by pitch." This knowledge he doled out to his players while also getting them to understand the importance of accumulating it on their own. That, to McGraw, was taking the game seriously.[7]

"My memory . . . has been my greatest asset," McGraw declared later. "I knew and remembered the weakness and strength of nearly every player in the big league . . . I never doped out any system of remembering things. I guess it is due to my intense concentration on anything in which I am interested."[8]

Two qualities mattered most to him: smarts and speed. His teams would run and put constant pressure on the defense. "The first thing I notice in youngsters when they report is their speed," he noted. "If they have it, I pay more attention." By the same token, "the first indication that a player is slipping comes from his legs . . . When I notice that an infielder or an outfielder has lost that quick spring of youth in going for a ball, I immediately begin looking for his successor."[9]

Every team had some fast men and stole some bases. McGraw differed from others in wanting speed up and down the entire lineup. Speed did more than grab extra bases. It put pressure on the pitcher to hold runners and on the infield and outfield to hurry their throws. It produced infield hits instead of outs, reduced the need to waste an out on a sacrifice, and put constant pressure on the pitcher and catcher alike.

But speed alone did not produce wins unless it was tempered by smarts. The smart runner could steal more bases than the man blessed with speed but not much else. Speed could not be learned, but smarts could if the player applied himself. For McGraw everything revolved around knowing when to do what. The ability of the base runner to read the pitcher, the catcher, the situation, and understand when to steal. The sacrifice, hit-and-run, delayed steal, bunt, even the Baltimore chop, were all tactical tools; the trick was learning which one to apply in a given situation. McGraw came to dislike the sacrifice because it wasted an out to get a base that could better be gained by other means.[10]

So, too, with defense. He liked to say that a fast, sure infield could handle 75 percent of fielding chances, especially behind a curveball pitcher.

Positioning was crucial for both infielders and outfielders, which required them to learn the propensities of every hitter. McGraw passed them along from the bench or the third-base coach's box through signals. He also developed signals for telling runners what to do and pitchers what to throw. Once a player learned enough to do the right thing, McGraw let him operate on his own most of the time; until then, however, he took his orders from the manager. "Ball players, as a rule," he declared, "can do a more workmanlike job when they feel that someone else is taking the responsibility."[11]

To get his message across, McGraw adopted an autocratic, unyielding style. "I have made it a point . . . never to blame a player for failing in a sincere effort to carry out instructions from the bench," he stressed, "but I also have made it a point to censure a player, even if he won the game, by failing to obey orders." On one occasion he fined outfielder Red Murray for not bunting as ordered even though Murray hit a home run. For McGraw, discipline and control mattered above all else. "I'd like to use fewer signs, or do away with signals entirely," he declared, "but I can't with so many young pitchers and fielders. The veterans can be directed by a wave of the hand. They know about what to expect or do. It's a slower process with these boys . . . but soon it becomes part of their natural skill, and they will be outstanding because of the firm foundation in tactics and strategy."[12]

The sharp, vitriolic tongue and biting sarcasm he unleashed on umpires lashed his players as well. "Players didn't know what to expect," observed Blanche, "and played their heads off to prevent it." Most responded well to the challenges McGraw thrust at them. "Sometimes Mr. McGraw would bawl the dickens out of me, as he did everybody else," recalled outfielder Fred Snodgrass. "Any *mental* error, any failure to think, and McGraw would be all over you. And I do believe he had the most vicious tongue of any man who ever lived. Absolutely! Sometimes that wasn't very easy to take." But, Snodgrass added, "he was a very fair man, and it was only when you really had it coming to you that you got it. And once he'd bawled you out good and proper, and I do mean proper, then he'd forget it. He wouldn't ever mention it again, and in public he would always stand up for his players. It was really a lot of fun to play for McGraw."[13]

Not everyone felt that way. "I didn't like John J. McGraw," admitted outfielder Edd Roush, who went on to the Hall of Fame. "I just didn't enjoy playing for him, that's all. If you made a bad play he'd cuss you out, yell at you, call you all sorts of names. That didn't go with me. So I was glad as I could be when he traded me to Cincinnati." But Roush had been a Giant only a few months. Shortstop Al Bridwell, however, thought he was a great manager "because he knew how to handle men. Some players he rode and others he didn't. He got the most out of each man. It wasn't so much knowing baseball . . . One manager knows about as much about the fundamentals of baseball as another. What makes the difference is knowing each player and how to handle him. And at that sort of thing nobody came anywhere close to McGraw."[14]

McGraw liked smart players who picked things up quickly and never had to be told something twice. He liked the fact that more players were coming to the majors from college rather than from the farm or factory. "With the same amount of natural common sense behind him," he observed, "the college boy has a full two years' jump on the town-lot boy. The difference is simply this—the college boy, or anyone with even a partially trained mind, immediately tries to find his faults; the unschooled fellow usually tries to hide his. The moment a man locates his faults he can quickly correct them. The man who thinks he is keeping his mistakes under cover will never advance a single step until he sees the light."[15]

McGRAW DISCOVERED EARLY THAT ONE PLAYER FIT his criteria perfectly even though Christy Mathewson was plagued with inconsistency. At twenty-two he had shown great promise but, as McGraw observed, "he had so many faults that it would be difficult to enumerate them. He simply knew nothing about pitching at all. His wonderful equipment was being wasted. Even as a boy, though, he had an unusual store of common sense and, being well educated, was eager to be directed." McGraw regarded Mathewson as "pretty nearly the perfect type of a great pitching machine." He stood six foot two, weighed about two hundred pounds, and had the handsome, blond-haired, blue-eyed looks of a matinee idol. He also had an incredible memory and never had to be told anything twice.[16]

A native of Factoryville, Pennsylvania, Mathewson was the eldest of five children born to staunch middle-class Baptist parents who believed in education as a way to escape the mines. At Keystone Academy in Factoryville he excelled at baseball and football. While there he earned money playing baseball in the summer at a dollar a game, which helped convince him that he was not destined for the ministry, as his parents had hoped. In the fall of 1898 he entered Bucknell University, where he excelled as both student and athlete. He seemed almost too good to be true: bright, handsome, multitalented, modest, and an overachiever. He remained at Bucknell three years before leaving to pursue a career in baseball.[17]

In June 1900, while pitching for Norfolk in the Virginia League, Mathewson learned that both the Giants and Athletics were bidding for his services. Aware of Philadelphia's strong pitching staff, he chose the Giants, saying, "I thought I'd have a better chance of getting a good workout with the inferior pitching staff of the New York team." Freedman anted up $1,500 for the pitcher, who then surrendered 35 hits and 14 walks in thirty-four innings. In December Freedman returned him to Norfolk, where Connie Mack put in an offer for him. However, Freedman asked Brush to acquire him for the Reds. Brush did so and promptly traded him back to the Giants for Amos Rusie, a once-great pitcher who had held out for two futile seasons; he never won a game for the Reds. Like it or not, Mathewson was stuck with the hapless Giants. For that, McGraw and Brush were profoundly grateful.[18]

During 1901 Mathewson compiled a record of 20-17 in 338 innings pitched. That winter his arm went so lame that, he admitted later, "I was haunted by the idea that the arm would never get into shape again." Although his arm strength returned, the experience left Mathewson with a firm conviction never to overtax his strength again. Several Giant veterans, jealous of his salary, urged Fogel to get him off the mound. Fogel obliged by putting him at first base and the outfield for several games in 1902. His tormentors responded by throwing badly to first base on purpose, pulling him off the bag and making him look bad. As late as June 30 the *Times* reported that "Christy Mathewson, the former pitcher, was again tried at first base. He did nothing remarkable."[19]

After McGraw arrived on July 17 the nonsense ended. The notion of putting Mathewson at other positions appalled the new manager, who called it "sheer insanity . . . any man who did that should be locked up." Mathewson was restored to pitching duties, and several of his tormentors found themselves on the list of those cut from the team. Mathewson finished the season with a record of 14-17 but led the league in shutouts with eight. During those last months of the season McGraw saw enough to conclude that he had a truly unique talent in the big fellow whose knock-kneed walk earned him the nickname of "Old Gumboots." During spring training at Savannah in 1903, McGraw went out of his way to forge a relationship with Mathewson. From this effort emerged one of the oddest couples in all sports.[20]

The two men could not have been more different. The one short, loud, pugnacious, and profane, the other tall, handsome, soft-spoken, and digni- fied; the one from a hardscrabble Catholic background, the other from a comfortable middle-class Protestant family; the one driving himself unmer- cifully to achieve his goal of victory, the other just as determined but harnessing his strength by extending himself only when necessary, making it all look effortless. For McGraw, baseball was all-consuming; Mathewson had other interests. He read widely and became so expert at checkers that he could play eight opponents simultaneously while blindfolded. He also excelled at almost every game or sport he took up. McGraw would do anything to win; Mathewson, for all his competitiveness, seemed a paragon of good sportsmanship.[21]

Yet, for all their differences, the two men had important qualities in common. They were both fierce competitors, Mathewson not only in base- ball but in all of his endeavors. They both understood how much work it took to excel and were students of the game. McGraw was eager to teach and Mathewson to learn. To McGraw's delight, the pitcher seemed able to grasp everything told him the first time he heard it and possessed a photo- graphic memory that could record every pitch he threw and what came of it. Once McGraw impressed on him the importance of knowing the weak- nesses and strengths of every batter, Mathewson began accumulating his own mental files on the men he faced. He became the one pitcher for whom McGraw never called pitches. He would be the only superstar McGraw would have on his team for another quarter century.[22]

Spring training before the 1903 season also served as Mathewson's honeymoon with his recent bride, Jane Stoughton, whom he had met at Bucknell. A bright, energetic young woman with gray eyes and dark brown hair, she came from a good family and taught Sunday school. Despite his background, Mathewson was not overly religious. He had promised his mother that he would never pitch on Sundays, a promise that was easy to keep given how few teams played Sunday ball in the major leagues, and he willingly changed from the Baptist to the Presbyterian Church at his new wife's request.[23]

In Savannah, Jane was one of the few wives present and somewhat lost in this strange new environment. She sat quietly in the lobby of the De Soto Hotel, at first exchanging glances with Blanche McGraw. Gradually they began going out shopping or sightseeing together and quickly became fast friends much as their husbands had done. At the end of spring training, the

McGraws and Mathewsons did an extraordinary, possibly unprecedented thing for a manager and player and their wives. Once back in New York, they rented a large apartment at Columbus Avenue and Eighty-fifth Street together for $50 a month. McGraw paid the rent and gas, Mathewson the food bill. The apartment was only a block from Central Park and close to the elevated that took them to the Polo Grounds.[24]

"He had an unusual mind," Blanche said of Mathewson, "a quick mind, and the stubbornness of a person with a trained mind. He had the ego of a great competitor and a deep-rooted belief that every opponent was his inferior ... He read a lot. Most interesting was his memory ... He could remember dozens of cards that had been played in a game, and a cribbage score. He played checkers by numbers. That is, the squares were numbered in his mind." During their time together on and off the field, McGraw happily emptied his store of knowledge about the game and other players into Mathewson's receptive mind, giving them yet another bond for their friendship.[25]

The 1903 season opened well for the Giants, who found themselves in first place at the end of May and drawing the largest crowds to the Polo Grounds in years. McGraw put Roger Bresnahan, who had played third base as well as catcher for the Orioles, in center field alongside Sam Mertes in left. Bresnahan hit .350 that season and Mertes led the league in runs batted in with 104. At second base he installed Billy Gilbert, another refugee from the Orioles. McGraw also hired his old friend John Murphy as groundskeeper. A quiet, older man, Murphy had groomed the field for the Orioles to fit a team devoted to speed and alertness. He manicured the Polo Grounds to suit McGraw's game just as McGraw did his players.[26]

If McGraw had hopes of playing more games in 1903, they were dashed early. His damaged left knee buckled again during spring training, and an unfortunate accident early in the season hurt him severely. While hitting grounders to his infielders, a stray throw from the outfield by pitcher Dummy Taylor hit McGraw in the face, smashing his nose and breaking a blood vessel inside his throat. He was rushed to a nearby hospital with blood gushing from his nose and mouth. The shattered cartilage in his nose never healed properly. For the rest of his life he would be plagued with sinus trouble and upper-respiratory infections.[27]

Still coming together as a team, the Giants gave the powerful Pirates, who had won the pennant in 1901 and 1902, a tough race. Mathewson and Joe McGinnity emerged as the most formidable pitching duo in the league with Matty absorbing lessons from his thirty-two-year-old colleague as he did from McGraw. McGinnity went 31-20 and led the league with an astounding 434 innings pitched; Mathewson was close behind at 30-13, hurling 366 innings and leading the league in strikeouts. Together they appeared in 100 of the team's 139 games and accounted for 73 percent of its 84 victories, a record never equaled. In the end, however, the Giants finished second, six and a half games behind the Pirates, a far cry from the previous season. McGraw still had some building to do, and he had an owner who supported everything he did.[28]

JOHN T. BRUSH—ONE WAG SUGGESTED that the T stood for "Tooth"— stood distinctly apart from the other owners in several ways. He was a man of definite ideas, as shown by his syndicate scheme, and did not hesitate to make decisions, even unpopular ones, or depart from the game's conventional wisdom. He had money and was willing to spend it if he thought the investment was sound. An unfortunate physical condition also separated him from his peers. He suffered from locomotor ataxia, a progressive disease that robbed him of the ability to control his bodily movements. By 1903, when he bought the Giants, he had already suffered its agonies for several years and needed two canes to walk. "But nothing ever stilled his active mind," said an admiring Blanche McGraw, "or lessened the fighting qualities of his tireless heart."[29]

Brush was another American success story. Born in Clintonville, Ohio, in 1845, he was orphaned at the age of four and sent to live with his grandfather in Hopkinton, Massachusetts. At seventeen he went to work in a Boston clothing store but left a year later to enlist in the First New York Artillery. After the Civil War, he clerked in different eastern clothing stores before moving in 1875 to Indianapolis, where he opened his own dry goods establishment, which evolved into one of the region's first department stores. He prospered at the business and involved himself in civic affairs. After his first wife died, leaving him with a daughter, he married an actress and had another daughter. In 1887 he bought shares in the Indianapolis Hoosiers of the National League, partly to advertise his store. When the National League dropped Indianapolis in 1890, Brush agreed to take over the Cincinnati franchise and also acquired shares in the Giants. In Cincinnati he encountered the hostility of local sportswriter Ban Johnson, who was to be his nemesis for years to come.[30]

Despite Brush's roots in Ohio, Blanche McGraw thought that "his eye was always on New York as a site for his baseball operations, and perhaps his clothing business as well." His ambition to enter the New York market was stalled by two unexpected developments: the onset of his illness and the surprise scoop of the Giants by Andrew Freedman. When he finally got there in 1903, he was not about to let even his physical disability stifle his plans. He did more than marry an actress; he married show business itself. "My father was definitely stage-struck," recalled his youngest daughter. "He married an actress and joined the Lambs Club. Almost every actor in New York had a pass to the Polo Grounds and the big stars had boxes." The passes were no mere pieces of cardboard but distinctive items fashioned by a jeweler with a different design every year.[31]

Brush rightly viewed baseball as another form of entertainment in what was the prime market for entertainment. He wanted not only a popular but a classy product, and liked to boast that his season boxholders were the same kind of people who purchased boxes at the Metropolitan Opera. The Giants did not start their games until four o'clock to enable the Wall Street crowd to make it to the Polo Grounds after the market's three o'clock closing. More women were also coming to games, suggesting that the fans were becoming more civilized. However, Brush did not want to lose touch with the common folk who flocked into the bleachers to cheer for their heroes.[32]

Above all, Brush wanted what New Yorkers of all classes craved most: a winner. One writer observed that "from the time that . . . Brush got into baseball he was madly infatuated with the idea of winning the championship." Whatever else it did for him, that goal made good business sense. He would do his part by giving McGraw the resources he needed and staying out of his way. In that sense he was the ideal owner for McGraw, and their partnership proved both fruitful and lasting. "He was heart and soul with me in my plan to build up a club," said McGraw. "Not once . . . did Mr. Brush ever interfere with me in the slightest way."[33]

At age fifty-seven Brush knew he would never be popular beyond a limited circle of friends. Both his personality and his illness prevented him from testing the social waters in New York. On one occasion Charles W. Murphy, who worked as a press agent for Brush before buying the Cubs in 1906, suggested that Brush get out and mix more with people to improve his popularity.

Brush smiled at the suggestion. "If the Giants win, I will be popular," he replied. "If they lose I will not be. All the personal popularity in the world gets the club owner nothing if his club is a loser."[34]

However, Brush had good reason to be satisfied. The play of the Giants in 1903 had brought eager crowds back to the Polo Grounds and to other parks when the Giants came to town. McGraw was largely responsible because of the controversy and enmity his belligerent style, and that of his team, aroused everywhere. For the first time in years the Giants had entered the mix of bitter rivalries, the kind that kept turnstiles spinning at home and elsewhere.[35]

As THE 1904 SEASON APPROACHED, McGRAW continued to improve his lineup. In what he later called "the most successful deal that I ever made," he gave Brooklyn two players for shortstop Bill Dahlen, a fiery competitor and a brilliant defensive player. In announcing the trade, he said: "There is no better shortstop in baseball . . . He is the kind of man every club needs to steady the infield." Third base, his old position, remained a problem until he found Art Devlin, who had left Georgetown University after his sophomore year to play professionally. The son of an Irish immigrant who worked as a harness maker and locksmith in Washington, D.C., Devlin impressed McGraw with his play at Newark in the Eastern League, where in 1903 he hit .287 and stole fifty-one bases. When McGraw brought him to spring training in 1904, some veterans sneered at him as "McGraw's college boy." Their derision only made him tougher and more pugnacious. McGraw also acquired outfielder Harry "Moose" McCormick, who had led the Eastern League in batting.[36]

For pitching, McGraw had the incomparable one-two punch of McGinnity and Mathewson. McGinnity seemed virtually indestructible. Somehow switching between overhand, sidearm, and a masterful underhanded curveball that he called "Old Sal" fed his amazing durability. "I've pitched for 30 years and I believe I've averaged over 30 games a season," he said, "and in all my experiences I've never had what I could truthfully call a sore arm." Unlike the refined Mathewson, McGinnity was a rough character who loved a good fight. Earlier in life he had operated a saloon and served as his own bouncer. McGraw also had Dummy Taylor, so called because he was a deaf-mute. Besides his pitching, Taylor contributed to the Giants in another important way: Former manager George Davis had the entire team learn sign language to communicate with Taylor, and McGraw did so as well. For a time McGraw used sign language as a backup signals system until other teams began catching on.[37]

To support this trio, McGraw brought on board two youngsters, Leon "Red" Ames and George "Hooks" Wiltse. Ames made an impressive if brief showing for the Giants late in the 1903 season; Wiltse was signed during the winter after a 20-8 season with Troy in the New York State League. Hooks got his nickname not from a good curveball but because his long arms and big hands made him an excellent fielder. It was Ames who possessed the outstanding curveball. Although Ames and Wiltse pitched only spottily in 1904, they became part of the core team McGraw was assembling for the long haul.[38]

Sportswriters saw early that McGraw's approach offered a striking change from past Giant teams. "Team work and speed on the bases is the result Mac is aiming at," wrote one, "which, in conjunction with good pitching, is calculated to repeat the success he achieved . . . last season." Asked his views, McGraw did not hesitate. "I have the strongest team I have ever led into a pennant race," he said. "I ought to come in first, but I don't want to go on record as predicting that—the game is too uncertain, injuries to players and the uncertainty that makes the sport so attractive sometimes proves too much of a handicap."[39]

Opening day on April 15, 1904, offered a preview of the quickening tempo of New York baseball and American life in general. Charles Ebbets, the Brooklyn president, hired two gasoline-powered automobiles to drive into Manhattan and carry John McGraw and other executives across the Brooklyn Bridge for the game at Washington Park. After lengthy pregame ceremonies the Giants downed Brooklyn 3–1 behind Mathewson.[40]

Opening day in New York did not occur until April 21. Prior to the team's arrival back from spring training, Brush had added six thousand seats to the bleachers and fitted out the offices and dressing rooms with electric lights and steam heat. A huge crowd thronged the Polo Grounds only to witness another first-time disappointment. The Phillies knocked Mathewson out in the fifth inning, in which he yielded six hits and had fans howling for his removal. Philadelphia scored seven runs before the carnage ended and thumped the Giants by the embarrassing score of 12–1. But McGraw knew it was an aberration. He had a veteran team that quickly proved its manager had made no idle boast. Despite the home opener fiasco, they raced to a 12-3 start and kept on winning until their record reached 53-18.[41]

Still McGraw wasn't satisfied. During May the team scuttled in and out of first place. McGraw thought the team needed another big bat, and on July 3 he got his wish in the form of "Turkey Mike" Donlin, so called because of his strutting walk. McGraw said wryly, "He was born on Decoration Day, and he's been parading ever since . . . But he can really field and hit and play anywhere." In 1901, Donlin had jumped from St. Louis to McGraw's Orioles and hit .347. For all his talent he was a troubled soul, having lost his parents at the age of eight when a bridge collapsed, and struggled with consumption as a boy. At an early age he developed a drinking problem that scarred the rest of his life.[42]

Despite this weakness, McGraw admired his fiery temperament and live bat. Donlin's future with the Orioles seemed limitless, but in March 1902 he went on a drinking binge that landed him in jail for six months and the team released him. Paroled a month early for good behavior, he was picked up by Brush's Cincinnati team in August. In 1903 he managed to stay out of trouble and gave Honus Wagner a run for the batting title. He got off to a great start the next season, batting .356, but then went on a bender that got him in trouble again. Joe Kelley suspended him for thirty days and decided that he had had enough of Donlin's antics.[43]

McGraw concluded that under his supervision Donlin could be a productive and reliable player. He induced his friend Kelley and Fred Clarke of the Pirates to pull off a three-team swap of outfielders with Moose McCormick going to the Pirates, who sent Jimmy Sebring to the Reds, who in turn unloaded Donlin on the Giants. Donlin blossomed into a star on the big stage of New York. "If you treat me right, I'll be on the up and up," he pledged the city's sportswriters, and he kept his promise.[44]

Content with his lineup, McGraw put himself in only five games all season as the Giants battled their way to the pennant their manager had said they should win. Everywhere on the road he played to the hilt his image of the archvillain bringing his stable of ruffians to town. Like the Orioles of old, the Giants became the most hated team in the league and relished the role. Mathewson thought that McGraw got "the most out of a throng by his clever acting . . . He can do more with a crowd, make it more malleable than any other man in baseball." The sportswriters dubbed him "Muggsy," a name he loathed as much as Donlin hated "Turkey," but he had no problem living up to his image as a profane, brawling, umpire-baiting agitator who also happened to know how to get his men to play their best. "It is the prospect of a hot feud," McGraw said blandly, "that brings out the crowd."[45]

"Probably no more wily general ever crouched on the coaching line at third base than John McGraw," said Mathewson. "His judgment in holding runners or urging them on to score is almost uncanny . . . He has formulated a list of regulations for his players which might be called the 'McGraw Coaching Curriculum.'" The first base coach took his cues from McGraw. "Around McGraw revolved the game of the Giants," added Mathewson. "He was the game."[46]

It had to be that way in McGraw's eyes. The players were still new to each other and had not fully digested his system or methods. "The result was that I had to play the game myself," he observed. "I directed it from the bench . . . We had a system of signals that governed every situation on the field. I know it was condemned by some managers; but in our case it was necessary . . . I was seldom seen on the coaching line that year. We won the pennant from the bench." From the bench McGraw gained a fuller view of the game with fewer distractions. "A real reason for his going to the bench . . . is because this increases the club's chances of winning . . . Many a game he has pulled out of the fire by going back to the bench and watching," said Mathewson. He especially watched pitchers, especially those new to him. "Pitching was my first love," McGraw admitted, "and I have never got away from it. To me it is the most fascinating art in the world."[47]

IN AUGUST THE GIANTS HEADED WEST ON a road trip to Pittsburgh, Chicago, Cincinnati, and St. Louis. In front of gratifyingly large, hostile crowds, the team swept twelve of fourteen games and all but clinched the pennant. Observed one writer: "The last Western trip of McGraw's men has developed into a sort of triumphant pennant march . . . The lion's share of the credit for the club's success belongs to John McGraw because of his good generalship on the field and his diplomacy in dealing with the players. Always master of the situation, McGraw has utilized his magnetic influence to advantage and has proven a more resourceful manager."[48]

Manager Frank Selee of the Cubs offered a generous assessment of McGraw's work. "Although McGraw is a rival," he said, "I want to say that he is to-day the wonder of the base ball world. When he took hold here the American League people said, 'We'll put him out of business in one season.' Now he is not only the ideal of New York City, but New York State."[49]

The Giants finished a shocking thirteen games ahead of the Cubs and dominated every aspect of the game. They scored the most runs (744),

allowed the fewest (476), and set a record for wins with 106. Although none
of the regulars hit higher than Dan McGann's .286, they led the league in
batting, doubles, homers, stolen bases, and fielding average. Their 283
steals were 56 more than the Cubs, who placed second. The pitching staff
led the league in earned run average, strikeouts, and shutouts. McGinnity
was magnificent, going 35-8 with a league-leading 1.61 earned run average,
408 innings pitched, 9 shutouts, and 51 appearances. Mathewson was close
behind, compiling a 33-12 record in 48 games with 368 innings pitched, a
2.03 earned run average, and a league-leading 212 strikeouts.

The only sour note came in the postseason. Since the peace agreement of
1903, interest had grown in staging some sort of championship contest
between the winners of both leagues. That year the owners of the winning
teams, Barney Dreyfuss of Pittsburgh and Henry J. Killilea of Boston,
agreed privately to hold a best-of-eight contest that in retrospect was labeled
the first World Series. Upstart Boston stunned the Pirates five games to
three. The following year Ban Johnson proposed that a similar series be
held with the formal blessing of the National Commission. Brush and
McGraw wanted none of it. As early as July 25, McGraw declared emphatically that under no circumstances would the Giants play an American
League team. Brush had never forgiven Johnson for shoehorning an
American League team into New York, and McGraw had his own list of
grievances against him.[50]

Despite widespread protests and criticism, Brush refused to budge on
the question. "There is nothing in the constitution or playing rules of the
National League," he said haughtily, "which requires its victorious club to
submit its championship honors to a contest with a victorious club in a
minor league." Much later McGraw explained that "having been one of the
main supports of the National League for years, he did not see why we
should jeopardize the fruits of our victory by recognizing and playing
against the champions of an organization that had been formed to put us
out of business."[51]

The players were disappointed because such a series would have put
money in their pockets. To slake their discontent, Brush helped arrange a
special benefit at the New York Theatre to celebrate the city's first championship since 1889. Brush bought the first subscription box for $5,000 and
attended along with a bevy of show business and political figures. Altogether
the public bought $20,000 worth of tickets, which was split among the
players. After a vaudeville show, the players marched onto the stage in dress

suits and were introduced individually. State Senator Thomas F. Grady delivered a ringing speech praising McGraw's leadership, then surprised him by presenting him with a silver loving cup on behalf of the team. It bore the inscription, FROM THE CHAMPION PLAYERS TO THE CHAMPION MANAGER.[52]

Earlier, in a little ceremony at the Polo Grounds, the players presented Brush with a loving cup engraved with an inscription along with all the players' names and those of Fred Knowles, the secretary-treasurer, and Harry Stevens, who ran concessions. By any measure Brush had treated the players generously, especially compared to some other owners. Still, Donlin told a newsman that the refusal to play a postseason series left a "sore bunch of ballplayers around the club house." They did not know that Brush was about to formulate a plan for such a series the following year, and that both he and McGraw expected the Giants to play in it. Asked whether the players should share in the receipts of such a series, Brush replied that they should.[53]

CHAPTER 4

Rivals

*"The idea of deciding baseball's destiny, game
by game, or season by season, through the
thrown or batted ball was an obsession with
John McGraw. Psychologists might call it a
fetish. He countenanced no other method and
fought to decide everything on the field, because
there he was master of his fate."*

—BLANCHE McGRAW

*"The science of managing . . . is in picking the
spots for attack. The idea that any field
manager can outline a plan of attack against
an entire team is erroneous . . . impossible. Like
the captain of a football team the baseball
manager quickly discovers the weak spots in the
enemy's lineup . . . Being aware of these spots
the trick is in waiting for the exact moment to
spring something that will double-cross the
particular player and throw the opposition off
balance . . . All you need is to fool just one
player—or maybe two."*

—JOHN McGRAW

AMERICANS GREETED THE NEW CENTURY with more than their
usual dose of optimism about the future. The depression of the
1890s had faded, the economy was flourishing, the tempo of
everyday life was speeding up, and change had already become a way of
life—especially in those fast-growing hotbeds of progress, the cities. A
nation of farmers was morphing into one of employees whose livelihood

depended ever more on an increasingly complex network of industrial, commercial, and financial giants that dominated the economy. For ambitious individuals opportunity beckoned everywhere on a scale never before seen, but so did the possibility of failure. The scale of everyday life seemed to be expanding and the role of the individual shrinking along with it. In the full flush of their enthusiasm about the future, Americans launched into yet another of their periodic spasms of reform, this one known as the Progressive movement. In 1901 the youngest president the nation had yet known took office in the wake of an assassination and proceeded to make himself a fitting icon for the era with his unabashed vigor and relentless energy.

Theodore Roosevelt was a card-carrying outdoorsman who loved to test his wits and physical stamina against nature. However, he cared little for baseball, probably because he had never played the game, and in that indifference he parted company with most American males. The game infatuated rural, small-town, and big-city America alike. In many a small town baseball had a virtual lock on the summer amusement market, while in larger cities it had to compete with several other forms of enjoyment. However, the target audience in cities grew steadily, swelled by two separate and very different streams of newcomers: immigrants from abroad and rural folk who poured into the cities in even larger numbers than the foreigners. One was largely ignorant of baseball, the other quite familiar with it.

Between 1850 and 1910 the nation's population mushroomed from just under 23.2 million to more than 92.2 million despite the loss of nearly an entire generation of young men during the Civil War. By 1920 more than half of all Americans lived in urban places (defined as 2,500 or more people), and the number of cities with 50,000 or more people jumped from 16 in 1850 to 144. Between 1870 and 1910 the middle class, consisting largely of the professions, managers, technicians, merchants, and white-collar workers, nearly quadrupled from about 2.3 million to nearly 8.9 million. The financial industry employed an army of people, especially in New York, who were among the most eager audiences for ball games. So were white-collar workers, the foot soldiers of commerce and bureaucracy: clerks, bookkeepers, stenographers, typists, store clerks, salespeople, drummers, sales agents in insurance, real estate, and other fields, and a host of others.[1]

In their rapid growth cities took on two striking characteristics: They emerged as the ultimate marketplaces and the most competitive arenas.

Everything from sin to salvation could be bought in the city. Every urban dweller peddled his skills to whoever needed them. Workers sold their labor and lawyers their acumen; politicos bought votes and sold influence; newspapers sold information, teachers education, and revivalists salvation. Pleasure and entertainment no less than other fields developed their own markets and professionals. The price of admission bought one a ball game, concert, recital, lecture, vaudeville show, nickelodeon, dance hall, amusement park ride or sideshow, or any number of other diversions. One could rent another person for everything from menial tasks to simple companionship to sexual gratification.

Such an environment offered the ultimate competitive arena for climbing the ladder of success, especially in business. Victory required unswerving dedication, daring, foresight, some measure of talent, ruthlessness, unflagging energy, and a modicum of luck. From its battles emerged a new and more virulent strain of American individualism. Where earlier generations had fought their toughest battles against nature, urban warriors fought each other or, even worse, the invisible but relentless forces of the marketplace.

For those who entered the baseball arena, the combat was direct and the outcome clear. The business world might be clogged with ambiguities, but on the field of play everyone understood what had to be done to achieve success. For the players the pressure was no less constant than for the titan of business or the Wall Street warrior. Fans came to amuse themselves for a couple of hours by watching them play, but for the players every contest helped define their livelihood and their future. A promising career could be cut short in an instant by injury or gradually by time's inevitable erosion of skills. Ability also declined from sheer mental and/or emotional fatigue or personal excesses, of which drinking was the most common. For the professional ballplayer uncertainty was a way of life and every season an ordeal for which strength, stamina, and perspective had somehow to be summoned and maintained. No amount of love for the game could alone guarantee survival, let alone success.

Of such stern stuff was John McGraw made. He had shown himself to be the ultimate warrior as both player and manager. He had willingly, even eagerly, placed himself in the most conspicuous and challenging position in the nation's largest city, one that demanded success. In looking over his team during the off season, he liked his chances of repeating. He had pretty much the same squad: McGann, Gilbert, Dahlen, and Devlin around the infield, Browne, Bresnahan, and Mertes in the outfield, and Donlin for a full season. Catching, however, remained a weak link.

Once it looked as if Donlin would pan out, McGraw came to an inspired decision: He put Donlin in center field and made Bresnahan his catcher. So well did Bresnahan do that McGraw later called him "about the best catcher of all times." He could hit, work walks, and steal a few bases, and, most important of all to McGraw, he had smarts and a quick mind. He had played every position in his day and so knew them all, and his memory approached that of Mathewson and the manager. Like them he was dedicated to winning and only had to be told something once. Like McGraw, too, he was hot-tempered and tactless; one writer described him as "highly strung and almost abnormally emotional."[2]

In February 1905, McGraw made his only addition to the team by purchasing Sammy Strang from Brooklyn. Besides being a decent hitter, Strang could play almost any position. Under McGraw he played at every infield position and the outfield as well in 1905 while also pioneering a new role in baseball: the pinch hitter, whose job was to bat for someone else.[3]

McGraw was hardly alone in his tireless effort to build a winning team. The National League races between 1901 and 1913 resembled those of the previous decade in one important respect: Only three teams won all the pennants. However, the three teams changed entirely, with Chicago, New York, and Pittsburgh rising to the top while Boston and Brooklyn fell to the level of doormats and Baltimore was dropped from the league. Two key managers remained winners: Frank Selee shifted from Boston to Chicago and McGraw from Baltimore to New York. Early in the 1900s both men took a backseat to Fred Clarke, player-manager of the Pirates, who guided his team to three consecutive championships.

WHEN THE NATIONAL LEAGUE VOTED TO DROP Louisville in 1900, it threatened the baseball future of the club's owner, a diminutive German-Jewish immigrant of thirty-four named Barney Dreyfuss. A 125-pound bundle of energy who spoke with an accent, Dreyfuss left Freiberg, Baden, in 1883 at the age of seventeen to join members of his family who had already moved to America. He worked as an accountant for a distillery in Paducah, Kentucky, owned by his cousins, one of whom had married his sister. Advised by a doctor to get some outdoor exercise, he discovered baseball and fell in love with the game. In 1888 he moved to Louisville and bought a few shares in the Colonels. When Louisville moved from the American Association to the National League in 1892, Dreyfuss gained control of the club and traded places with its president, Harry Pulliam, who became secretary-treasurer. In 1899, Dreyfuss bought out the other interests to become sole owner.[4]

Fascinated by the inner workings of a big-league club, Dreyfuss vowed to make the team a winner in the new league despite having its smallest market. "Smartness pays off in baseball, as well as in any other activity," he declared, "and I think I'm a pretty smart fellow." However, he had no answer for the decision to drop his team from the league. Earlier in 1900, Brush had informed him that Pittsburgh's owners wanted to sell. They offered Dreyfuss a half ownership in the Pirates provided he brought with him the best of his Louisville players. Since Louisville had not yet been officially dumped from the National League, the deal took the form of a trade in which four players and $25,000 went to Louisville in exchange for thirteen of its players.[5]

The influx of new talent for Pittsburgh was stunning. It included Fred Clarke, second baseman Claude Ritchey, third baseman Tommy Leach, catcher Charley "Chief" Zimmer, pitchers Charles "Deacon" Phillippe and Rube Waddell, and an outstanding outfielder by the name of Honus Wagner. One key Pirate who left in the trade, pitcher Jack Chesbro, returned to the team. Pittsburgh's management reorganized with Dreyfuss as president and Pulliam as secretary. Clarke became the manager as well as left fielder. "In the baseball business," Dreyfuss proclaimed, "an owner must act quickly and secretly. He does not have time to consult a board of directors. He must act on the jump and talk afterward." That approach had netted him Clarke, Leach, and his ultimate prize, Honus Wagner. "So you see that the chief factor in baseball success is the ability to pick good players," Dreyfuss added. "That's the game the owner plays—and it's a game that turns his hair gray."[6]

In 1898 and 1899 the Pirates had finished eighth and seventh in the twelve-team league. Under Clarke's strong leadership and exemplary play, the revitalized team finished second in 1900 and then swept to three straight pennants. The incomparable Wagner, whom McGraw pronounced the greatest player he had ever seen, won batting titles in 1900 and 1903 and, after playing all over the diamond, settled in to become the greatest shortstop of all time. He looked like anything but a great ballplayer with his placid expression, hulking frame, severely bowed legs, and gorilla arms with their huge hands. Yet he was surprisingly graceful and fast, stealing a total of 723 bases in his career, and in the field he got to balls no one thought possible. He had all the tools: speed, smartness, quickness, anticipation, and incredible stamina. Unlike his fiery American League rival Ty Cobb, he was shy and modest.[7]

While Wagner's presence could make any team a contender, he had an imposing supporting cast early in the decade. Clarke provided sound, shrewd leadership as well as good hitting and fielding. Center fielder Clarence "Ginger" Beaumont hit .357 in 1902 to wrest the batting title from Wagner for a year. The small, slight Leach, too often called "Tommy the Wee," shuttled between third base and the outfield and for a time had trouble even getting into ballparks because the guards refused to believe he was a player. But he could run and hit; in 1902 he actually led the National League in home runs with six and finished second in triples with twenty-two. Claude Ritchey was a solid second baseman and Chief Zimmer a dependable catcher. In 1901 the Pirates acquired William "Kitty" Bransfield, who filled a hole at first base for a few years. The pitching staff was anchored by Phillippe, Chesbro, Sam Leever, and Jesse Tannehill.[8]

When Chesbro and Tannehill jumped to the New York Highlanders after the 1902 season, Phillippe and Leever shouldered an even greater load, going 25-9 and 25-7 respectively. A native of Goshen, Ohio, Leever worked as a schoolteacher for seven years while pitching Sundays for a semipro team. In 1899 he led the National League in games and innings pitched, an effort that left him with a sore right arm that plagued him for the rest of his career. During the run of three pennants, Leever piled up a 55-19 record while Phillippe did even better at 66-28.[9]

Along with Wagner, Ginger Beaumont keyed the Pittsburgh offense. During the three magical pennant seasons he batted .341, .357, and .332. For all their presence, Clarke remained the glue to the team, batting .324, .321, and .351 while playing a stellar left field. Although he had trouble going back on fly balls, he made up for it by playing deep and diving for catches on shorter balls. Only twenty-nine years old in 1901, Clarke was a farm boy from Iowa and Kansas who made it to the Louisville Colonels in 1894. Three years later, at only twenty-four, he was named player-manager; that season he batted .390. He was a fearless and intense player who knew how to inspire his men. A successful manager, he told a reporter, needed "shrewdness, cheek, information, and money" to get good players, and then have the ability to shape them into "a happy whole both on and off the field." Dreyfuss supplied the money; Clarke took care of the other qualifications.[10]

In 1904, Pittsburgh stood poised for a run at a fourth straight title, but a series of injuries and other misfortunes plagued the team from the start. The dispirited Pirates tumbled to fourth place, behind not only the Giants but the Cubs and Reds as well. Bransfield slipped badly and was shipped to Philadelphia. For the rest of his managerial career, which lasted until 1916, Clarke searched in vain for a hard-hitting first baseman. Nevertheless, in December, Dreyfuss boasted about the upcoming 1905 season that "McGraw and his Giants will be sitting by the side of the track watching the Pittsburghs whiz by in the limited." As the season wore on, McGraw made him eat his words.[11]

CONVINCED THAT HIS TEAM WAS PRIMED TO repeat in 1905, McGraw worked more than ever to mold them into a reincarnation of the old Orioles, especially in their attitude. He prodded them to be aggressive, belligerent, and ruthless in their style of play, to seek every advantage, exploit every opening or weakness, and give no quarter to either rival players or the umpires. Later in life he said almost coyly, "It was a team of fighters. They thought they could beat anybody and they generally could. As a result of this fighting instinct we got into much trouble."[12]

Sporting Life took a jaundiced view of the McGraw style. "The so-called 'Baltimore ball' of the middle 80's," it observed, "marked the beginning and culmination of real rowdy ball, the principle of which was to get the best of everything by consistent and persistent bull-dozing, with or without cause. At this day Managers Kelley, McGraw and [Clark] Griffith are the remaining exponents of the old-style of rowdy ball that has fallen into universal disfavor." McGraw and his Giants were about to demonstrate that, however universal the disfavor, the effectiveness of rowdy ball remained powerful.[13]

New York celebrated opening day with a parade of sixteen automobiles carrying Brush, McGraw, Boston manager Fred Tenney, and the two teams on a round trip from the Polo Grounds to Washington Square and back. Before a large crowd of about twenty thousand eager fans, McGinnity stifled the hapless Boston hitters, Donlin smacked a homer, and the

Giants romped 10–1. Next day they walloped Boston again 15–0 behind Mathewson.[14]

The Giants were literally off and running and they did not let up all season, winning 105 games while losing only 48, finishing 9 games ahead of the Pirates while leading the league in runs scored (778), batting average (.273), slugging average (.368), doubles (191), home runs (39), and stolen bases (293). Donlin hit .356 to finish third behind Cy Seymour of Cincinnati (.377) and Wagner (.363). Mathewson was magnificent, going 31-8 with a minuscule earned run average of 1.27 in 339 innings pitched. McGinnity faltered somewhat with a record of 21-15. Red Ames emerged as a team stalwart at 22-8, Hooks Wiltse went 15-6, and Dummy Taylor 15-9. Small wonder that late in life McGraw hailed the team as "the greatest ball club that I have managed . . . I have handled other clubs that were greater hitters and greater base runners. I hand the laurels to the 1905 team for its smartness. We did not have a really slow-thinking ball player on the club."[15]

Mathewson had clearly mastered his craft, thanks in large part to McGraw's tutoring. "Knowledge of batsmen and their supposed weakness is essential in the success of any twirler," he said in a newspaper article that April. "Pitchers try to discover and remember the pronounced weaknesses of batsmen . . . Catchers must also have knowledge about the batters . . . If he knows nothing of the batsmen he must be governed largely by the man's position at the plate . . . The way he holds his bat may show to the pitcher the kind he is most likely to meet. Then the position of the batsman in the box is of vital importance. He may stand at a certain angle from which he can scarcely be able to connect with a fast high ball or a slow one."[16]

As the season progressed, McGraw concluded that most of his players had learned their lessons well enough to make decisions on their own in many cases. Mathewson noticed the change in him. "After winning the pennant in 1904 by sitting on the bench, keeping away from the coaching lines, and making every play himself, McGraw decided that his men were older and knew the game and that he would give them more rein in 1905," he said. "He appeared oftener on the coaching lines and attended more to the base runners than to the game as a whole. But in the crises he was the man who decided what was to be done."[17]

The Giants lived up to the legend of the old Orioles by earning the dubious honor of the nastiest, rowdiest team in the league. Only eight days into the season McGann got into a fight with Phillies catcher Fred Abbott, who had tagged him out. Umpire George Bausewine tossed McGann from the game, prompting McGraw to rush bellowing at Bausewine while a large Philadelphia crowd clamored for his scalp. After the Giants' 10–2 victory an unhappy mob pelted the carriages carrying the Giants back to their hotel with bricks and rocks until the police managed to restore some semblance of order.

The Pittsburgh press abused McGraw nearly all summer, slackening only when the Pirates finished a disappointing fourth to the Giants that year. But McGraw had targeted the Pirates as the team to beat in 1905, and he encouraged rather than downplayed the growing enmity between the two clubs.[18]

In May, McGraw was introduced to one of the league's new umpires, Bill Klem, who went on to become a member of the Hall of Fame. Prior to the game with the Cubs at the Polo Grounds, McGraw graciously presented Klem with a silver ball and strike indicator, a gift from some friends in Rochester, New York, his hometown. "He had real charm," said Klem, "and he could turn it on when he wanted to." Three innings into the game, however, one of Klem's calls so incensed McGraw that he unleashed a torrent of profanity, prompting Klem to throw him out. The next day another Klem call went against the Giants. On his way past the rookie umpire McGraw hissed, "I can lick any umpire in baseball, you know." When still another argument broke out the following day, McGraw growled, "I'm going to get your job, you busher." They would play out the role of antagonists for the rest of McGraw's managerial career, abusing each other on the field while becoming close friends off of it. In private McGraw praised Klem as the league's best umpire, while Klem conceded that McGraw was a "champion" among managers.[19]

"John J. McGraw left behind him millions of admirers," said Klem late in his life. "He left none who fought him as often as I did and he left none who had as many pleasant hours with him as I did. John McGraw, off the field, was a man in every old-fashioned sense of that word. He helped his friends; he fought for his rightful due with words, fists or whatever came readily to hand; his charity knew neither restraint nor publicity; and he practiced a pure democracy. It was McGraw's insistence that his players were just as good as he was that got decent hotel and train accommodations for ballplayers. McGraw, so many years ago, tried to get Negroes into the big leagues. But John McGraw on the field was a detriment to baseball . . . He would fight with the cash customers, the umpires, the opposing ballplayers and members of his own team. Nothing was sacred when he unloosed his tongue."[20]

McGraw's critics, and they were legion, complained that he was trying to intimidate umpires and certain players on other teams. "He had got the job of umpires who preceded me," said Klem, "and he was to get men fired who were my colleagues . . . . I was not the only umpire to fight McGraw. Most of them tried to get along with him to the complete detriment of their work and self-respect . . . McGraw could understand me. When he got choleric, I did too. When he hammed it all over the field protesting a called strike, I gave it a little of the showboat too—as I tossed John out of the game."[21]

McGraw's ugliest and most controversial episode that summer involved the Pirates and their owner. The bad blood between the two teams extended back to July 1904, when the Pirates realized that the Giants posed a serious threat to their dynasty. Allen Sangree reported that no one in the Pittsburgh press box had voiced complaints about any of the Giants or McGraw until the team visited the city that July. Then a parade of vicious articles began appearing daily in the Pittsburgh papers. Even Mathewson was sneered at by being called "Sis" for his rather high voice that didn't fit the rest of his image.[22]

For the rest of 1904 every Giant visit to Exposition Park in Pittsburgh brought ugly exchanges between fans and the team, which McGraw accepted as the natural outcome of the rivalry and certainly a boost to the gate. He seemed little disturbed by the situation. "It was seldom that we went to Pittsburgh without having some kind of run-in with fans," he said later. "I suppose we did antagonize them too much, but it certainly was a lot of fun."[23]

"I have seen McGraw go on to ball fields where he is as welcome as a man with the black smallpox," said Mathewson, "and face the crowd alone that, in the heat of its excitement, would like to tear him apart. I have seen him take all sorts of personal chances. He doesn't know what fear is . . . His success is partly due to his indomitable courage."[24]

In those days teams dressed at their hotels and traveled to and from the park in their uniforms. After one tough game with the Pirates the fans started getting on the Giants as they boarded their open carriages for the trip back to their hotel. "Of course, we were not altogether blameless," said McGraw. "If the fans started razzing us we would razz right back at them. To tell the truth, we sort of delighted in tantalizing the overheated rooters." The response was a shower of gravel and rocks until the carriages passed the public market, where the missiles changed to old potatoes, onions, tomatoes, and cantaloupes. At one point McGinnity stood up to quiet things down and was plastered in the seat of the pants with four large tomatoes. Sammy Strang took an overripe cantaloupe in the head. Yet McGraw insisted that the players enjoyed running the gauntlet. "They loved to lick the Pirates . . . and then drive by the market," he claimed.[25]

On the field the intensity only ramped up during 1905. After a game with the Giants in Pittsburgh, a writer stationed himself by the visitors' carriages to see how they dealt with the hostile crowd around them. "Every New York player in an open carriage seemed to be taking a fall out of fans all around him—and the sarcasm was not gentle, either," he reported. "John McGraw was a ring leader in the nagging . . . Five carriages of sneering, carping Giants drove off the field. At least three-fourths had cigarettes stuck in their mouths, and those too busy puffing away at these coffin nails to answer the shots from the spectators."[26]

Exasperated by the constant kicking, league president Harry Pulliam issued an edict on May 22 directing his umpires to allow no questioning of judgment calls. Henceforth only the captain of the team could challenge the construction of a rule. "The umpire will recognize no one as captain unless he is a player actively engaged in the game," Pulliam emphasized. "No manager . . . will be allowed to question the construction of the rules, except he also is captain of his team and is actively engaged as a player in the game."[27]

By then McGraw had already set off another firestorm. "Pitchers were McGraw's favorite target, next to umpires," observed Klem, "and for the same reason. He was working on their confidence and coordination, using personal abuse as his weapon." During Pittsburgh's first visit to the Polo Grounds in May, McGraw and Clarke almost came to blows when McGraw started riding pitcher Mike Lynch as he headed for the bench. Umpire Jimmy Johnstone separated them and ejected McGraw. An inning later Mathewson protested a decision and was also banished. Before the next day's game, Barney Dreyfuss was sitting with some friends in a box behind third base reserved for visiting-team officials. McGraw yelled some sneering remarks and suggested that Dreyfuss umpire the remaining games.[28]

The next day Dreyfuss stood at the main entrance to the Polo Grounds talking with some friends when McGraw, who had been thrown out of the game, went to the grandstand upper deck, leaned over the railing, and shouted, "Hey, Barney." When Dreyfuss ignored him, McGraw chanted "Hey, Barney" in a singsong voice, then charged him with welshing on his gambling debts and manipulating the umpires through his former minion, Harry Pulliam. Furious, Dreyfuss lodged a formal protest with Pulliam against McGraw's behavior. "The time has come when the leader of the Giants must be put on the rack for his conduct," he told a reporter. "He has been defiant to the rules entirely too long."

When Pulliam handed the matter off to the league's board of directors, McGraw called him on the phone and berated him as "Dreyfuss's employee" and "hand-picked president." Pulliam responded by fining McGraw $150 and suspending him for fifteen days.[29]

On the same day McGraw received his suspension, a telegram arrived from his sister informing him that their father was dangerously ill at her house in Fulton County, New York. McGraw caught a train to visit the father he had seen so little of since his boyhood, and ended up attending his funeral as well. The experience did nothing to lift his mood for the clash with Dreyfuss and Pulliam. Brush offered his support as well as legal assistance, knowing that McGraw was determined to fight the Dreyfuss charges.[30]

When the directors met on June 1, McGraw appeared with his lawyer and the general counsel of the Giants. He herded in half a dozen witnesses to the affair who swore that McGraw had said nothing offensive. Three directors, Brush, Arthur Soden, and Jim Hart, voted to absolve McGraw of the charges and formally disapprove of the undignified course of President Dreyfuss in "indulging in an open controversy with a ball player." Soden and Hart then turned around and joined Dreyfuss in praising Pulliam for fining and suspending McGraw for his behavior on the phone. Unappeased, Brush and McGraw got a court injunction in Boston to prevent enforcement of the fine and suspension. A frustrated Pulliam could do nothing.[31]

Some New York writers rushed to McGraw's defense. "The life of a ball club is enthusiasm," wrote Arthur James of the *New York Evening Mail*. "Crush this and you have embalmed baseball . . . The present attitude of the National League umpires, who take their cue from President Pulliam, is that baseball is a step-sister to parlor tennis and a foster-brother to drop-the-handkerchief. No proper citizen believes in rowdyism on the field but by the same token no proper citizen has a wish to see the national game put on a pink tea basis."[32]

In the long run the big loser was Dreyfuss himself. "What I did was for the good of the game," he muttered as he stalked out of the meeting. A few days later he admitted that "had I been sitting on my own case at Boston and have heard the evidence that McGraw brought to bear I would have been compelled to decide against myself, just as that Board of Directors did." After a game at Exposition Park, Brush approached Dreyfuss with an outstretched hand only to be told to go to hell. After delivering some choice words to Brush, Dreyfuss turned on his heel and stalked out of the stands.[33]

For years Dreyfuss had to endure sneering chants of "Hey, Barney" from hostile crowds around the league. For McGraw, in retrospect at least, "that whole club had the spirit of skylarking college boys and I was just as bad as any of them. On the field, though, they thought like men of affairs. Always they were on a hair edge ready to get into a row if anybody pulled the trigger." No one was a better triggerman than McGraw. The "Hey, Barney" episode only made him more aggressive. In August he got ejected from three games in a row. In Pittsburgh he and his infield protested a call at third base for so long that umpire Bob Emslie pulled out a watch and, when the Giants did not resume play, forfeited the game. As the crowd swarmed onto the field and trapped the Giants near their bench, it took the efforts of Clarke and several of his players to hold them back long enough for the Giants to get to their carriages safely. One writer called it "one of the worst riots ever seen at a base ball game in Pittsburg [sic]."[34]

Writers also became a target—at least, those who put out stories that displeased McGraw for some reason. *Sporting Life* complained that "legitimate sporting writers are still being excluded from the Polo Grounds at New York, and this time at the command of John McGraw." James Bagley of the *Evening Mail* was told that his presence was not welcome, and Sam Crane got his second notice to stay away. Unlike the New York Highlanders, who welcomed reporters regardless of their views, the Polo Grounds had become "the only place where reporters have been banished for expressing their opinions."[35]

In every city the turnstiles clicked merrily as crowds came out to vent their displeasure on McGraw's antics. On another day in Pittsburgh, McGraw threw a ball at Emslie. In Cincinnati he offered to fight everybody in the stands, leading Mike Donlin to quip that "he's a wonder. He can start more fights—and win fewer—than anybody I ever saw." But the team continued to win.[36]

BY EARLY SEPTEMBER *SPORTING LIFE* declared that the Giants had clinched the pennant. This time Brush and McGraw were ready, even eager, to take part in what would be the first official World Series, if only because it promised handsome profits and, hopefully, proof of the Giants' superiority. Brush helped formulate the plan on which the rules governing such a series would be based, ensuring its continuation in later years. McGraw outfitted his team in stunning new black flannel uniforms with white trim and a large "NY" across the chest in white. "I will never forget the impression created in Philadelphia," he recalled, "and the thrill that I got personally when the Giants suddenly trotted out from their dugout ... I have heard army men say that the snappiest-looking outfit is usually made up of the best fighters. I can well understand that. The psychological effect ... was immediately noticeable upon the players."[37]

Opposing the Giants were the Philadelphia Athletics, managed by Connie Mack, who could not have been more different from the feisty McGraw. Tall and thin, dressed invariably on the bench in a suit with an old-fashioned high starched collar, Mack was subdued, unruffled, and easy with his players, pointing out the errors of their ways quietly in private and without sarcasm. His gaunt, angular frame contrasted sharply with the short, scrappy man whose belly was already expanding from too much good food and whose narrow gray eyes seemed ever wreathed in suspicion. The one pugnacious, vitriolic, given to cursing and brawling, the other serene and dignified, almost ascetic, with obscenities seldom leaving his lips. But Mack was a shrewd, observant leader whom his players adored, and his manner worked no less magic with them than did McGraw's harsher style on his team. Together they remained the yin and yang of managerial styles for more than a quarter century.[38]

Like the Giants, the Athletics were a team not of superstars but of solid, hard-nosed players fortified by four top-notch pitchers, Eddie Plank, Andy Coakley, Chief Bender, and the childlike, irrepressible George Edward "Rube" Waddell, whose enormous talent was matched only by his erratic behavior. Mack considered him one of the greatest of all pitchers—and his biggest headache. In 1905, Waddell had his best season, going 26-11 with a 1.48 earned run average, leading the league in strikeouts, throwing seven shutouts, and picking up eight of his victories in relief. But Waddell had hurt his shoulder horsing around and was not available for the World Series.[39]

Even without Waddell the Series turned into the finest display of postseason pitching in history. It went five games, every one a shutout. Mathewson pitched three of them in six days, a performance that has never been approached. In twenty-seven innings he allowed only fourteen hits, walked one, and struck out eighteen. McGinnity lost the second game 3–0 to Bender, who surrendered only four hits, then came back to best Plank 1–0 in game four.[40]

"Mathewson was the lion of the hour," marveled *Sporting Life*, "and that no greater pitcher ever pitched a ball is the verdict of all." An awed Grantland Rice—then, like Mathewson, only twenty-five years old—concurred. "I marvel at what Matty has done," he wrote. "In those few days he was the greatest pitcher I've ever seen. I believe he could have continued to pitch shutouts until Christmas!" The *Times* agreed. "Be it recorded here," ran one article, "New York possesses the pitching marvel of the century, Christy Mathewson." Later in life McGraw had his own estimation of his star. "There never was another pitcher like Mathewson," he said simply. "I doubt if there will ever be."[41]

The final game took slightly over ninety minutes, after which the Polo Grounds erupted in celebration as fans charged onto the field and tried to carry the players to the clubhouse beyond the outfield. In victory both McGraw and Brush were gracious to Mack and his team. At a banquet honoring the Athletics in Philadelphia, Brush brought his listeners up short by toasting the lasting friendship of the rival leagues, admitting at long last that "there is room for two major leagues." For their feat the players collected a payoff of $1,142 each along with a diamond-studded gold emblem. A month after the season ended, Brush rewarded McGraw with a new three-year contract for a reputed $15,000 a year.[42]

Brush's generosity did not extend to Harry Pulliam. At the owners' meetings in December he joined Garry Herrmann in opposing Pulliam's reelection as president of the league. "I opposed Mr. Pulliam because I think he is incompetent and ignorant of the law and the rules of the National League," he said bluntly. When Pulliam gained reelection anyway, Brush stopped attending the owners' meetings. His absence became an ominous sign to the other owners.[43]

To the surprise of many, McGraw, who seemed to regard his Orioles as legendary, declared that his Giants were "the fastest baseball team that was ever organized. I played on the old Baltimore team of 1893, 1894, and 1895. I have often heard the Orioles spoken of as the fastest team ever organized. In my opinion, the Giants of 1905 can do anything the champion Orioles did—and have a shade on them besides." After the World Series he declared his intention of keeping the team intact for the coming season.[44]

New York burst into an orgy of celebration. In a city of big reputations McGraw had become the king not only of baseball but of Broadway and the entertainment world as well. In only two years he had given the city a pennant, in three a World Series championship. He and the Giants had become heroes in a town that adored winners and that worshipped style as much as or more than substance. Politicos, stage actors and other entertainers, Wall Street types, jockeys, boxers, and other athletes all sought his company. Mathewson underwent a different but no less worshipful expansion of image. He was elevated into the role of all-American boy made good, the handsome, modest, good-natured fellow who could serve as a perfect role model for America's youth. That he smoked an occasional cigar or pipe, drank an occasional beer, and even let fly an occasional obscenity went unnoticed in his exalted new image. No player had ever become a public idol of quite this type.

For his part McGraw was discovering that an oversized life in an oversized city suited him just fine, that he relished being a big fish in a big pond. Among other things it brought out even more of the showman in him, a quality that had always been there but had never been given its head. He was no less intense and deadly serious about baseball, but off the field a new lifestyle beckoned, one that would lay to rest the slower, quieter patterns of Baltimore and even his early New York years with their leisurely walks along Fifth Avenue or Sunday night dinners out or small gatherings of friends in the apartment shared with the Mathewsons. The days of a carriage ride through the streets capped by ice cream sodas were long gone, never to return.

Having reached the top of the mountain, he faced the ageless problem of how to stay there in a sport that was as fiercely competitive as any other business. McGraw was sure that he could keep winning. All the attention, the distractions of victory, had done nothing to dull his competitive instincts. If anything they only made him more certain that his methods and approach were the proper ones. Fred Clarke's Pirates had managed to win three in a row; why couldn't he, especially with the personnel he had and their fighting instincts?

He was about to find out why not.

CHAPTER 5

Fresh Blood

*"Sportsmanship and easy-methods are all
right, but it is the prospect of a hot fight that
brings out the crowds. Personally I could never
see this idea of taking a defeat philosophically. I
hate to lose and I never feel myself beaten until
the last man is out. I have tried to instill that
same fighting spirit in all the teams I have
managed."*

—JOHN MCGRAW

NEW YORK OFFERED THE GRANDEST STAGE on which McGraw could ever strut, and he was not slow to take advantage of it. Gradually the McGraws forged a lifestyle that both suited their tastes and catered to McGraw's habits and disposition. They ate out most of the time, favoring Italian restaurants such as Mama Leone's but also Guffanti's, Zucca's, and Enrico & Paglieri. McGraw was an eager trencherman who could not restrain himself around good food or sweets. During spring training in Savannah in 1903, Bozeman Bulger of the *Evening World*, who had just met McGraw, watched in amazement as he emptied an entire one-pound box of candy on the walk from the Pulaski Hotel to the ballpark. "That's probably the last candy I'll have for a month," McGraw said. "But I always believe in shooting the works. Can't stop once I start."[1]

Compulsive in some things, a control freak in others, McGraw offered a fascinating profile to the observer. During the off season he could be a bon vivant among his growing legion of friends. Along the Gay White Way, the stretch of Broadway between Thirty-fourth and Forty-fourth streets, he became a familiar figure in the bars and dining rooms of the fashionable hotels and the lobster palaces that had become all the rage. He developed a reputation for never letting anyone else pick up the tab. Even during the season he and Blanche went to the theater, mostly vaudeville, in the evening as a way for McGraw to wind down from the day's game. He admitted to Mathewson that after managing a tough game he was as tired as if he had played himself.[2]

His companions included not only the theater crowd, politicos, and sports figures but gamblers, bookies, and denizens from the underworld. Running with shady characters never bothered McGraw, who simply didn't make any such distinctions. He liked to gamble and won some $400 or $500 from Athletics rooters betting on the Series. Gambling and swindling establishments thrived in New York at the turn of the century, ranging from high-toned houses for the rich and careless to mean dives catering to whatever victims they could attract. One posh place, the House with the Bronze Door, was reputed to be owned by a syndicate headed by Frank Farrell, who along with his partner Big Bill Devery bought the old Orioles and moved them to New York.[3]

Mindful of his success in Baltimore, McGraw opened a billiard parlor on Herald Square at the intersection of Broadway, Sixth Avenue, and Thirty-fourth Street. The place boasted fifteen tables described as "works of art and the highest-priced ever placed in a billiard-room," and opened for business in February 1906; the invited guests included billiards champ Willie Hoppe. When not at the billiard parlor McGraw could often be found in a drinking establishment such as Diamond Dan O'Rourke's, a place in the Bowery owned by Dan O'Rourke at 156 Park Row. The décor, unchanged since the 1880s with its ornate chandeliers with gas fixtures, large mirrors, and splashes of jockey silks, offered a pleasant setting for socializing and was off-limits to the Giants players.[4]

What had he accomplished in that magical season of 1905? From various sources he had plucked the right players to create a superior team and then molded them into a smoothly working machine by the sheer force of his personality and leadership. He had helped transform Mathewson from a good pitcher to the best in the league, rescued Donlin from the scrap heap of self-disgrace, and moved Bresnahan to the position at which he achieved greatness. His success had buried the Highlanders, who finished sixth in the American League, in obscurity in New York, and in doing so he thumbed his nose at Ban Johnson, reminding him that he might have had McGraw as manager of that club. He had put Dreyfuss and Pulliam in their place, terrorized umpires, and further stuck it to Johnson by running away with the World Series.[5]

Since boyhood McGraw's life had been hard enough that he had learned never to take anything for granted. After 1905, however, those restraints seemed to loosen. To his boasts about the greatness of the Giants, the benevolent despot that was his owner smiled and nodded. If McGraw grew too full of himself, no one in New York could rein him in and the rants of his enemies only fueled his self-assurance. For the coming season he ordered new uniforms with the words "World's Champions" emblazoned across the shirtfronts. He also saw to it that whenever the team traveled between their hotel and the ballpark in other cities, they rode four to a carriage pulled by horses wearing yellow blankets with "World's Champions" embroidered on them. This bit of showmanship enraged local fans, which suited him just fine.[6]

The team trained in Memphis that spring. As it wound its way north toward opening day, reporters asked McGraw the inevitable question: Did he expect the Giants to repeat as champions? "I do," he answered. He was convinced that he had the best team and he expected them to demonstrate their superiority. However, two factors, eternal in the game itself, rose to taunt him: the emergence of a formidable new rival and the vagaries of fortune.

NOT UNTIL FRANK SELEE ARRIVED in 1902 did Chicago's prospects improve. That year Albert Spalding finally sold the club to his protégé, Jim Hart, who had been its president for a decade. The team even struggled for a nickname, being called the Colts and then the Orphans before a newspaper began calling them the Cubs in 1902. Selee arrived with impressive credentials. He had put together the great Boston teams of the 1890s and won five titles in a dozen years. "Few men in baseball," wrote an admirer, "were ever more popular than Frank Selee . . . He was a gentleman by birth and breeding. He ruled his players gently, yet firmly." Once in Chicago, Selee undertook the same patient creation of an advanced baseball machine.[7]

Frank Chance joined the team in 1898 as a catcher and outfielder. Only twenty-one years old, he was the son of a banker in Fresno, California. A handsome, strapping six-footer, his fearless style of play behind the plate and at bat shortened his career. "Chance is the sort of athlete who is likely to get injured," observed Mathewson. "When he was a catcher he was always banged up because he never got out of the way of anything." Johnny Evers noted that Chance's recklessness, especially his crowding the plate, twice almost got him killed. "When he was given an opportunity to work behind the bat," wrote Ring Lardner, "he stopped the pitched balls with the ends of his fingers, the foul tips with his knees and the wild pitches with the top of his head." His teammates called him "Husk" because of his solid build.[8]

Although he hit well, Chance seemed destined to be no more than a backup catcher when Johnny Kling arrived and Selee made him the regular catcher. Selee had to decide what to do with Chance, whose attributes were not as obvious as they seemed later. He was, recalled Evers, a "big, bow-legged, rather awkward young player ... Quiet, good-natured, rather retiring off the field, serious, and in deadly earnest while playing, honest and sincere in everything ... Anyone who at that time had predicted that Chance was to become the leader of the greatest club ever organized would have earned a laugh."[9]

Selee saw real potential in Chance as well as the need to get him away from catching if he was to survive physically. In the spring of 1903 he persuaded a reluctant Chance to take over first base; he played 121 games, batted .327, and became a mainstay of the team. That same season Selee acquired two more new regulars: Jim "Rabbit" Slagle, a quiet, patient left-handed hitter to lead off and play the outfield, and a young third baseman named Joe Tinker.[10]

The son of a contractor, Tinker hailed from a tiny village north of Topeka, Kansas. Like so many players, he graduated from school to semipro to minor-league baseball before spending the full 1901 season at Portland in the Pacific Northwest League. During spring training in 1902, Selee, whose shortstop had jumped to the American League, auditioned a dozen replacements in vain before turning to Tinker, who switched positions with the greatest reluctance. During his first season he made seventy-four errors, but his fielding improved steadily until in 1906 he led the league's shortstops.[11]

Late in the 1902 season Selee acquired an intense, dour young shortstop named John J. Evers from Troy of the New York League. When Evers made his debut on September 1, Selee put him at shortstop and shifted Tinker back to third base. The arrangement lasted only three days, after which Selee moved Tinker back to shortstop and tried Evers at second base. Evers did not impress, batting only .222 in twenty-six games. However, veteran second baseman Bobby Lowe suffered a severe knee injury and was not ready to play when spring training began in 1903. Having won the job by default, Evers performed well. Writer Hugh Fullerton described him as "a bundle of nerves with the best brain in baseball." No one suspected even remotely that Selee had put together what would become the most famous infield combination in baseball history.[12]

Selee enlisted as a scout George Huff, the athletic director at the University of Illinois; he paid dividends immediately by recruiting Carl Lundgren, who had pitched the university to two championships. Quiet, studious, a close student of batters, Lundgren's deliberate style led to his being called the "Human Icicle." In 1904 Selee took his greatest gamble yet by giving St. Louis two talented if troublesome players, pitcher Jack Taylor and catcher Larry McLean, for a pitcher named Mordecai "Three Finger" Brown. Taylor had gone 21-14 in 1903, Brown an uninspired 9-13 for a last-place team. Because of Brown's deformity Selee saw in him a potential for greatness that had escaped other baseball men.[13]

Brown was born in 1876 in Nyesville, Indiana, a small farming and coal-mining town north of Terre Haute. At age seven he caught his right hand in a corn shredder on his uncle's farm; the accident severed his index and part of his little finger and damaged the middle finger as well. Despite his deformed hand, Brown took eagerly to baseball. He played semipro ball while working in the coal mines, which earned him a second nickname, "Miner." He went 23-8 for Terre Haute in 1901 and 27-15 for Omaha of the Western League the following year. St. Louis manager Patsy Donovan picked him up for 1903, impressed by Brown's "freak ball" but never suspecting the depth of talent he possessed.[14]

The mutilated hand gave Brown a unique grip on the ball, from which evolved a curveball that Ty Cobb called "the most devastating pitch I ever faced." It was a pitch no one could duplicate. To it he added speed and masterful control. "Brown is my idea of the almost perfect pitcher," said Mathewson. "He is always ready to work." For years he and Brown hooked up in some of the greatest pitching duels of the era, with Brown coming out on top more often. "Brown . . . was one of the wonders of base-ball," said shortstop Al Bridwell. "What a tremendous pitcher he was. Just as good as Matty, in my book. Better, maybe."[15]

Late in the 1904 season Selee dispatched Huff to scout a player in Syracuse. Huff wired Selee to forget him but take two other outfielders, Mike Mitchell and Frank "Wildfire" Schulte. Mitchell went to Cincinnati; Schulte became an anchor of the Cubs outfield. Evers called him "one of the rarest baseball treasures, a 'third batter.' The third batter in any team is the most important. He must hit long flies, hit hard, bunt and run, because ahead of him in a well constructed team are two batters who are on the team for the ability to 'get on,' and the third man must be able either to move them up or hit them home."[16]

Schulte was a rare bird in many ways. One of the only batters who did not choke up, he held the bat at the very end and swung from the heels in the style that became current much later. His bat "Nellie" weighed forty ounces but, unlike other bats, it had a thin handle. He could hit for power, steal bases, and had one of the strongest arms in the league. The son of a building contractor, Schulte hailed from a small village in western New York and played his early ball for a succession of obscure small-town teams. A quiet, modest man, he had a droll sense of humor that appealed to Ring Lardner, who said, "Frank Schulte hated anything false or tinged with 'bull.'" He was also an eccentric who scoured the street for hairpins, believing that the larger the ones he found, the greater the hits he would get.[17]

Late that season Huff traveled to Des Moines and discovered a shortstop named Arthur "Circus Solly" Hofman, who had not impressed in a brief trial with Pittsburgh in 1903. One of five sons of a St. Louis father who managed a local ball club on which they all played, Hofman's strength proved to be his versatility. Like Sammy Strang of the Giants, he played every position except pitcher and catcher for the Cubs over the next several years.[18]

Selee did not develop a winner but he laid the foundation for one. The Cubs finished third in 1903 and second the following year. When Selee needed a new captain, he took the unprecedented step of asking the players to make the decision. His personal choice was third baseman Doc Casey; the other candidates were Kling and Chance, who had led the team again with a .310 average in 1904. To his consternation the players chose Chance by a wide margin. Evers thought the vote was "the turning point in the career of Chance and in the development of the club." Having elevated himself into a great first baseman, Chance began showing the qualities that would earn him the sobriquet of "Peerless Leader."[19]

Although disappointed, Selee had little choice but to lean increasingly on Chance. Selee was seriously ill with consumption, the dreaded "white death" that killed more Americans than any other disease. Gradually his condition began to impair his judgment. He lasted only sixty-five games into the 1905 season before illness forced him to surrender the managerial reins to Chance, who compiled a 55-33 record in leading the team to a third-place finish. "We need pitchers," he said when taking charge, "we must have a new third baseman, and a hitting outfielder before we can win the pennant."[20]

During the season Huff had uncovered one promising pitcher for the Cubs. Tall, strapping Ed Reulbach had a terrific curveball and a technique for hiding the ball in his windup. A native of Detroit, Reulbach entered Notre Dame in 1901 and became a star outfielder and pitcher. He passed on his senior year and enrolled in medical school at the University of Vermont, where he also starred on the baseball team. Huff found him there and signed him for the Cubs in May 1905. He finished the season 18-13 with a 1.42 earned run average. During the 1906–1907 seasons he would run off a personal seventeen-game winning streak. For three seasons, 1906–1908, he led the National League in winning percentage. Writer J. C. Kofoed called him "one of the greatest pitchers that the National League ever produced, and one of the finest clean-cut gentlemen who ever wore a big league uniform."[21]

Major changes reshaped the Cubs at both upper levels during the season. In August 1905, when Selee handed his duties over to Chance and went to Colorado to fight his disease, word leaked out that Jim Hart had sold his shares to Charles W. Murphy, former press agent for John Brush. Soon after Murphy's arrival, questions arose as to how, at age thirty-seven, he had managed to find the money to buy the Cubs. The fear was that New York money was behind him and that syndicate ball might be rearing its ugly head again. Murphy dispelled that rumor by identifying his backer as Charles P. Taft, William Howard's brother and one of the wealthy Ohio Tafts. He soon established himself as one of the league's most controversial owners, but he had the good sense to give Chance free rein in building a winner.[22]

Their relationship began as a lovefest broken only by occasional spats. Chance, said Murphy, "has the heart of a child and the courage of a lion . . . He is serious and inspires players to their best efforts . . . asks his players to do nothing that he is not himself willing to do." He did not pretend to know everything and allowed players to disagree with him and offer suggestions. "Chance is a good listener," Murphy added. "He has often listened to me and possibly then he has gone and done just as he pleased." Especially was this true with personnel changes. "I have never in any way tried to tell him his business," Murphy claimed. "He would not let me, and if he did I would not want him as a manager."[23]

After the season Chance went hunting for the players he had in mind. He wanted Jimmy Sheckard, the much traveled outfielder who was popular but unhappy in Brooklyn. In a stunning deal he swapped two outfielders, his third baseman Doc Casey, and a pitcher along with $2,000 for Sheckard. The trade enabled him to install Sheckard in left, keep Slagle in center, and move Schulte to right, his best position. Evers called Sheckard "one of the brightest ball players in the business." For third base Chance coveted an unlikely candidate, Harry Steinfeldt, who was unhappy in Cincinnati and playing indifferently. He was twenty-eight and slow, but he could hit and field well and had a strong arm. Chance had played with him in California and knew the Reds were anxious to trade him. He asked Murphy to make the deal. It took Murphy three attempts to trade two players for the controversial third baseman.[24]

On the same day that Steinfeldt signed his contract, Chance allowed that if he had more pitching he could win the pennant. Thanks to Huff and his own sharp eye, he got two more stalwarts. John Hagenbush lost both his parents at age three and was raised by an uncle, Fred Pfiester, whose name he took. Jack Pfiester had brief auditions with the Pirates in 1903 and 1904 before being exiled to Omaha of the Western League. Huff found him there, pitching well and with a nonreserve contract, meaning that he could sign with anyone. A side-arming lefty with a devastating pickoff move, Pfiester had gone 49-22 over two seasons in Omaha, and Huff was quick to scoop him up.[25]

Orval Overall had gone a dismal 17-22 for Cincinnati in 1905 with 318 innings pitched. Although he stood six foot two and weighed 214 pounds, Chance was convinced that his weak record stemmed from overwork. Overall had been a star athlete at the University of California, where he was an excellent student and class president. When he opened the 1906 season with an unimpressive 4-5 record, Chance traded pitcher Bob Wicker for him. Overall possessed a wide, sweeping overhand curve ball that some players thought was even better than Brown's. Finally, in February 1906, Chance acquired catcher Pat Moran from Boston to back up Kling.[26]

By the spring of 1906 Chance had the team he wanted, one capable of winning it all with a little luck. Although the Cubs had managed second place the previous year, he reckoned that McGraw would be more concerned with the Pirates. The sterling play of the Cubs would quickly change that focus.

CHANGES WERE COMING FOR THE McGRAWS. When Jane Mathewson learned that she was pregnant that winter, she and Christy found their own apartment for the season. The McGraws moved into the Washington Inn, a residential hotel at 155th Street and Amsterdam Avenue not far from the Polo Grounds.[27]

In February 1906, Mike Donlin landed in jail for getting drunk and brandishing a pistol aboard a train. During spring training in Memphis he took to slipping out of his room late at night for a night on the town. When he showed up at five o'clock one morning thoroughly drunk, McGraw suspended him and barred him from the hotel. It took two days for a repentant Donlin to wheedle his way back into McGraw's favor. The harsh truth was that his bat was needed, and he had become a celebrity to New Yorkers in his own right. As much as he hated the nickname "Turkey," kids in the city made a fad of imitating his strut.[28]

A more serious problem arose when Mathewson came down with diphtheria, the same dread disease that had claimed five members of McGraw's family in his boyhood. He was quarantined from the team and his wife, leaving a distraught McGraw to fear for the life of his close friend. For three weeks the sports pages issued daily reports on his condition to anxious readers. Not until May 5, still weak from his ordeal, did Mathewson make his first start for the Giants.[29]

Early in the season, on April 18, catastrophe struck the nation when a huge earthquake devastated San Francisco. For McGraw and the Giants the season soon devolved into a series of aftershocks. Ten days after Mathewson's return, Donlin broke his ankle sliding into third base. At the time he led the league with a .349 average. Then Bresnahan took a pitch in the head and was slow to recover, and Dan McGann broke an arm. Ames and Wiltse both suffered ankle injuries. At thirty-six Bill Dahlen was slowing down and Billy Gilbert's performance fell off as well. George Browne's average dropped by thirty points. To bolster his outfield, McGraw traded Sam Mertes to the Cardinals for William "Spike" Shannon and induced Brush to buy Cy Seymour, the batting champion of 1905, from Cincinnati.[30]

Seymour was familiar to McGraw. A native of Albany, New York, he broke into the National League in 1896 as a pitcher for the Giants, posting records of 18-14 and 25-19 for a bad team. Like so many others, he also ran afoul of Andrew Freedman. When his arm went bad, Seymour in 1901 jumped to McGraw's Orioles as an outfielder and hit .303. The following year he moved to Cincinnati as their center fielder and hit over .300 every year. The only player in major-league history to compile a more impressive record as both pitcher and batter than Seymour was Babe Ruth. Sensitive and high-strung, Seymour was rumored to have a drinking problem. He had an aloof personality, but McGraw liked his spirit as well as his talent.[31]

Despite this run of bad luck that contrasted so sharply with 1905, the Giants played well enough to win ninety-six games. That number of victories put them three games ahead of the Pirates and would win a pennant in most seasons, but in 1906 it didn't even come close. The newly retooled Cubs swept their way to the most remarkable season in baseball history, winning a record 116 games and losing only 36. The Cubs seized first place on May 28 and never relinquished it. Instead of a pennant the Giants found themselves twenty games out of first place. Chicago also set an attendance record by drawing some 654,300 fans to West Side Park that season, while the Giants declined to slightly over 400,000—20,000 fewer than the despised Highlanders attracted.[32]

The seeming decline of the Giants led some writers to view McGraw's antics in a less tolerant light. Joe Vila in particular became an implacable critic of McGraw and the team. He castigated rowdyism, questioned McGraw's decisions and leadership, and called the team much weaker than fans had been led to believe. To his thinking Mathewson was washed up and the team would be lucky to get $100 for him. Strangest of all, Vila insisted that Andrew Freedman remained the primary force in the team's front office, with Brush as little more than his minion. This stream of criticism from Vila flowed nonstop for the next two years and grew steadily uglier.[33]

McGraw would not admit that the Cubs were superior to his club or that the Cubs were one of the best teams ever assembled, although he conceded that "the bitter rivalry that had existed between the Giants and the Pirates immediately shifted to a war of wits between the Giants and the Cubs. Those were hot days—just as hot as we had gone through on the many visits to Pittsburgh."[34]

It was not that the Giants had played poorly but rather that the Cubs had played spectacular ball all year. In winning more games than any team before or since, they led the league in batting, fielding, and pitching. They were the first team to commit fewer than two hundred errors in a season. Their pitchers compiled a team-earned run average of only 1.76. Mordecai Brown led the way with an amazing 1.04 runs per game, the second lowest ever. Steinfeldt had a career year, tying for the league lead in runs batted in with 83 and finishing second to Honus Wagner in batting at .327. Chance led the league in stolen bases with 57. The only blemish to their season came in losing the World Series to their crosstown rivals, the White Sox, four games to two. Known as the "Hitless Wonders," the White Sox finished dead last in team batting and led the league in nothing except shutouts and walks issued.

That fall Arthur Soden sold the Boston team to George B. Dovey, whose name prompted writers to call the club the Doves. At the owners' meeting in December, Pulliam pledged to fight "the brand of sportsmanship known as 'McGrawism'" and won reelection, with Brush casting the only vote against him. However, Brush also offered a more positive proposal in persuading the rules committee to require every team to provide facilities for visiting teams so that they would not have to dress at their hotels.[35]

After New Year's Day, McGraw and his wife traveled to Los Angeles, where he arranged for the Giants to hold spring training. He persuaded Brush that the venture would not only fetch good publicity but make money as well. What seemed like a good idea turned out to be a flop. Lousy weather for much of the three-week stay in California kept attendance low, and several exhibition games on the return trip were undermined by poor arrangements and McGraw's own temper. The journey started off badly with a wire from Donlin, who, smitten with show business and the possibility of becoming an actor, skipped spring training to remain in Chicago as assistant manager of a theater where his wife, actress and comedienne Mabel Hite, was performing. "They'll be actors, all right," grumbled McGraw. "Bad actors!" Donlin offered to sign a contract for 1907 if the Giants would pay him the $3,300 he received in 1906 plus a $600 bonus for remaining sober during the season. Brush dismissed the offer as little more than blackmail.[36]

Joe Vila kept after McGraw with a salvo that soon became another of his primary themes. "McGraw left here the other day for Los Angeles," he wrote. "Of course, McGraw will not bet on horses while in Los Angeles. Oh, no! He will only peep through the fence because he does not believe in letting the hungry bookmaker know that he is so near at hand with a bunch of real money in his pocket. But can he stand such temptation? Hardly, when he begins to see familiar faces."[37]

In New Orleans nearly everything went wrong thanks in part to another McGraw confrontation with an umpire that resulted in the forfeiting of one game in the first inning and the canceling of another. Later the Giants were fined $1,000 for the escapade. Donlin decided to hold out for the entire season, during which he and Mabel put together their own show. "I can act," he said. "I'll break the hearts of all the gals in the country." Most critics thought otherwise, but his absence left a major hole in the Giants outfield.[38]

Convinced that the Cubs could never duplicate their performance, McGraw saw little need to tinker with his roster. The only regular to go was Billy Gilbert; McGraw thought he was "losing his speed" and released him after the 1906 season. He could find no suitable replacement until July, when he sent his old teammate Dan Brouthers to Springfield, Illinois, to scout a promising youngster named Larry Doyle. Springfield's president had shrewdly lured Detroit and Washington into a bidding war for Doyle's services. On a favorable report from Brouthers, McGraw bid $4,500, the highest price ever paid for a minor leaguer at the time, and secured Doyle's services.[39]

Not quite twenty-one when he arrived in New York on July 21, Doyle was as raw as they came. He hailed from Caseyville, Illinois, and for five years had worked in the coal mines near Breese, Illinois, east of St. Louis, while playing semipro ball on weekends. "Working in a mine is like going up in a balloon, only in the opposite direction," he said afterward. "You don't think anything of it if you are used to it, but when you first go down into the earth there comes a sudden realization of what might happen to you . . . When you get caught without a light in some deep labyrinth in the bowels of the earth it's no picnic." He recalled that playing his first game in "fast company" earned him a fat $3.50 and was "quite a big event in my otherwise colorless existence."[40]

In 1906, Doyle took the plunge by quitting the mines to play professionally for Mattoon, Illinois, in the Kitty (Kentucky-Indiana-Tennessee) League. On Christmas Eve that year six miners in Breese lost their lives in a disaster. In 1907, he moved up to Springfield in the Three-I (Illinois-Indiana-Iowa) League and was hitting .290 when the call to the Giants came. After the train discharged him in Jersey City, Doyle made his way to Manhattan and was told to take the elevated to the Polo Grounds. He got on in the wrong direction and ended up at the shore. Once he reached the Polo Grounds, McGraw took him to a hotel where the unmarried men stayed, and then into the bar for a beer. "I was scared to drink beer with him around," Doyle said later. "I ordered pop." The next day he found himself playing second base against the Cubs, a position he had never played. His hesitation on a play gave Chicago a crucial run. "Forget it," said McGraw. "When you learn more about second, you won't make mistakes like that."[41]

In sixty-nine games that season Doyle batted .260 but made twenty-six errors for the lowest fielding average of any starter in the league at his position. His performance did not impress the city's sportswriters given his hefty price tag. "Doyle was so streaky last year that it was almost out of the question to get any fixed line on his ability," said the *New York Evening Telegram*. "One day he would be a dead wall which nothing could pass, and the next he wobbled on every hit that came to him, like a boxcar on a coal railroad. Some days he could hit the ball on both sides of the seams, and on other days he missed all sides." As usual McGraw saw more than the managers on temporary duty as sportswriters. The youngster had a shaky glove but a live bat, and he could run. More important, he had a great disposition and was eager to learn. In time he drew the nickname "Laughing Larry" because of his good nature. He had to be nurtured and encouraged, and McGraw knew how to do that as well as criticize.[42]

At May's end the Cubs and Giants had identical records of 24-5. Then the Giants marched into West End Park and absorbed three straight losses to Chicago. By mid-July the Cubs were still going strong while New York slid backward until they trailed Chicago by fifteen games and scrambled to keep ahead of the surging Pirates. McGraw was right: The Cubs could not possibly match their performance of 116 wins in 1906, but they won 107 games and finished 17 games ahead of Pittsburgh. Although Mathewson won 24 games with a 1.99 earned run average, the Giants finished fourth, twenty-five and a half games behind the Cubs as Philadelphia jumped ahead of them by four games. None of the regulars hit higher than Dan McGann's .298. Even the workhorse McGinnity fell off to an 18-18 record. Ames regressed to 10-12 and Wiltse to 13-12.[43]

In July, Vila unveiled a new theme with his acid pen. "The passing of McGraw is not far distant," he predicted. "The disorganized Giants have lost caste with the metropolitan base ball public and there is nobody to blame but the rowdy manager who has four-flushed his way to the front only to drop a million miles into the Slough of Despond!" The Chicago series "proved beyond peradventure that he was not a good sportsman; that he was a cowardly, bulldozing bluffer; that he had a yellow streak a yard wide; that he did not know the first rudiments of clean base ball and that as a user of vile language and personal abuse . . . was a class by himself. Steeped with an insane desire to gamble on the race track, Muggsy McGraw has lost all interest in the welfare of the Giants . . . He knows that he has run his race as a manager here."[44]

Gleefully Vila quoted a headline from the *Evening Journal*: "Base Ball or Racing—To Which Is McGraw Giving the Most Time?" In pounding home his belief that McGraw was on his way out, Vila claimed that "the New York base ball public today is anxious to see one Roger Bresnahan made manager and captain of the Giants. Bresnahan is a popular idol. He is on the ball field actually doing something. He thinks of nothing but base ball and doesn't play the races."[45]

The Cubs had replaced the Giants as the team with drive, determination, and even feistiness. Chance matched McGraw's intensity on the field and seemed actually to relish encounters with the man others in the league feared most. Even more, he drove his players to give the Giants no quarter in baiting them. "He had us all doing it," said Evers. "If we didn't ride McGraw and his players, Husk would have fined us and maybe beat hell out of us."[46]

Through it all, McGraw seemed to lose his fiery edge. He did spend more time at the racetracks, going so far as to send two players up to Yonkers to lay down a bet on a 10–1 horse on a day when Pittsburgh massacred the Giants 20–5. Other reporters joined Vila in commenting on his time at the tracks and apparent indifference to the team. In June he mused about retiring after the season, admitting that "the very sight of a railroad train appalls me . . . I am a slave to the Pullman sleeper and the tender mercies of the hotel in the next city." During much of the 1907 season he sat in uncharacteristic silence on the bench, more unhappy with his players than with the umpires.[47]

However, regardless of anything he said aloud, retirement was not an option for McGraw. Nor is it likely he ever considered it seriously. He was only thirty-four. The game was all he knew; if he quit, what would he do? He had gained an enviable status in life, found a comfortable lifestyle, and made good money, all of which depended on his continuing in baseball at a high level of performance. Having reached the peak of his profession, he was not about to abandon it even though he knew that staying there was even more demanding than the struggle to get there.

What bothered McGraw more than anything else during that lost summer of 1907 was the realization that the team he loved and had built so carefully had outlived its usefulness. No matter how much he admired or cared for his men, they were of no use once they lost their ability to perform at the level he had come to expect from them. The team had to be dissolved and most of its parts discarded in favor of new ones. Only a few of them, the most obvious being the irreplaceable Mathewson, could be retained. "It was in 1907 that I discovered my players were growing old and beginning to slip," he said later. "Always I have made it a point never to let a club grow old on me. A manager must start reconstruction quickly or several years will be required to bring a ball club back." He did not mention that he had not started quickly enough, or that this experience had brought him to this conclusion.[48]

The most interesting aspect of his response was his decision as to what kind of team would replace the current one. He would put together one built almost entirely on speed and youth, one capable not only of playing his brand of baseball but of growing and learning so that it could endure for a longer haul. It was a bold and demanding plan because it meant starting over almost from scratch. Instead of veterans who did not have to be told what to do, he would seek youngsters who had to be taught everything. The demands on himself would be greater than ever, and there would be growing pains along the way, but he thought it was the only way to move forward.

No sooner had the 1907 season ended then McGraw washed its scars from his mind and began the challenging task of reconstruction.

CHAPTER 6

Starting Over

*"The test of managerial ability in baseball is
not in winning a first pennant. It is in
discarding the worn-out parts of an old
machine and putting together a new set of
championship cogs without losing momentum.
That is what McGraw had to do at the end of
1906, after the Giants had lost the pennant to
the Cubs."*

—BOZEMAN BULGER

BASEBALL AS A CURE FOR INSANITY? So claimed a Dr. Harmon, super-intendent of an insane asylum near New York. "This game has worked wonders in many cases of insanity," he reported, "in that it gives these unfortunates healthful exercise and diverts their minds from the channels into which their maladies have sunk them." However true his argument was, Major League Baseball sometimes seemed more to promote insanity than reduce it.[1]

Especially in New York. During 1907 Joe Vila kept hammering away at the theme of McGraw at the racetrack. Calling McGraw an "alleged base ball manager, alleged gold mine operator, alleged stockbroker, alleged race track plunger and alleged other things," Vila insisted that the team's fans would not be satisfied until McGraw was sent packing in favor of Roger Bresnahan. His crusade against McGraw and in favor of Bresnahan slowly picked up support in other quarters. On November 10, 1907, the widely circulated Hearst morning paper, the *New York American*, roused the sports fans among its readers with a startling headline: BRESNAHAN TO SUCCEED M'GRAW AS MANAGER OF THE NEW YORK GIANTS. The story lingered a few days but proved to be a false alarm.[2]

However, the John McGraw of this postseason was a changed man. The 1906 and 1907 seasons taught him a harsh lesson in humility, reminding him anew never to take anything for granted. He had built a great team, done the Pirates one better, but the Cubs had trumped them both in spectacular fashion. Between 1906 and 1910 the Cubs swept to victory every year except 1909, when they lost out not to the Giants but to the resurgent Pirates. One of those seasons ended in a nightmare that saw the Giants snatch defeat from victory in humiliating fashion. For the decade the Giants managed only two pennants, while the Pirates grabbed three and the Cubs four. Chicago had become the league's darling, while New York developed a reputation as a perpetual bridesmaid.

Once it became clear to McGraw that he would have to build another team from scratch, he began the search for parts best suited to the machine he had in mind. He knew veterans would be needed to maintain standards and mentor the younger players, but they had to be men capable of a leadership role until the youngsters came of age.

What is the value of a player? Some expressed it in monetary terms, others in performance statistics. But the most important measures were more subtle and intangible: reliability, consistency, attitude, judgment, wits, knowledge of the game, speed, determination, grit, dedication, focus, a hunger to do well. The manager's toughest job was to evaluate all these factors and put together a roster of not just the best players but the best blend of players to perform as a team. How to compare the value of experience to that of youth? No player ever gets younger but neither does he necessarily get smarter as he gets older. A manager also had to measure a player's package of skills against his ability to wring the most from them. At all these tasks McGraw excelled.

In surveying his roster at the end of the 1907 season, McGraw found only a few names that were keepers for the long haul. Bresnahan and Devlin could still play, although Bresnahan had slowed somewhat. Young Doyle looked promising at second base. Mathewson was still brilliant but McGinnity and Taylor were wearing down. Ames and Wiltse were young but erratic. At thirty-six, McGann had begun to drop off and was injury prone. Dahlen was as savvy and fierce as ever, but at thirty-eight he was ancient for a shortstop and slow. No one in the outfield suited McGraw. Bowerman at forty still carped constantly about not being the regular catcher, a resentment that soared when Bresnahan caught every game of the 1905 World Series.[3]

In November McGraw received one bonus when Mike Donlin agreed to return from his theatrical sabbatical and play ball in 1908. McGraw rewarded him with the new responsibility of captain, making him the team's spokesman on the field with a $500 bonus to enhance his $4,000 salary. The manager also had an intriguing rookie purchased for $2,500 in September. Fred Merkle was only nineteen and as raw as they came, but he was smart, fast, athletic, and eager to learn. In time he might give the Giants a strong presence at first base, but he needed grooming and McGraw did not think McGann was the man for that job.[4]

On December 10, while the National League magnates gathered for their annual meeting in New York, McGraw collared other managers about trades. On Friday the thirteenth he struck a blockbuster deal with his old friend Joe Kelley, who had just become Boston's manager. McGann, Browne, Bowerman, Dahlen, and pitcher George Ferguson went to Boston in exchange for first baseman Fred Tenney, shortstop Al Bridwell, and catcher Tom Needham. Although Tenney was thirty-six and had played for thirteen seasons, he was still a smart hitter and one of the finest fielders at his position. He had invented the 3-6-3 double play in 1897 and for seven seasons led the National League in assists for first basemen while averaging .308 at the plate. Equally important to McGraw, he had been Boston's manager from 1905 through 1907. He was a reliable leader in the clubhouse and ideal mentor for Merkle even though he wore what Sam Crane called "a Cotton Mather visage."[5]

A native of Friendship, Ohio, Tenney quit school at thirteen and went to work in a shoe factory, putting in ten hours a day six days a week for $1.25. By age eighteen he had advanced to $3 a week, all the while playing baseball for amateur and semipro teams. In the fall of 1902 he jumped at a chance to earn $125 a month playing for Columbus of the American Association. Two years later he got picked up by Cincinnati, then was traded in 1905 to Boston, where he spent two uninspired seasons with a weak team.[6]

The sportswriters applauded the acquisition of Tenney but didn't know what to make of Bridwell, who was only twenty-four years old and had a reputation as good field, no hit. Vila called it a "fool deal" and sneered that "Bridwell . . . can't hit an airship with a shotgun charge." The Press conceded that "Bridwell has always been rated as a clever fielder, but fans belittled his abilities because he did not knock down fences." McGraw wanted him because of his sweet glove work, his speed, his bunting ability, and his way of waiting out a pitcher at the plate. He was smart and a man of good habits.

Although he hit only .227 and .218 for Boston, McGraw was convinced that he would improve with some work.[7]

"In many of these trades it was said that I made mistakes," said McGraw. "I may have done so, but I don't think I made many. My principle has always been, if I need a particular player for a certain place, to go out and get him at any price. They say that I have let a lot of good players go. I have. But I have never yet discovered any plan by which a manager can get a crack player without giving up a good one in exchange. I may have a crack player who is not absolutely necessary to the machinery of my club. I will trade him in a minute, if I see a chance to get the one man who completes the cogs for my machine."[8]

In January 1908, McGraw took Blanche to Los Angeles for a brief vacation. The trip allowed him to visit the tracks there and also hunt up a promising young player he had seen the year before. During spring training in 1907 the Giants had played three exhibition games against St. Vincent's College. While umpiring the games, McGraw was impressed by the catcher for the college team, Fred Snodgrass. On this vacation he offered Snodgrass a contract and told him to talk it over with his parents. In March a naïve Snodgrass journeyed to spring training with a salary of $150 a month. He was twenty years old, a native of Ventura, California, the son of a private patrolman who had come west from Kentucky.[9]

Like most rookies, Snodgrass found it a chore to get time at the plate for batting practice. Few veterans mentored the kids, but Snodgrass was lucky enough to find one in Spike Shannon. "He took me under his wing, helped me, encouraged me, and told me what to do and what not to do," he said. "I doubt if I'd have made the club that year if it hadn't been for Shannon." Snodgrass became the third-string catcher behind Bresnahan and Tom Needham, but he got into only six games and went to bat only four times, producing a lone hit.[10]

In his search for talent, McGraw happened on a third baseman in the New York–Pennsylvania League. Charles "Buck" Herzog was a Baltimore native who played shortstop for the University of Maryland alongside third baseman Frank Baker, later a star for the Philadelphia Athletics. A German Presbyterian, his prominent nose and last name misled some New Yorkers, including the Yiddish newspapers, into thinking he was Jewish. His work in spring training prompted one writer to observe, "It is seldom that a minor league recruit in his first year in fast company shows enough class to win a regular position, but this may be the fortune of Charley Herzog. He covers considerable ground around short position, is a sure fielder, and a fast and accurate thrower." Above all, he hustled and was a fierce competitor. "No player ever got more out of the equipment his Maker gave him," wrote one columnist.[11]

Although McGraw did not go out of his way to seek pitching help, he did sign one youngster purely out of sentiment, or so he later claimed. In glancing over a list of players the Giants could draft, he saw one from a familiar minor-league team. "That's the fellow I'll take," he told Fred Knowles, the Giants secretary, "and I'm taking him simply because he comes from Cedar Rapids. That's where I got my start." To a reporter he said, "I had never seen another ball player from the old town, and when I ran across the name of Crandall I decided that I would just try him out.[12]

James Otis Crandall was a twenty-year-old farm boy from tiny Wadena, Indiana, which had a long baseball history. His father had played local ball and did not mind his son doing so once his chores were done. He jumped from local to semipro teams before turning fifteen and made it to Cedar Rapids in 1906. One of the last rookies to arrive in Marlin, he had to shag flies in street clothes for a couple of days because the Giants had run out of uniforms. "His head hung down on his chest," observed Mathewson, "and, when not playing, a cigarette drooped out of the corner of his mouth." But nothing seemed to ruffle him. McGraw soon discovered that he was much more than a pitcher.[13]

Reporters learned from Crandall that his control came from shucking corn. "It teaches you to put them over the plate," he said, "and gives you a free movement. Why, I have shucked corn all day with my head down and never once missed hitting a target on the sideboard with every ear. I'd have a circle about a foot in diameter as a mark, and I got so I didn't even have to aim at it. That's good practice for those snap throws to first base where you don't have to locate the bag before you heave the ball." Sid Mercer of the *New York Globe* asked Crandall what he had been called at Cedar Rapids. "Nothing but Otis," replied Crandall. "Well," said Mercer after a short pause, "you're Doc from now on."[14]

Although camps usually included a liberal share of rookies, some of whom invariably made a splash early on, rarely did one make the team, but McGraw did things differently in 1908. He liked the team he had and the way it was coming together, but he also knew that the key to its future lay with the young players, who had to be brought along properly. Merkle, Doyle, and Herzog impressed the writers with their play, but Vila offered his usual sour assessment of the team's chances and predicted that "the Giants will slide down pretty close to the second division."[15]

As the team headed north, Bresnahan prepared another innovation for the coming season. On opening day in 1907 he had startled observers by wearing huge shin guards like those used in cricket to protect his legs. After the inevitable ridicule, the gear gradually caught on among catchers. This season Bresnahan attached leather-bound rolls of padding to the wire rim of his catcher's mask to cushion the shock of foul balls. For the Giants the most startling innovation was the number of young players McGraw kept on the roster. Doyle moved in as the regular second baseman, sharing time with Herzog. Merkle and Snodgrass rode the bench, but Crandall got pressed into duty as a starter.[16]

Ahead lay what has since come to be considered the most remarkable season in baseball history. The Cubs remained the same powerhouse that had copped two pennants in a row and in 1907 crushed the Tigers four games straight in the World Series. Pittsburgh had retooled with a strong pitching staff and solid regulars, but Honus Wagner skipped spring training and talked of retiring from baseball. Tommy Leach thought that "Hans merely wants to dodge the strenuosity of the training season, and I don't blame him." Wagner rejoined the team on April 18 and went on to lead the league in batting and slugging average, hits, runs batted in, doubles, triples, on base percentage, total bases, and stolen bases.[17]

Few people expected the Giants to match these two teams, but McGraw insisted that his club could compete. "We are going to be every bit as strong as we were in 1904 and 1905," he insisted. Chance countered that "we have taken two pennants straight with this team, and there is nothing to indicate we will not make it three in a row." Clarke admitted that "without Hans Wagner . . . I am worried." When Wagner joined the team in Cincinnati, noted a reporter, "tears almost came to Clarke's eyes."[18]

On a cold opening day in Philadelphia, Mathewson bewitched the Phillies in a 3–1 victory. "The Phillies simply could not touch Christy Mathewson," noted the *Philadelphia Inquirer*. "That's the whole story." The *New York Evening Mail* thought that "the game brought out the significant fact that the Giants are to be feared this year. The men, new and old, worked so well together that McGraw must be congratulated. The infield was like a stone wall." Early in May, when the Giants were playing uninspired ball, McGraw admitted to being worried about the team. Vila agreed entirely. "I predicted several weeks ago that the Giants would finish sixth," he wrote.

"Now I'll say they have an excellent chance to wind up in seventh place, if not in the tail-end division!" Bresnahan fractured a finger, Bridwell and Ames fell ill with fevers, Seymour was hobbled by a charley horse, and Mathewson endured four poor starts. "McGraw's misfits look pretty small now," crowed Vila. "Just as I told you, the Giants are outclassed simply because McGraw didn't get new and competent players when he had the chance."[19]

Doyle became a storm center of controversy with his mercurial play in the field and on the bases. But as the summer wore on he began to hit, and attitudes toward him started to shift. However, on June 21 the Giants were to play an exhibition game in Elizabeth, New Jersey. Herzog balked at going, saying his wrist was too sore to play and he didn't want to make the trip just to watch the game. McGraw lit into him with such vehemence that Herzog went home to Ridgely, Maryland, vowing never to play for the Giants as long as McGraw was manager. With Herzog gone, McGraw counted on Merkle to be his key utility player, but early in July he pulled up lame with a mysteriously swollen foot that turned out to be blood poisoning. He underwent two operations and fended off complications that threatened amputation. Not until July 22 did he recover enough to be on crutches and talk of returning to the team.[20]

Still the Giants continued to win. Early in July only a game and a half separated first-place Pittsburgh, Chicago, and New York. Wiltse celebrated the Fourth by hurling a ten-inning no hitter in which only one Phillie reached first base. A restless McGraw, convinced that his club had a shot at the pennant, brought Moose McCormick back to the Giants and put Shannon on waivers. After the 1904 season McCormick had dropped out of baseball for three years to work as a salesman for a steel company. Slow and burly, he did not fit McGraw's ideal for an outfielder, but he batted .302 for the Giants. McGraw also went hunting for another pitcher and a catcher to back up Bresnahan.[21]

He found an intriguing prospect pitching for Indianapolis of the American Association. Left-hander Richard "Rube" Marquard stood six-three and weighed 180 pounds. He got his nickname not from being a country hick but from a teammate who chided him for carrying a "typical farmerish carpet bag." In fact, he was a city boy, the son of a city engineer in Cleveland. Like Chief Meyers, he later claimed to be younger than he was, saying he was born in 1889 when a birth certificate showed the date to be 1886. His parents had come from Germany in 1874 and settled in Cleveland, where his father, Ferdinand Marquardt, learned the butcher's trade, then got a job in the city's fire department while he studied engineering. By 1895 he had done well enough to buy a house for his family.[22]

His family were giants for their time; Marquard had three brothers and a sister, who at six feet was the shortest among them. He lost his mother at thirteen and, to his father's dismay, showed more interest in baseball than in schoolwork, finishing only five years of grammar school. "Ballplayers are no good," his father would growl at the end of their constant arguments, "and they never will be any good." Although Marquard did not smoke or drink, he hung around poolrooms and smoke shops to mingle with older players. In 1906, at age nineteen, he snuck away from home and rode the rails to Waterloo, Iowa, where the local team had offered him a tryout. He got the tryout but no contract and had to make his way back home.[23]

The following spring Canton of the Central League gave him a contract. He won twenty-three games and earned a promotion to Indianapolis, where he did even better, winning twenty-eight games in 1908, including two no-hitters, one a perfect game. After the latter, the team's owner put him up for bid to several eager big-league teams. It was, Marquard recalled, "like a horse being auctioned off." To get him, Brush paid $11,000, a staggering figure far above anything paid for a minor leaguer in the past. It was a bold gamble; Marquard would not report to the Giants until September and would not likely figure in the pennant race.[24]

The search for a catcher brought the Giants to a most improbable candidate. John Tortes "Jack" Meyers was a member of the Cahuilla tribe and a unique personality. Like others of his blood, he was inevitably tagged with the nickname "Chief," which he despised but grudgingly accepted. Much of what the public came to know or assume about him turned out to be wrong, partly because of what Meyers himself told reporters. He was born in 1880, not 1882 as he originally claimed, because in 1908 he did not want to be seen as a twenty-eight-year-old rookie. His father, John Mayer, was of German ancestry and hailed from Terre Haute, Indiana. Sometime in the 1870s he moved to Riverside, California, where he acquired a saloon. He married Felicité Tortes, a member of the Cahuilla tribe and a remarkable woman.[25]

Jack's pilgrimage to the major leagues was more convoluted than most. After his father died in 1887, his mother worked as a cook and maid in Riverside. For a time Felicité took her children to live on the Santa Rosa Reservation, where she was the first Cahuilla woman to take individual title to communal lands. That experience imprinted Jack with a thorough acquaintance of his heritage and language. His mother spoke English, French, German, and several Cahuilla dialects, and prodded her children to speak their language correctly. After a few years at Santa Rosa she moved the family back to Riverside and managed to buy a small house. Jack attended Riverside High School but did not graduate.

Baseball already claimed his attention. He played for a reservation team and for different Riverside teams. Joining a team sponsored by the Atchison, Topeka and Santa Fe Railway provided him with a job in the company's shop. One of the rival teams, Olinda from Orange County, featured a teen-aged pitcher named Walter Johnson, of whom he later said, "Walter's right arm was different than yours or mine. It was special, like Caruso's lungs or Einstein's brain." Between 1902 and 1904 Meyers kept his Santa Fe job while playing for different teams in southern California.[26]

Through an acquaintance Meyers gained admission to Dartmouth in September 1905 but left school shortly before the end of his first year and regretted the decision the rest of his life. In the summer of 1906 he hooked on with the Harrisburg Senators of the Tri-State League for $250 a month, "more money than I had ever seen in my life," then moved to Butte, Montana, of the Northwestern League. His odyssey took him in 1908 to St. Paul; the team lost more than a hundred games but Meyers performed well. In July he was hitting .292 when word came that the Giants had bought the rights to him for $6,000.[27]

Altogether McGraw and Brush had shelled out the unheard-of sum of $17,000 for two unproven minor leaguers who could not be expected to provide much if any help in the pennant race. Clearly McGraw had in mind building for the following season and beyond regardless of what happened in 1908. No one without a long-range plan would have stocked his team with so many young players who had potential but were not yet ready to become regulars. Late in the season he added another recruit, plucking a diminutive twenty-year-old outfielder named Josh Devore from Newark.[28]

Even so, McGraw believed that, given a few breaks, the Giants could win that season. After sweeping four games from Philadelphia, including the no-hitter by Wiltse, the Giants headed out on their western swing. When they returned on July 23 after going 8-7 on the trip, they had moved up to second place. Merkle was on crutches and Herzog had signaled his willingness to return; McGraw took him back on July 25. "Not in years has the National League had such a contest as is being waged at present," observed the *Tribune*. "In the last two years the Cubs clinched their hold on the pennant by August 1 . . . The story is altogether different this season."[29]

The gritty battle for the pennant by the Giants did much to restore McGraw's reputation as the best—if most obnoxious—manager in baseball. "Few people, even the most rabid fans, realize what a wonderful fight McGraw has made this season," said the *Evening Mail*, "and that the Giants are second is due far more to his wonderful generalship than to the playing of the team. Everywhere McGraw is feared by opposing players, and there is not a fan . . . who down in his heart would not like to see McGraw leading their team."[30]

The Cubs, riddled with injuries, opened August by losing to lowly Boston 14–0. Dissension in the ranks became a theme for writers covering Chicago. Word spread about an ugly clubhouse fight involving Sheckard, infielder Heinie Zimmerman, and Chance. Evers had a sour disposition that earned him the nickname "Crab," and he and Tinker did not speak to each other except during a game. Yet the Cubs refused to let tensions or anything else stand in their way and closed the month with a nine-game winning streak that included a three-game sweep of the Giants. However, at month's end New York held a slim half-game lead over Chicago and one game over Pittsburgh. Ahead lay the challenge of playing forty games in twenty-nine playing days.

Writers began jumping on the Giants' bandwagon. Even Vila conceded that "the Giants have been the surprise of the year. I admire them for their pugnacity and earnestness. McGraw has the laugh on all of us who tried to show he erred in his trade with Boston . . . Tenney never played better, while Bridwell has developed into a good hitter and a brilliant shortstop."[31]

On September 4 an incident occurred in a game between Chicago and Pittsburgh that was to loom large in the pennant chase. A pitching duel between Miner Brown and Vic Willis remained scoreless until the bottom of the tenth inning, when Chief Wilson shot a single into right field with the bases loaded. Fred Clarke scored easily from third base but Warren Gill, the runner at first, ran only halfway to second base, then headed for the Pirates dugout as soon as he saw the hit land safely. Watching Gill change course, Evers alertly yelled to Slagle to throw him the ball and touched second base with it. Under the rules, a run cannot score if there is a force out on the play. Evers tried to get the attention of the lone umpire, Hank O'Day, but O'Day could only say that Clarke had scored and he had not seen what Gill had done. The Cubs protested the game but Pulliam abided by the umpire's decision not to call something he had not seen.[32]

At the time it seemed a minor event in the heat of the pennant race. The Giants took five straight games from Brooklyn at the Polo Grounds. Larry Doyle was severely spiked and laid up indefinitely, but Herzog stepped in and performed well. To accommodate the overflow crowds that had become a constant, Brush replaced a thousand bleacher seats with a new stand that held three thousand people. St. Louis came to town and the Giants whipped them three in a row to extend their record to a sparkling 85-46, but they could not shake either the Pirates or the Cubs, the next teams due at the Polo Grounds.[33]

On September 18, before what the *World* called "the greatest throng of humanity ever attracted to a baseball game," the Giants stung the Pirates in both ends of a doubleheader, thanks to a shutout by Mathewson in one and a twelve-run outburst in the other. The victories ran the Giants winning streak to eleven games. "The double victory," predicted the *Times*, "practically assures the Giants of winning the National League pennant." Then the Giants lost the next two games to Pittsburgh. "We are in the fight for the flag until the last inning of the last game of the season," promised Clarke, not realizing how prophetic his words were.[34]

Tempers flared when Chicago arrived at the Polo Grounds on September 22 and swept a doubleheader from the Giants. "The baseball played yesterday," reported the *Times*, "was the kind that makes the National sport so popular. Brilliant fielding, punctuated with an occasional phenomenal play, added to clean, hard hitting, were the characteristic features of the two games." The home team clung to first place by only a few percentage points, having played six fewer games than the Cubs. The stage was set for what became the most controversial game in baseball history, one that has almost as many versions of what happened as there are tellers of the tale.[35]

The day started badly for the Giants when Fred Tenney was scarcely able to bend or walk and had to sit; it was the only game he missed all season. Fred Merkle, who had spent most of the summer watching and learning from the bench, went to first base for this crucial game. Not surprisingly, the game boiled down to a pitching duel between Christy Mathewson and southpaw Jack Pfiester, who had begun to earn a reputation as "Jack the Giant Killer."[36]

The score stayed at 1–1 into the ninth inning. Mathewson retired the Cubs in order, having faced only twenty-nine batters. With one out Art Devlin stroked a single. Moose McCormick bounced to Joe Tinker, who was upended by the sliding Devlin before he could complete the double play.

Merkle delighted the crowd with a liner to right, sending McCormick to third. With two outs and men at the corners, Al Bridwell belted one over second base for a clean hit, allowing McCormick to trot home with what appeared to be the winning run, McGraw doing a celebratory dance alongside him. At that point sheer pandemonium broke out on playing field.

With the crowd cheering wildly and pouring onto the field, some of the Giants began heading for the clubhouse in center field. Merkle, seeing them moving that way, followed suit before he reached second base. Umpire Bob Emslie had tumbled to the ground to avoid being hit by Bridwell's drive and did not see Merkle veer off course, but the alert Johnny Evers did. For him it must have been déjà vu all over again: the same situation that had happened in the September 4 game against the Pirates and with the same umpire, Hank O'Day, who was in position to see what Merkle did. With the fans milling around him, Evers screamed for the ball but Art Hofman threw it over his head. Joe McGinnity rushed in from the first base coaching box, retrieved the ball and heaved it as far into the crowd as he could.

While fans scrambled for the ball, a husky Chicago pitcher named Floyd Kroh waded through them, retrieved the ball—or some other ball—and handed it to Harry Steinfeldt, who got it to Evers for the force out at second base. After Bridwell's hit, O'Day had run to the pitcher's mound for a better look at the play. Evers, standing on second base with the ball, yelled to O'Day that Merkle never touched second and should be called out, which meant the run didn't count.

By O'Day's own account, Emslie said he had not seen the play and asked him whether Merkle had touched second base. O'Day said he did not, whereupon Emslie called Merkle out and O'Day, although surrounded by celebrating Giants fans, declared that the run didn't count. Emslie concurred, and the two umpires relied on a wedge of policemen to reach their dressing room. Six years later O'Day claimed that "we did not make the decision because Evers touched second when Merkle started for the clubhouse, as is commonly supposed. We did it because Joe McGinnity, when the ball was thrown back to the infield by Artie Hofman, interfered with Pfiester, a Cub player, who had picked up Hofman's throw. McGinnity wrested the ball from Pfiester and threw it into the crowd, which by this time was swarming onto the grounds back of third base. Steinfeldt retrieved the ball and ran to second base with it, tossing it to Evers just before reaching the bag."[37]

By this time most of the large crowd had left in the belief that the Giants had won the game. As umpires left the park, reporters demanded an explanation. O'Day was evasive at first but in leaving shouted over his shoulder, "Merkle didn't run to second; the last run don't count. It's a tie game." At first, no one believed that O'Day had nullified the run, leaving the game tied and unfinished. Frank Chance insisted that the game continue, but O'Day refused. Asked later why he had called the game, O'Day said he had done so on account of darkness. In his report he said that "the People ran out on the Field. I did not ask to have the Field cleared as it was too dark to continue play."[38]

According to one account, McGraw had gone to his office and was sitting at his desk when someone rushed in to tell him what O'Day had ruled. "That dirty son of a bitch!" McGraw yelled. "O'Day is trying to rob us of a game. How the hell did he know Merkle didn't touch second? He was at home plate and never saw a damn thing. The fucking ball was out in center field." More to the point, McGraw insisted that "if Merkle was out, the game was a tie and O'Day should have cleared the field and resumed play. If not, we won the game." On this occasion, at least, his adversary Bill Klem fully agreed with him. Writing years later, he called O'Day's ruling "the worst decision in the history of baseball . . . Any judge will tell you that it is the *intent* of a law which counts, not the phraseology. The intent of this rule applied to infield grounders and such. It does not apply to cleanly hit drives to the outfield that make a force-out impossible unless the runner on first drops dead."[39]

In veering away after a walk-off hit, Merkle had only done what others had done hundreds of times, and umpires ignored the rule. But the rule was clear, however much it had been ignored in the past. Chance, supported by Murphy, argued just as vehemently that the Giants had forfeited the game because it was their responsibility to make the field playable for carrying on the game. Neither umpire required that the field be cleared before they departed the grounds.[40]

The *Times* was unforgiving in its account: "Censurable stupidity on the part of player Merkle in yesterday's game . . . placed the New York team's chances of winning the pennant in jeopardy . . . The result of this game may prove to be the deciding factor in the championship race." *Sporting Life* called it "the stupidity of a player who failed to obey one of the elementary rules of the game . . . absolutely inexcusable in view of the fact that only a few weeks ago the very same play was made the subject of a protest, of press discussion, and of an official Presidential report." Charles W. Murphy stirred the pot by telling a reporter, "We can't supply brains to the New York Club's dumb players."[41]

Pulliam summoned both umpires to a meeting that evening. Their written versions were quite similar, suggesting that they had either agreed on a story or saw events in the same light. Pulliam listened to them, then announced that he supported their version of events and declared the game a 1–1 tie. Since neither team had an open date, the game would not be made up. The decision pleased no one. Brush promptly appealed the ruling, as did Murphy, who demanded that Pulliam declare the Cubs victors by a 9–0 forfeit. If Pulliam had decreed a makeup game, it could have been played the next day as a doubleheader.[42]

In making his protest, Murphy had unwittingly prevented Pulliam from ordering the game to be made up the next day. The league constitution decreed that a protest and all accompanying evidence had to be furnished to the other team, which then had five days to reply. Informed of his blunder, Murphy tried to withdraw his protest the next morning, but Pulliam said it was too late to give both teams enough notice that the game must be replayed that day. The Giants beat Chicago 5–4 in the scheduled game on September 4, keeping them in first place. By that morning news of the controversy had spread across the nation, making it fodder for front pages and a prime subject for heated debates everywhere. But the season had by no means reached its climax. Pulliam had not yet ruled on the appeals from both sides, and the teams still had more than a dozen games to play.[43]

The Giants were in poor shape to play those games. As *Sporting News* put it, "Tenney, Donlin, Seymour and Bresnahan ought to be in the hospital with Larry Doyle." Donlin nursed a charley horse, Bresnahan suffered from a sciatic nerve problem, and Doyle was still on crutches from his spiking. For his part, McGraw greeted his men daily by asking, "How are the cripples? Any more to add to the list of identified dead today?"[44]

The distraught Merkle was the worst case of all. He began losing weight and asked McGraw to send him back to the minors or release him. McGraw refused and assured him that his best days as a major-league ballplayer lay ahead. But the immediate road ahead looked rocky. "Oh, joy! oh, joy! [Manager] John Ganzel and his Reds will be our guests in two games this afternoon, and Honest John will take his medicine like a sport," crowed the *American*. But the Reds proved to be uncharacteristically rude guests, sweeping both games on September 25. The losses left the Giants again clinging to first place by mere percentage points over the Cubs and the Pirates.[45]

In the first game Rube Marquard made his debut with the Giants. Cincinnati greeted him with six hits for five runs (two earned), aided by a hit batsman and wild pitch. Marquard retired after five innings of what he later called the worst day of his life. "I was so badly rattled I didn't get over it all winter," he said later. "I lost confidence in myself completely and those calls, 'take him out' . . . and so on, they ring in my ears yet." The writers who had labeled him the "$11,000 peach" were quick to rebrand him the "$11,000 lemon." He did not appear in another game that season.[46]

The Giants rebounded the next day to sweep a doubleheader from the Reds. Mathewson cruised to victory in the first game for his thirty-fifth win, but it brought his innings pitched to 365. The Cubs had six games left to play, the Pirates seven, and the Giants eleven. But eight of New York's games were with Philadelphia, a team they had already whipped eleven out of fourteen games.[47]

On September 28, the Giants led the league by one percentage point but were half a game behind the Cubs and half a game ahead of the Pirates. That day they eked out a win over the Phillies 7–6 and the next day split a doubleheader with them. In the second game an obscure lefty named Harry Coveleski blanked the Giants 7–0. A newcomer to the Phillies, Coveleski was so green that in a previous game he let a man steal second easily. Asked why he didn't hold the runner, he replied, "I didn't know he was there." Manager Billy Murray called his infielders together and told them solemnly, "From now on, we'll have no further secrets on this club. Whenever a runner gets to base on Harry, I want you to tell him. Do you understand?"[48]

If Coveleski was good for a joke, the Giants weren't laughing. By a fluke of the schedule they had to play the Phillies eight straight times, including two doubleheaders. With his pitching staff exhausted from four double-headers in eight days, McGraw saw no choice but to call on Matty twice during that stretch. The Giants beat the Phillies on September 30 but split a doubleheader the next day. Pitching on one day's rest, Mathewson stag-gered to a 4–2 victory. In the second game Coveleski again bested the Giants, 6–3. Red Ames managed his second straight win over the Phillies on October 2, leaving the Giants in second place with one critical game left against Philadelphia and three against Boston.[49]

Having just used Mathewson on one day's rest, McGraw saw no choice but to do it again, so important was the final game against the Phillies. To his surprise, Murray opted for Coveleski, also going on one day's rest. Despite a gallant effort by a weary Matty, Coveleski beat the Giants for the third time in five days, 3–2. He won only one other game that season, but he was now officially a Giant Killer.[50]

Writers agreed they had never seen anything like this race. "The baseball public is on the verge of dementia doperina," said William F. Kirk of the *American*, "and the players of the three leading clubs are worn to a frazzle." Of the Giants he observed that "the team is now a sadly battle-scarred lot of ball tossers." The last crushing loss to the Phillies put the Giants in a bad place. Pittsburgh and Chicago had one game left to play, and it was against each other. If Pittsburgh won, they would take the pennant regardless of what the Giants did. If the Cubs won, the Giants would have to win all three games against Boston just to finish in a tie with them. The elephant in the room remained the disputed game of September 23. Not until October 2 did Pulliam rule "that this game ended in a tie score and that Chicago has no claim for a forfeited game on Sept. 24." Two days later the Cubs beat the Pirates, giving the Giants a glimmer of hope if they could sweep Boston. The Giants proceeded to do just that without using Mathewson, leaving them tied with the Cubs for first place.[51]

If 1908 was a season for the ages, September qualified as a month unlike any ever seen. During its hard-fought days the Cubs compiled a record of 23-8, the Giants 24-8, and the Pirates 25-8. "Never before in this league has a situation existed," gushed *Sporting Life*, "wherein three clubs had almost equal chance within two days of the close of a race." In the American League a mere game and a half separated Detroit, Cleveland, and Chicago on September 30. It was as if the rival leagues were dueling to see which race could be closer and more exciting. On that point the National League had an edge: Its pennant chase was not simply close but deadlocked.[52]

Never before had a season ended with two teams tied for first place. Only then did the full impact of the outcome of the September 23 game register. The National League board of directors met on October 6 to consider Pulliam's decision and the evidence. Its decision admitted freely that "the game should have been won by the New York Club had it not been for the reckless, careless, inexcusable blunder of one of its players," but it upheld Pulliam and the umpires, declared the game a tie, and decreed that a playoff game should be played on October 8, only one day after the Giants' last victory over Boston.[53]

McGraw was furious at the board's decision; the players, like himself, believed they had won the pennant and should not have to play another game for it. But when McGraw let them decide whether or not to play, they voted to send a delegation to see Brush and ask his opinion. "I am going to leave it to you," Brush said. ". . . But I shouldn't think you would stop now after making all this fight." The players huddled briefly and told Brush they would play. "I'm glad," he said. "And, say, boys . . . I want to tell you something. Win or lose, I'm going to give the players a bonus of $10,000."[54]

The first playoff game in National League history was about to unfold, one game to settle a long ordeal of struggle, strife, anxiety, and determination. The largest crowd ever seen at a sporting event began filling every space of ground around the Polo Grounds. By two o'clock "Coogan's was loaded to the gunnels," noted the *Times*, "and the tens of thousands stretched along the entire semi-circle from the Jumel Mansion [160th Street and Edgecombe Avenue] to Eighth Avenue." For nearly a mile a mass of people lined stairs, viaducts, streets, Speedway, bluffs, crags, rocks, peaks, grass, plots, trees, and any other available space not previously occupied. "There were fully twice as many persons immediately outside the fence around the grounds as there were inside," declared the *Evening Telegram*. To control the mass of humanity, three hundred city police and five mounted police arrived to reinforce the fifty special policemen hired by the Giants. At twelve forty-five the gate to the grounds was ordered closed because capacity had long since been reached.[55]

The Cubs arrived by the elevated and made their way into the clubhouse largely unrecognized in their street clothes. Brown had in his coat pocket half a dozen letters warning that he would be killed "if you pitch and beat the Giants." He showed them to Chance and Murphy, saying he wanted to pitch just to "show those so-and-sos they can't win with threats." From the stands a steady roar of abuse rained down on the Cubs in their dugout.[56]

Chance had designated Jack the Giant Killer to start for the Cubs, who had enjoyed four days of rest since their last game. Predictably, McGraw chose Mathewson, thinking that he might be at his best after four days' rest even though he had pitched in nine of the fifteen games before that. But Matty had not slept well the night before. "I'm not fit to pitch today," he admitted to Jane before leaving for the ballpark. "I'm dog tired." At the park he told McGraw succinctly, "I'll go as far as I can."[57]

The clubhouse was quiet as the players put on their bandages and uniforms. McGraw told the men, "Chance will probably pitch Pfiester or

Brown. If Pfiester works there is no use trying to steal. He won't give you any lead. The right-handed hitters ought to wait him out and the left-handers hit him when he gets in a hole. Matty is going to pitch for us." Outside the crowd continued to heap abuse on the Cubs. "They called us everything they could think of and some things we have never heard before," said Kling. When the umpires decided to start the game fifteen minutes early because the crowd was so immense, McGraw took the time from the twenty minutes allotted to the Cubs for batting practice. To impartial observers it seemed a mean, petty trick, but Chance ordered his players to "cross 'em up. No matter when the bell rings to end practice, come right off the field. Don't give any excuse to quarrel."[58]

In the clubhouse before the game Chance also told his players to pick out one of the Giants for their special attention. "Call 'em everything in the book," he said. The Cubs needed little encouragement to repay the McGraw brand of abuse in kind. "Chance and McGraw were born to battle on baseball fields," observed Joe Tinker. "If you didn't honestly and furiously hate the Giants, you weren't a real Cub."[59]

Mathewson started well enough, retiring the Cubs in order and striking out two in the first inning. A nervous Pfiester stumbled out of the gate, hitting Tenney with a pitch and walking Herzog. Bresnahan struck out and Kling rifled a throw to first base to catch Herzog off the bag for the second out. The bill for Herzog's blunder came due at once when Donlin smacked a double down the right-field line. Tenney scored, as would Herzog if he had still been on base. Seymour then walked, prompting Chance to replace Pfiester with Miner Brown, who fanned Devlin to end the inning.[60]

Leading off the third, the irrepressible Tinker smashed a ball to left center that Seymour misjudged. "Probably forty-nine times out of fifty Seymour would have caught that ball," said a sympathetic Mathewson. Tinker reached third and scored on a single by Kling. If Seymour had caught Tinker's hit, the inning would have been over. As it was, Evers walked because, Matty declared, "I was afraid to put the ball over the plate for him," and both Frank Schulte and Chance followed with doubles. Steinfeldt fanned, but four runs had scored.[61]

"None of the players spoke to one another as they went to the bench," said Mathewson. "Even McGraw was silent. We knew it was gone." From behind the watercooler Merkle said, "It was my fault, boys." As Brown began mowing down the Giants, the crowd grew increasingly silent. Matty kept the Cubs at bay for another four innings; in all he struck out nine batters. In the seventh Devlin singled, McCormick followed suit, and Bridwell walked to load the bases with nobody out. In a questionable move McGraw sent Doyle, who had not played in weeks, to bat for Mathewson, a decent hitter. Doyle hobbled to the plate on his bad foot and fouled out to Kling, who made the catch despite dodging a pop bottle and cushion thrown at him. Tenney plated one run with a sacrifice fly, but Herzog grounded out to Tinker. In the ninth Brown set them down on four pitches.[62]

Once again the game and the pennant belonged to Chicago. The Cubs went on to whip the Detroit Tigers, who had also won the pennant on the last day of this magical season, in five games. In their struggle to leave the Polo Grounds after the game, Chance was struck in the neck and suffered broken cartilage, but he recovered enough to play in the series two days later. Afterward, Evers happened on him sitting quietly, lost in thought. "The big, hearty, joyous boy who had come from California a dozen years before was battered, grizzled, careworn and weary," he recalled. "Still young, his fine face showed lines of care and worry and a few gray hairs streaked his head. He was thirty-two and looked old."[63]

Chance sat musing for a long while, then looked up at Evers with a grim smile. "This business," he said, "is making a crab out of me."

McGraw, too, felt the strain of the season's long, constant struggle with the other contenders, the umpires, the enemy fans, and sometimes the players, to say nothing of the travel that took its toll on endurance and mental alertness. At age thirty-five he had already managed for a decade, for part of which he played as well. He looked older and his middle had begun to spread, but however tired or discouraged he got, he always bounced back to the role he had fashioned for himself. Crushing as the outcome of this season was, he turned his sights toward next year.

Amid the gloom in the clubhouse on that last day, a haggard-looking Merkle came to him and said, "I've lost you one pennant. Fire me before I can do more harm."

"Fire you?" answered McGraw. "We ran the wrong way of the track to-day. That's all. Next year is another season, and do you think I'm going to let you go after the gameness you've shown through all this abuse? Why you're the kind of guy I've been lookin' for many years. I could use a carload like you. Forget this season and come around next spring. The newspapers will have forgotten it all then. Good-bye, boys."[64]

CHAPTER 7

Bitter Aftertastes

"Baseball is always played out in the sunshine,
where the air is pure and the grass is green,
and there is something about the game—or at
least I have always found it so—which teaches
one to win or lose as a gentleman should, and
that is a very fine thing to learn."
—CHRISTY MATHEWSON

THE SEASON JUST CONCLUDED WAS EASILY THE most exciting and unpredictable in baseball history. The nation's love of the game, which had grown sharply if unevenly over the decades, reached new heights of interest and excitement by the time of the playoff game. Attendance soared and publicity broadened to the point where even the staid *Times* reported the outcome of the playoff game on page one, the first time the paper had dignified the sport in that manner. Baseball had long been labeled America's national sport; in 1908 it demonstrated that role as never before. The owners should have been ecstatic at how the season turned out, and for a brief time they were, but events conspired to rob them of joy.

Under a cloud of unresolved issues the magnates gathered at league headquarters, 1133 Broadway, for their annual meeting on December 8. One owner was conspicuously absent even though the gathering was in his own city and he had come back to town days earlier. Brush continued to boycott meetings while Pulliam remained league president. Annoyed as they might be by this imperious attitude, the magnates continued to tread softly around Brush because of the gate receipts New York provided them. Attendance in 1908 had soared 15 percent above that of the previous year. By one estimate the Polo Grounds attracted 880,700 customers compared to 619,807 for the Cubs. Philadelphia ranked third with 415,171, Pittsburgh fourth with 366,427, and Boston a poor last with a measly 245,284.[1]

No one was prepared for what developed during the meeting. After hearing Pulliam's report, the owners reelected him president. Pulliam thanked them, then launched into a strange monologue that betrayed the strain he had endured for months past. Painfully aware that his administration had been controversial, he admitted freely to having made mistakes, "but I have suffered indignities and humiliations in this job that I would not have suffered were it not for a sense of duty, and from the fact that I did not have the money that I wished to have."[2]

Pulliam rambled on for some time before finally turning to the recommendations in his report. "I cannot emphasize too strongly that portion of my report that deals with gambling at your ball games," he said. There was good reason to be even more concerned than usual. While gambling had always flourished in New York City, the threat to baseball had increased sharply since the Hart-Agnew Law of June 1908 banned gambling in the state. New Jersey had banned gambling and horse racing a decade earlier, and Pulliam predicted that the closing of the New York racetracks "may cause the National League to fall into disrepute" as gamblers turned their eyes toward baseball.[3]

Then, well into the meeting, Pulliam observed abruptly that "the umpires I do not think are given the consideration they deserve by the club owners." Only then did he inform the owners for the first time that an attempt had been made to bribe the umpires who worked the playoff game on October 8. During the World Series rumors had surfaced that someone working for the Giants had tried to bribe their way to the pennant in the late-season games with Philadelphia and Boston. Nothing came of them and they might have faded away entirely had not Pulliam stunned the owners with the revelation he had been keeping secret.[4]

Bill Klem had umpired the Giants' game with Boston on October 7. Afterward, as he and Jimmy Johnstone, the other umpire, approached the exit underneath the grandstand on their way to the umpires' dressing room, Dr. Joseph Creamer, the Giants' team physician that year, said to him, "I have been designated to hand you five five hundred dollar bills, and if we win the game you keep it, and if we don't you give it back to me; and you can suit yourself about giving any of it to Johnstone." He assured Klem that "it ain't going to hurt you, because McGraw or the players don't know anything about it."[5]

"This is my bread and butter," Klem replied, "and I could not think of doing that." Creamer said he would try to up the amount to $3,000. Next morning Klem reported to the league office and was told he would be umpiring the game along with Jimmy Johnstone, who was also there. Klem asked to speak with Pulliam only to find he was in Cincinnati. Instead he told the league secretary, John Heydler, and asked him to get other umpires for the game. "My God," Klem said, "if we make a mistake against the Chicago Club we would be ruined for life." Johnstone agreed, but Heydler told them that the only other umpires were in the West and could not get there in time for the game. Heydler had heard that some $40,000 had been wagered on the game, "probably by this race course crowd." He told the umpires, "Here we are, boys. All depends on your honesty."[6]

Seeing no choice, the two umpires agreed to work the game and went to the Polo Grounds to dress quickly, hoping to start the game early because of the huge crowd. Unable to get through the grandstand, they went underneath it. Creamer was waiting for them. He grabbed Klem's hand and pressed the money into it. "Now, take that, will you, Bill," he said. "I hope that my mother may drop dead in the Grand Stand if I ever mention it to a soul." Klem shoved it back to him and kept going toward the field, saying he wouldn't take it if it were ten thousand. "I can get you a job here for all the winters of your life," Creamer persisted. "Well, I cannot do anything like that," Klem said adamantly. ". . . I can umpire only one way, and that is to call them as I see them."[7]

Fortunately for the umpires, the game proceeded without any controversy involving them. On the fourteenth, when both men were in Chicago, Klem went to Pulliam's hotel room and told him the whole story. Pulliam asked him to put it in writing and sealed the statement in an envelope, deposited it at the Lincoln Trust Company, and said nothing about it to anyone. For seven weeks he sat on the story, uncertain of what to do. On December 1, a week before the owners' meeting, Johnstone came to see him on another matter. Pulliam asked whether Klem had told him anything, and whether he had witnessed a bribe attempt. Johnstone said he had, and Pulliam asked him to write out what he had seen.[8]

"I saw Creamer of the New York Club try to hand money to Klem on two different occasions, October 7th, 8th, as a bribe for the New York Club to beat Chicago," Johnstone wrote. "I was also approached twice on the 59th street elevated station on the evenings of October 6th and 7th, by two different men, and was told there was money in it for Klem and I if we seen

that New York would beat Chicago. I told them there was nothing doing."
Johnstone didn't know any of these men, but he recognized Creamer.[9]

Pulliam was at a loss as to what to do. Not until the day before the
meeting did he broach the story to Charles Ebbets, who was furious and
insisted he tell the others in executive session. After Pulliam spelled it out,
the owners were appalled. "This matter is of such importance that there
should have been no hesitation on your part in telling us right away, not to
put us in the position of forcing it out of you," said Herrmann. Murphy
thought it "the most sensational and important thing . . . affecting the
National League since I have been in it . . . It rocks the very foundation of
our sport." It was also something, he added, that had to be kept secret until
the magnates figured out what to do.[10]

The situation was more complex than it appeared. They needed to find
out who had bankrolled Creamer and was behind the bribe. Should they go
public with the story? If so, when and on what basis? They did not yet have
any evidence beyond the word of the two umpires. But if the story was withheld, it would look like a cover-up. And what could they actually do about it?
A bribe had allegedly been offered but refused; had any crime occurred? No
one had convincing answers to these questions or a clear course of action to
suggest.

On one point they agreed: No one believed that Brush or anyone else on
the Giants was responsible. "I believe . . . that John T. Brush is as absolutely
innocent of any knowledge of this thing as a newborn babe," said Murphy
firmly. Stan Robison, who had taken charge of the Cardinals since his
brother Frank's death in September, agreed and suggested that Herrmann
take the letters to Brush and brief him on what had happened.[11]

The owners sent Ebbets and Herrmann to see Brush. They asked him to
join the meeting and help find some intelligent line of action. Brush agreed
that the matter was very serious but did not commit himself at first. Creamer
had already been dismissed for other reasons, he said, and would never
work for the Giants again. On October 10 he had submitted a bill for $2,800
to Brush for services rendered. "I almost fell off the chair," said Brush. He
thought the bill was padded but paid it and told Creamer his services were
no longer needed. As for the bribe story, Brush said that Creamer was "just
the kind of a son of a bitch that would do a thing like that."[12]

Brush conceded that he didn't know what should be done or what action
should be taken. At least, he added, it showed that the umpires were
completely honest, and that was no small thing. "My opinion is very strong

that we must do something," Herrmann told the other owners, "but just what to do I do not know . . . If it once gets out that we have done nothing, we are in awfully bad shape." In their absence the discussion among the other owners had arrived at the same conclusion. Dreyfuss pushed for taking the matter to the district attorney.[13]

Murphy reminded him that no crime had been committed and that "our League has no standing in court, because it is a voluntary association. We cannot go into a civil court; we are not a corporation." Ebbets observed that if they went to the district attorney and could not substantiate a charge, they would face a libel suit. Finally they agreed that nothing could be done that night. When the owners took up the matter again on the eleventh, Brush was present. Pulliam repeated for Brush everything he had told the board earlier. Heydler read Klem's letter aloud and recounted his meeting with the umpires on the morning of the game. Johnstone's account was also read aloud. When they had finished, Ebbets suggested calling the roll to get each owner's opinion on what to do. Brush asked to go last so he could hear all the others first.[14]

George Dovey said only that he would join the majority in whatever was decided. Herrmann agreed and stressed anew the urgency of doing something. Murphy followed suit, saying it would be a disaster to try to deceive the press, but he had no remedy to offer, either. Dreyfuss reiterated his desire to turn the umpire's statements over to the district attorney. He also wanted to give everything to the press and "not conceal anything at all." William Shettsline, president of the Phillies, wanted the case "thrashed or probed to the bottom" but had no ideas on how best to go about it. Robison agreed with Dreyfuss and favored criminal prosecution.[15]

Ebbets doubted that taking it to the district attorney would work, "for the simple reason that there is no corroboration." He, too, believed that gambling interests were behind Creamer and wanted the whole thing given to the press. But names had been bandied about that he thought were not involved and should be suppressed, most notably those of Big Tim and Little Tim Sullivan. He wanted even Creamer's name kept out of the minutes because the evidence was not sufficient to avert a libel suit. Having heard the others, Brush admitted that he had no course of action to suggest.[16]

"I hardly know him," Brush said of Creamer. "I have hardly known any of the physicians that we have ever had in the club. We have had a new one nearly every year . . . I never saw him at a game in my life; never had any conversation with him." He agreed with Ebbets that not enough proof existed to take it to the district attorney. "We are really in the dark," he admitted, "and being in the dark . . . I really do not think it would be politic for the League to rush into print with a case that it did not know or understand itself." He suggested creating a committee to try to obtain more information.[17]

Pulliam endorsed Brush's suggestion and added, "I want to say what I think, and what everybody thinks, that Mr. Brush is an honest man. We think you are just as much interested in this as we are, and we think you won't stand for a wrong condition. As proof of that I am willing to make you chairman of that committee with full power to act." Murphy renewed his argument for full publicity, Dreyfuss his for going to the district attorney. "If we give out this information . . . we cannot go any further because we have no power," stressed Dreyfuss. "We cannot ask Creamer to come here."[18]

"If we do not give it out, and it leaks out through one of our umpires telling some gate-tender a month or two or three weeks from now," countered Murphy, "it is going to hurt us all." The reporters were downstairs in the lobby waiting for news of what was happening upstairs. Shettsline agreed, believing that "if we take it to the District Attorney we will find that no crime has been committed. It is only an attempt to bribe." Robison thought publicity would show that the league was trying hard to get to the bottom of the affair. Ebbets suggested drawing up a public statement giving all the facts but withholding names to avoid the appearance of an accusation. Dovey objected, saying, "I think it is untimely to publish before you know what steps you are going to take."[19]

Ebbets wanted a statement released that afternoon. If so, advised Dreyfuss, "name the man. The moment you say this happened they will want to know who; the papers will demand it." Murphy conceded that whatever they did would be misconstrued by someone, but he did not think there was "a chance in the world to convict this man." The object rather was to prevent any future attempts, and publicity would accomplish this best. Brush agreed that going to the district attorney would be futile. "I am not a lawyer," he said, "but I know this is ex parte, what you have got here, you have not got the other side of it at all. You do not know what might be brought in to offset that."[20]

Herrmann then outlined a possible statement for release. No names would be included, but it would emphasize that none of those withheld included officials or players of the Giants, Cubs, or any other club. Brush approved the outline, the others agreed, and a motion passed to appoint a special committee, chaired by Brush, to investigate the entire matter with authority to employ counsel and present facts to the district attorney if deemed advisable. Herrmann, Pulliam, and Ebbets were named to the committee, which prepared a statement for the press. After reciting the facts of the bribe attempt, it called for "the most thorough and searching investigation . . . to maintain the high standard and honesty of the game throughout the entire country. . . . To make it such an investigation as the unsigned desire, we deem it unwise to give out any names of persons claimed to have been connected with this matter, as we have grave doubts as to the truths of certain statements alleged by the person who approached one of the umpires . . . We desire, however, to state that none of the persons whose names are withheld at this time are in any way connected with organized baseball."[21]

After commending the umpires for their honesty and integrity, the statement closed by listing the names of the committee members. As part of their vigilance the magnates had every mention of Creamer and other names cut out of the official minutes, but whoever did the job overlooked one reference to Creamer on page 347. The public would not learn his name until the following spring. The owners pledged mutual silence on the whole affair until the committee did its work, and adjourned to await its report.[22]

The reporters lounging in the lobby and the bar had no notion of what was going on upstairs or why the meetings stretched over so many days. When Heydler handed out the release, it created an immediate sensation. "Not since the senior base ball organization of the country went into session," said *Sporting Life*, "had there been anything like the excitement that was created among the hundred-odd base ball men who waited in the lobby of the hotel to hear the result of the meeting." Since the ban on racetrack betting, it added, "it has been feared that the gamblers . . . would turn to base ball as a new field of operations." Columnist W. A. Phelon said emphatically that "gambling at or on ball games must be stamped out ruthlessly and immediately, and the race track element must be kept out of the ball park with a heavy club." The problem, as always, was how to go about it.[23]

GAMBLING HAD ALWAYS BEEN A SMOLDERING ember in baseball that on occasion burst forth into flames. In New York it had become a big business, almost corporate in its organization, its efficiency interrupted only by the earnest but usually ineffectual arrival of a reform administration and sporadic turf wars. A long parade of personalities dominated the business in the city during these years. Few had more influence than Big Tim Sullivan, who started his career as a saloonkeeper, graduated to politics, built an impressive organization largely around his own family, and became a master of the shakedown.[24]

Sullivan was a world unto himself. "His money and power were wrung from what would come to be called organized crime," wrote David Von Drehle. "From his customary table at the Occidental Hotel on the Bowery, Big Tim skimmed the first cream from all the vices south of Fourteenth Street. Immensely charming, Sullivan was also extremely tough. He reigned by muscle . . . Big Tim owned the cops and the crooks. He was the smiling, genial face of political corruption." He neither smoked or drank, was fond of serious literature, and was notoriously generous. His philanthropies included a huge annual Christmas dinner for unfortunates in the Bowery. A compulsive gambler himself, he sustained his habit by combining with Bill Devery and Frank Farrell to shake down all types of gambling in the city. That alliance naturally brought him close to baseball. His name was one of the first to surface in speculation about who had bankrolled Creamer, although he had defenders as well.[25]

Ebbets had the temerity to broach the question in private to Little Tim Sullivan, adding hastily that the owners did not believe they were involved. "Charlie, we would not do anything like that," protested Little Tim. "It is an outrage; we would not do anything of that character. Everything and anything that happens in the City of New York is ascribed to the Sullivans." Ebbets believed him, and so did Herrmann, who had heard an even more disturbing story alleging that the men behind Creamer were John McGraw, Roger Bresnahan, and Christy Mathewson. That charge bordered on the fantastic; none of the owners believed it, but it could not be dismissed out of hand.[26]

In February, *Sporting News* called the appointment of Brush as chairman "unfortunate" and repeated the call for a full investigation as promised. Long a supporter of Pulliam, the paper applauded his efforts to get at the truth. Rumors spread that Fred Knowles would resign as secretary and treasurer of the Giants. Joe Vila thought he knew why. "I have always contended that Knowles' connection with the New York Club was wholly due to the fact that Freedman was the real owner and that Sir Frederick simply represented Andy's interests. If Knowles gets out, therefore, I believe it will be due to the fact that Brush has finally acquired complete ownership of

Freedman's stock." Brush denied the story, but when Knowles was reelected it merely confirmed for Vila that Freedman was still in charge.[27]

AMID THIS MOUNTING TIDE OF CRITICISM the magnates reconvened their adjourned meeting on February 16, 1909, this time at the Auditorium Annex hotel in Chicago. Brush did not attend even though the committee's report was a main item on the agenda along with some proposed changes in the constitution. Herrmann noted that Brush had always opposed one of the changes but still would not come as long as Pulliam remained president. Had Brush known what was about to occur he might have changed his mind. Before a day's business was finished, Pulliam had thrust himself onto the agenda as a major item.[28]

That evening Pulliam hosted a dinner for the Baseball Writers' Association of America, which had just been formed in October. The fifty-one guests included Ban Johnson, but the National League magnates were pointedly barred from the event. It soon became painfully obvious that Pulliam was undergoing a mental and/or emotional breakdown. On the first day of the meeting Ebbets had chastised Pulliam for his behavior at an earlier session in Cleveland when, together with Dreyfuss, they put together the schedule for the coming season—always a subject of contention. After agreeing on a plan, the three men met with a committee from the American League to set the opening day dates. When the meeting ended, Pulliam abruptly left the room saying over and over in a loud voice that the National League was a joke.[29]

When it came time to sign the report, Ebbets had to go down to the hotel bar to find Pulliam, who was in no condition to discuss it. At a dinner that night, Ebbets reminded him, "All you could think of . . . was to tell Jew stories of a respected member of this League [Dreyfuss]." After leaving Cleveland, Pulliam called Dreyfuss on the phone, fell into an argument, and hung up on him. Dreyfuss did not come to Chicago for the meeting but sent William Locke, the team secretary, instead; Ebbets thought it was because of how Pulliam had treated him.[30]

The owners adjourned early and convened at two o'clock the next afternoon. Pulliam surprised them all by saying immediately after the roll call, "Gentleman, I am going to ask your indulgence to permit me to retire." Charles Comiskey was hosting a dinner that night at eight, and Pulliam felt obliged to be there. "When I get back from Philadelphia I hope to get back a well man," he said enigmatically. "Otherwise I am not afraid to meet my God. I am not afraid to die."[31]

Pulliam hurried out of the room, leaving Ebbets furious. Herrmann admitted that "we are confronted with a serious condition and situation . . . We see things occurring every day, and the time has come now where we . . . ought to take it in hand." Pulliam was, after all, their employee, he stressed. "It is not for him to tell us what we should do, but it is for us to tell him what he shall do." Pulliam's behavior led Herrmann to believe that something was wrong with him.

Recently Pulliam had grown melancholy and despondent, wanted to be left alone, and refused to talk. "I believe the time has come," Herrmann said, "when we . . . ought to get together and agree upon some proposition as to how to handle him, and what to do with him. My own judgment is that Pulliam should be taken care of by . . . those who know him well." Heydler knew there was a problem; so did the American League and the newspapermen. He cited some examples of Pulliam's erratic behavior and wild talk and said, "If you let him go along as he is doing you will have a scandal in the League before your season commences."[32]

"We ought to take care of this man," Herrmann repeated. "He has lost his mind. He is not right." He recited the story of Pulliam's odd behavior with a lady he took to the theater, some extravagant dinners he gave, tipping waiters $5 every other course instead of once at the end, and lavish tips handed to cabmen and bellboys. "The chances are that he is down in the bar room, abusing every one of us as he did last night, using language that Harry Pulliam never used before," Herrmann said. "I never heard Harry Pulliam swear. He says 'They are a lot of bastards; they are a lot of cocksuckers; they are a lot of crooks; and in the presence of fifteen or twenty people at a time. That indicates to me that he has lost his mind."[33]

Everyone agreed that Pulliam could not continue as president, and that it was imperative to get him help of some kind. The owners agreed to give Pulliam an indefinite leave of absence in hopes that he could recover his balance. Heydler would serve as interim president in his absence, and the public need not be told the specific reasons for the leave. Murphy emphasized that Pulliam should not be allowed to perform any official function in his current condition.[34]

The magnates then turned to the report of the Brush committee, which Ebbets read aloud. He and Brush had taken the matter to DeLancey Nicoll, a prominent attorney and former district attorney, who told them that under

New York law no crime had been committed and no district attorney would attempt an investigation on the basis of so little evidence. After receiving Nicoll's letter to that effect, Brush drafted a report laying out the facts but mentioning no names. It affirmed the integrity of the game, commended the umpires for their honesty, and declared that "there was no possible chance for an umpire to take from the Chicago Cubs the victory of October 8th if he had desired or promised it. This fact is known to all who witnessed the event ... What is said of umpires applies equally to players ... Any corrupt agreement on the part of player or umpire involves collusion and the danger of subsequent exposure which would mean eternal banishment from organized base ball."[35]

The report was quickly approved, and the owners again voted to delete the names from the minutes of the present meeting as well. Two statements had to be given out, one on the attempted bribes, the other on Pulliam's leave of absence. The key sentence was parsed to read, "The National League grants the request of President Harry C. Pulliam for an indefinite leave of absence, owing to illness, and hope that he will return wholly restored to health." On the nineteenth the owners convened again to brief Ban Johnson on the whole affair. Johnson agreed with omitting all the names except that of Creamer, which he urged be put in the statement. Without accepting his suggestion, the board voted to refer the report to the National Commission for whatever action it chose to take.[36]

Once in reporters' hands, the statements provoked both criticism and confusion. Unaware of the inside details, most writers rallied to Pulliam as a brilliant president undone by his nerves and the pressure of the job. Pulliam himself told the *Sporting News* that, "owing to the many glaring incorrect and cruel statements concerning my condition, permit me to say I am neither a mental nor physical wreck. I am simply worn out through the arduous and trying duties of my position as president of the National League, which, by the way, I have served faithfully without profit to myself. My nerves were worn to a frazzle at our last meeting through the uncalled-for nagging that I was subjected to." For his part Heydler insisted that "I am not president of the National League ... I am merely representing Mr. Pulliam during his absence."[37]

Through the winter the owners steadfastly refused to give out the name of the individual despite persistent efforts by reporters to get it. Not until April 19 did the National Commission release its decision on the matter. Not surprisingly, it sustained the report and with it the allegations of Klem and Johnstone, and banned the unnamed perpetrator from every major-league ballpark in the nation. As one reporter quipped, it complimented the umpires "for their disinterested honesty in this age of graft, and asserts that the culprit deserves to be boiled in oil, but unfortunately the commission is powerless to buy enough oil." He criticized the commission's decision as merely deepening "the mystery surrounding the case and left the damaging impression in the minds of the people untouched."[38]

The writer of this unsigned article in the *Chicago Tribune* was Harvey Woodruff, who four days later revealed the identity of the "mysterious stranger" as "Dr. Creamer" of New York. Notices bearing that name, without first name or initials, had been sent to every president in both major leagues as the man to be barred from their parks. Woodruff likely saw one of the notices sent to Murphy or Comiskey. Some digging in New York turned up the full name, Joseph H. Creamer, as well as his background. The son of a coroner, he had been the official physician for some boxing clubs, then turned to cycle racers. He was also said to be a staunch Tammany man and a henchman of Big Tim Sullivan. Once the name had leaked, the National Commission and New York teams released the affidavits of Klem and Johnstone to reporters.[39]

Creamer strongly denied the charge. He told reporters, "It is a job to ruin me . . . I cannot understand why the umpires have mixed me in this unless it is a conspiracy of some kind." He threatened to file suit for libel. The story circulating through the baseball world also included "the positive assertion that the $2,500 . . . belonged to three members of the New York team who wanted to make it a sure thing that the Giants would get into the World Series . . . and thereby secure a part of the large gate receipts." Early in May the *Evening Journal* began asking each day on its sports page, "Who were the men behind Doctor Creamer?" A few other New York papers jumped briefly onto the bandwagon. Under different circumstances the cloud of suspicion might have descended on McGraw, given his penchant for gambling and his long association with gamblers and other dubious characters. However, *Sporting Life* dismissed the case as having "taken a turn disgusting to all decent and fair-minded men owing to the despicable efforts of several sensational New York papers to implicate New York Club officials or players."[40]

The National Commission shared Brush's desire simply to make the whole thing go away, especially with the lack of more concrete evidence. The only man who knew the whole story was Creamer, and he steadfastly refused to reveal it before his death in 1918. Neither did he bring suit or take any other steps to clear his name. McGraw walked away from the episode untouched, and the new season soon swallowed the story. The primary casualty of the episode turned out to be Harry Pulliam.[41]

The overwrought president spent his convalescence in Tennessee and Florida, saying in March he would soon be fully recovered and in better shape than he had been in years. To the public the owners professed their desire to have him resume his post. Pulliam returned to New York on June 28 and took up his position again, seemingly recovered even though some friends found him still moody and uncommunicative. Exactly one month later he went to his office in the St. James Building and started working his way through some correspondence. He stopped abruptly and began staring out the window. At one o'clock he told his stenographer that he felt unwell and went home to his apartment on the third floor of the New York Athletic Club, where he had lived for some time. That night around nine thirty, clad only in his underwear, he put a revolver to his right temple and fired. A physician arrived and concluded that Pulliam was too severely wounded to be moved to a hospital. He clung to life until seven forty the next morning. He was forty years old.[42]

On August 2, in an unprecedented move, both the National and American Leagues postponed all their games in tribute to Pulliam. The funeral in Louisville attracted a large number of baseball people and players. Brush could not attend because he had sailed for Europe on July 30 to spend five weeks recuperating at Carlsbad. An hour after the service the league board met and named Heydler as Pulliam's successor. By then the league was reeling from its losses. On June 19, George Dovey, long a Pulliam ally, died suddenly aboard a train at the age of forty-eight and was replaced as president by his brother John. Nine days later Israel W. Durham, who had replaced Shettsline as president of the Phillies, succumbed to a lingering illness at age fifty-two.[43]

AT THE END OF THE 1908 SEASON the players filed out of the clubhouse and scattered to their fall and winter lairs. Donlin took to the stage with his wife and pulled down a reported $2,000 a week for his efforts. Bresnahan returned to his hometown of Toledo to run a large hotel in which he had an interest. McGinnity was involved in an iron business in Oklahoma that had supposedly made him wealthy apart from baseball. Dummy Taylor retired to a grocery store in Kansas. Snodgrass hurried back to California and Crandall to his farm in Ohio. Bridwell planned to spend much of the winter hunting in Ohio. Doyle talked of doing some mining in the Cripple Creek district. Herzog headed back home to ready his Maryland farm for spring planting. Devlin and Seymour, having no outside business interests, stayed in New York. Wiltse went home to Syracuse and Ames to Ohio. McCormick returned to his longtime job as sales agent for a steel company in Philadelphia.[44]

Mathewson had already involved himself in some business ventures with McGraw and opened an insurance firm in lower Manhattan. A reporter stopped by his office hoping for an interview and was greeted by a smiling, broad-shouldered man in a well-cut business suit who motioned him to a chair and offered him a cigar. "It is quite different," marveled the writer, "looking at a diamond god in a chair three feet away from watching him from the grand stand; it is a new sensation to hear his voice disturbed only by the clucking of a typewriter . . . Mathewson is now a business man. When you see him behind a roll-top, you can hardly make yourself remember that he is a ball-player."[45]

In January, Matty went home to Factoryville to visit his parents and his brother Nick, nine years younger than Christy, who some considered to be an even better pitcher. McGraw loved him and sometimes sent him packages of Giants equipment or used uniforms, which Nick sold to local kids. Hughie Jennings had already tried to sign him for the Tigers, but his father insisted that he start college instead. Tall, rugged, and handsome like Christy, he seemed to have everything needed for a good life. Nick chose not to attend Bucknell and that fall enrolled at Lafayette College in Easton, Pennsylvania. A few months later, having pitched for the freshman team, he returned home complaining of feeling ill and run-down. No one thought much of it until January 15, 1909, when Nick walked into the family barn, scribbled a few lines on a sheet of paper, climbed up into the hayloft, and shot himself in the head.[46]

It was Christy's sad fate to discover the body and convey the news to his parents. Nick had been brooding over falling behind in his schoolwork, but no one suspected even remotely that he was so distraught. "We never realized just how much he was worried," said his father glumly, "and we didn't appreciate that his mind was becoming so unsettled." Christy had to bear this tragedy through the winter, and some feared its weight might affect his performance in the coming season. It was a cruel capstone to the most brilliant season of his career to date, and a ghastly burden to carry for the rest of his life.[47]

CHAPTER 8

Coming Together

"If John walked you to the corner, he wanted to get there first."
——BILLIARD JACK DOYLE

"Aggressiveness is a great thing in base ball, and McGraw is the personification of aggressiveness."
——FRANK SELEE

AFTER THE PLAYERS WENT THEIR SEPARATE WAYS, McGraw settled into his winter's work. In doing his annual postmortem of the season, he found much that pleased him. Donlin had played a full season, hit .334, and drove in 106 runs to finish second in both categories only to the inevitable Honus Wagner. Tenney proved to be the consummate professional McGraw had hoped, leading the league in runs scored even though he hit only .256 and serving as an anchor for the infield. Doyle had been a pleasant surprise with a .308 average in 104 games even though his glove remained shaky. Bridwell proved McGraw right by upping his average to .285, and Seymour knocked in ninety-two runs even though his average dipped to .267. Bresnahan remained a force at the plate and behind it, hitting .283 while collecting a team-leading eighty-three walks. Even more impressive, he appeared in a career-high 140 games despite his wounds.[1]

Among the pitchers Mathewson was more than ever in a class by himself. Just turned twenty-eight, he posted an astonishing 37-11 record, a 1.43 earned run average, 12 shutouts, 0.97 walks per 9 innings, 391 innings pitched, 34 complete games, 56 appearances, 259 strikeouts, and 5 saves. In every one of these categories he led the league, yet he would remember most the one game he had to win and could not. Hooks Wiltse came into his own with a 23-14 record, and Crandall showed both poise and promise far above his 12-12 finish. That McGraw put him into thirty-two games and started him in twenty-four showed the manager's belief that he had the stuff to play in the majors as well as his urgent need for another reliable pitcher.[2]

Beyond this trio, however, the pitchers disappointed. McGinnity was worn down and finished 11-7. At thirty-three Dummy Taylor went 8-5 in his final season, and Ames struggled with his control to finish 7-4. Marquard, the $11,000 peach turned lemon, took a pasting in his only game. Except for Doyle, McGraw was content to nurse the other youngsters along on the bench. Snodgrass got into only six games with four at-bats, Devore five games with seven plate appearances. Herzog, pressed into service when Doyle got hurt, played in sixty-four games despite his midseason sabbatical and hit .300 while filling in at four positions. Meyers did not play and Art Wilson got into only one game.[3]

Merkle, the youngest man on the team, was, after his nightmare moment, also the most fragile. The son of immigrants, he grew up in Toledo, Ohio. In school, under his Americanized name of Frederick Charles Merkle, he became a star pitcher in baseball and a halfback in football. After playing for semipro teams in Toledo, he joined the Tecumseh team of the South Michigan League in 1906. The following season he hit .271 with six homers for Tecumseh and was purchased by the Giants for $2,500. He made his debut with the team on September 21 at the tender age of eighteen and in fifteen games batted .255 despite his lack of experience in professional baseball. Nothing in his background prepared him for the intensity and pressure of the 1908 season.[4]

He played in thirty-eight games at first, second, third, and the outfield, and hit a respectable .268 while handling sixty-eight chances without an error, but his confidence was devastated by the enormity of his mistake and the "bonehead" label imprinted on him. He told a reporter, "I only lost fifteen pounds since the affair . . . but it is all over now and will have to be forgotten, like all the other great national crimes." McGraw was wrong on one point: The sages of Punditsville did not forget, and neither did the fans in hostile ballparks, all of whom heaped abuse on Merkle whenever he appeared. McGraw showed his stripe by giving Merkle a $500 raise for the coming season, but he realized that under the circumstances Merkle was far from ready to be thrust into the lineup as a regular. However, McGraw did not waver in his belief that he would excel in time.[5]

Despite the bright spots, McGraw realized that the roster needed revamping for the coming season. Donlin again posed a problem. After the season he had been awarded a trophy as the team's most popular player, and at a dinner in his honor John Barrymore, a good friend, had performed one of Hamlet's soliloquies—a fitting tribute for a man trying to decide whether to play or not to play. Eager to resume his theatrical career, Donlin opened a one-act show with his wife, Mabel, called *Stealing Home* at the Hammerstein Theater on October 26. Its success fed his growing conviction that he could make a better living on the stage than on the field, and the life of a celebrity suited him.[6]

The outfield had to be rebuilt. Donlin's defection left a serious hole in right field. Seymour had done well in center but at thirty-five was nearing the end of his career. McCormick had hit well but was slow, and McGraw wanted speed. The infield looked to be in better shape with Devlin, Bridwell, and Doyle solid and Herzog in reserve. The only question was whether Tenney could keep going long enough until Merkle was ready to replace him. Catching posed a dilemma. Although Bresnahan was only twenty-nine, he had absorbed a lot of physical punishment over the years. He was among McGraw's closest friends but, sentiment aside, he wanted very much to manage a team and that wasn't going to happen on the Giants. He all but begged McGraw to let him go to a team that needed a manager.

While his scout, Dick Kinsella, scoured the minors for hidden talent, McGraw made his first move at the annual owners' meeting in December. Rumors abounded that McGraw wanted outfielder John "Red" Murray of the Cardinals as well as a pitcher. St. Louis owner Stan Robison needed a manager to replace John McCloskey, who was regarded as a poor disciplinarian. Earlier, McGraw had promised to let Robison acquire Bresnahan as his manager. He found Robison in the bar at the Waldorf and renewed the offer. "Bresnahan will make a great man for you," said McGraw. "He hasn't had a chance to manage a ball club yet, but he's capable of managing one. And he'll be a drawing card for you, too. With him out there, you'll get some fans in your park next year." Robison agreed, and a deal was struck.[7]

In return for Bresnahan St. Louis gave McGraw Murray, pitcher Arthur "Bugs" Raymond, and catcher George "Admiral" Schlei, who Robison first had to acquire from Cincinnati. Although he hated parting with Bresnahan, McGraw realized that he had done his friend a favor by getting him a managerial post, and he had done himself an even bigger favor, albeit one with a hefty dose of aggravation attached. Even Joe Vila conceded that McGraw had got the best of the deal. *Sporting Life* was even more positive. "The more we figure out that trade," it said, "the more forcibly we are impressed with the exceptional trading ability of John McGraw."[8]

At twenty-five, Red Murray had established himself as one of the league's better outfielders. In 1908 he played in all 154 games and hit .283, finishing third in home runs and total bases, fifth in slugging average, and second in stolen bases to Wagner with forty-eight. Although he led the league's outfielders in errors with twenty-eight, he had a strong arm and a sure sense of the ball. With his impressive combination of power and speed he could bat cleanup and fill Donlin's place in right field. A native of Arnot, Pennsylvania, Murray was another college man, having spent two years at what is now Lock Haven University and two more at Notre Dame.[9]

The wild card in the deal was the irrepressible Raymond. Pitching for a last-place team that suffered a dozen shutouts while he was on the mound, Bugs had led the league in losses with twenty-five but with a 2.03 earned run average. His baggage included a killer spitball, a tendency to be a clown, and an unquenchable thirst for booze. "Raymond . . . was one of the greatest natural pitchers that ever lived," said McGraw much later. "He had his odd ways of thinking while off the field, but once in the box he knew exactly what he was doing. All we had to do was to keep him in physical condition . . . He could make the ball do the queerest of stunts and never did he hesitate to pull one of these tricks when his team was in a hole."[10]

A native of Chicago, Raymond turned twenty-seven in February 1909. His major-league debut occurred in 1904 with Detroit but he was let go after five games, reportedly because of rumors about his drinking. In 1907 he displayed his spitball for the first time and compiled a 35-11 record for Charleston of the South Atlantic League despite his erratic behavior. The call to St. Louis came near the end of the 1907 season. McGraw knew about Raymond's problem but decided to take the chance that he could keep him in line enough to exploit so marvelous a talent. He gave Raymond a good contract and promised him bonuses if he stayed sober. If not, he warned Raymond that spring, "I'll get rid of you so fast it will make your head swim. And you know that if I get rid of you, nobody else will give you a chance. You'll be through."[11]

During the winter McGraw reluctantly let McGinnity go and picked up Art Fletcher, a skinny twenty-four-year-old from Collinsville, Illinois, across the river from St. Louis. His father had worked his way up from a breaker boy in the coal mines to superintendent and did not want his son following in his footsteps. He was also religious and did not approve of Art playing baseball, especially on Sundays. At his parents' insistence Art went to business school, earned a degree in stenography, and found a job at Ingersoll-Rand while playing baseball on weekends. In March 1908 he took time off to play shortstop for Dallas of the Texas League. That spring Dallas played some exhibition games against the Giants, and McGraw got his introduction to a brash kid who took no guff from anybody, even major leaguers. Whatever lip they gave him he returned in kind; he slid hard into bases with spikes high and continued to crowd the plate even when the Giant pitchers brushed him back. "I was a pretty fresh busher," he admitted years later.[12]

McGraw liked what he saw, perhaps because Fletcher reminded him of himself as a belligerent rookie. "That's my kind of player," he is reputed to have said, and took an option on Fletcher's contract for $1,500. That summer Fletcher hit .275 and stole thirty-five bases for Dallas as their shortstop. Although the Giants were well stocked with infielders, McGraw saw to it that Fletcher joined the team for spring training in 1909, and he did well enough to earn a place on the roster. Still not content, McGraw added yet another outfielder to the team, plucking Bill O'Hara from Baltimore of the Eastern League. O'Hara had toiled seven years in the minors and was fast if not much of a hitter.[13]

In February, McGraw set a precedent as the first manager to hire a full-time coach. Arlie Latham was an old-time ballplayer with the St. Louis Browns and Reds who was notorious for being both a brawler and a prankster. Latham knew his baseball but he was also a clown who earned the nickname "the Freshest Man on Earth." During the March exhibition games Latham played a practical joke on Seymour, who did not take it kindly and proceeded to beat him up in front of some other players. Much as he liked a good fight, McGraw felt obliged to suspend Seymour for the first eight weeks of the season, which did not help his outfield situation. The scribes were also beginning to notice Chief Meyers as something more than an oddity. "Myers [sic] going to make the greatest hit around New York that the old town has seen for a long time," McGraw told them. "In addition to being a good catcher and a hard hitter, Myers [sic] is so chock full of life and ginger that he gets the whole club upon its toes."[14]

Brush did his part by overhauling the Polo Grounds in fine style. The park featured a circle of seats surrounding the field with tiers of new seats connecting the fifty-cent bleachers to the twenty-five-cent ones. By moving the diamond farther out, seven new rows of seats were added in front of the

existing grandstand. The stalls that had served as boxes in the upper grandstand were replaced by 166 overhanging boxes accommodating four
persons each. Under the watchful eye of John Murphy, seven thousand
carloads of dirt were spread behind the infield to eliminate a slight slope in
the outfield. New players' benches were installed on cement floors. A tunnel
from each dugout led to an open area behind the grandstand where pitchers
could warm up unseen. The first level of the grandstand had telephone
booths with operators standing by.[15]

The team that emerged from spring training approached McGraw's ideal
of youth and speed, though not yet wise in the ways of the game. The only
players over thirty were Tenney at thirty-seven, Seymour, thirty-six, and new
catcher Admiral Schlei, thirty-one. Unfortunately, the first two were the
ones who faltered most in 1909. Thanks mostly to injuries, each managed
to get into only eighty games and declined in almost every performance
category. In his first game back from suspension, Seymour collided with
Murray and injured his knee. Mathewson thought he was never the same
player afterward. Schlei shared catching duties with Chief Meyers, who
outhit him .277 to .244. By season's end it was clear that Meyers would be
the catcher of the future. *Sporting Life* noted that "this is the first time the
Giants have ever had a real Indian in their line-up."[16]

It proved an exasperating season for McGraw. The older players were
slipping and the youngsters, except for Doyle, were not ready to move into
the lineup full-time. Raymond proved a constant source of aggravation,
promising solemnly to reform, then reverting to his old habits. Other
players annoyed McGraw with their habits so much that, for the first time
in five years, he decreed no more late nights or dice playing or even
moderate drinking. After being fined heavily Raymond made his peace with
the manager, saying he didn't mind having his money taken from him
because "I never have none, nohow." Unknown to him, McGraw sent all of
Raymond's lost pay to his wife. Mathewson performed in brilliant fashion
but even he could not salvage a lackluster season. McGraw bought a big
right-hander named Louis Drucke who, after graduating from Texas
Christian University in 1909, had put together a 14-4 record for Dallas in
the Texas league. He came to the Giants late in the season and went 2-1.
When Tenney got hurt, McGraw thrust Merkle into the lineup.[17]

By September Raymond looked to be overweight and out of condition,
and his pitching showed it. On the twenty-fourth McGraw suspended
Raymond for the rest of the season despite his winning record. By one

estimate $1,700 of his $4,200 salary had been swallowed by fines. Attendance at the Polo Grounds fell away steadily. The Giants capped a discouraging season by playing a postseason exhibition series with the Boston Red Sox and losing four of five games before crowds so thin that each player took home only $133.[18]

After their spirited run and near miss of 1908, the Giants and their fans were disappointed at dropping to third place, eighteen and a half games behind the rejuvenated Pirates, who went on the beat Detroit in the World Series, and the omnipresent Cubs. *Sporting Life* attributed New York's poor showing to "a miserable start, which in turn was due to experimental condition of the team—a condition which endured almost the entire season." Doyle emerged as a reliable star, batting .302, leading the league in hits and stealing thirty-one bases. Murray proved as solid as expected. Bridwell and Devlin had their usual solid seasons, but Herzog broke an ankle in July, slumped to a ghastly .185 in forty-two games, and spent most of the season on the bench, where his cantankerous attitude made him a thorn in McGraw's side.[19]

Among the pitchers Mathewson overcame his winter tragedy with yet another sterling season, going 25-6 with a breathtaking earned run average of 1.14. He ran off a thirteen-game winning streak and saw a streak of twenty-four consecutive wins over St. Louis end on May 24; the Cardinals had not defeated him since May 1904. Raymond managed to compile an 18-12 record despite the repeated clashes with McGraw. Wiltse remained solid at 20-11 and Ames improved to 15-10, while Crandall went 6-4 in thirty games, only eight of which he started. The biggest disappointment once again was Marquard, who appeared in twenty-nine games and amassed a sorry record of 5-13. Clearly he had not adjusted to pitching in the major leagues. "His main fault," said McGraw, "was of putting the ball over the plate with nothing on it . . . So fearful was he of not being able to get the ball over when it came down to two-and-three that he would simply toss it over as straight as a string . . . He had so much stuff that he was afraid to use it."[20]

Once again McGraw nursed the youngsters along mostly on the bench. Merkle saw the most action except for Meyers, getting into seventy-nine games at first, second, or pinch-hitting while batting an anemic .191. Fletcher, Wilson, and Devore appeared only occasionally with unimpressive results. Devore posed a different kind of problem for McGraw. He grew up near Terre Haute, Indiana, and became the best and fastest ballplayer of the

village, but at five feet six inches he seemed too small for a future in baseball. In 1906 an older brother heard that the Meridian, Mississippi, team
was looking for an outfielder. Josh beat out all the other candidates and
played two seasons with Meridian, hitting only .242 and .241. Nevertheless,
the Giants agreed to buy him in the spring of 1908. He spent the 1908
season with Newark, where his .290 average earned him a trip to Marlin in
the spring of 1909, but an attack of appendicitis sidelined him. However,
McGraw kept him on the Giants roster all season.[21]

The young outfielder had speed to burn and some power but neither the
smarts born of experience nor the concentration needed to develop it. A
left-handed hitter, he had the bad habit of bailing out against lefties and so
did poorly against them. Both problems had to be fixed if Devore was to be
of any use to the team, and McGraw was convinced it could be done. Critics
wondered why the youngsters were not down in the minors honing their
skills. They looked at the Giants' bench and saw only deadweight or basic
training, neither of which helped in a pennant race. On that point they may
have been right, but McGraw saw something else entirely: the future.[22]

NOT UNTIL 1910 DID THE MCGRAWS FINALLY land in a place they could
call home in New York. Until then they had been content to move from one
residence to another. That year they moved into a six-room apartment on the
fifth floor of a building at Broadway and 109th Street and remained there
for eleven years. The new place encouraged McGraw to put down roots of a
sort in the city of constant change. "Home must have given John a feeling of
security and perhaps thanksgiving," Blanche thought. Shortly after the
move, McGraw came home one day with a small, quivering Boston terrier
acquired from a friend who bred them. He received the name Truxton, as
did his four successors in the apartment, all of them devoted to the master
who spoiled them unabashedly.[23]

The good life had two enduring effects on McGraw: It expanded his
waistline and increased his penchant for charity. Always a generous man,
his informal philanthropy took on a new dimension. He had always been a
sucker for a handout, and early in his career he began slipping a ten or
twenty into a player's locker as a reward for some extra effort or outstanding
performance. In the league and around town he developed a reputation as
the softest of touches. A year or so after moving into the new apartment his
first vest-pocket book appeared with a growing list of names and the amount

"loaned" to each one. The mini-ledger did not include everyday handouts; McGraw recorded only larger amounts and started a new book each year with what seemed a never-ending stream of entries on which little or no effort was made to seek repayment.

Blanche didn't know what to make of it. "I never knew the exact nature of John McGraw's financial philosophy," she admitted, "and I never worried about it. He gave me everything I ever asked for or failed to ask for. I wanted for nothing, and so I never questioned his income or what he did with it. Naturally, I had a wife's concern that his generosity might hurt him, yet I had no fear that it would hurt me."

Late in life, when McGraw was ill and the couple was downsizing, Blanche saw her husband feeding a stack of papers into the fireplace. She grabbed a few of them and saw to her astonishment that they were "a fantastic collection of checks and notes and apologies. 'No account' . . . 'Insufficient funds' . . . 'Protested—deducted from your account' . . . 'Not known at this bank.'" He shrugged. "They'd have paid, Blanche," he said, staring at the flames. "They just didn't have it." How much? she asked. "I don't know," he replied. "Ten or fifteen thousand, I guess."[24]

No one paid McGraw's generosity a more lavish tribute than, of all people, a Chicago writer. "Off the field McGraw is the kindliest, most generous and most sympathetic of men," he wrote. "The supporter of a herd of pensioners—a long list of poor creatures, who, if McGraw should die or be reduced to sudden poverty, would at once fall into utter destitution. [He is the] most loyal of friends, the most steadfast of good fellows . . . Fifty percent of John McGraw's money goes direct to the support of sick, crippled, helpless dependents, mostly people who have no claim on him but were brought to his notice by sympathetic friends. The little manager has a charity list that would make most millionaires look like pikers . . . McGraw's great heart contracts to the dimensions of a bean when he gets on a ball field . . . How do you figure it all out?"[25]

MORE CHANGES CAME TO THE NATIONAL LEAGUE leadership. At the winter meeting in 1910 the magnates replaced Heydler with a compromise candidate put forth by Brush. Thomas J. Lynch had been a league umpire from 1888 to 1902. During that time he had fought many a pitched battle with McGraw's Orioles. Since a major task of the president was to oversee the umpires, Brush observed, who better to do the job than the man once known as the "King of Umpires"? Heydler resumed his old post as secretary.[26]

Relations among the owners soured even more after Pulliam's death, and Lynch provided a convenient lightning rod. A surprise sale of the Phillies brought them an improbable new president who scarcely warmed his new seat before complaining about Lynch and his handling of the umpires. He was none other than Horace Fogel, erstwhile newspaperman and short-lived manager of the Giants who had put Mathewson on first base.[27]

While the magnates played out their latest round of intrigues and vendettas, they changed managers as well. Former Giant shortstop Bill Dahlen took charge of Brooklyn and catcher Red Dooin of Philadelphia. One rumor asserted that Brush lay near death, another that he would retire from baseball and yield his presidency to Fred Knowles. The first proved utterly false and Brush was quick to squelch the second. "I do not intend to resign," he said flatly. "Secretary Fred Knowles is not slated for the presidency of this club; indeed, he is a very sick man in the Adirondacks. I have relieved him of a great deal of his responsibility pending absolute recovery." Since Knowles suffered from tuberculosis, recovery seemed unlikely. Brush had hired William M. "Billy" Gray to serve as secretary while Knowles was gone.[28]

The coming season posed a dilemma for McGraw. Despite finishing third, the Giants had done well. Pittsburgh trumped them with a fabulous season in which nearly everything went its way, winning 110 games and all but clinching the pennant by Labor Day. Pitchers Howie Camnitz (25-6), Vic Willis (22-11), and Lefty Leifield (19-8) all had superb years, while rookie Babe Adams went 12-3 and achieved immortality by winning three games in the World Series. The Pirates led the league in most offensive categories, with Honus Wagner at the top in batting, slugging, runs batted in, total bases, and doubles. The infield had been bolstered by an impressive rookie second baseman, John "Dots" Miller, who idolized Wagner and formed a good double-play combination with him. Fred Clarke remained solid both on and off the field. He, Wagner, and Tommy Leach had played together for twelve years.[29]

Against this juggernaut the Cubs fell short even though they won 104 games. The vaunted Cub machine that had produced three straight pennants was starting to creak. Slagle was the first to go, released in March 1909 and replaced in center field by the man for all positions, Circus Solly

Hofman. A month later pitcher Carl Lundgren was put on waivers and Johnny Kling, considered by some the best catcher in baseball, got into a salary dispute with Murphy and sat out the season. Chance found a splendid replacement in Jimmy Archer, whose arm many considered the strongest in the league. He didn't hit as well as Kling or provide the same field leadership, but he threw rifle shots to second base from a crouched position. Chance himself had suffered a broken shoulder in June and seemed unable to shake the string of injuries that had slowed his performance.[30]

Against these formidable adversaries McGraw had to field what amounted to a team in transition. He recognized that the time had come to insert some of his youngsters into the lineup and teach them to play together. In November McCormick returned to his steel company job, and O'Hara was released. Several clubs were sniffing around the younger players, but McGraw wasn't about to let go of the men he had spent so much time cultivating. Tenney remained with the team until May, when McGraw put him on waivers and installed Merkle at first.[31]

In April, on the eve of the season, McGraw sent Herzog and outfielder Bill Collins to Boston for outfielder Beals Becker. Although McGraw loved Herzog's talent and hard-nosed approach, he had grown tired of bickering with him. The move confirmed that Fletcher would be the reserve infielder in 1910. Becker hit only .246 and led the league in striking out eighty-seven times in 1909, his first year in Boston, but he also stole twenty-one bases. McGraw liked his blend of speed and power along with his potential as a pinch hitter and backup outfielder.[32]

The infield was set with Doyle, Bridwell, Devlin, and Merkle. In the outfield only Murray was penciled in as a starter. Seymour could not be counted on to play full-time, and McGraw did not yet see Becker as a regular. He decided to entrust left field to the diminutive Josh Devore despite his shortcomings, which included a tendency to be dogged by injuries. "Devore has been pursued by the worst kind of luck of any man in the business," wrote a sympathetic scribe, "and every time he has tried to make the Giant team he has been up against some ill turn of nature." Nevertheless, McGraw wanted his bat and his "dazzling speed in the outer garden" in the lineup.[33]

The wild card in the lineup turned out to be Snodgrass, who as fourth-string catcher grew miserable sitting on the bench and expected to be traded or demoted. Instead McGraw began using him to spell Merkle at first base and platooned him in left with Devore when the Giants faced a southpaw.

Late in May he asked McGraw to send him down to the Eastern League so that he could play regularly. McGraw had no intention of sending him anywhere because in the few games he played Snodgrass was hitting beyond anyone's wildest dreams. On June 2 his average of .407 topped the league. It was clear to McGraw that he had to play every day. By contrast, Seymour was batting .268. When the team reached Cincinnati on its first western swing, McGraw said, "Snow, how would you like to play center field?"[34]

Taken aback by an offer that had never occurred to him, Snodgrass blurted out, "With what club?"

"Why, *this* club, of course," McGraw replied.

"You mean you're going to take Cy Seymour out of center field?"

"Yes. Would you like to try it?"

It was a bold gamble by McGraw. Snodgrass had rarely played the outfield, but he was smart and had good instincts, a strong arm, and the speed the manager craved. On July 13, Snodgrass first appeared in center field; for the rest of the season he indulged in on-the-job training there while sometimes spelling Merkle at first base. "I preferred playing first base," he admitted later. "I didn't particularly like the outfield. You can be out there all day without a chance . . . I like to be in the middle of things and fight a little bit." But he made himself into an excellent outfielder and surprised the league with his hitting as well. In particular he developed a knack for getting hit by a pitched ball. Late in August Snodgrass was still batting a lusty .387 and *Sporting Life* called him "the greatest thing in the batting line that the National League has seen for years."[35]

Pitching remained a problem. Wiltse had enjoyed a good season in 1909 but struggled to maintain the workload of earlier years. McGraw concluded that he fared best in cooler weather and simply wore down during the hot summer months; he would have to be used judiciously. Ames, he of the devastating curveball that he had trouble harnessing, had also developed a reputation as a cold-weather hurler as well as a hard-luck one. Giants bats seemed to go dormant whenever he took the mound. Crandall proved to be a good listener, a quick learner, and an unshakable presence on the mound. Mathewson called him "the sort of pitcher who is best when things look darkest."[36]

Apart from these stalwarts, two very different unpredictables remained, Raymond and Marquard, and the promising rookie Louis Drucke. McGraw had spotted him in the spring of 1908 when Drucke pitched the only exhibition game the Giants lost in Texas. He became a favorite of New York writers, some of whom hailed him as the next Mathewson. Despite his brush-ups with McGraw, Raymond had appeared in more games in 1909 than any other Giant pitcher. Although Marquard had proved a major disappointment, Meyers insisted that he had more stuff than any other Giant pitcher.[37]

The 1910 season saddled McGraw with another bout of frustration leavened by hints of promise. Marquard again flopped, starting only eight games and compiling a record of 4-4. "Marquard is still a mystery," declared *Sporting News.* "He seems to have everything a pitcher needs in his line, except control of the ball." After a poor start, Raymond imploded at midseason on his way to a 4-11 slate. On occasion Bugs showed flashes of his talent, but drinking again undermined him. In desperation McGraw hired a former Pinkerton detective to accompany Raymond everywhere and keep him out of trouble, but Raymond found ways to elude his shadow. In June, after being sent to warm up, McGraw summoned him to relieve Drucke, who held a 3-2 lead against Pittsburgh. Bugs then gave "about the worst exhibition of pitching he has ever been guilty of," letting in four runs for a 6-3 Pirates victory.[38]

Afterward a furious McGraw learned that Raymond, instead of loosening up, had hurried to a familiar saloon across Eighth Avenue and traded the warm-up ball for a few shots of cheap whiskey. He slapped an indefinite suspension on Raymond but relented after a few weeks. Raymond then walked in the winning run at Pittsburgh, sending the Giants to a fourth straight defeat and, late in July, showed up drunk for a game in St. Louis and refused McGraw's order to take off his uniform. When McGraw suspended him for the rest of season, Raymond returned to Chicago and tried pitching for a semipro team under an alias.[39]

Matty the Magnificent was once again just that, pitching 318 innings with a 1.90 earned run average on his way to a 27-9 record. Wiltse lost six weeks after a shot hit him in the elbow and fell off to 14-12. Crandall burnished his reputation as a pitcher who finished what others started. In forty-two games he started eighteen while finishing twenty-one on his way to a sparkling 17-4 record, but he also gave up ten home runs, the most in the league. As a bonus he also hit .342. Ames struggled through another up-and-down season that culminated with a sore arm and a 12-11 mark.[40]

Despite their erratic pitching, the Giants made a race of it for a few weeks, partly because both Chicago and Pittsburgh stumbled out of the gate as well. The pitching that had carried the Pirates to victory in 1909 deserted them almost entirely. "Barney Dreyfuss doesn't talk base ball at all these days," said *Sporting Life* in June, when the Pirates languished in fourth place. "The poor showing of the Pittsburgs [*sic*] has made him very weary. But he is waiting patiently for the inevitable brace to come, and then he says he will have the laugh on everybody." But the brace didn't come. No one hit up to their usual standard during the first half of the season; as of June 17 even Wagner was batting only .238.[41]

The Cubs seemed also to be climbing uphill until the end of May. Chance got into only eighty-eight games and hit .298, but his wounds were fast catching up with him. Although Evers played in 125 games, he seemed at times to be coming unraveled. In May a car he was driving crashed, leaving him unhurt but killing his passenger, a Chicago sportswriter who was a close friend. Those who knew Evers said the shock of the accident stayed with him all season. On the field he became nastier and more argumentative than ever. "Johnny Evers is having a row of some kind every day," said *Sporting Life*. After a second suspension along with several banishments, the Cubs held a team meeting and told Evers bluntly that he was hurting their pennant run. The Cubs had problems enough without Evers throwing tantrums. Chance went down with the shoulder injury, Tinker was hurt midseason, Ed Reulbach contracted diphtheria, and Orval Overall's arm went lame.[42]

Yet the Cubs kept winning. The pitching staff remained shaky, prompting Murphy to acquire two veteran hurlers, Lew Richie from Boston and Harry McIntire from Brooklyn. After a slow start Miner Brown regained his form. On August 11 his record stood at 14-10; he finished at 25-13 with seven saves. Rookie sensation Leonard "King" Cole emerged as an ace with a sparkling 20-4 record and an earned run average of 1.80, tops in the league. Richie chipped in by going 11-4 and McIntire 13-9, while Pfiester went 6-3 before breaking his wrist in midseason. All their performances were bolstered when Kling returned on May 8. Archer split the catching duties with Kling and also filled in for Chance at first base.[43]

The pennant race turned out to be no race at all after the first month. On May 25 the Cubs charged into the lead and were never again headed. Pittsburgh dropped thirteen of nineteen games and found itself in a losing battle with the Giants for second place. Dreyfuss made no attempt to mask his unhappiness at the team's performance. "Our 1910 team was my biggest disappointment in baseball," he told Fred Lieb. "Never did I see a great team fold so quickly."[44]

The Giants fared little better. By June E. H. Simmons concluded that "neither Merkle nor Doyle were of championship caliber. To these names must now be added that of Myers," who, he added, "cannot stand the racket every day in the week . . . In the catching department alone New York's weakness is fatal." The Giants chased Pittsburgh for second place, caught the Pirates at the end of August by sweeping three games from them, and clinched it after the Pirates stumbled badly on their final eastern swing.[45]

For Brush the summer was also disappointing in that his health suffered a downturn. Having wintered in San Antonio, he did not return as usual to New York for the season. When the doctors finally pronounced him strong enough to travel, he went first to Chicago and placed himself under the care of a specialist in locomotor ataxia. He remained there through August and claimed not to be taking part in management of the Giants. However, he agreed to let the team do something the fans in New York had long been clamoring for: a postseason series against the Highlanders, who had surprised everyone by finishing second to the Athletics and stealing some attention from the Giants.[46]

The pressure was on McGraw to beat the upstart Highlanders, who had played second fiddle to the Giants since their arrival in New York. The battle for Broadway bragging rights was staged as the best four out of seven like the World Series, alternating between the Polo Grounds and Hilltop Park. Mathewson proved too much for the Highlanders, earning three victories and a save as the Giants took the series. The Giants maintained their supremacy in the big city, and players picked up a nice paycheck of $1,110.62 each for their efforts. For Art Fletcher, known as "Chisel Chin" for his elongated jawline, the extra payday enabled him to go home to Collinsville, Illinois, and marry his sweetheart. Mathewson gained something more than money from the series: On a smaller scale it was 1905 all over again for him. The players chipped in to buy Matty a $500 gold watch for his performance. Afterward he and Meyers went off to perform a vaudeville routine during the winter, of which Sporting Life felt obliged to report that, "to the surprise of the New York fans and dramatic critics, the Indian catcher, Myers, speaks his lines in the sketch he plays with Mathewson, much better than the big pitcher delivers his words."[47]

IN DECEMBER THE RANKS OF THE MAGNATES underwent an important shift. John Dovey sold his team to a group headed by William Hepburn

Russell, a New York lawyer, but including three prominent Bostonians. The Doves became the Rustlers. As the hot-stove season unfolded, Lynch gained reelection as National League president but only for one year. During the season he had hired one new umpire, Mal Eason, who had done a good job, and plucked Bill Finneran from the Eastern League for the coming year.[48]

McGraw approached this off season in a very different mood from previous years. For the first time in years he made no deals. Having assembled this team and taught it to play his way, he was content to stand pat. "If McGraw was willing to part with some of his youngsters," observed E. H. Simmons, "he could get a lot of good deals." But he was not willing, as the Giants had shown marked improvement during the last six weeks of the season. Brush was certainly pleased with his manager. Before leaving to winter in San Antonio, he secured the heart and soul of his team with a new contract for five years at $18,000 a season. At about the same time Mathewson accepted a three-year contract for $9,000 a season.[49]

Brush also made Billy Gray the permanent secretary. Fred Knowles, still ill with tuberculosis, retired from the club. The move convinced *Sporting Life* that Brush "is at last the real controlling power in the New York Club, and that Mr. Freedman no longer has the slightest voice in the affairs of the club." Brush also managed to obtain a new ten-year lease on the Polo Grounds from the Coogan estate, which gave him enough longevity to sink more money into improvements. As the team prepared to migrate to Marlin for spring training, he would be close enough to meet with McGraw and watch them occasionally.[50]

As the time for departure approached, McGraw seemed more confident of his team's chances than he had been since 1905. Signed contracts for the year flowed steadily into the team office with no sign of a holdout. Just prior to the National League meeting in December he abandoned the caution of past years and argued that the Giants should be the favorites to win in 1911. No club had been better during the last two months of 1910, he pointed out. Earlier he had announced that Raymond would be given one last chance to make the team in spring training.[51]

The news appalled Simmons, who blamed Raymond more than anyone else for New York's failure to win the pennant. "The one criticism that it seems can be justly made against McGraw is that he hangs on too long to old favorites," he wrote. "Bugs Raymond, Ames, and Arlie Latham appeared to the writer to belong to this class." Raymond offered his usual disclaimer: "I have cut out the booze," he said, "and will prove this season that I can pitch as well as any one." Simmons reminded his readers that the Giants had weaknesses, most notably their fielding. While they led the league in hitting, they finished next to last in fielding. "It wasn't that the Giants were poor fielders all the time . . . Their errors when they were made came in bunches," he observed. Doyle was the primary culprit, finishing dead last among second basemen, but he was not alone. No Giant regular stood out except Bridwell, who was second among shortstops to Mickey Doolin of the Phillies.[52]

Simmons also stressed that McGraw based his confidence largely on the belief that the Cubs and Pirates would be weaker in 1911. "What chance has Chicago to beat us?" McGraw asked. "None, absolutely none! A lot of nice fellows, and I don't want to use the hammer on them, but on the level that combination has busted up—simply outlived their usefulness." As for the Pirates: "There are a lot of veterans in this club like the Cubs, and they are sure to play inferior ball to the brand they displayed last season."[53]

McGraw understood that his was a team on the rise, while his two great adversaries had begun to slide downward and had yet to rebuild. By his own calculations, drawn especially from his experience after the triumphs of 1904 and 1905, McGraw figured that neither of them could continue their pace of past seasons. On the eve of his departure for Marlin he enthused, "I don't see how we can be beaten if we get an equal break with Dame Fortune. I intend to have a substitute for every man . . . And I am sure we will get at least one more good pitcher out of the big bunch of young twirlers who are going to Marlin, and also one more backstop. I believe that Meyers will be much better this season, and I look for Wilson to do grand backstopping. He was sick all last year and could not play at full speed. But watch that boy this season." Evers, always ready with an observation, departed from his Cubs teammates in saying, "The team that wins in the National League the coming year will have to beat the Giants to do it."[54]

PART TWO

THE SEASON

CHAPTER 9

April: All Fired Up

"Base ball, like war, is for the boys."
— MR. DOOLEY

*"There is another feature about the new
stadium which no theatre could ever have. This
feature is its massive beauty. Take it away from
the background of the lofty rocky bluff behind
it and stretch it on a plain, and it would
command the same air of respect that is held by
the pyramids built in all their silent grandeur
on the shifting sands of the desert. There is
nothing like it in baseball, and even New York,
with all of its marvels, pauses a moment to take
a fresh breath and brag about the 'biggest
baseball yard in the world.'"*
— BASEBALL MAGAZINE

ON THE EVE OF OPENING DAY IN 1911, *Sporting Life* looked across the broad expanse of the United States and enthused, "There is not one cloud in sight. Business conditions in the country at large are again normal, and there is no disturbing national political situation or financial crisis. Also, within the line of 'organized ball' there is now peace, harmony, unity of purpose, and concert of action in every quarter . . . and so firmly is the 'organized ball' family united that outlawry has been practically eliminated as a dangerous factor, or of harmful effect upon the great union of leagues, or upon the clean and beautiful sport itself."[1]

The United States in 1910 had just under 92 million people, 47.3 million of them male, 44.6 million female, and 13.3 million foreign born. Of their number 1.04 million were immigrants, of whom 39,448 were naturalized in 1910. Males had a life expectancy of 50 years, females 51.8. The median age for men was 24.1 and for women 23.5. Some 42 million Americans lived in urban places (2,500 or more people), 9.1 million of them in New York State. New York City dwarfed other cities with 4.77 million people, more than twice the number of Chicago and three times that of Philadelphia. These three cities alone had populations exceeding a million. Education beyond the basics remained out of reach for most people. Only 156,000, or 8.6 percent of those seventeen and under, graduated from high school.[2]

Most people went to work at an early age. The labor force totaled 36.9 million, or 57.4 percent of the population over the age of fourteen. An average worker took home $575 a year. To get their pay, manufacturing workers put in 56.6 hours a week (50.1 hours if unionized), coal miners 51.6 hours, and those in the building trades 45.2 hours. The hourly wage of manufacturing workers came to 26 cents (40.3 cents if unionized) compared to 29.9 cents for coal miners and 52 cents for the building trades. With that pay they could buy five pounds of flour for 18 cents, a pound of pork chops for 19 cents or bacon for 26 cents, a dozen eggs for 34 cents, a half gallon of milk delivered for 17 cents, or ten pounds of potatoes for the same 17 cents. To enter the Polo Grounds cost 50 cents for a bleacher seat until Brush installed the quarter seats—no small sum for a workingman, even assuming he could find time to go to the ballpark in a city that banned Sunday baseball. If he wanted to splurge, a reserved grandstand seat went for a dollar and a box seat for $1.50.[3]

New York City boasted 600,000 factory workers, an amazing 290,000 shopkeepers, and 220,000 laborers and mechanics. Another 58,000 worked in the liquor business, 45,000 in offices, and 40,000 in the printing trades. Educators totaled 24,000 and church workers 8,000. The city's 6,000 lawyers outnumbered its 5,000 physicians and 3,000 dentists of all stripes and training. Many of the lawyers did not practice but scrambled to earn a living as agents, collectors, promoters, loan procurers, or process servers. Those in search of a drink had their choice of an astounding 11,000 establishments of one kind or another that sold alcohol. They were supplied by 112 firms that manufactured or prepared liquor and beer for sale. A goodly supply found its way into the hands of Harry Stevens, who dispensed it to eager customers at the Polo Grounds. If the reporters could be believed, those customers made up a broad and varied sample of New Yorkers in what had become a baseball-crazed city.[4]

Some workers were directly involved in the business of baseball by manufacturing the equipment that made the games possible. "The baseball is one of the big crops that this country produces," proclaimed the *Press*. "One factory alone turns out 6,000,000 every year; others turn out millions more. The various leagues that play professional baseball use up nearly $100,000 worth of baseballs a year. How much more is consumed by the millions of boys and men who play in the fields and vacant lots is beyond calculation . . . 20,000,000 is the average of the guesses of those familiar with the matter." By one estimate a major-league club ran through at least forty dozen balls a season. At the end of the 1910 season, organized baseball had forty-nine professional leagues with more than three hundred teams.[5]

"The cheap ball is made by the million and with little care . . . But the 'league' ball is quite another matter," added the *Press*. "It is the result of years of careful study and endless experiment, and the 'league' ball of this year is an evolution of more than half a century of thought. The cork centre ball is this year's novelty that has been productive of some heavy hitting in the professional leagues. It has aroused some complaint."

An A. G. Spalding "Official National League" ball with the patented cork center sold for $1.25. An ordinary ball, mass produced with a center of ground-up carpet rags, went for 85 cents or less. One New York store put two thousand baseball gloves on sale at prices ranging from 25 cents to a dollar along with men's baseball uniforms at $1.25 and boys' versions at 85 cents. Spalding in its many stores offered a variety of gloves at prices from 25 cents to $8, the latter for the "professional model" catcher's mitt. Baseball shoes ranged from $2 for the junior version to $7 for the "Featherweight" model or Sprinting model made of kangaroo leather. Claflin, a rival company, had a line of five shoes beginning with the canvas model at $2.50 up to the Sprinter at $7.50. Spalding also featured sliding pads for $1.50 and leg guards for catchers at $6 a pair.[6]

The Spalding empire also offered eight different "Gold Medal 'Players' Autograph'" bats for a dollar each. The signees included Frank Chance, Roger Bresnahan, Johnny Evers, and Fred Clarke. The Chance model was the most imposing, a thick-handled club thirty-five inches long and weighing forty-five to forty-eight ounces. Even the smallest, the Willie Keeler model, weighed between thirty-six and thirty-nine ounces although it was only thirty-one inches long. "SPALDING'S Trade-Mark on any article used on a ball field," boasted the company, "is proof that the article that you have is better than the other fellow's."[7]

The best bats were made of white ash, the supply of which came largely from Michigan. Once cut, it had to be seasoned for four to seven years out of doors. No respectable player would even look at a bat dried in a kiln. Once seasoned, it headed for the lathe, where many players personally oversaw the cutting of the club to their specifications. A major-league team used about seventy-five bats a season. "I went to Spalding's in New York," recalled Heinie Groh, who began his career with the Giants in 1912, "and we went down in the basement and right there we whittled on a bat until it was just what I needed." McGraw took a wholesale approach. Just before spring training in 1908 he ventured into the Spalding cellar and selected six dozen bats. "It is the bats that tell the story and make ball players," he explained. "Pitchers may be all right, but give me the bat I want—the one that feels good to me—and I will make the other fellows extend their grounds."[8]

IF NATURE COULD HAVE BEEN COMMANDED, THE Polo Grounds would have been drenched in warmth and sunshine on opening day, April 12, in 1911. The sun honored the event with its presence but in the company of chilly temperatures and a stiff wind that kept everyone but those in the roof-less bleacher seats shivering. "It was a champagne cocktail of a day," wrote young Fred Lieb of the *Press*, "with a sky blue as Cork's or Milan's and a tang in the atmosphere that gave a fillip to the blood." That tang was too much for the *World*'s man. "Cold—awful cold . . . very, very cold at the Polo Grounds," he moaned.[9]

The park itself never looked better. Glistening from a fresh coat of paint, fortified by the addition of still more bleacher seats going for a quarter apiece, the biggest park in baseball boasted a smooth, level playing field, carefully trimmed grass, and borders of freshly planted geraniums and creeping ivy along the stands, thanks to the skill of John Murphy. The *Tribune* said he had "excelled even himself in his efforts at landscape gardening to make what has already been considered one of the most attractive ballparks in the United States more attractive than ever." Red, white, and blue bunting adorned every reachable surface, and as a special touch Murphy planted old Irish flags with golden harps set against a green backdrop at second base and right field, the positions occupied by Doyle and Murray. Whatever other teams thought of the Giants, they relished playing in Murphy's garden.[10]

Since taking charge of the team, John Brush had enlarged the park until it could hold thirty thousand to thirty-five thousand people. To get standees off the playing field, he had in recent years extended the bleachers and the grandstand until they fully encircled the field. The new twenty-five-cent seats completed this work, adding another four thousand seats. On the upper tier of the grandstand, Brush installed 165 boxes with six seats each. Gates were placed at every aisle so that the crowd could enter and exit more quickly. New technology had also been installed at every ticket booth in the form of machines that could print the date on every ticket as it was used. Even the turnstiles sparkled in a new coat of white enamel paint. By one estimate the most recent work had cost Brush $100,000. Despite his debility, he had come back from Texas in time to watch the opening game.[11]

Well before the gates opened, Harry Stevens had his army of waiters and vendors readying their wares. He had met McGraw in 1891 in Columbus, Ohio, where Stevens started his concession business with a hundred pounds of peanuts that he roasted, bagged, and sold along with printed scorecards. Once in New York, he developed concessions into a fast-growing business. His vendors dispensed generous wedges of pie for a dime, hot dogs for the same price, and scorecards with lineups and lots of advertising for a nickel. Waiters dressed in black coats with white aprons roamed the aisles with trays holding glasses filled with beer at ten cents apiece. The glasses tended to disappear in a hurry, especially on hot summer days.[12]

Murphy and his helpers removed the tarpaulin covering the infield and strapped down the bases. The previous June he had spent a day in Pittsburgh learning how they spread their cover, and had ordered one for the Polo Grounds. Players filtered in, many if not most of them unrecognized in their civilian clothes by the waiting crowd. The umpires went to their own room to dress. By noon the stage was set.[13]

The chilly weather did not discourage an enormous crowd from flowing in as soon as the gates opened at noon even though the game itself was four hours away. In the rush for bleacher seats old friends and familiar faces, most of them wearing derbies or caps, greeted each other cheerfully in anticipation of another season of camaraderie. While waiting for the game to start, they indulged in an opening-day tradition of pelting each other with paper missiles of every kind. A large number of women could be seen making their way into the grandstand and boxes, many of them wearing hats not appreciated by those sitting behind them. The crowd was estimated at thirty thousand and beyond. "While all classes and phases of humanity were represented," noted the *Herald*, "all distinctions were checked at the gate." It was a friendly crowd, full of laughter and song and anticipation for the fun to come.

Around two thirty cheers burst forth from the stands as McGraw led his troops across the field from the center-field clubhouse for their batting practice. It was a large contingent; most of the youngsters were still with the team. A short time later the Phillies followed suit behind their capable manager and fine catcher, Red Dooin, who was about to sign a new three-year contract. Since finishing dead last in 1904, Philadelphia had been respectable, usually winding up fourth and no lower than fifth. They had a solid team: young Fred Luderus at first, hard-nosed Otto Knabe at second, Mickey Doolin at short, and Hans Lobert at third. The outfield featured hard-hitting, temperamental Sherry Magee in left, fleet Dode Paskert in center, and silent John Titus in right. Dooin was an outstanding catcher and splendid manager. During warm-ups the two teams mingled freely on the field; the hard feelings that existed between the Giants, the Cubs, and the Pirates did not extend to the Phillies.[14]

While the players loosened up, many in the crowd did their own rehearsing with bells, rattles, whistles, or squawkers punctuated with the inevitable war whoops when Chief Meyers stepped in for batting practice. At three o'clock the Seventh Regimental Band started playing tunes to amuse the crowd. Josh Devore drew laughs by grabbing a bat and dancing a little jig to one number. A loud cheer broke out around three forty-five when Mayor William Gaynor, wearing a silk hat, entered a gate and strolled across the field with Giants secretary Billy Gray, treasurer John Whalen, and other dignitaries to their seats in one of the boxes. In distant Washington, President William Howard Taft, who enjoyed baseball, threw out the first ball of the season for the second year in a row, launching a tradition. In New York Mayor Gaynor did the honors.

The most impressive lineup of rookies this day could be found not on the field but in the crowded press box. One of them, twenty-three-year-old Fred Lieb, had just wangled the job of baseball writer for the *Press* and would carve out a distinguished career in the field for more than sixty years. His fellow newcomers were three men who all became giants in journalism: Damon Runyon of the *American*, Grantland Rice of the *Evening Mail*, and Heywood Broun of the *Morning Telegraph*. Runyon and Rice had been writing sports for a decade but had just come to New York, Runyon from the West and Rice from the South. Broun, a hulking, unathletic, slovenly giant, stood six-three and weighed around 225 pounds. The same age as Lieb, he had spent time at Harvard before turning to sportswriting.[15]

The four men could hardly have been more different from each other. Lieb was a somewhat prim, ambitious young man with an insatiable love of baseball. Rice, the gracious Southerner, made friends with everyone and had a gift for language; Lieb called him "the poet of the press box." The bespectacled Runyon seldom smiled and wore the air of an intellectual who seemed amused by whatever paraded before him. He had a marvelous insight into character and could find the human drama unfolding before his eyes, but he could not master the intricacies of the box score. More than once he asked Lieb, "Freddy, will you let me copy your box score? I never did learn to get up one of those damned things." Broun was notorious for his voracious appetite. "He liked to eat," said Lieb, "and he ate often and well."[16]

Scorekeeping was an art in itself, and one not yet consistent in form. Box scores varied in details from one reporter to another, both in form and content. One goal of the Baseball Writers' Association of America was to standardize as much as possible the keeping of records, but that hallowed goal had not yet been reached. The *Times* box score tended to be cleaner and clearer in print than the other papers', but it also frequently differed from them in the statistics it offered for the simple reason that every reporter made his own judgments and did not always pay attention to what the official scorekeeper among them decided on a given play.

Most of the veterans in the press box had been covering the game and/or the Giants for some time. Their ranks included Sam Crane of the *Journal*, who had the honor of being banned from the ballpark when he offended Andrew Freedman; Bozeman Bulger of the *Evening World*; George Tidden of the *World*, Harry Cross of the *Times*, the snarky Joe Vila of the *New York Sun*, Sid Mercer of the *Globe*, John Foster of the *Evening Telegram*, Jack Wheeler of the *Herald*, and Walter Trumbull of the *Evening Sun*. Few had bothered trying to interview McGraw or the players before the game. McGraw posted a large former policeman at the clubhouse door to keep interlopers away, and was even more adamant after games.[17]

As the hands of the clock above the bleachers touched four o'clock, Murphy rang the bell by the dugout, Gaynor stood on cue and tossed a ball to umpire Jimmy Johnstone, and the band struck up the national anthem. As the notes faded, Johnstone bellowed the batteries for the day, then shouted "Play ball!" as a mighty roar erupted from the stands. At long last the season was under way.

McGraw had decided early on a lineup and stuck pretty much to it. Devore led off and played left, followed by Doyle at second, Snodgrass in center, and Murray in right. Merkle hit fifth and played first, Bridwell sixth at shortstop, Devlin at third, Meyers catching, and the pitcher. For the third year in a row McGraw chose Red Ames as the opening-day pitcher. Ames was a good cold-weather hurler and had done well the two previous openers only to lose both because of poor support. The dreaded term "jinxed" had already been fastened to him, but McGraw decided to defy it. His opponent was Earl Moore, beginning his eleventh year in the majors, most of it in the American League, coming off an impressive 22-15 performance in 1910.

For six innings Ames held the Phillies hitless while Moore allowed the Giants a lone single by Doyle. While Ames struck out nine with only one walk, Moore surrendered eight free passes. He walked the bases full in the fifth but wriggled out of trouble. In the seventh Dode Paskert got the first hit off Ames, but the game remained scoreless until the ninth, when a double by Fred Luderus chased home two runs for a 2-0 Philadelphia lead. Merkle walked to open the ninth but watched the next three batters fly out. "The opening day hoodoo hovered over 'Red' Ames again," said the *Herald*, and Ames agreed. "If I was to wear a uniform trimmed with four leaf clovers and a horseshoe in my glove I couldn't win an opening game," he told McGraw in disgust.

"That's all right," McGraw assured him. "You pitched good ball, and I don't blame you for losing the game."

With the season off on the wrong foot, McGraw sent Mathewson to the mound the next day. Gleeful fans and sports writers alike expected the Phillies to get their comeuppance for opening day, but no such thing occurred. To their horror, Philadelphia clobbered Matty for fifteen hits and six runs in eight innings and coasted to a 6–1 win. Jack Rowan, who would win only one other game that summer, held the suddenly toothless Giants to three hits. Compared to the raucous clamor of the first game, noted the *Tribune*, the park "seemed as quiet as that famed deserted village." Two games, two losses to a team the Giants once dominated. Was it the curse of 1908 and Harry Coveleski come again, or had the Phillies improved enough to be serious contenders? Whatever the case, the Giants figured that their luck could not get any worse than it had in these opening games. On that point they could not have been more wrong. Before their next game the team suffered an even greater loss.[18]

To CALL A PLAYER "FIERY" IS TO praise him for his intensity and aggressiveness. To regard him as "fired up" is to see him as bristling with energy and confidence. The most driven players are said to have "fire in their bellies." A team "on fire" is one playing at the top of its game and winning most of the time. In sports, fire was a positive metaphor for performance; in society it remained one of the most feared and destructive forces, especially in cities. During 1911 these polar opposites came together in unexpected fashion, especially in New York.

Like all big cities, New York had endured its share of disastrous fires. One of the worst occurred at the Brooklyn Theatre in December 1876, claiming 289 lives. Hotels seemed especially prone. Forty-five people perished at the Windsor Hotel in March 1899, twenty-eight at the Hotel Royal in February 1892, and twenty-one at the Park Avenue Hotel in February 1902. The worst disaster of all took place in June 1904 aboard the *General Slocum*, a steamboat that caught fire in the East River and sank with a loss of an estimated 1,021 lives. On March 25, 1911, while the Giants were in Dallas watching rain cancel their exhibition game, Manhattan suffered the horrific Triangle Shirtwaist Factory fire in which 146 people, mostly young immigrant women working in a garment sweatshop, died either inside the building or leaping in desperation from eighth- or ninth-floor windows. The impact of this nightmare traumatized the city for weeks and triggered a fight for reforms to eliminate such nightmares.[19]

Buildings in cities burned because many of them still used considerable wood in their construction, had inflammable materials inside them, took construction shortcuts to save money, and ignored steps to prevent or fight fires such as sprinkler systems. Ballparks, too, were made primarily of wood except for the first two models of a new breed constructed of steel and concrete: Forbes Field in Pittsburgh and Shibe Park in Philadelphia. In May 1901 what became known as Robison Field in St. Louis lost parts of its grandstand, pavilion, and offices to a fire. On March 17, 1911, eight days before the Triangle fire, flames engulfed the grandstand and bleachers of League Park in Washington, home of the Senators. The owners moved quickly to start work on steel stands, but it took until July 24 to complete work on what became Griffith Stadium.[20]

Sometime around twelve thirty on the morning of April 14, three weeks after the Triangle fire, a watchman at the Polo Grounds noticed a glare and went to investigate. Seeing tongues of flame licking up from the end of the south grandstand, he ran to fetch two nearby policemen. Together they tried in vain to contain the fire with hand extinguishers before putting an alarm in to the fire department. By the time the first unit arrived, the flames had spread to the bleachers. The captain turned in three more alarms while his men struggled to get their gear past the fences. Water pressure was low because the High Bridge pumping station was partly closed for repairs. A newly built water tower, supposed to be ready for filling the next day, stood empty just north of the park. The scene resembled a giant bonfire as the fast-moving flames consumed the grandstand and much of the north and south bleachers. Doggedly the firemen fought to save the clubhouse and about half the bleachers on either side of it.[21]

For the next ninety minutes the Polo Grounds turned into a madhouse. John Murphy, aroused from his bed, thought first of the six English setters kenneled underneath one of the threatened bleachers and rushed to their rescue at his own peril. A strong south wind spread sparks widely and pushed the fire toward the elevated railroad structure and car repair shops just north of the park. The shops housed some five hundred cars, and flames soon devoured the nearest line of them. A group of motormen and conductors braved the intense heat and flames to move some forty trains of five to seven cars each out of the sheds and down the storage spur to the main line at Eighth Avenue. The line was closed above 135th Street to all trains except those being salvaged. Once the remaining bleachers and club-house appeared safe, the firefighters turned all their efforts toward the elevated platform and the wooden shops.

Within a short time thousands of people crowded onto Coogan's Bluff, the Speedway, and the shore of the Harlem River to watch the spectacular blaze. Hastily summoned police reserves struggled to handle the crowd and the mass of vehicles piling into the area. John McGraw was shooting a game of pool at his billiards parlor when he got the news and hurried to the park. Harry Stevens arrived to watch his entire store of concessions vanish in the flames. Several players from both the Giants and Phillies drifted in and stood watching the fire in silence. Bugs Raymond told reporters that during the previous game he and Murphy had noticed a small fire under the grandstand and quickly put it out. He thought the cause had been a cigar or cigarette butt dropped onto a layer of dried peanut shells. McGraw confirmed the story and said he had wanted the piles of old shells removed.

Fire Commissioner William J. Wright, one of the first to reach the scene, looked around helplessly for something to salvage. He settled on second base, stamped out a flickering flame, and tucked the charred bag under his arm. Fred Merkle was among the players watching the disaster unfold. While firemen had managed to save the tarpaulin spread over the infield after games, a stray spark had reached second base. Noticing it smolder before Wright picked it up, Merkle said with a grim chuckle, "They can't say it wasn't touched that time."[22]

By two A.M. the firemen finally contained the blaze in both the park and on the elevated structures. Miraculously, no one died in the fire, and no one cared to contemplate what might have been the case if the fire had broken out during a game when the park was filled with people. Had that happened, editorialized the *Tribune*, "there might have been a loss of life compared with which the death roll of any other fire would have seemed almost insignificant." Although several theories were advanced, no one discovered the actual cause of the fire. The best guess remained the smoldering combustion of dried peanut shells.[23]

As dawn broke and revealed the full extent of the disaster, more spectators showed up from all directions to gawk at the smoking ruins. All of the players' equipment and uniforms were in the clubhouse and so escaped the fire except for their supply of bats, many of them newly acquired by painstaking selection for the coming season. The umpires were not so lucky: Their room burned along with two new suits and other equipment. Harry Stevens stared glumly at the remains of the space that had housed his seat cushions, printing plant for scorecards, beverages, and concession foods that included two tons of peanuts and four barrels of liquor. Having just laid in supplies for the new season, he reckoned his loss at $25,000 to $30,000, all of it uninsured. Fire adjustors figured the overall loss conservatively at $250,000, about a third of it the elevated railway facilities.[24]

The third game with the Phillies was canceled, and the Giants found themselves homeless with a series against Brooklyn due to open the next day. McGraw had no answer to the question of what was to be done. The decision of whether or not to rebuild belonged to Brush, who was in neither the best of health nor the best of spirits. Frank Farrell, of all people, solved the immediate problem. The president of the Highlanders was in Atlantic City when news of the fire reached him. Without hesitation he called Brush and offered him the use of Hilltop Park until the Polo Grounds could be put back into service. Brush was surprised and grateful that the man whose team he had tried so hard to keep out of New York had come to his aid. Charlie Ebbets made a similar offer of Washington Park, but the Dodgers and Giants had numerous scheduling conflicts, while the Giants and Highlanders had none until August. For an unknown period of time the Giants would be playing still farther uptown, in a much smaller park.

The question of whether to rebuild presented Brush with a major dilemma. For some years he had wanted to expand the Polo Grounds into an even bigger facility, one capable of holding fifty thousand people. What had stopped him was not the expense or even the annual threats by politicos to run a street through the park or that of the Manhattan Railway to get the property condemned for its own use, but rather the fact that his lease on the grounds, renewed the previous year, had only nine more years to run. He had just lost most of the money he had recently plowed into upgrading the park and hesitated to invest a huge sum in a new stadium without a longer lease. City officials made it clear that any new park would have to be constructed of steel and concrete to eliminate the fire hazard. The cost would likely exceed half a million dollars.[25]

The fire, warned *Sporting News*, "may mean the end of the famous Polo Grounds" in favor of a park "so far removed from the crowded city that the fans can feel they are enjoying an afternoon in the country." Even more, the loss of the home grounds "seriously upset calculations of those who had picked the Giants as most probable pennant winners . . . may, in fact, change the entire aspect of that race." They had thirty-two games scheduled at home before June 1 in the park *Sporting News* called "a veritable fortress to McGraw." Hilltop was more foreign to them than any park in their own league.[26]

Sixty-five years old, his disease continuing to progress, John T. Brush was a tired man wracked with constant pain. It would have been far simpler to take the insurance money and run, but Brush was a fighter whose will was as strong as his body was frail. According to his daughter, Brush drove to the Polo Grounds with his wife, Elsie, and rolled onto the field in his wheelchair. After surveying the ruins for a time, he said, "Elsie, I want to build a concrete stand, the finest that can be constructed. It will mean economy for a time. Are you willing to stand by me?" When Elsie nodded assent, Brush went right to work. As a crucial first step, he had Whalen negotiate a new arrangement that extended the lease another twenty-five years beyond the nine still on it. Within two days he had architects working on plans for what he conceived as a grand replacement park.[27]

On May 3, Brush announced that the new lease had been signed and that work on the new Polo Grounds would proceed. He also lavished thanks on Frank Farrell for his generosity in providing a temporary home for the Giants "even while the embers of destruction were still glowing in the early hours of the morning of April 14." New York's two major-league teams, once the most implacable of enemies, would share a bandbox that some people still called simply "American League Park."[28]

HILLTOP PARK STOOD AT THE SOUTHWEST CORNER of Broadway and 168th Street, a site overlooked by Freedman and Brush in their campaign to scoop up every conceivable location for a ballpark to prevent an American League team from entering the city. They ignored the site because it was so rocky and unlevel that the cost of transforming it would be prohibitive. However, Farrell and his partners grabbed the nearly ten-acre parcel overlooking the Hudson River and spent $200,000 blasting it down to level and another $100,000 to erect a ballpark made entirely of wood. By allowing standees behind the foul lines and across the outfield, its capacity could be stretched from fifteen thousand to nearly twenty-five thousand. A portion of the bleachers down the left-field foul line had just been roofed over and new trapezoid-shaped bleachers added in front of the center-field fence for the coming season, eliminating the dark batter's background and shortening the distance to the center-field fence to about 370 feet.[29]

To this park the Giants came as near strangers to play all but three of their remaining games in April. They knew it only from the three games played there against the Highlanders the previous fall. It helped that most of the games were against the East's two weak sisters, Brooklyn and Boston, interrupted only by three games in Philadelphia. The first game attracted an overflow crowd of both Giant and Superba fans eager to see their teams and a park into which few of them had ever ventured. The big Texan Louis Drucke drew the start and lasted only four innings as Brooklyn reached him for six hits, two walks, and three runs. With the score tied 3–3, Doc Crandall came on and stifled the Superbas on two hits the rest of the way while driving in two runs with a pair of triples as the Giants gained their first win, 6–3.[30]

Next day, Sunday, the Giants traveled to Newark and mashed Joe McGinnity's Indians 14–6 in an exhibition, collecting sixteen hits and stealing seven bases—one of them by pitcher Dick Rudolph—in the process. On their return to Hilltop the team reeled off three straight wins over Brooklyn. In the first one on the seventeenth Hooks Wiltse started but left in the second inning after a line drive hit the wrist of his pitching hand. McGraw decided to give Raymond his first opportunity and was pleased when Bugs shut the Superbas out the rest of the way in a 3–1 victory. Five different Giants stole a base in the game.[31]

That same day a much more sorrowful scene played out in Toledo, where members of the Cleveland Naps and Detroit Tigers gathered at the funeral of Addie Joss, a brilliant pitcher who had died of tubercular meningitis at the age of thirty-one. The two teams had a game scheduled that day; Ban Johnson insisted that they play until the Naps threatened to strike, and for once the president relented. "No better man ever lived than Addie," said team captain George Stovall. Before a huge turnout, former pitcher turned evangelist Billy Sunday delivered the sermon. Two months later a group of American League all-stars played an exhibition game against Cleveland and raised $12,914 for the benefit of Joss's family.[32]

In the third game with Brooklyn, McGraw sent Marquard to the mound and was rewarded with a 7–1 win. "He had wonderful speed," said the *Tribune*, "a beautiful drop ball which fooled the opposing batsmen time and again and a cross fire delivery that was an enigma." He walked five but struck out eight; in the last inning he walked the bases loaded, then struck out the side. "Marquard, under the tutoring of McGraw, is a new pitcher," proclaimed the *Times*. "He has laid aside that pretzel wind-up, which threw him into a sailor knot every time he tossed the ball ... His assortment yesterday had variety and much mystery." McGraw was quick to credit Marquard's spring tutorial with Wilbert Robinson for the good performance. "We've put weight on Marquard at last," he told reporters afterward. "Wilbert Robinson is largely responsible for his good showing. He has worked over him all spring. I guess we can keep him from going up in the air after this."[33]

In the final game of the series, played in a cold rain, hard-luck Ames held the Superbas in check until the ninth inning, when they pushed across three runs for a 3–2 lead. The Giants responded with two runs of their own to steal the game 4–3 and complete the four-game sweep. The ninth-inning rally gave McGraw a taste of the brand of ball he wanted this team to play. Merkle opened with a single. Bridwell popped out but Devlin drew a walk. After Dahlen brought in a new pitcher, Meyers shot a single to center, scoring Merkle. McGraw sent Becker up to bat for Ames and the fleet outfielder beat out a slow roller down the first base line. With the bases loaded and the winning run on third, McGraw dispatched Art Fletcher to run for the slower Devlin. Devore chopped one to shortstop, allowing the speedy Fletcher to outrace the hurried throw home. The play was close enough that Devlin would have been out if he were the runner. Speed and timeliness—that was the formula McGraw wanted to see implemented.[34]

"In winning four straight games from the Brooklyn Superbas the Giants proved last week that the handicap of new bats and strange grounds could be overcome," reported the *Tribune*. The writer praised Marquard's performance and reminded readers that "almost everybody except McGraw lost confidence in the wonderfully speedy but erratic twirler long ago . . . It will take more than one game to convince the rank and file. It is quite possible, however, that Marquard's year has come, and that he will prove a strong asset."[35]

Marquard wanted desperately to succeed. "I think I've got the words 'eleven thousand dollar lemon' memorized better than any other four words in the language," he told a reporter years later. "If I'd open a paper the first few words I'd see on the sports page were those . . . I'd get it in the baseball grounds whenever I'd show my face. I'd get it in the hotel when I'd catch little scraps of conversation. If I went to a show some comedian would be sure to have something about it. The fans were full of it." He stopped reading the papers and hesitated even to show himself on the street, but "the one thing I couldn't sidestep was my mail. I'd get 12 or 15 letters a day. I'd call 'em 'big-stiff' letters because they always commenced, 'You big stiff, go back to the plow.'"[36]

After the game the Giants traveled to Philadelphia for that team's home opener, but cold weather and wet grounds deferred it for a day. Mathewson warmed up but told McGraw his arm didn't feel right and Doc Crandall was again tapped on short notice. He pitched well enough to win most games, but Earl Moore again baffled the Giants, this time on a lone bloop single sprinkled with five walks as the resurgent Phillies took their third straight from New York, 3–0. Rain washed out the next day's game, but on the twenty-fourth Jack Rowan duplicated his earlier feat by holding the Giants to only one run on nine hits as the Phillies romped 4–1 even though Wiltse allowed them only six hits. Four straight losses to Philadelphia prompted the *Sun* to attribute it to the "Quaker hoodoo."[37]

Sunshine finally greeted the Giants in more ways than one on their return to Hilltop. Boston, that refuge for former Giants players, came to town for four games and dropped three of them. Already the rumors had started that Mathewson had lost his magic and was going downhill. In the first game he silenced the cynics by scattering eight hits for a 3–1 win in a brisk game that took only an hour and twenty-five minutes. Next day Raymond got his first start and yielded eleven hits but only three runs as the Giants won again, 6–3. McGraw had Wilson do the catching, aware that Meyers disliked handling spitballs. Although Raymond struck out seven and walked only two, the *Herald* observed that "he looked as if he was dragging his anchor more than once." A skeptical E. H. Simmons noted that "Raymond has disappointed us so often in the past that it will take considerable more than one game to restore complete confidence in him."[38]

Marquard took the mound on the twenty-seventh and quickly reverted to form, giving up four runs, five hits, and two walks in only two innings before being replaced by the busy Doc Crandall, who stifled Boston on three hits the rest of the way. New York romped 12–5 by slugging five doubles, a triple, and a monster home run by Merkle and stealing six bases, including a delayed steal by Meyers and a double steal by Devlin and Crandall. Merkle's homer was the first to clear the newly double-decked left-field wall. "It went over the left field fence," said the *Herald*, "as if it was an express and the first stop was Yonkers." Only in the final game did the Giants falter, losing 9–3 as they stranded nine runners.[39]

On Saturday the twenty-ninth, in weather finally fitting for baseball, the Giants crossed the bridge to Washington Park to take on Brooklyn again. Thousands of Giant loyalists followed suit, giving Charlie Ebbets a rare full house with customers strung out along the field as well. McGraw's men ripped off four runs in the top of the first and coasted to a 7–3 victory behind Mathewson, who eased up as he often did with a big lead and gave the Superbas ten hits but only the three runs in the sixth inning, by which time he had a six-run lead. Murray had four hits and Doyle three to lead the assault. The last day of April being a Sunday, the team had the day off.[40]

The first returns of the season told McGraw little about his team. The Giants had won eight of nine games against the two weakest teams in the league and dropped four in a row to a team they were supposed to beat. The hitters had not yet warmed to their task, and the pitching had been uneven. But the team had stolen twenty-six bases in thirteen games and shown the speed he craved up and down the lineup.

STANDINGS APRIL 30

	Won	Lost	Pct.		Won	Lost	Pct.
Philadelphia	11	3	.786	Cincinnati	4	6	.400
Pittsburgh	8	4	.667	Boston	5	10	.333
New York	8	5	.615	St. Louis	3	7	.300
Chicago	8	6	.571	Brooklyn	4	10	.286

CHAPTER 10

May: Home Away from Home

*"Our team last year was no team at all and
New York should have beaten us easily. We
won a lot of games for earlier pennants with
sacrifice hits, and that was what they expected
last year. When I saw my pitchers were weak, I
told the boys to play hit and run and slam the
ball out, and by this scheme we generally got so
far in front at the start the other teams could
not catch us . . . Still, I think we will win the
National League pennant again, with all our
bad luck last year."*

—FRANK CHANCE

B Y 1911 SPEED HAD BECOME AN AMERICAN craze. The pace of urban
life quickened steadily, driven in part by the impact of instant
communication in the form of the telegraph and telephone.
Production lines moved faster as more newfangled machines moved into
factories, forcing those working alongside them to step up their pace as
well. Language grew more crisp and succinct, thanks in large part to the
telegraph, where words cost money. Nothing revealed this tendency more
than the growing presence of automobiles. Although their speeds seem
slow to later generations, they shocked many Americans at the time even as
they frightened horses. Here was the machine to top all machines, made
increasingly available to ordinary Americans after the introduction of Henry
Ford's iconic Model T in 1908.

Inevitably the automobile became an instrument for racing and endurance contests as well. Newspapers filled their columns with details of every
contest just as they did every accident on city streets. As early as 1895,
France held the first sanctioned automobile race between cities,

but a disastrous contest in 1903 killed eight people and ended the wild enthusiasm for open-road racing. As the sport moved to enclosed tracks, William K. Vanderbilt Jr., a rabid motorcar enthusiast, sponsored the first American international race for the Vanderbilt Cup in 1904. By 1906 racing cars were already topping a hundred miles per hour in speed. Two years later Savannah hosted the first American grand prix race. Huge crowds mobbed the events, turning speed into a major spectator sport.[1]

In 1909 Carl Fisher spent $155,000 repaving his racing oval in Indianapolis with more than three million bricks. Two years later organizers put forth $25,000 in prize money to make the city and its track a major player in automobile racing. They intended to overshadow the Vanderbilt Cup and grand prix events with a longer race running five hundred miles, the distance calculated as the longest that could be done in one day while allowing spectators to leave for home in the daylight. On Memorial Day in 1911 the first Indy 500 took place and was won by Ray Harroun in a disputed finish that received surprisingly little attention from the press. Harroun's Marmon Wasp featured a rearview mirror, the first ever in racing. He finished with an average speed of 74.6 miles per hour.[2]

Throughout the summer of 1911, racing drew enormous crowds everywhere, with little thought given to their protection. On September 16 a huge throng flocked to the track at the New York State Fair in Syracuse. President William Howard Taft attended and enjoyed a quick spin around the track, which was wetted to keep the dust down despite protests from the drivers. On the forty-third lap a car driven by Lee Oldfield (no relation to Barney), traveling at seventy-miles an hour, crashed through the fence and plowed into the crowd, killing nine people and injuring many more. The accident served notice, not for the first time, that speed could kill. Speed on the base paths, it seemed, was much safer if not without its own perils.[3]

ALTHOUGH DISPUTES AROSE EVERY YEAR over some aspect of the schedule, the basic pattern could not have been more simple. The four eastern (Boston, Brooklyn, New York, Philadelphia) and four western (Chicago, Cincinnati, Pittsburgh, St. Louis) clubs first played home and away series against every team in their group. When that was done, one group went on the road to play a series against every team in the other group. After finishing those games, the home group played some games against teams in its own area before heading out to make the rounds of their recent visitors. That done, the traveling group returned home to complete its round against its own area teams. The full cycle, once completed, was then repeated, augmented by an unpredictable number of makeup games for rainouts and other causes that were worked in as part of a doubleheader. By May an ominous pattern had developed, as bad weather had already created the need for sixteen doubleheaders later in the season.[4]

For the Giants this pattern gave them a favorable schedule in May. After two more games in Brooklyn and four in Boston they returned to Hilltop for the rest of the month to play the four western clubs and then Philadelphia and Brooklyn. In June they would find themselves on the road for most of the month. Hilltop would take some getting used to; Al Bridwell pronounced it the fastest field he had ever played on.[5]

In the two games against Bill Dahlen's Superbas the Giants extended their mastery to seven consecutive wins. After sitting idle during yet another day of rain, McGraw sent Wiltse to the mound on a chilly May 2 and got another short but almost sweet performance. Holding Brooklyn hitless and fanning eight through four and a third innings, Hooks surrendered a double and proceeded to load the bases with two walks. With a 3–0 lead McGraw summoned Doc Crandall, who hit a batter for one run and had another score when Doyle muffed his grounder. Crandall clung to the 3–2 lead until the eighth, when he allowed two runs. In the bottom of the ninth Becker batted for Devlin and singled, stole second, and took third when Meyers drove a shot off the pitcher's hand and made it safely to first. McGraw replaced him with Fletcher, who lost no time stealing second. McGraw let Crandall hit for himself and again he came through, this time with a hot grounder past second that scored both runners.[6]

The next day, facing Brooklyn ace Nap Rucker, Devore led off with a triple and scored on Doyle's sacrifice fly. Although the Giants got two more runs in the seventh, Bugs Raymond didn't need them. His spitball was dancing despite a cold, raw wind as he shut out the Superbas on four hits and five walks. No Brooklyn runner even reached third. More cold and wind greeted the Giants in Boston on the fourth but Mathewson, given a six-run lead, allowed the Rustlers nine hits and five walks in a 7–2 win. Then came the sort of game McGraw despised most. A struggling Red Ames carried a 5–3 lead into the ninth despite issuing seven walks along with six hits. After getting the first two men out, he yielded a bloop single and proceeded to walk the next three batters, forcing in a run. An irate McGraw summoned Wiltse, who walked in the tying run and allowed a single to give Boston a 6–5 lead and the game. "Leon Ames's old hoodoo paid him a friendly visit in the ninth inning," reported the *Press*.[7]

The game got even weirder on Saturday the sixth. "The Bostons and New York gave a fine exhibition of how baseball shouldn't be played this afternoon," quipped the *Sun*. Crandall started but lasted only six innings while being mauled for seven runs and eleven hits. Marquard followed him and promptly surrendered two more runs, but the Giants, too, went on a hitting spree and won the game 15–9. They made four errors, Boston five, and umpire Bill Klem threw out two Rustlers along with Doyle and McGraw. "Taken as a whole," concluded the *World*, "the work of this arbitrator was of the rankest kind . . . He was hooted off the grounds when the game was over." One aspect of the game went unnoticed by the reporters. Amid the offensive fireworks the Giants stole an astonishing ten bases.[8]

Having completed their first round of series against the eastern teams, the Giants occupied third place as they prepared to welcome the western teams to their home away from home. Before their arrival McGraw pared his roster down to size by shipping out nearly all the rookies and one veteran. Admiral Schlei was sent to Indianapolis while six pitchers were dispatched elsewhere—Rudolph and Tesreau to Toronto, Jenkins and Shontz to Newark, and Nagle to Syracuse. Hendricks was released outright, leaving only the two catchers, Hank Gowdy and Grover Hartley, as survivors from spring camp.[9]

The first western visitor to Hilltop was none other than Chicago. By 1911 the Cubs had arrived at that unhappy place McGraw's Giants had been in 1907. A game but aging team was no longer performing to its high standards, and one crucial part after another was falling away. Harry Steinfeldt, whose performance had been slipping, did not report for spring training, and neither did Johnny Kling. Although Steinfeldt did report to camp belatedly, Chance put him on waivers and sold him to St. Paul. His departure marked the first break in the infield that had dominated the league since 1906. Kling, too, finally signed and turned up at camp but found that he had to share catching duties with Archer.[10]

Chance himself was in poor shape. The endless string of injuries, coupled with the stress of managing, had steadily eroded his playing time. He never matched his outstanding performance of 1906 and played fewer games every year after 1908. Someone calculated that he had been hit in the head twenty times in his career. "There are pains that shoot through his head and other parts of his body too numerous to mention," noted a writer, "which make it just about impossible for him to take an active part, a playing part, in the game at which he is so expert." By 1911 he had lost all hearing in one ear and part of it in the other. Another beaning this season left him with severe headaches and the feeling that the left side of his head was filled with sawdust. At thirty-five his career was drawing to a close; he saw action in only thirty-one games, yielding his position to rookie Vic Saier.[11]

Nor did the casualties stop with Chance. A few days before the series with New York, Evers, after being ejected from a game, fainted dead away on the clubhouse floor and suffered a nervous breakdown. Later he attributed it to the loss of nearly all his money in the collapse of his shoe business. His recovery was slow; he was said to be home in Troy, New York, in bed and deeply discouraged over his future. Although Chance played in the series against the Giants, Joe Tinker remained the lone survivor of the original infield. Jimmy Doyle took over third base and Heinie Zimmerman, a slow-witted utility man with a perpetual scowl on his face, replaced Evers at second. Kling managed to get in only twenty-seven games before being traded in June to the Rustlers, who also picked up Steinfeldt. In Boston, Steinfeldt lasted only nineteen games before coming down with a serious illness in July that all but ended his career.[12]

The vaunted Cubs pitching staff fared no better. Miner Brown continued to be a workhorse but was wearing down. Reulbach remained a stalwart but was as wild as ever; in one April game he was lifted after throwing ten straight balls. Pfiester arrived in spring training with stomach trouble thought at first to be a heart ailment. Giant killer no more, he never found his groove and went 1-4 for the season. Orval Overall took his sore arm to the magic fingers of Bonesetter Reese and claimed to be recovered, but a contract dispute with Murphy led him to sit out the season working in a California gold mine he owned with Brown. With so much uncertainty Chance admitted freely that his hopes depended on the pitching.[13]

The Cubs arrived in New York with a new lineup and batting order as well as new dark-blue uniforms. The first game featured another matchup between Mathewson and Brown, who had won eleven of their eighteen contests. Rain delayed the start and remained steady, but McGraw decided to play anyway and Hank O'Day did not call the game once it started. Three errors on each side in sloppy, wet conditions did not detract from a hard-fought struggle before a hardy crowd of about seven thousand. This time Matty prevailed 5–3, allowing seven hits and no walks.[14]

Next day Hooks Wiltse limited Chicago to four hits while his mates raked the struggling Pfiester for six in less than three innings and Fred Toney for another seven on their way to an 11–1 romp. With the Giants ahead 7–0 after four innings, both managers started taking their veterans out of the lineup. However, the Cubs won the final two games to split the series.[15]

A minor ear operation kept Merkle out of the lineup for the last Cubs game, but he was back on the thirteenth when St. Louis came to town. The Cardinals also wore a fresh look in two very different ways. Since taking charge of the team, Roger Bresnahan had improved their personnel and their play. His core of solid players included first baseman Ed Konetchy, feisty second sacker Miller Huggins, third baseman Mike Mowrey, and outfielder Steve Evans, along with himself. Three pitchers topped his staff: the capable Bob Harmon, Bill Steele, and the unpredictable Harry "Slim" Sallee, yet another performer with a drinking problem. Other than Harmon, the staff lacked consistency, but they had the expertise of Bresnahan to help them along.[16]

The most striking change occurred not on the field but in the front office. To the astonishment of everyone, Stan Robison's will left controlling interest in the team to his niece, Helene Robison Britton, and the remaining shares to her mother, the widow of Stan's brother Frank. Observers expected her to put the shares on the market, and Chicago businessman Charles Weeghman fully expected to buy them, but she decided not to sell. Ignoring the media gibes and cold shoulders of the other owners, she declared her intention of not only owning but also running the team. As a first step she announced her entire satisfaction with Bresnahan as manager. For the first time in history, a major-league team had a female owner, and one who was not merely a figurehead.[17]

The Cardinals came into New York with a record of 7-13 and ran into a buzz saw as the Giants sent seventeen men to the plate in the first inning to score thirteen runs and added three more in the second in a 19–5 massacre. Every Giant scored a run; Murray tallied twice in an inning that lasted half an hour. Merkle drove in six runs in the big inning alone, and the Giants added six stolen bases to the damage. Sallee and Harmon both toiled and together got only four outs. Mathewson opened for New York but McGraw lifted him after the first inning and sent Marquard in for the rest of the game. He also put five reserve players on the field in short order. On Monday, New York resumed its siege with a 10–6 win in which they scored in every inning but two. Drucke allowed eleven hits and three walks but staggered to the win as the Giants stole four bases to go with their twelve hits, nine walks (four by Devore), and a Merkle home run. "It was such a listless game," quipped the *Herald*, "that the bricklayers on the new armory overlooking the field went right on working."[18]

The Giants were not alone in piling up the runs. That same day the Phillies overwhelmed Cincinnati 21–5 with twenty-one hits good for forty-eight bases. A day earlier four American League teams scored more than ten runs. On May 11 eight games in the two leagues together produced 126 runs and 177 hits, a record for any one day. "How about this beating the hide off the ball and scattering it all over the lot?" asked the *Times*. "Is the batting talent improving, or are the pitching wings getting glassy?" The *Times* had another answer. "It's the new cork centre in the ball. The resiliency of the sphere is so pronounced that a good poke is worth a base or two more than it used to be." At this early date batting averages had soared, both in size and number of hitters above .300. Young Stuffy McInnis of the Athletics led the American League with an astounding .455, teammate Eddie Collins followed at .431, and Ty Cobb at .392. Red Dooin topped the National League at .397.[19]

Most of the experts pointed to the cork-centered ball as the reason for the outburst of scoring. "One thing is certain," said *Sporting News*, "the dear old public no longer complains of the lack of batting." However, after conceding that the pitchers might not yet be in form and some fielding had been mediocre at best, the paper called attention to another factor: "the development of base running. Managers of the modern school are picking men for their speed on the bases as well as their hitting and fielding, and are getting results . . . The success of managers who regard base running as important as batting has established a solid precedent." No manager was getting more out of the running game than McGraw; the Giants had already stolen sixty-two bases in their first twenty-six games.[20]

The *Chicago Tribune* predicted that the "heavy batting which has been the wonder of fans and the despair of pitchers since the opening of the 1911 baseball season will be curtailed by natural causes in the near future . . . It can be stated as authority . . . that the next supply of official balls for the clubs of the major and minor leagues will not be as lively as the ones now in use . . . The present lively ball which is breaking down fences and produced

367 runs in three days in the major leagues was due to a tip from the base-ball powers that there was not enough batting to suit the fans."[21]

If McGraw expected more of the same in the third game, he was soon disappointed. Bugs Raymond lasted only an inning as the Cardinals ran up a 6–0 lead and coasted to an 8–6 win. Freshman umpire Bill Finneran got his first taste of the McGraw style in the first inning and banished him to the center-field bleachers after enduring a lengthy harangue. There McGraw joined Joe Tinker, who had come to the game while serving a three-game suspension for a transgression in Brooklyn. A short time later Cardinals shortstop Arnold Hauser, also ejected by Finneran, and Raymond, who had yielded four walks and two triples in his lone inning, joined them. Afterward, Thomas J. Lynch, who had promised to protect his umpires from kicking, slapped a three-day suspension on McGraw.

With McGraw absent, the Giants dropped the final game of the series 3-1 as lanky Slim Sallee's crossfire limited them to six hits. McGraw was not pleased. It was one thing to split a series with Chicago, quite another to do so with lowly St. Louis.[22]

On the eighteenth the parade of western visitors continued with New York's other bitter rival, the Pirates. After their triumph in the 1909 World Series, Barney Dreyfuss had told Fred Clarke, "I guess we have a team that'll stay up there for some time, like our team of 1901." Clarke agreed. "There are a few of us getting older," he said, "but those Cubs aren't getting any younger, either. We're a great team, and there's nothing in sight that should finish ahead of us in 1910." But the Cubs did just that, and McGraw had added insult to injury by pushing Pittsburgh into third place that year.[23]

Clarke himself had talked of retiring after the 1909 World Series to spend more time with his family, but Dreyfuss had persuaded him to stay on. At thirty-eight he could still play at a high level but not as often. His outfield still had the irrepressible Tommy Leach, Chief Wilson, and a prom-ising newcomer named Max Carey. The infield boasted the incomparable Wagner, still going strong at thirty-seven; Dots Miller at second; and dimin-utive Bobby Byrne at third. First base remained the black hole of the Pirate lineup. George Gibson was an excellent catcher, Adams continued to excel after his stunning three wins in the 1909 Series, and Clarke hoped that Howie Camnitz and Lefty Leifield would revert to earlier form.[24]

The Pirates occupied second place, two games behind upstart Philadelphia and three games ahead of New York, when they arrived at Hilltop Park.

Thunder and lightning enlivened the first game but the rain held off until the eighth inning, by which time the Pirates had banked a 6–1 victory. Mathewson coughed up ten hits and all six runs in seven innings while Adams breezed along with a five-hitter. Five errors contributed to Mathewson's poor day. That Marquard came in and struck out the side in the eighth offered little solace. "There's no use talking," said the *Sun*, "the Giants miss McGraw. They flopped around in an aimless way yesterday and in one inning threw the ball around in a crazy way."[25]

After that fumbling start the Giants reeled off three straight wins against Pittsburgh. In the first game, with the score tied 3–3 in the seventh, Wiltse, who had pitched well, split his hand knocking down a drive by Clarke and retired after throwing him out. Raymond relieved and struck Wagner out. In the bottom half Beals Becker doubled to drive in what proved to be the winning run. McGraw returned the next day but did not appear in the coach's box until the fourth inning of a pitching duel between Leifield and Drucke. An overflow crowd, the largest of the season, saw Leifield hold the Giants hitless until the seventh while his teammates sprayed ten hits off Drucke but could score only one run, and that without a hit. With the score tied 1–1 in the ninth, Devlin singled and Fletcher again went in to run for him. A wild pitch moved Fletcher to second, and the ever versatile Crandall, batting for Drucke, promptly stroked a single to win the game.[26]

On Monday, Bugs Raymond, "the well-known inventor of the Croton highball, baffled the Pirate batsmen with an assortment of wet and dry tosses," and the Giants gained revenge on Adams with a 5–1 win. Raymond had the Pirates beating the ball into the ground; Merkle wound up with fifteen putouts. The final visitor, former Highlander manager Clark Griffith's Cincinnati Reds, arrived on the twenty-third to the delight of Mathewson, who had defeated them seventeen straight times and had not lost to them since May 18, 1908. He added to the streak as the Giants coasted to a 7–2 win. The next day, before a small, shivering crowd, Marquard struck out eight Reds and hurled a two-hitter, both in the first inning, for a 2–1 victory called by one writer "the best game . . . he ever pitched for the Giants." For the first time since May 1910 the Giants moved into first place as Philadelphia dropped its sixth straight game.[27]

The stay was brief as the Reds bested New York 6–1 the following day. Drucke lasted only three innings. "His offerings to the batters were as undraped as a barefoot dance," commented the *Herald*. "The ball had practically nothing on it." The Phillies, who snapped their losing streak by beating St. Louis to reclaim first place, happened to be the next team due at Hilltop for three games. Already McGraw realized that this Phillies team was stronger and tougher than the patsies of earlier years. So, too, were the Cardinals, who were playing spirited ball under Bresnahan. But McGraw liked what he saw from both Raymond and Marquard, and his boys continued to run. Although limited by Gibson of Pittsburgh to five steals in four games, they collected eight in the three games against the Reds. Speed, often in the form of pinch runners, was winning games.[28]

WHILE CONSTRUCTION WENT STEADILY FORWARD at the Polo Grounds, the scourge of fire continued to torment the East Coast and Manhattan. May first brought news of a conflagration that ravaged downtown Bangor, Maine, taking two lives and wiping out much of the business district along with the town library and many of its finest residences. On May 3 a small fire in a five-story Broadway sweatshop sent five hundred terrified girls, mindful of the Triangle fire, fleeing in panic; fourteen were hurt when a flimsy balustrade in a stairwell collapsed. Ten days later a fire destroyed several buildings at Rockaway Beach, causing a loss estimated at $100,000. Early on the morning of the 27th a huge blaze broke out at an entertainment venue quite the opposite of baseball. The target for this disaster was Dreamland, the immensely popular attraction at Coney Island.[29]

Few places in the city attracted more people. As the season opened, the *Press* reported that "a hundred thousand electric lamps have been added to the entrance of Dreamland, forming a network above the heads of the ingoing crowd ... Ballroom and restaurant are now housed in a new building near the main entrance and in front of the tower ... Everything looks new, if it isn't. The babies in the incubators are guaranteed to be strictly new ... Luna Park and Dreamland provide every amusement for the crowd ... Last season there were more than 10,000,000 visitors to Steeplechase and Dreamland, not even mentioning Luna Park. Coney can take care of them all and more."[30]

Hell Gate, a watercourse through which boats floated by gravity, lay near the entrance to Dreamland. Repairs had to be done in the wee hours because crowds roamed the park until its midnight closing. Around two A.M. some men were tarring one of the troughs through which the boats moved when a slight explosion occurred and a cluster of lights went out. In the confusion someone knocked over the pot of hot tar, and apparently sparks from the failed lights set it ablaze. Fed by the flimsy construction of the trough, the flames moved quickly and forced the workmen to flee. From this accident erupted what was called "the biggest fire this city had seen since the great one which wiped out the lower part of Manhattan in 1835." It led a fire official to sound the dreaded "2-9" alarm, the most drastic of all, which brought to the scene thirty-two engines, ten trucks, and two water towers in a desperate attempt to contain the fire. Before it was harnessed at around five A.M., the blaze destroyed a hundred buildings and flattened sixteen acres of amusements, for a total loss estimated at nearly $5 million.[31]

Across from Hell Gate stood two of Dreamland's most popular attractions, the infant incubators and the Colonel Joseph G. Ferrari wild animal show. A small structure housed the newfangled incubators, which contained five babies ranging in age from two weeks to six months and a boy weighing less than a pound that had just been born the night before. The night nurse had just summoned two wet nurses for the regular two A.M. feeding when Dr. S. Fischel, the presiding physician, rushed in with news that fire was approaching the building. Together they gathered up the infants, threw blankets over their heads, and hurried them to the nearby residence of another physician, where the nurses did their feeding as if nothing had happened. Fischel raced back to alert three other sleeping nurses, who were led to safety through the smoke by a police sergeant. He also told a fireman of his Saint Bernard dog, locked in his office. The fireman got him out. Fourteen ponies tied less than a hundred feet from Hell Gate were also untied and led to safety.

Joseph Ferrari was aroused from bed in his sleeping wagon parked outside the entrance to the animal arena; the rest of his staff slept in upstairs rooms and were already coming down to look after the "stuff," their affectionate term for the menagerie they tended. Ferrari first got his wife and daughter to safety and then ordered his helpers to move as many animals as possible from their performance cages to moveable ones that could be hauled away. Already the smoke and heat had terrified the animals, which were snarling and screaming with fear. Jack Bonavita, Ferrari's assistant, who had lost his left arm to a lion, scooped up a favorite lion cub and handed her off to someone outside for safekeeping. Then he plunged back into what had become a scene of nightmarish horror.[32]

As the smoke grew thicker, the men tried desperately to get the frantic animals to move, pushing and beating them into the traveling cages. Their efforts managed to rescue five lions, four leopards, two llamas, six ponies, an armful of monkeys, and the bloodhound that served as watchdog. As flames drew nearer, the handlers realized their time was running out. Suddenly the skylight in the roof collapsed, sending shards of glass into the cages and maddening the terrified beasts even more. Ferrari loved his menagerie; they had made him a good living but he was also deeply attached to them, as were Bonavita and the other helpers. Grudgingly, bitterly, he realized that the heat and smoke made it impossible to get any more of them out. In their frenzy the animals were clawing at the bars of their cages and tearing at each other.

Ferrari ordered everybody out, and they hurried to the lobby where Little Hip, the young elephant who sometimes handed out programs with her trunk, was shackled. They undid the shackle, and five of them pushed furiously to get the beast to move the short distance to safety outside. But the elephant was so terrified that she refused to budge; she pressed her head against the wall and trumpeted pitifully. "No good, boys," said Ferrari wearily. "Get out. Jack, you stay." In black smoke too thick to see clearly, they groped their way back to the cages, revolvers in hand, and went grimly from cage to cage shooting as many of the shrieking animals as possible before the heat became too much for them. One monkey scratched his head and looked at them with a sad, quizzical expression. "I can't do it," said Ferrari. "I'm damned if I can."

They left the building gagging with smoke and watched mournfully as the monkey burned to death along with Little Hip and seventy or more other animals. The casualty list included lions, leopards, pumas, hybrids, bears, hyenas, the elephant, monkeys, birds, Virginia deer, a wolf, an antelope, a jaguar, a kangaroo, and a sea lion. None of the men could forget their agonizing screams as flames consumed the building. A lion and leopard had escaped their cages. The leopard made its way to Surf Avenue, where a policeman shot it. The lion, its mane on fire, howled in pain as it raced through the smoke and a crowd of people to the dark building of the Rocky Road to Dublin, a scenic railway. Policemen found it near some cars about twenty feet in the air where, whimpering from several bullet wounds as well, it crawled along the incline and into a depression where a policeman, out of ammunition, finished it with an axe and rolled the body down to the street. Almost at once members of the crowd began pulling out its claws and teeth as souvenirs.

The flames spread quickly because so much of Dreamland was made of cheap, flammable materials. With merciless speed they devoured one flimsy building or shack after another while firemen raged furiously at the failure of the high-pressure water system to live up to its name. "It failed us completely," said the deputy fire commissioner in disgust, "and from what I have heard from firemen and other trustworthy witnesses the first hydrant gave us only a trickle of water instead of 75 to 100 pounds we should have." Later an inspector claimed that too many hydrants had been opened at once and taxed the system beyond its capacity. "We had to put our fingers across the weak stream as it came from the nozzle . . . just as if we [were] handling a garden hose, so that the stream would shoot further," said a fireman. The famous observation tower, a landmark since the 1876 Centennial though unused in recent years, collapsed with a roar.

Luna Park, which had its own saltwater system, protected its property and threw streams of water over the giant roller system, whose steel structure helped stop the fire at its edge. Elsewhere the flames halted at some large ovens used to cook frankfurters. To the east and south, however, almost everything was lost: Jolly's Hotel, several restaurants, the L. A. Thompson Oriental Scenic Railway and Pike's Peak Railway, concession stands, Johnson's Carousel, Stubbman's Carousel, the Great Whirlwind ride, shooting galleries, a motion picture house, two bathing pavilions, Lent's Music Hall, game shacks, souvenir stores, candy stores, photographic studios, Mark Lee's Gypsy Camp, the boardwalk, and the new iron steamboat pier. Along Sheridan's Walk the displaced Gypsies, who spoke no English, milled about in confusion. Stubenbord's Hotel barely survived but lost its restaurant. Some unfinished municipal baths caught fire but were saved by the firemen.

Miraculously, no human lives were lost even though people began flocking to the scene as soon as word of the fire spread. Most were content to watch; some tried to snatch souvenirs from the debris in the confusion. The fire took place early on a Saturday morning. Sunday was the busiest day at Coney Island, and this Sunday was no exception. By eight A.M. the cars of the elevated were packed to suffocation with people eager to view the five blocks of ruins and other sights offered by Coney Island. By one estimate some 350,000 visitors poured onto the streets, nearly twice the average Sunday crowd. In the crush it took twenty minutes to get from the train to the street. Others arrived by automobile, carriage, wagon, hack, or on foot.[33]

Between Surf Avenue and the ocean, and from Sheridan's Walk to the municipal baths, was a wasteland except for a lone group of buildings.

Although firemen still sprayed water on some smoldering areas, Dreamland was far from dead. Few of its denizens had insurance for their loss, but they were tough-minded people who had seen adversity before; one man claimed to have been burned out six times. The hardy souls who made their living from the park scarcely paused for breath before setting out to get something ready for Sunday. Ghoulish as the scene was with its debris and remains of cremated animals, it also boasted a bizarre array of hastily improvised attractions. Anticipating the crush of gawkers, the police were out in force and had roped off the burned-out district. Amid the ruins and around them, however, tents were going up, stands thrown together, and equipment assembled. The proprietor of Stubenbord's Hotel arranged some tables and chairs around a standing oven, the lone survivor of his restaurant, rigged up some electric lights on poles, and welcomed patrons with beer and food.

Fred Schue's small refreshment booth was gone, but on its site he put up an old tarpaulin and began dispensing beer to thirsty roamers. Henry Tarr had a crude version of his photographic studio ready for business, and the "Seven-in-One Show," described as "an old-fashioned circus exhibit of freaks," was preparing to resume shows under canvas. Louis Gordon reopened his grotesque "Hit the Nigger" show in which patrons got three balls to knock the hat off a black man. "Except for police interference," noted a reporter, "[he] would have had the crowd tossing balls at him." Half a dozen other concessionaires managed to devise some sort of open bars to serve the public. Candy stands displayed their wares along Surf Avenue, and the surviving frankfurter ovens were dusted off and put to work making hot dogs and roast beef sandwiches.

Joe Ferrari, too, wasted no time in mourning his losses, dear as they were to him. While his two surviving wagons cruised about the street empty, he dumped two wagonfuls of sawdust over the ashes of his arena, pitched a large tent, and announced that the surviving animals would be performing. At the same time he looked into ordering new stuff from Cuba and Europe. Next to his tent, Sultan, the lion slain on the Rocky Road tower, had already been stuffed and put on exhibit, a performer even in death. Ferrari understood, as did most of his fellow amusement merchants, that the show must go on regardless of their personal feelings or sense of loss.

Nearly everyone reporters spoke to talked of rebuilding even though Coney Island had been ravaged by thirteen fires since 1893. Despite the heavy financial losses, no lives had been lost in any of them. "It appears," observed the *Tribune*, "that its amusements are more dangerous to human life than are its fires." Dreamland was "justly named," added the editor, "a fairy palace set in the night of New York's beautiful bay, a bit of wonderland to gaze upon with ever renewed appreciation from passing steamers and from the shores and hills of Staten Island, its outlines rising in airy, graceful lines and arches of light out of the dusk. Those who entered its gates found it a well ordered place of harmless tinsel and innocent frivolity." The *World* agreed that "the value to health of this incomparable city of summer plea-sure so close to the crowded tenements is not easily calculated. There is no reason," added the editor, "why Coney Island should not be as solidly and substantially built as English Brighton."[34]

WHILE THE CONEY ISLAND TRAGEDY PLAYED ITSELF out, the Giants enter-tained the Phillies at Hilltop Park. A trade with the Reds in February had brought the Phillies two key players, Dode Paskert and Hans Lobert, along with pitchers Jack Rowan and Fred Beebe. The bandy-legged Lobert was a solid third baseman who had hit .309 in 1910, while Paskert emerged as one of the finest outfielders of his generation and had batted .300 for the Reds. Both could run; Paskert swiped forty-six bases for the Reds, Lobert forty-one in only ninety-three games.[35]

Paskert proved a perfect fit between two outstanding outfielders. Hotheaded Sherry Magee, what a later generation called a five-tool player, was coming off a career season in which he snatched the batting title from Wagner while also leading the league in runs, runs batted in, on-base percentage, and slugging. His forty-nine stolen bases placed him fourth in the league. John Titus, a man so quiet that a teammate once said, "He doesn't even make any noise when he spits," was a lefty with an uncanny batting eye and an arm so strong that he accumulated more than twenty assists for seven straight seasons. He wore a thick mustache and chewed a toothpick when on the field. Now thirty-five, his average had slipped to .241 in 1910 but he was off to a strong start this year. To complement them Dooin also had fine young first baseman Fred Luderus, acquired from the Cubs in 1910.[36]

Pitching had long been the weakness of the Phillies, but Dooin had two invaluable additions to the staff. George Chalmers had come up late in 1910 and impressed enough in spring training to stick with the club. More important, Dooin unveiled a tall, sandy-haired, freckle-faced rookie named Grover Cleveland Alexander, who quickly earned the nickname "Alexander the Great." A farm boy from Nebraska, Alexander had pitched for Indianapolis, the same team that had sold Marquard to the Giants for a record price a year earlier. No one seemed to appreciate his talent: Indianapolis sold him to Syracuse, where he went 29-11. Dooin did not hesitate to compare him to a young Mathewson. The Phillies got Chalmers from Scranton for $3,000 and, almost as an afterthought, drafted Alexander from Syracuse for $500. The teams that overlooked him would all regret their oversight: By the end of his career Alexander finished in a dead heat with Mathewson with 373 victories. In 1911 he commenced what proved to be a record-breaking season for a newcomer.[37]

Painfully aware that Philadelphia had swept the first four games with the Giants, McGraw was eager to repay the wound in kind. Bugs Raymond took a 3–1 lead into the eighth inning, allowing only three hits. Then he yielded a walk and three straight singles, sending home the tying runs and leaving men on second and third with one out. McGraw summoned Mathewson. Shortstop Mickey Doolin smacked a long fly ball that looked certain to give the Phillies the lead, but Devore raced back, caught the ball, and uncorked a throw that nailed the runner at the plate for one of the game's six double plays. In the bottom half Devore beat out a bunt and Doyle let a pitch hit him. Dooin tried to catch Devore off second but his throw bounced off Doolin's knee into right field, moving the runners up to second and third. Dooin then brought in his prize rookie, Alexander, to face the Giants for the first time. Unimpressed, Snodgrass belted a single to left, his fourth of the game, sending both runners home in a 5–3 win.[38]

The win moved the Giants past the Phillies into first place. On the twenty-seventh, the day after the Coney Island fire, a record crowd estimated at twenty-two thousand, with several thousands more unable to get through the gates, filled the seats and spilled over onto the field to watch a duel between Earl Moore and Mathewson. They got their money's worth as Matty scattered eight hits and issued no walks in cruising to a 2–0 victory. During the game Philadelphia center fielder Harry Welchonce hit a dribbler down the first base line. Matty grabbed it just as the runner arrived and, unable to straighten up, stuck a shoulder into Welchonce and knocked him down. Magee, the next batter, threw his hat on the ground and started calling Mathewson names. "He is bad when irritated," noted Mathewson, "and tolerably easy to irritate." When Matty did not respond, Magee hit a slow grounder to the infield and made a wild slide at first in an obvious attempt to spike Merkle.[39]

After the obligatory Sunday day of rest the Giants had to play the series finale without McGraw, who was called away at the last minute because Blanche had fallen ill, and without Doyle or Meyers, both nursing injuries. Philadelphia rapped Doc Crandall for four runs in the second inning and coasted to a 6–4 triumph. The loss enabled the Cubs, who beat Pittsburgh, to ease into first place by half a game. "The lead in the National League," declared the *Times*, "is getting to be a Chinese puzzle. There is a new face peering over the pennant pinnacle every morning now."[40]

New York had one more series to play at Hilltop, this one against the team it loved to beat. In a Memorial Day doubleheader, cheered on by two large crowds, the Giants swept hapless Brooklyn 4–1 and 3–0 to move back into first place. In the first game Marquard pitched well enough to win despite giving up nine hits. Raymond started the nightcap despite feeling poorly and held Brooklyn at bay for four innings. In the fifth Wilson signaled McGraw that Raymond could not continue. "He got ptomaine poisoning from eating ice cream," Wilson explained with a smile. Ames took his place and held Brooklyn to two hits, one more than Raymond had allowed. The month ended as it had begun, with a rainout, and the Giants prepared to leave for an exhibition game in New Castle, Pennsylvania, on June 1.[41]

In May the Giants went 17-9 and stole sixty-five bases, good enough to give them a share of first place in what had become a four-team race. McGraw had seen enough to know that what the team lacked so far was consistency. Especially was this true of the pitching. Marquard and Raymond had shown promise; Drucke had been a disappointment. Ames and Wiltse had their moments, and Crandall seemed to do better in relief than as a starter. Becker and Fletcher needed more playing time, and McGraw was not yet sure how to make that happen. Wilson had shown him enough as a catcher to let Admiral Schlei go; he had appeared in only one game and that briefly. He also still had Grover Hartley and Hank Gowdy.

One thing was already clear: This season was not to be like any other in that the fight for the pennant extended beyond the usual suspects. Philadelphia had already made its mark, and St. Louis was showing signs of life. That would mean fewer easy games and more strain on the pitching staff, which still lacked a reliable second to Mathewson. But McGraw's emphasis on speed was paying off. Devore, Snodgrass, Merkle, and Murray led the way but everyone was running, and already the extra bases had paid off in wins.

STANDINGS ON MAY 31

	Won	Lost	Pct.		Won	Lost	Pct.
New York	25	14	.641	St. Louis	19	18	.513
Philadelphia	26	15	.635	Cincinnati	17	21	.448
Chicago	23	15	.603	Brooklyn	14	26	.350
Pittsburgh	23	17	.575	Boston	10	31	.244

CHAPTER 11

June: Dogfight

*"A club of base runners will do more to help a
pitcher win than a batting order of hard
hitters, I believe. Speed is the great thing in the
baseball of today . . . They must be fast starters,
fast runners, and fast thinkers."*
—CHRISTY MATHEWSON

*"The man who is his own worst enemy needs
no others."*
—BUGS RAYMOND

"THIS SEEMS TO BE A PARLOUS SEASON for the crippling or the incapacitating elsewise, of base ball stars," observed *Sporting News*. "The club that has not had one of its reliables on the hospital list is the exception, rather than the rule." The two most conspicuous casualties in the National League were Evers of the Cubs and John Titus of the Phillies, but other teams had suffered losses as well. In the American League the toll was more devastating. Cleveland had lost Napoleon Lajoie, Joe Jackson, and Cy Young along with the stunning death of Addie Joss. Boston missed Tris Speaker, New York Hal Chase, and Philadelphia Eddie Collins. Washington's Walter Johnson missed time because of illness, and Detroit had to do without its promising first baseman Del Gainor. So far the Giants had been spared the scourge of major casualties, but no one could predict how long that good fortune would last.[1]

For the Giants, June meant nearly a month on the road. Hilltop Park had served them well; the Giants compiled a record of 21-8 there. McGraw hoped that this first sojourn into the West would give him a better idea of what kind of team he had. The fact that they were so young was a mixed blessing, and it was much too early to see how they would respond to the pressure of a tight pennant race. The long trips by train created dynamics of their own and could be wearing, as he well knew. At least they would be staying in first-rate hotels and eat well, and he had few problem children on the roster compared with some years. The days of dressing at the hotel and riding to the park in open carriages that invited abuse were past.

The first stop was Chicago, one of three western cities that permitted Sunday baseball along with Cincinnati and St. Louis. McGraw did not go west with the team because Blanche still had not recovered and he did not want to leave her. Team captain Larry Doyle served as acting manager. The first game, and the whole series, proved to be a portent for the month. Playing under a glowering sky on a wet field only partly dried by liberal coats of sawdust, Bugs Raymond walked the first batter he faced, hit the second, and, after a sacrifice, issued another walk before young Jimmy Doyle cleared the bases with a ringing double. In the second inning he yielded two singles and a walk before being replaced by Ames, who allowed two runs before getting the Cubs out. In the third Doyle, still nursing a sore ankle, left the game in favor of Fletcher. For four innings King Cole held the Giants helpless atop a 6–0 lead.[2]

In the fifth the Giants got a single from Bridwell, two walks, a muffed grounder by Tinker, two more walks from Lew Richie, who replaced Cole, a double by Murray that cleared the bases, and another single by Bridwell, who was thrown out trying to take second. Seven runners crossed the plate, and Ames held on for a 7–6 victory.

The next day, before a huge overflow crowd, the Giants staked Marquard to a four-run lead in the first inning against an ineffective Miner Brown, who was ejected early along with Heinie Zimmerman. Ed Reulbach came in and surrendered a two-run double to Devlin. But Marquard fared little better. In the third, when the Cubs scored their third run, umpire Mal Eason tossed Meyers, Becker, and Raymond for protesting too strenuously. The Cubs tied the game in the sixth, and in the eighth Wildfire Schulte blasted a majestic grand-slam homer off the scoreboard in right field.[3]

The weirdness continued on Sunday as another overflow crowd braved the hottest June 4 on record. The Giants raced to a 5–2 lead against Brown and Larry Doyle was ejected for the third straight day. Despite making five errors, the Cubs tied the game in the eighth, thanks in part to Tinker's line drive off Wiltse's stomach, and won it with a run in the ninth. Art Devlin took charge of the team for the final game after Doyle was slapped with a three-game suspension for his antics. Once again strangeness prevailed. Mathewson and Harry McIntyre hooked up in a scoreless duel until the Cubs managed a run in the seventh. Brilliant fielding and errorless ball on both sides kept the game close until the ninth, when the Giants exploded for three singles, three doubles, a triple, and a walk for another seven-run inning and a 7–1 win. Rarely had a four-game set featured so many dramatic finishes. Neither Chance nor Evers played for the Cubs. Chance's headaches had grown worse, and he talked of consulting a specialist.[4]

On June 4 the Giants learned that the National Commission had approved Mike Donlin's petition for reinstatement. He had been suspended for failing to report to the team in the spring of 1909 and had not played since then. While he still belonged to the Giants, few observers expected McGraw to keep him for long. No one knew what shape he was in or whether he could regain his old skills after two years' absence. McGraw met him and sent him back to New York to discuss a contract with John Brush. He returned in time for the next series with Cincinnati but saw little action. The harsh truth was that McGraw liked his outfield and had no place for an older, slower Donlin.[5]

McGraw rejoined the team on the sixth for the first game in Pittsburgh and did not like what he saw. Already the pundits were observing that the team seemed lost when he was not present to direct them. "Every time the manager turns his head," said one, "a game is lost through the inability of his machine to move without him right at the throttle. Probably no other club in either big league is so thoroughly dependent upon its leader as the homeless Polo Grounders, and yet no one will deny that it is a good ball team."[6]

He planned to start Raymond, but Bugs was missing and no one had seen him on the train from Chicago. While a series of frantic telegrams flew back and forth to Chicago, Raymond strolled into the hotel lobby and wondered what the fuss was about. He claimed that the engineer on the train was an old friend of his, and Bugs decided to make the trip in the cab with him. Under threatening skies he allowed the Pirates four runs before giving way to Crandall after the fifth inning. To McGraw's chagrin the Giants played sloppy ball, making three errors along with Snodgrass and Murray watching a fly ball drop between them. New York botched a chance to score in the second when Merkle, leading off third, avoided being picked off by raising his shoulder in front of the catcher's throw and was called out for interference. Bridwell then hit what would have been a sacrifice fly. The Giants lost 4–3.[7]

The defeat bumped New York back to second place. The next day McGraw winced at another sloppy game in which the Pirates made seven errors and the Giants five miscues, all by Bridwell and Devlin. Pittsburgh also set a record with an astounding twenty-seven assists, one for each out, but New York drove Babe Adams from the box and Lou Drucke pitched well enough to win 9–4.[8]

On June 8 the Giants eked out a 4–3 victory in eleven innings, thanks in part to what the *Times* called "a carnival of sensational base running." They stole six bases, including two double steals, and were aided by four Pittsburgh errors. Bridwell redeemed himself by rapping four hits, and Doyle returned from exile. In the final game of the series Mathewson scattered eight hits and won 6–3 despite losing Chief Meyers in the third inning when he objected too strenuously to Bill Klem's calls behind the plate. The writers covering the Giants had begun to notice one outstanding feature of the team's efforts, the one on which McGraw had placed so much emphasis. "Speed of Giants Again Crushes Slumped Pirates," proclaimed the *World*. The *Times* was even more explicit: "It was a case of the badly slumped Pirates against a team that is just now hitting the fastest kind of a stride and is overwhelming teams with its speed on the bases."[9]

This was precisely the kind of game McGraw wanted his club to play. Altogether they stole nine bases against the Cubs, ten against the Pirates. They continued to run themselves out of rallies at times and got caught napping too often; Snodgrass in particular had a bad habit of being picked off base. But their speed rattled pitchers and forced infielders and outfielders alike to hurry their throws. Although bedeviled by inconsistency, Marquard and Raymond were at least winning some games. Drucke remained the biggest disappointment. He was involved in a curious lawsuit against the Interborough Rapid Transit Company, suing them for $2,500 on the grounds that while going to his seat he had been thrown against a stanchion violently enough to damage his pitching arm. His performance so far seemed to substantiate the claim.[10]

Although well seasoned in 1910, it was still a young team that needed close direction. Writer Hugh Fullerton complained that the game needed "more dash, less mechanical work, more brains by individuals, and fewer orders from the bench," but McGraw knew better. Some of his players had matured enough to think on their own and react instinctively to situations, but most needed constant attention to keep their focus in the right place. Snodgrass had his weaknesses but was a quick learner and had already mastered the art of getting hit by a pitch. "I had baggy uniforms," he recalled, "a baggy shirt, baggy pants—any ball thrown close inside, why I turned with it and half the time I wasn't really hit, just my uniform was nicked. Or the ball might hit your bat close to your hands and you'd fall down on your belly, and while you were down you'd try to make a red spot by squeezing your hand or something. If you had a good red spot there, the umpire might believe you."[11]

That, too, was vintage McGraw ball, as was the necessity for following orders. "The first thing that every manager teachers his players now is to obey absolutely the orders of the coacher," affirmed Mathewson. "When the batter was at the plate in a critical stage, he would stall and looked to the 'bench' for orders . . . He would tie his shoe or fix his belt, or find any little excuse to delay the game . . . A shoe lace has played an important role in many a Big League battle." None of the Giants had broken base running down into a science as Johnny Evers had done. "Hours spent in snapping split second watches," he declared, "have proved that every base runner, if properly held up at first base, ought to be caught stealing second base. Yet the same timing proves that not one pitched ball in ten, during actual play, is pitched, relayed by the catcher and handled by a second baseman in three seconds."[12]

Evers thought that base running was "fast becoming one of the lost arts of baseball . . . In the old days the motto of every manager was 'run and keep running; make the other fellow throw' . . . The modern manager recognizes the same thing. He knows that if he can make the other team throw, it is only a question of time until they throw away the game." Yet few managers did this in practice. The reason, thought Evers, was that "more and more every year, individual effort is being sacrificed to team work . . . The modern ball player has been so trained to team work that only a few with brain and daring pull off the brilliant individual feats that are necessary to win pennants." McGraw was the exception to this trend. He harnessed his players to team effort but even more to his will, telling them when to run and not chastising them when they were thrown out if they did what they were told. If, however, they ran on their own and were caught, they heard plenty from him unless he thought the situation called for their taking the chance.[13]

On the tenth, Cincinnati, which had been playing poorly, managed five runs off Marquard in one and a third innings and coasted to a 5–2 win. That same day news came that the Cubs, playing Boston at home, had pulled off a major trade with the Rustlers. Chicago shipped Johnny Kling, outfielder Al Kaiser, and pitchers Orlie Weaver and Hank Griffin to Boston in exchange for outfielder Wilbur Good, catcher Peaches Graham, outfielder Bill Collins, and pitcher Cliff Curtis. The trade gave the Rustlers a lineup that looked like a joint Cub-Giant alumni club. "This had to come," said Frank Chance. "I don't know when I'll be able to return to my position—perhaps I'll be out of it for months. That meant we had to have a first class baseman and outfielder if we want to win the pennant." His thinking was to put Good in the outfield to free Solly Hofman for first base, but most observers thought the outfield was stronger with Hofman in center.[14]

Wiltse celebrated Sunday ball in Cincinnati by blanking the Reds on six hits 5–0. That same day the Cubs swamped Boston 20–2 amid complaints from the latter's vice president that he had not been consulted on the trade and thought it a bad one. Johnny Evers got into the game for one inning but still was in no shape to play. According to one report, "He cannot stand more than 20 minutes without an overpowering dizziness." The Reds then pushed the Giants back to second place behind Bobby Keefe, who outpitched "Hard Luck" Ames 3–1. The next day Mathewson took the mound for the series finale and continued his mastery over the Reds, cruising to a 5–2 win behind a homer by Merkle and four stolen bases, three of them by Murray. In typical fashion Matty allowed the Reds eleven hits and even three walks but kept them from scoring when it counted.[15]

Both teams had an off day on the fourteenth, and Brooklyn was in town to play the next series with the Reds. Although McGraw was not pleased to have gained only a split with the lowly Reds, he agreed with the other managers to take their teams together to the Latonia Race Track to play the ponies. McGraw was reported to have won $942, Reds manager Clark Griffith about $400, and Bill Dahlen $225 on what was hailed as "Baseball Day" at the park. Most of the players pocketed a few dollars as well. That evening the Giants boarded a train for St. Louis and the final series of their western swing. They were greeted by a St. Louis heat wave with temperatures in the mid-nineties at game time. Heat was one thing that could slow a running team down as the season wore on. In the first game the Giants stole only one base but Crandall shut the Cardinals out 3–0, beating Slim Sallee in a game that took only an hour and thirty-seven minutes.[16]

Bresnahan took the defeat harder than usual. After the game a few of his players had gone out on the town. When Bresnahan found out, he suspended two of them and fined two others "for leading the strenuous life." Still stewing over the loss and the behavior of his players, he punched a hotel night clerk in the face and was hauled off to the police station, where matters were worked out. McGraw could sympathize, if only because his number one problem child had finally driven him to the brink.[17]

The second game turned into a fiasco for the Giants. Drucke started and walked the first three batters before McGraw dismissed him in favor of Raymond, who hit a batter and surrendered a single and sacrifice fly that, along with an error by Bridwell, gave St. Louis four runs in the first inning. He calmed down until the fifth, when he gave up four more runs. When Marquard replaced him in the seventh, no one suspected that the "Human Insect," as the writers called Bugs, had just pitched his last inning in the major leagues. In all, McGraw used sixteen players—something almost unheard-of—in an effort to salvage the game, but New York lost 8–4. After the game he slapped Raymond with a $200 fine and an indefinite suspension for "breaking training rules and not being in condition to pitch effectively."[18]

Although it should have been an important story for the writers, only the *World* reported McGraw's action. Since spring training the writers had cooperated with McGraw in concealing the fact that Raymond's rehabilitation had not gone as smoothly as everyone had been led to believe. "His fondness for companionship was his downfall," McGraw concluded later. "I think he knew every man and boy in every little town we ever played in as well as in the big league cities." Raymond had an endless bag of tricks for getting drinks. McGraw tried cutting off his money supply and warning writers never to lend him money, but somehow Bugs always found a way. A sympathetic Blanche referred to him as "a spitball pitcher who used 86-proof saliva."[19]

Although there had been other incidents, the first major lapse in spring training occurred on the team's visit to Dallas for an exhibition game. The hotel always served cocktails with Sunday night dinner but McGraw told the steward to take them all back to the kitchen. Raymond knew the steward and went to pay him a visit during dinner. Once in the kitchen, he spied the trays of drinks and started sampling them until he had gone through more than a dozen. The next day it rained and Raymond was nowhere to be found. He finally turned up around midnight, saying he had been with some old railroad friends. McGraw had a detective follow Raymond for twenty-four hours and give him a detailed account. The detective reported on only twelve hours, during which time Raymond downed forty-eight glasses of beer, a peck of pretzels, and eight Bermuda onions.[20]

McGraw was in a quandary. He could expose Raymond to the writers, who had been praising his recovery, or take one more shot at reforming him. "I didn't expect to keep him entirely sober, of course," he reasoned, "but I figured if I could keep him in half-way condition he could win some ball games for us at the beginning of the season." He hit upon the clever device of rousing the writers from bed to act as a jury hearing Raymond's case. The jurors included Sam Crane, Sid Mercer, Bozeman Bulger, Damon Runyon, and some others. "I want you to hear the evidence," he told them, "and then it will be up to you to decide whether you shall expose his weakness in your papers and tell the world that he's no good, or whether you will overlook it and give him one more chance."[21]

Raymond sat with downcast, bloodshot eyes, unshaven face, and tousled hair while McGraw read the detective's report. The jurors took careful notes. Asked for his response, Raymond said, "It's a damned lie, Mac! . . . Of course, I might've had a coupla dozen glasses of beer, but I'm tellin' you it's a lie—I ain't eat an onion in seven months!" At that the jury and McGraw burst into laughter. Then the jury voted solemnly to say nothing if Raymond would promise to swear off the booze. "Bet your sox I will!" Raymond cried. "Fellows, I'm through." Thus acquitted, he celebrated by going out and getting drunk that night, but the writers stayed mum on his antics. He fell off the wagon again in Atlanta but straightened up enough to pitch some good games into June.

But his behavior was growing as erratic as his pitching. During one game McGraw handed him a new ball and sent him out to the bullpen behind the bleachers to warm up. When he did not return in half an hour, McGraw sent the batboy to fetch him. He was nowhere to be found. The trainer joined the search and reported that Raymond was sitting in an Eighth Avenue saloon, drinking beer. He had traded the new ball for drinks. After his shabby performance against St. Louis, McGraw concluded that his usefulness had come to an end. The suspension had the effect of exiling him permanently from organized baseball. He could play only for New York, and McGraw would not take him back. Thus ended the career of a pitcher of whom even Chief Meyers, who did not like to catch his spitball, said, "That fellow can do more tricks with a baseball than any man in the world."[22]

Mathewson took the mound for the third game against St. Louis and allowed no hits until the seventh inning, when a single and a triple by Steve Evans plated a run. But the Cardinals had cadged a run in the first when pesky Miller Huggins got hit by a pitch, stole second, went to third on a errant throw by Meyers, and scored on an accidental squeeze play when Matty had no play at home. Bob Harmon, having what proved the best season of his career, pitched one of the best games of his career, shutting out the Giants until the ninth, when they managed a lone run. Harmon gave up three hits, Mathewson only two. It did not help that Bridwell was sick and Art Fletcher nursed a charley horse, forcing McGraw to play Doc Crandall at shortstop.[23]

In the final game the Cardinals pummeled Wiltse for fourteen hits and grabbed an early 3–0 lead, but the Giants fought back with ten hits and the gift of eight walks to prevail 5–4 when Murray slammed a two-run double in the ninth. The first western swing concluded with another split series and one lost pitcher. McGraw would actually be short two pitchers, since Crandall had to play shortstop for another four games. For the rest of the month the Giants figured to have easier pickings with seven away games against Boston and Brooklyn and a three-game set at home against Boston. They headed homeward in second place, a game and a half behind the Cubs, with a record of 9-7 on the trip. The good news was that when they finally played at home on the twenty-eighth, it would really be home. Although far from finished, work on the Polo Grounds had progressed to a point where games could be played there.[24]

After the western swing he deemed successful, McGraw talked openly about winning the pennant. "We have won a lot of games that the other fellows thought they had cinched," he said. "Our pitchers are getting better right along and we have kept up front without calling upon Matty to pitch out of his turn. This is a great advantage, for 'Big Six' will be able to go in top form during the months of July and August when the race will be decided. Yes, we ought to cop, with Pittsburg and Chicago fighting it out for second." Boasting it might have been, but it was also McGraw issuing a challenge to his own team to fulfill it.[25]

FRED TENNEY HAD NAMED JOHNNY KLING AS Boston's new captain as the cellar dwellers welcomed the Giants to town. His presence behind the plate helped Al Mattern wage a tight pitching duel with Marquard. With the score deadlocked at 1–1 going into the ninth, Devore singled, stole second when Kling could find no one to throw the ball to, and tallied the winning run when Doyle hit one over the head of Big Jeff Pfeffer, a pitcher filling in at center field. Things went more smoothly the next day when Mathewson, bolstered by three first-inning runs, stifled the Rustlers 4–0 on seven hits to run his record to 12–3. In the final game, however, Boston got its revenge in the ninth on a walkoff home run by Harry Steinfeldt. In doing so he kept his old team, the Cubs, atop the standings by half a game despite their losing to the Pirates 12–3.[26]

Frank Chance was struggling to keep his patchwork team afloat. "With his regular lineup shot to pieces and his pitchers going at a pace that is anything but satisfactory," observed the *Chicago Tribune*, "the P. L. [Peerless Leader] is working might and main to hang on to the lead which has been gained by some of the best baseball ever played by a crippled squad." Hofman was the latest to join the procession of wounded. "Chance has been experimenting," added the *Tribune*, "buying and swapping players until it takes one man nearly all his time to keep track of the P. L.'s operations on the baseball board of trade." Pittsburgh was in town to play the Cubs, and Frank Clarke displayed his own troubles, most notably at first base. Fred Hunter, brought up from Kansas City "touted as the best there ever was," had been put on waivers. John Flynn was the latest candidate, and rumor had Wagner moving to the position.[27]

On the twenty-third, while the nation followed in the papers the elaborate coronation of England's George V, the Giants traveled to Washington Park for their last road series against Brooklyn. Having won nine straight from the Superbas, McGraw's men found themselves locked up in a pitching duel between Wiltse and Nap Rucker, each of whom yielded only four hits. No Giant reached third base, and no one scored until Brooklyn broke the curse by pushing across a run in the bottom of the ninth for the win. Doyle was spiked in the first inning but managed to limp through the game. He had little choice; no substitute was available except perhaps McGraw himself. Rarely had Dahlen's men played a better game, and it proved to be their lone glimmer of glory in the series.[28]

In Cincinnati a furious ninth-inning rally by the Cardinals fell one run short and precipitated an ugly incident. With four runs in and the tying run on third, Bobby Keefe threw the batter two strikes. From the coaching box Bresnahan protested loudly that the second one had been a balk. While he and the batter argued, Keefe tossed a third strike and Bill Klem called the batter out. An infuriated Bresnahan rushed Klem, who stopped him with a fist to the face. The players separated them before any more damage could be done. An embarrassed Tom Lynch, who had worked so hard to protect his umpires, fined Klem $50, saying that he "forgot the most essential part of an umpire's duty, that of keeping his temper."[29]

Brooklyn's largest crowd of the season, an estimated eighteen thousand, turned out next day to watch Mathewson subdue the Superbas 7–4 in one of his workmanlike performances that saw him flit in and out of trouble. He also contributed three hits, an honor he shared with Murray, and injected a rare moment of humor in the third inning when Zack Wheat swung so hard at a fadeaway pitch that his bat flew out to the mound. Mathewson fielded it cleanly and tossed it to Merkle at first. Not in the least amused, Wheat swatted the next pitch he saw for a double. The victory edged New York back into first place as the Cubs dropped their third in a row to Pittsburgh. Doyle was in no shape to play, but Bridwell pronounced himself ready to go and played shortstop with Crandall shifting to second base.[30]

That same day in Winsted, Connecticut, Bugs Raymond was scheduled to pitch a game for the local team against Torrington. Arriving in town the night before, he amused a crowd in the street with his antics and kept most of the guests at his hotel awake for much of the night before friends finally got him to bed. Awakened shortly before the game, he fell back into his routine of pranks and pitched only seven innings before being removed. The locals made it clear that he would not be invited back.[31]

Rain washed out the Monday game, forcing the Giants and Superbas to play a doubleheader on June 27, which New York swept. As the *Times* observed, the club "conclusively demonstrated to thousands of home rooters, reinforced by many thousands of tube travelers, that it is as easy to take the Dodgers' measure twice in the same afternoon as it is to chalk up a single victory." Marquard took the first game 6–3, Ames the second 7–1. In the second game, after rolling up six runs in the fifth inning, McGraw continued his recent practice of emptying the bench by sending Crandall, Becker, Wilson, and Donlin in for four starters. Few teams had a bench strong enough to enjoy such a luxury.[32]

On the twenty-eighth the team finally got a close look at the progress made on the Polo Grounds as they prepared to make their first appearance there since the fire. Billy Gray, the team secretary, invited the baseball writers to an automobile tour of the park, followed by lunch at the Claremont Hotel. They saw an enlarged grandstand over a thousand feet in length and eighty feet high to the balustrade, shaped like a horseshoe. The massive steel-and-concrete structure extended back twenty-five feet farther than the old one and contained thirty-two rows of seats compared to twenty-one in the wooden one, yet the rows were raked in such a way that someone in the last row could get a better view than a person in the middle of the old stands. The upper deck had yet to be finished; the club hoped to complete it before the Giants returned from their next western swing. The most glaring unfinished item was the lack of a roof.[33]

The southeast section of the grandstand did not yet have chairs, and the Giants planned to open it to standees if the crowd was large enough. The work of replacing the bleachers with steel-and-concrete versions remained to be done after the season ended, as did all the finishing work. "The new stadium will be faced with a decorative frieze in the façade containing a series of allegorical treatments in bas relief in polychrome," said a club statement, "and the box tiers are designed upon the lines of the royal boxes of the Colosseum [sic] in Rome, and pylons in the Roman style will flank the horseshoe on either side." Like the team itself, the park was a work in progress, exciting visitors with its promise.[34]

Hapless Boston had the dubious honor of being the first team to play the Giants in their refurbished lair. Summer heat had descended on the city, roasting not only those in the bleachers but everyone in the uncovered grandstand as well. "It was so hot yesterday," reported the *Times*, "that many persons were fearful that the fire was still burning." Thanks to the ministrations of John Murphy, the field itself was in beautiful shape, the grass a sparkly emerald green. A pleased John Brush took his usual place in his automobile in deep right field. Surprisingly, only about six thousand fans by one estimate and ten thousand by another ventured to the park for the opener.[35]

Before the game, friends of Mike Donlin presented him with eight large floral pieces, and pictures were taken of both teams arranged around them. On this first trip back to the Polo Grounds, Donlin remained a fan favorite even though he played little. Fittingly, McGraw tapped Mathewson to pitch what some billed as "second opening day." He needed little help, breezing to a 3–0 win in his usual style, scattering nine hits and walking nobody. He also had to break in a new umpire named Ralph Frary, who did well enough to arouse no protests. "It is about as hard for Matty to beat Boston," intoned the *Times*, "as it is for you to eat strawberry shortcake."[36]

Doc Crandall returned to his pitching chores the next day in a game that revealed what the *Tribune* liked to call "the fine Italian hand of McGraw." Tenney chose to start a rookie southpaw named Eddie McTigue. Aware that the lanky hurler was prone to wildness, McGraw ordered his troops to take a full complement of pitches without swinging. As a result, eight Giants struck out without a murmur and the team got only two hits through the first five innings. In the sixth McGraw told them to start swinging at the first pitch. They responded with a vengeance, shelling McTigue and his successor, Buster Brown, for nine hits and nine runs en route to a 10–4 win. After the outburst, Donlin was sent in to replace Snodgrass and managed to get a hit, steal a base, and score a run, to the delight of the fans.[37]

The month ended on a sour note as the Giants suffered their first loss in the refurbished Polo Grounds. "Fred Tenney's Forlorn Hopes came to life on the Polo Grounds yesterday," smirked the *Press*, "and startled 6,000 sons and daughters of Old Pop Knickerbocker by throwing a jolt into McGraw's pennant chasers by a score of 7 to 4." Boston's lineup consisted of two ex-Giants and seven former Cubs. Mindful of the McGraw approach, the *Sun* observed that "the psychological moment business which the Giants have been able to spring on many an opponent, this thing of concentrating the attack when the other side is about to or near a break didn't work out today."[38]

During the fifth inning some special guests of the management arrived to take their seats in the new stand behind third base. A dozen members of the baseball team from Waseda University in Tokyo, one of several Japanese teams that had come to the States to play American universities and other amateur clubs, took a keen interest in the game even though they did not see the home team at its best. Baseball had already been popular in Japan for several years, and its university teams looked forward to tours in the United States, where they were well received.[39]

In Cincinnati that same day Frank Chance, concerned by his team's recent poor performance, inserted himself into the lineup and received a warm round of applause. "I don't know how long I will be able to stand the pace, owing to my headache and the nervous affliction which recently seized upon my feet," he admitted, "but I'm going to try to stop our losing streak." He also intended to get his pitchers "into form where they can go the whole route. This thing of 'blowing up' in the sixth and seventh innings will have to stop." Although Chance went hitless, the Cubs rode Mordecai Brown to a 3–2 victory that day. However, after practicing with the team under a broiling sun the next day, Chance started toward the bench and collapsed. He was partially revived, then taken to the clubhouse to await a doctor.[40]

Giants players walking along train tracks during 1911 spring training. (National Baseball Hall of Fame Library, Cooperstown, N.Y.)

From on high: the Polo Grounds from Coogan's Bluff.

Speed merchants: the 1911 New York Giants.

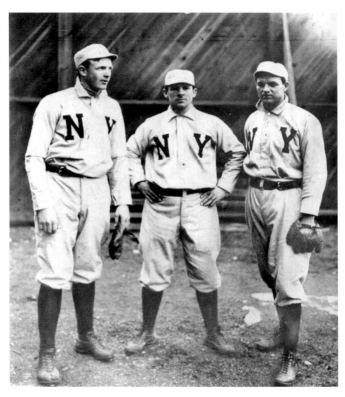

A king with two aces: Christy Mathewson, John McGraw, and Joe
McGinnity. (National Baseball Hall of Fame Library, Cooperstown, N.Y.)

Man of controversy: New York Giants owner John T. Brush.

Left to right: John McGraw, John T. Brush, Blanche McGraw, concession king Harry Stevens, and Mary Stevens. (National Baseball Hall of Fame Library, Cooperstown, N.Y.)

Idol for all seasons: the incomparable Christy Mathewson.

Contrast in styles: Ty Cobb and Christy Mathewson.

Late bloomer: the unpredictable Rube Marquard.

The first fireman: James "Doc" Crandall.

Failed experiment: Arthur "Bugs" Raymond.

Hard luck: Leon "Red" Ames.

Man of character: George "Hooks" Wiltse.

Slow but steady: the hard-hitting John "Chief" Meyers.

Man for all positions: Roger Bresnahan here behind the plate.

erated but unbowed: Fred Merkle bats during the 1911 World Series.

Honest showboat: the peerless umpire, Bill Klem.

Umpire Hank O'Day, who seemed to find every controversial play.

John "Red" Murray, a key piece in McGraw's 1911 machine.

Big hit: Fred Snodgrass, who made an art of getting hit by pitches.

Finishing touch: Art Fletcher, the final piece of McGraw's machine.

"Laughing Larry" Doyle, the spirit of the 1911 Giants.

Twin warriors: John McGraw and John "Chief" Meyers.

Curtain call: Mike Donlin and wife Mabel Hite.

Return engagement: Mike Donlin welcomed back to the Polo Grounds.

Two chiefs meet: John Meyers and Charles Albert Bender.

Peerless leader: Frank Chance at bat.

The "Tall Tactician": Connie Mack.

Matty's master: Mordecai "Three Finger" Brown.

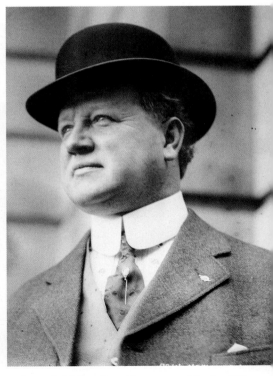

Second fiddler: Brooklyn owner Charles Ebbets.

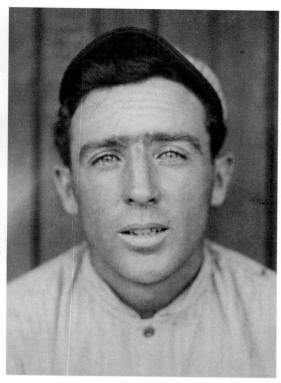

Chicago crab: the brainy but
surly Johnny Evers.

Matty's nemesis: Cub shortstop Joe Tinker.

adership personified: the Giants follow McGraw off the field.

The National Baseball Commission, January 1909. Left to right: Harry Pulliam, president of the National League; August Herrmann, president of the Cincinnati Reds and unofficial commissioner of baseball; Ban Johnson, president of the American League; and J. E. Bruce, secretary to the commission.

Players inspect fire damage at the Polo Grounds, April 14, 1911.

McGraw's manor: the Polo Grounds.

Cheap seats: the right-field bleachers at the Polo Grounds.

Getting the word out: Telegraphers' Row at the Polo Grounds.

Fans lining up at the Polo Grounds at 7 A.M. to buy 1911 World Series tickets.

Dr. H. H. Hines, the Cincinnati club physician, ordered him back to the hotel for rest. An examination convinced him that Chance had a blood clot on the brain that might prove fatal if he got too excited. He told the Peerless Leader that his playing days were over and that he should confine himself to managing from the bench if he wanted to stay alive. Fiercely competitive as he was, Chance conceded that he was in no shape to play ball. Although he put in a few token appearances in future years, he was done as a player and somewhat limited as a manager as well. The *Times* hailed him as "a born fighter, a determined, able, and magnetic leader of men, who could always inspire his men with extraordinary enthusiasm, get the best work out of them, and always hold their good will . . . His departure from the field will leave a big void in baseball."[41]

New York closed out the month with a 16-10 record and fifty-one stolen bases. The club had lost Bugs Raymond and regained Mike Donlin. Art Fletcher was ready to return to duty, giving McGraw the spare infielder he badly needed. For all their big innings and late-game heroics in June, the Giants had not hit well. At the month's end the team was batting a combined .248, putting them seventh in the league ahead of only Brooklyn. Four teams had scored more runs, although no one came close to New York's 138 stolen bases. Chief Meyers at .318 was the only regular hitting above .300, although Doyle hovered nearby at .296; Merkle at .251 and Snodgrass at .250 brought up the rear. Mathewson's record stood at an impressive 13-3, second only to the Philadelphia sensation Grover Cleveland Alexander's 15-3. No other Giant pitcher came close to matching Matty, although Marquard was a pleasant surprise at 6-3.[42]

The larger question for McGraw was whether the Giants could maintain the pace. He was painfully aware of how thin his pitching had become in the past few years as the season wore on. Drucke had disappointed, Ames and Wiltse had their well-known limitations, and Crandall could only do so much. As the dog days of summer approached, he still had no answer to the question of who would emerge as a strong second starter to Matty. The pennant race remained a dogfight between five teams, something the league had not seen in many years. By month's end the Phillies, far from fading, actually shoved themselves into second place by a hair.

Even Cincinnati could not be taken for granted. Although six games back of the fifth-place Cardinals, the Reds' team batting average of .264 was only a point behind Pittsburgh's league-leading .265 and a point ahead of Philadelphia. If their wobbly pitching came to life, they could inject themselves into the pennant chase. McGraw realized that first place would remain a short-term rental space for weeks to come, and that the competition for it would once again be a war of attrition. The key question was whether a team built around youth and speed was suited to such a contest.

STANDINGS ON JUNE 30

	Won	Lost	Pct.		Won	Lost	Pct.
New York	41	23	.641	St. Louis	35	29	.547
Philadelphia	39	25	.609	Cincinnati	29	35	.453
Chicago	38	26	.593	Brooklyn	22	41	.349
Pittsburgh	37	26	.587	Boston	14	50	.219

CHAPTER 12

July: Dog Days

"The race is becoming a grind to the mathematical intellect, and if the see-saw argument keeps up the season will end with three or four teams matching pennies for the streamer."
— THE NEW YORK TIMES

"The two major leagues are now engaged in their third intersectional series—an exchange which is bound to have the greatest effect upon the ultimate results. Especially is this the case in the wonderfully close National League race, in which we have now five real contenders owing to the remarkable advance of the Cardinals, who for a month have played the most consistent ball in the league."
— SPORTING LIFE

THE DOG DAYS ARRIVED EARLY IN THE summer of 1911, blanketing New York with a killer heat wave during the first two weeks of July. The city had not suffered a major heat wave since 1901 and nothing like this one since records started being kept in 1871. The temperature on July 2 reached 94.5 degrees, the highest recorded mark for that date. For the next ten days or so the weather became front-page news, with some papers printing grim lists of those who had died or collapsed from the heat. The discomfort stretched across the nation from the East Coast to western Kansas. Between July 2 and July 6 Chicago ranged between 98 and 102 degrees. A temperature of 87 at eight A.M. on July 3 gave New York the dubious distinction of being the hottest spot in the United States. That day a hundred people died from the heat across the country, ten of them in New York, where the mercury hit 96 degrees. Chicago had a staggering fifty-one deaths, Philadelphia and Pittsburgh twelve each. By one count heat-related causes killed 431 Americans between July 1 and July 5 alone.[1]

The instruments of the Weather Bureau were located in a tower atop the Whitehall Building in Battery Place. The *Times* had a thermometer in the lobby of its building to record temperatures at street level. On July 3 that instrument displayed readings ranging from 99 to 106. The national holiday became the hottest Fourth on record at 93 officially but as high as 103 on the street. Chicago reported 101, Topeka, Kansas, 106, Atchison, Kansas, 108. The casualty list mounted steadily, not only of people but of animals, especially workhorses. During the first six days of the heat wave, horses, many of them in harness, fell dead across the city at the rate of more than a hundred a day. So many died that complaints rolled in because the city could not remove the carcasses fast enough; the work required horse-drawn wagons. Many owners kept their horses off the street and sprayed them with water, the same treatment given to the menagerie at the Central Park Zoo.[2]

People desperate for relief flocked to the seaside or parks and slept on balconies, in parks, or even in alleyways to escape their stifling hovels. No one suffered more than the mass of humanity crammed into the tenements on the Lower East Side, the most crowded space on the planet with eight hundred people per acre in some city blocks. The small, poorly ventilated apartments teemed with flies and dirt blown in through doors and windows left open in hopes of catching a wisp of breeze. With the dirt came the stench of sweating, unwashed bodies, garbage, sewage, and manure from the horses, all of it amplified by the heat. "It sizzles in the neighborhood of Hester Street on a sultry day," observed one writer, and it also rang with the interminable noise of clopping hooves, bellowing peddlers, crying babies, the rumble of elevated trains, and a hundred other street dissonances floating in the still, oppressive air. A huge demand arose for pure milk and ice to save babies in the tenements.[3]

New York had more than a hundred thousand tenement buildings, with twice that number of rooms that had no windows. About a quarter of their occupants lived five or more to a room, sleeping on floors, chairs, pallets, or even doors taken off their hinges. Many slept in shifts, depending on their work hours. Women, who were the backbone of the city's immigrant work-force, especially in the clothing industry, often toiled seventy or eighty hours a week for pitiful sums and took home piecework at night. For those trapped in these hellholes a heat wave seemed like a preview of Hades itself.[4]

Throughout the day and well into the night the streets of Manhattan rang with the clang of ambulances summoned to help those who had fainted from the heat. Thousands fled to the beaches or rode the ferry to Staten Island, Coney Island, West Point, or Rockaway just to get a sea breeze. An estimated four hundred thousand people flocked to Coney Island on the Fourth and another two hundred thousand to Staten Island. Those hoping for relief at the beach found instead sand that was hot enough to blister. That night some thirty thousand slept on the beach at Coney Island under the watchful eye of twenty-five patrolmen called out by the island's police station. Steeplechase Park opened its beach, pier, and pavilions to mothers with children for the night. The owner hired extra watchmen to stand guard over them. Despite a growing water shortage, the city filled park fountains with water and the police allowed children to splash away in them.

By the fifth, bathing clothes had become commonplace on the city streets, at least for men. Businessmen with offices on high floors hurried to them in hopes of catching breezes at higher altitude. A brief shower on the evening of the sixth did nothing to lift the heat and humidity. That morning thousands of subway riders found themselves trapped in their airless cars for up to half an hour during the morning rush because of a signal malfunction. As the death toll continued to mount, the heat wave broke suddenly on Friday afternoon the seventh with the thermometer dropping ten degrees in half an hour. But a day later the lethal heat returned and lasted through July 12. That night the humidity dipped rapidly and a southwesterly wind brought relief to the city. Altogether the heat wave killed at least 221 people in the city while making life miserable for everyone else.

"The heat wave is broken," proclaimed the *World* on July 13. "There were twenty-nine deaths today. Cooling showers are imminent. The pavements yesterday were strewn with the bodies of dead and dying horses, overcome by the heat. The weather forecaster promises breezes from the north. The parks were filled to overflowing last night with men, women, and little babies panting for a breath of fresh air."[5]

Playing ball in extreme heat presented challenges of its own, especially for a team that liked to run. Flannel uniforms grew heavy with enough sweat and dirt to slow the fastest man down. The merciless sun made it difficult to concentrate in the field, and everyone seemed to move more slowly in air so heavy that it was hard to breathe. Tempers frayed, both on and off the field. Fans coming to the Polo Grounds had to endure constant roasting in the seats still unprotected by a roof. Sound judgment was impaired by fatigue as the game wore on. Every movement took more energy that grew more challenging to summon. Each player had his own ways of dealing with the heat, but no one had endured a spell like this. Whatever their discomfort, the teams had no choice but to play. The show must go on.

On July 1, the Giants brushed aside Boston 9–1 in the final game of that series. Josh Devore, who had been slumping and had fanned three times when he last faced Al Mattern, smacked a home run on Mattern's first pitch, hit another one along with a double, got hit by a pitch, and scored four runs. "I guess that pays part of the score," he said to Kling while crossing the plate after his first homer. Although Marquard won easily, he yielded twelve hits and had constantly to pitch out of trouble. The next day in St. Louis, Slim Sallee shut out the Pirates and beaned Fred Clarke, knocking him unconscious. Coming only a day after Frank Chance collapsed, the casualty list of playing managers doubled. The loss to Pittsburgh was a severe one. As of June 29, Clarke was batting a hefty .351, second in the league only to Wagner.[6]

Before their long home stand against the western clubs the Giants went to Philadelphia, where it was just as hot, for five games, including back-to-back doubleheaders. In the single game on the third, fifteen thousand fans cheered raucously as Mathewson wilted in the heat, allowing thirteen hits and seven runs in a 7–3 loss. In the morning and afternoon doubleheader the next day the Phillies seemed far more alert and less affected by the heat as they swept New York to claim first place for themselves while shoving the Giants down to third. "It was simply a Philadelphia day," sighed the *Tribune*, "and nothing could stop it."[7]

An even larger and noisier crowd turned up for the afternoon game. Urged on by their fans, the Phillies battered Doc Crandall for fourteen hits and seven runs before knocking him out—literally—in the seventh inning when Red Dooin hit a shot off his forehead that traveled far enough into left field for Devore to narrowly miss catching it. Crandall lay out cold for a brief time, then was able to walk to the clubhouse. Making his first start against the Giants, Alexander did a fine imitation of Mathewson, scattering nine hits and four walks while keeping them at bay until Merkle stung him with a three-run homer in the seventh. By then he enjoyed a 7–2 lead, thanks in part to two home runs and a single by Fred Luderus. "The heat was severe on the players," observed the aptly named *Sun*. "In the closing rounds Paskert, Dooin, Bridwell, Devlin and Doyle staggered back and forth to their positions hardly able to walk."[8]

On the fifth both teams faced another doubleheader on a scorching day with their pitching staffs in tatters. Desperate for a win after three straight losses to Philadelphia, McGraw elected to bring back Mathewson for a rematch with Burns. It quickly became obvious that Matty did not do well in extreme heat as he surrendered fourteen hits, four of them by Paskert, and lost 6–4. The only consolation was the appearance in the ninth inning of the doughty Crandall, who had recovered enough to pinch-hit for Mathewson and drive in a run with a single. Desperate to avoid a sweep, McGraw was at a loss for someone to pitch the second game. Marquard walked up to him and said, "Give me a chance." Without hesitating, McGraw sent him to the mound. Marquard rewarded him with a sharp six-hit performance and the Giants came alive to flatten Philadelphia 10–1 with an eleven-hit barrage. Having stolen a total of six bases in the first four games, New York swiped seven in salvaging the final game of the series.[9]

"There on that sweltering July afternoon, when everything steamed in the blistering heat, a pitcher was born again," said Mathewson. "Marquard had found himself." The long hours spent with Wilbert Robinson in spring training and after had begun to pay dividends. He had drilled Marquard on mixing his pitches, improving his location, and, above all, learning the grooves and weaknesses of every batter. "Robinson was the coacher, umpire, catcher and batter rolled into one," said Mathewson.[10]

As the club returned wearily to New York to welcome the visiting Cubs in the intense heat, Sid Mercer observed that "the Philadelphia experience just melted the vitality out of them and wore their dispositions to a frayed edge." The Giants occupied third place yet stood only a game behind the Phillies and half a game behind Chicago. Pittsburgh was four games out and St. Louis a half game behind the Pirates. The race still belonged to anyone.[11]

Despite the last win over Philadelphia, it was obvious to McGraw that the Giants were not playing well—that they were, if anything, more inconsistent than they had been earlier in the season. In searching for weaknesses that might be improved, his eye fell on Art Devlin. The tough veteran was working as hard as ever but struggling in the heat. Pitching also worried him considerably. The Philadelphia series had forced him to use Mathewson three times in one week, twice in three days, and Matty had not responded well, losing both games and being hit hard. The combination of extra games and unprecedented heat could sink any pitching staff. For all his faults Raymond had given McGraw innings, and no one had yet stepped up to replace him. The one bright spot was Marquard, who seemed finally to be overcoming his inconsistency. McGraw sensed that July might well be the pivotal month in the season, if only because the rest of it would be spent playing western teams, first at home and then at their parks.

THE HEAT THAT ENVELOPED THE POLO GROUNDS was choking, and the lack of a roof kept the crowd small for so crucial a series. Chance donned a uniform for the first time since his collapse but, still plagued by severe headaches, stayed on the bench for the game. Evers, looking "rather pale and weak" according to one writer, was on the field during the Cubs' practice and shook hands with McGraw but did nothing more than coach. As it turned out, he wasn't needed. Heinie Zimmerman, his replacement, belted three hits, including a home run, to lead Chicago to a 6–2 victory over a logy Giants team. "When the two teams came on the field," said the *Tribune*, "it was a toss-up as to which appeared the most lifeless. The sun beat down mercilessly." The slim crowd of perhaps five thousand in the roofless oven watched Hooks Wiltse yield ten hits before being chased in the seventh. "It is not Frank Chance's smoothly oiled machine that made up the Cubs of today . . . Nevertheless, it is a hard hitting, energetic ball team," observed the *Times*.[12]

A brief respite from the heat with threatening skies on Friday the seventh seemed to galvanize the slumping Giants, especially Red Ames. "It has been strongly intimated in certain quarters that Leon Ames was through and was threatened with the discard by the waiver route," said the *World*. If so, he earned a reprieve by blanking Chicago 5–0 without allowing a runner to reach third. As a bonus he slammed a triple over Frank Schulte's head in the second inning to drive in two runs before a small crowd. Saturday brought out a huge crowd that was rewarded by another stellar performance from Marquard, who allowed nine hits but stranded eleven Chicago runners and for good measure poled a home run over the right field wall in the third inning. It proved to be the only one of his long career. Abetted by two of Chicago's four errors, the Giants scored four runs in the sixth en route to a 5–2 victory. The kranks, crowed the *World*, "all realized—from the fan octogenarian to the fan infantile—they all realized that yesterday's victory means that once again, dear friends, We are on TOP!"[13]

Once again the stay was brief. After the usual Sunday day of rest, the Cubs handed Mathewson his third straight defeat 3–2, thanks largely to four errors by the New York infield, two of them by Bridwell, whose fumble in the tenth inning allowed the winning run to score. "There were holes in the Giants' infield defense . . . big enough to drive a hay wagon through," commented the *Times*. Matty gave up nine hits but pitched well enough to win most games; however, his mates did little with Richie except for a home run by Fletcher. While the Cubs escaped town with a split in the series and a tenuous hold on first place, St. Louis took three out of four games from the Phillies. "The real sensation of the season in the big leagues," said the *Press*, "is the St. Louis Cardinals."[14]

As the season neared its halfway mark, a mere three and a half games separated the first-place Cubs from the fifth-place Cardinals. The Giants occupied third place only a game behind Philadelphia. In the American League Connie Mack's Athletics had finally gained first place over the Tigers despite the sensational batting of Ty Cobb, whose average on July 5 stood at an incredible .444. Behind him came Joe Jackson of Cleveland at .384 and Eddie Collins of the A's at .383. No one in the National League even approached those figures; Honus Wagner topped the hitters at .357. But the National League had the excitement of the pennant chase. Unfortunately, two ugly incidents marred the race in mid-July.[15]

Despite all of President Lynch's efforts to support his men, the umpires had been having a rough season. He had added new umpires to the staff so that most games would have two arbiters, but the new men invariably got harsh treatment from both teams and fans. "They just won't let those new umpires get along," complained Lynch. Managers had little patience for the inevitable mistakes made by both new and veteran umpires. Fred Clarke had vowed to protest every game his team lost by a miscall and had already filed four grievances in the previous six weeks. Chance declared that "umpires should be instructed to learn the rules, instead of being instructed to put players out of games for the slightest sign of insubordination."[16]

At Washington Park in Brooklyn on July 8, newcomer Ralph Frary "gave the punkiest exhibition of judging balls and strikes that has been seen here for many a day," according to the *World*. In the ninth inning of a tie game, Frary's calls enabled the Pirates to score the lead run. When howls of protest rose from the Brooklyn bench, Frary ordered it cleared. As six players and the team mascot marched across the field to the clubhouse, the fans unleashed a barrage of pop bottles from the right- and left-field bleachers. Some came close to Frary and were knocked away by Pirate second baseman Dots Miller. After the Pittsburgh victory a squad of police escorted Frary to his dressing room while a host of fans kept up loud protests outside the park.[17]

"I am very sorry this thing occurred," said a less-than-contrite Charles Ebbets, "but I don't see how I can prevent disturbances if President Lynch insists on sending his new umpires to Washington Park to try them out in running games. Bad umpiring will drive our patrons away from the games, but I am helpless in the matter."[18]

A *Tribune* columnist disagreed strongly. "Scenes of the kind which marred the game on Saturday do more harm to organized baseball in one day than can be repaired in months, and are to be deplored," he wrote. ". . . Hardly a day passes in the National League without the umpires being called on to send some manager or player to the bench or off the field for insubordination." Scarcely had his words reached print when another, much worse incident occurred in Philadelphia. Bill Finneran was also a new National League umpire but one with five years' experience in the Eastern League. He had already gone through some rugged initiation rituals with McGraw and other managers. Some critics thought him unduly combative with players and, as one writer observed, inclined "to decide plays before they are made."[19]

During the game between Philadelphia and St. Louis on the eighth, Sherry Magee was thrown out in the first inning for disputing a call. Two days later he was called out in the second inning by umpire Cy Rigler while trying to steal second. During his next at-bat Finneran called him out on strikes. Enraged, Magee tossed his bat in the air and headed away from the plate. When Finneran ordered him to the clubhouse, Magee turned and rushed toward the umpire. For a moment they clinched; then Magee pushed Finneran back and punched him hard in the mouth, knocking him to the ground. Dazed, Finneran finally got to his feet and, blood flowing from his lip, went after Magee, but several players intervened. Finneran retired to his dressing room, leaving Rigler to finish the game alone, and had to go to the hospital when the bleeding could not be stanched.[20]

Magee claimed that Finneran had called him an offensive name. The umpire denied the charge, saying he had simply ordered him out of the game. "I will leave it to Roger Bresnahan," he added, "who stood near and heard all that was said." Horace Fogel weighed in by saying, "Finneran invited the attack. Magee promptly accepted the challenge. In Boston on Memorial Day Finneran wanted to whip Manager Dooin. I will fight to the limit for Magee, and if they punish Sherwood they have got to give it to Finneran, for he has been taunting players to fight him. If we lose Magee it will hurt us."[21]

Lynch was furious at the whole episode. "I'll stop this sort of thing," he vowed after hearing of the incident. For the present Magee was suspended indefinitely while Lynch and the National Commission considered his case. Red Dooin found himself not only short of pitching but without one of his best hitters in Magee and another key outfielder, John Titus, who was just returning from a broken leg and could only pinch-hit. "Magee . . . is one of the hardest batters that I ever have had to face," said Mathewson, "because he has a great eye, and is of the type of free swingers who take a mad wallop at the ball, and are always liable to break up a game with a long drive."[22]

SOMETIMES THE SHOW COULD NOT GO ON despite the best of intentions. That was true the day after the Polo Grounds fire, and it was so again on July 11 for an entirely different reason.

Around three thirty in the morning on July 11, the *Federal Express* of the New York, New Haven & Hartford Railroad was running its regular route from Washington to Boston. At Philadelphia the St. Louis Cardinals boarded the fourth and fifth coaches from the engine for the run to their next series in Boston. In Manhattan the train had been cut into four sections of three coaches each, and the team's sleepers were mistakenly hitched to the rear of the train. This seemingly trivial detail turned out to be a godsend for the players.[23]

The train was in the hands of a substitute engineer because its usual one had been laid off. A. M. Curtis normally drove a highball freight train and was getting his first shot at passenger service. An hour behind schedule, he barreled along at sixty miles an hour toward his next stop, Bridgeport. The train approached a crossover switch near the city much too fast and plunged down a twenty-foot embankment onto a city street. Fortunately, the coupling between the sixth and seventh cars broke, leaving the last three sleepers still standing on the track as the other cars crashed onto the street below. None of the players suffered more than bruises and cuts. Shaken rudely from their sleep and stunned by the cries and shrieks, they heard Bresnahan order them to throw on clothes and get out of the car, saying there was work for them to do.

"Some of us went out just as we were, in our night clothes," said Steve Evans, "but most of us put on our trousers and shoes." Outside it was pitch-black except for the fire engulfing the baggage car. "Women were running about frantically," said Evans. "Some of them had lost their babies and seemed to have been driven insane." The players grabbed axes from the sleepers and hacked their way toward the dead and injured inside the tangle of cars below, toiling in the dark after the fire was extinguished. Groping through the debris, rookie Wally Smith stumbled across two babies and carried them out in a vain search for their mothers. Bresnahan and catcher Ivey Wingo managed to pull a woman from the wreckage of one car just as it caught fire. For two hours or more they struggled at the grim task of helping the wounded to safety and laying out bodies on a nearby lawn. "I don't know how much good we did," said a weary Bresnahan, "but I do know that I saw enough horrors to last me all through my life."

Sixteen bodies, including the engineer and fireman, were pulled from the wreckage, and forty-five passengers were rushed to the local hospital. When the team finally reached Boston later that day, some members of the Rustlers were at the station to congratulate them on escaping harm. Bresnahan saw that telegrams were sent to the wives and families of the players and the *St. Louis Post-Dispatch*, assuring everyone that the players were safe. Fred Tenney obligingly called off the day's game, but that meant the next day the teams would have to play yet another doubleheader.

WHILE THESE EVENTS PLAYED OUT, PITTSBURGH arrived at the Polo Grounds on the eleventh and buried the Giants beneath a nineteen-hit barrage, twelve for extra bases, for an easy 13–4 triumph. Wagner and George Gibson led the charge with four hits each, the same number compiled by Fred Snodgrass in a losing cause. "The climate of Zanzibar was like cold storage compared to the toasted grill under Coogan's Bluff," moaned the *Times*. Several disenchanted fans amused themselves by chanting any time Hank O'Day made a questionable decision, "We'll get Magee on you." Wiltse absorbed his fifth straight loss and fourth time driven to cover. Devore also heard from the kranks for whiffing three times. Nobody bothered braving the heat to steal a base for either team.[24]

Once again Rube Marquard came to the fore, beating Pittsburgh 4–3 for his sixth straight win. Within a single week he had stopped Chicago, Philadelphia, and Pittsburgh. He gave the Pirates nine hits and three walks but struck out nine. In two consecutive innings, with men on base and none out, he bore down and whiffed the side. He also allowed consecutive homers in the sixth by Wagner and Miller. With the score tied 3–3 in the ninth, the Giants scrounged a run on a single, sacrifice, error by Wagner, and a grounder on which Devore beat Wagner's throw home. The game was marred by what the *Times* called "the biggest wrangling match that the umpires have encountered at the Polo Grounds this year." The chief target was Frary, whose work behind plate aroused everyone's hackles. Along the way he tossed Bobby Byrne of the Pirates and banished McGraw from the coach's box to the bench.[25]

For the third game McGraw elected to go with Drucke, who couldn't seem to beat anybody except the Pirates. In the first inning Devore set the tone by walloping Lefty Leifield's first pitch for a triple and then speeding home when catcher Gibson dropped the relay. Doyle followed with a home run on Leifield's next pitch and the Giants romped to a 9–4 win. It was the Pirates' eighth loss in eleven games with the Giants. The win edged New York back into a tie for first place with the Phillies as the Cubs, plagued by "a frightful nightmare of walks and boots, and bungles and 'bones,'" dropped a second game to Brooklyn.[26]

Rain canceled the fourth game of the series on the fourteenth, giving both teams blessed relief, and Cincinnati arrived at the Polo Grounds the next day. Concerned about Mathewson's July slump, McGraw and the scribes alike figured the Reds to be the perfect antidote. "As Cincinnati hasn't beaten Mathewson since the neolithic period, or something like that ... the horoscope reads that Mathewson's losing streak is over," quipped the *Sun*. The reading was accurate, but barely. A large crowd turned out to see not only Mathewson but two exotic new players the Reds had plucked from Cuba: Armando Marsans and Rafael Almeida. Nearly every mention of their presence revolved directly or indirectly around their race. "Fans who expected to see Cuban ball players looking like Pullman porters were surprised," observed the *Times*. "Almeida is descended from a Spanish grandee class."[27]

Backed by a three-run homer from Merkle, who had three hits and drove in all the Giant runs, Matty took a 4–1 lead into the ninth in his usual manner of yielding hits but not runs. Then the Reds scored two runs and had two men on base with two out, moving the fans to the edge of their seats. But Mathewson bore down, getting Marsans to ground to Bridwell for the final out. The stumbling Cubs committed a ghastly eight (or nine) errors in losing a slugfest to Boston, 17–12, dropping them to third place. The Phillies seized first by downing Pittsburgh 2–1 thanks to two home runs by hitting sensation Fred Luderus. The sixteenth was a Sunday and rain washed out the game on the seventeenth, giving the Giants two days of leisure. During that time events in Boston gave McGraw fresh food for thought about his lineup.[28]

The Boston team now belonged to William Hepburn Russell along with two Boston publishers, Louis and George Page, and a Boston insurance man, Frederic Murphy. Once president, Russell wanted Fred Tenney for his manager only to be told, "I don't want to manage your team. You've got a rotten ball club." But Tenney owned some shares in the club that he was trying to unload, and he accepted the job when Russell agreed to buy them. The season had gone badly for the Rustlers, and problems simmering beneath the surface burst out on the sixteenth when two of the team's best players, Buck Herzog and Roy "Doc" Miller, quit and threatened to go home. Tenney had fined Herzog fifteen days' pay or $300 for "indifferent play" during the last series in New York but agreed to remit the fine if his play improved.[29]

Russell promptly suspended both players indefinitely. Herzog had managerial aspirations, said Russell, and was a disturbing element on the team. He had been suspended the year before on similar grounds. Tenney charged that Herzog had been a troublemaker and enjoyed the reputation of being one. Herzog denied these accusations, saying all he wanted was a square deal financially. Russell said that he would not sell or trade Herzog, that he would play for Boston or not at all. After a lengthy parley with Russell and Tenney, both players declared on the eighteenth that they would return to the team.[30]

While this uprising played out, Bobby Keefe breezed to his third victory over the Giants by a score of 8–2 as Marquard faltered and saw his winning streak end. "They played a debilitated and frowsy game," said the *Sun* in unsparing terms. "They were stagnant on the bases, sterile with the bat and pawed and booted the ball in the field." Marquard was "unsteady with men on base, hits were bunched on him and he had Meyers bending, stretching and stooping for his area scouring assortment."[31]

The final game of the series produced a much cleaner performance as Ames, who seemed to have found himself, stifled the Reds on eight hits to win 4–2. Merkle again provided the main support with three hits including a homer into the left-field bleachers. The Reds spent much of the game complaining to umpire Jim Johnstone, who banished three of them, including manager Clark Griffith. Both "dusky Cubans" played, as did Mike Balenti, described as a "Carlisle Indian." The *Times* had its own brand of fun with the Cincinnati roster. "With Indians, Cubans, Norwegians, Celts, Teutons, and Britons," it said wryly, "Clark Griffith has the distinction of rounding up the greatest congress of all nations ever seen on a ball field." A separate column offered the opinion that "with a Chinaman and a Jap or two, the Cincinnati team will be complete."[32]

Watching the game from his automobile parked in deep right field, John Brush was joined by Boston president Russell. One writer thought Russell was shopping for players, and he was at least partly right. Two days later McGraw reenacted his own version of the return of the prodigal son. The Giants stunned the baseball world by announcing that they had traded Bridwell and Gowdy to Boston for Herzog, sending the two infielders back to their original teams. No one had seen any such deal coming. Bridwell was popular in New York, the quintessential good soldier who had played well since coming to the Giants. Scribes wondered why McGraw would trade so reliable a hand for a troublemaker so cantankerous that he had already managed to antagonize three managers, including the Little Napoleon.[33]

The answer lay in McGraw's shrewd, cold appraisal of what he needed for the pennant run. He had replaced the popular Devlin at third with Fletcher because Devlin had slowed on the bases and in the field. Fletcher had done well since becoming a regular and was hitting .309, but he fared better at shortstop than at third. Like Devlin, Bridwell had lost both speed and range. "Bridwell has played brilliantly and consistently for the Giants," noted the *Tribune*, "but in the last few weeks has been slowing up, due to bad feet." Balls that he and Devlin once gobbled up were scooting through the hole for hits, and he no longer ran the bases as well as before. "Al Bridwell has been a credit to the Giants and to baseball in this city," said the *Tribune* in farewell, "and his passing is cause for keen regret." However, the writer conceded, "there is little place for sentiment in a business transaction. Bridwell, because of trouble with his feet, has been slowing up, just as Fred Tenney did, and no doubt McGraw, who has few, if any, equals as a manager, acted wisely."[34]

Personality aside, Herzog gave McGraw exactly what he wanted. He was difficult to handle, noted the *Tribune*, but this season he had "developed wonderfully as a player of the first magnitude ... Herzog has developed remarkable base running ability, and it is this as much as his hitting that has attracted McGraw." So far he had stolen twenty-four bases, tying him with Merkle for fourth in the league, and he was batting .302 compared to Bridwell's .267. With him on board the Giants had six of the league's top ten thieves, and Fletcher could run as well. Herzog was also solid at third base, enabling McGraw to put Fletcher at short. The *Times* declared what became a standard refrain from the pundits: "From every angle McGraw seems to have the better of the trade." The *Sun* thought that "if McGraw can handle him and make use of his ability to fit him into the machine he will strengthen the team 10 per cent."[35]

McGraw didn't want to give up Gowdy and had already spurned several offers for him, but he was the key to the deal for Boston. He could hit, and a weary Tenney wanted someone solid to take his place at first base. Even a slower Bridwell would strengthen the Boston infield, which had just lost Steinfeldt to illness. As McGraw had said many times, he would trade even good players to get what he thought he needed to perfect his lineup. The only question was whether he could get along with Herzog well enough to bring out the best in him.[36]

Having both Fletcher and Herzog in the lineup gave McGraw no less than seven speed merchants. The only starter with a lack of speed was Meyers, but he stole an occasional base, led the team in hitting, and had improved his handling of pitchers. "Chief Meyers is doing pretty well for a man regarded at one time as a 'joke' catcher," observed the *Sun*. "He could always hit; he is throwing as well as any of them and he ranks second in fielding among the National League backstops with an average of .988."[37]

The surprises in the National League kept coming. Lynch announced that Sherry Magee would be suspended for the rest of the season, a decision that the Phillies took to court. On Saturday the twenty-second, Barney Dreyfuss made the blockbuster announcement that the Pirates had just paid $22,500 for Marty O'Toole, a star pitcher for St. Paul who had recently fanned seventeen batters in one game. The price more than doubled the amount New York had paid for Rube Marquard. It also dwarfed the second highest figure of $12,000 paid by the Philadelphia Athletics for pitcher Lefty Russell in 1910. The slumping Pirates, who had dropped to fifth place behind St. Louis, hoped to revitalize the team for the pennant chase.[38]

The resurgent Cardinals came to New York for the final series in the current home stand. Bresnahan entered to a lavish fanfare of praise from the local scribes, both for his past years with the Giants and his work in rejuvenating the lowly Cardinals, who had just swept three games from Philadelphia. "All St. Louis is singing the praises of Roger Bresnahan," chirped the *Press*. ". . . The brilliant spurt of Roger's men has put St. Louis on the National League map again, and, whereas in former years the team played to slim crowds, the attendance this season has broken all records for the city. Great is Bresnahan, the King of the Cardinals." The Cardinals emphasized the point by abusing Mathewson en route to an 8–5 victory in the first game. Matty had nothing on the ball and asked to be removed with one out in the second inning after yielding five hits to eight batters. Crandall replaced him on short notice and was rudely treated until the fifth; Slim Sallee held the Giants in check long enough to win.[39]

"You'd rather have expected the big midweek crowd of 12,000 persons to be there with the big boo and sodawater bottle resentment against Big Beak Roger and his Resilient Rowdies," said the *World*. "But no! They like Roger up there. They remember when Roger was one of US, and it was during the time that we won the pennant . . . Friendly joshing and friendly cheers. Quite remarkable quite remarkable, truly."[40]

The win put St. Louis only three games out of first place and a single game behind the third-place Giants. A sweep would vault them past New York and into regions wholly alien to the franchise. With high hopes Bresnahan sent his ace, Bob Harmon, whose 14–4 record outdid that of Mathewson, to the mound against the much-abused Wiltse, who had lost five straight games. Wiltse responded with a masterpiece, throwing a no-hitter for six innings and allowing only two harmless singles. He walked two but Meyers gunned them both down trying to steal, and Wiltse faced only twenty-nine men in the 4–0 victory under glowering skies that unleashed rain on the unprotected crowd after the sixth inning.[41]

On Saturday the twenty-second a huge crowd turned out to watch not only the upstart Cardinals but also the return of Buck Herzog in a Giant uniform. Marquard was due to pitch, but Mathewson, unhappy over his last outing, asked to take the mound and McGraw agreed. With impressive efficiency he throttled St. Louis on seven hits before departing after the seventh as the Giants roared to a 10–2 win with four stolen bases in the bargain. Herzog made an impressive debut, belting a triple and a single, stealing a base, and making a key play in the field to squash a potential Cardinal rally. "Herzog's re-entrance to the local game was spectacular," said the *Times*. "He covered his territory with the quickness of a shadow, romped the bases with speed, and hammered forth a hilarious three-bagger. He got a warm reception from the crowd, and was so pleased with his new job that he smiled through the nine innings without the grin once leaving his frontispiece." This was not the Herzog anyone remembered, but he had served his time with a cellar dweller and was thrilled to be back in the pennant hunt.[42]

Sunday was getaway day as the Giants headed west for their next swing around the circuit. The first two stops were Cincinnati and St. Louis. Chicago still clung to first place by a half a game over the Phillies with the Giants a game behind and St. Louis three and a half games out. The *Tribune* noted that "the number of 'fans' who are rooting for the St. Louis Cardinals is arousing comment in almost every city in the circuit . . . All good sportsmen are filled with admiration for the fighting spirit which Bresnahan has instilled into his men." Sid Mercer joked that "they're getting so close now we'll have to start rooting against them." The fact that five teams were still in the race continued to amaze observers, who had never experienced such a thing.[43]

On Monday the twenty-fourth, while St. Louis was thumping the Phillies and Alexander the Great 10–2 before a record crowd, Marquard set down the Reds, who had defeated him two out of three starts this season, with nine hits and five walks while his mates drove their nemesis, Bobby Keefe, from the game with five runs in the second inning and won 8–3. The Giants were running again and stole four bases while smacking thirteen hits that included four triples, two by Marquard himself. Murray, who had been slumping, was the only regular not to get a hit, though he did steal a base. However, the next day George Suggs, who had won twenty the previous year, outpitched Ames for a 3–2 victory in which the Reds scored the winning run in the eighth and the Giants left the bases loaded with one out in the ninth amid a blinding rainstorm. McGraw subjected Jim Johnstone to a five-minute harangue, saying among other things that the umpire had been drunk all summer, before being exiled.[44]

The pennant chase took yet another unexpected twist on the twenty-sixth when Red Dooin suffered a broken leg in a collision at home plate with outfielder Rebel Oakes of St. Louis and was lost to the Phillies as a player for the rest of the season. The heart and soul of the team, he handled not only the players but especially the pitchers in expert fashion. Despite a desperate rally, the Phillies lost the game 7–6 while the Cubs swept a doubleheader from Boston. For their part, the Giants scrambled to defeat the Reds again 5–3 with a two-run rally in the ninth. When Wiltse faltered in the eighth, McGraw summoned Mathewson, the Reds killer, to squelch the rally. In the ninth he stroked a double down the right field line to score one of New York's runs and came home on Doyle's double.[45]

Before the final game of the series McGraw received word that he had been suspended three days for his harangue of Johnstone. He retreated to a seat beneath the grandstand to run the game as best he could. Clark Griffith decided to bring Keefe back on short rest and was rewarded with a solid performance and a 7–4 victory. On the Giants went to St. Louis, where Mathewson faced off against Sallee and scattered eleven hits only to be victimized by five Giants errors, two by Devore. "The defense of the Giants was moth eaten and full of holes," said the *Sun*. A sympathetic St. Louis writer agreed that "it seems that he has no friends on the team." Fighting rain that began in the third inning, Sallee pitched well enough to win 5–2, maintaining a shutout until Herzog tripled in both runs in the ninth.[46]

Then, as hopes soared in St. Louis, the worm turned with a vengeance. Before a huge crowd Marquard shut out the locals 8–0 on four hits while the Giants battered three Redbird hurlers for thirteen safeties, two by Marquard, and stole no less than nine bases while playing errorless ball. Dissatisfied with Murray's play both in the field and at the plate, McGraw sent Beals Becker to right field and got from him three hits, two runs scored, and a stolen base. The next day Wiltse outdid even Marquard's fine performance by blanking the Cardinals 6–0 before the largest crowd of the season, yielding only two hits while the Giants stole five more bases while again playing errorless ball. On one attempt an errant throw from catcher Jack Bliss hit umpire Bill Brennan in the head and knocked him out for five minutes.[47]

The two recent series against St. Louis convinced McGraw that the Cardinals could not hit lefthanders. This reasoning led him to send Marquard back out for the final game on only one day's rest. Bresnahan, who had sat out the first three games, inserted himself in the lineup and countered with Slim Sallee, hoping to salvage a split. But Marquard held St. Louis to five hits, two by Bresnahan, and the Giants eked out a 3–2 win with another errorless performance. Unimpressed by Bresnahan, they again stole five bases. Marquard, who had been batting left-handed, turned around to the right side and collected three of his team's twelve hits. Rube, it seemed, could do it all.[48]

At the end of the day and month the Giants found themselves in third place, while St. Louis had been shoved back into fifth, thanks in part to a twelve-game winning streak by the Pirates, who had become the hottest team in the league. Despite occasional lapses and missing personnel, the Cubs kept winning enough to occupy first place with the Phillies slightly behind. But how long the Phillies could stay in contention without Magee and Dooin, with an overworked Alexander, and with Titus still not in shape to play every day remained doubtful. The Pirates seemed to have caught fire despite the loss of Clarke, but pundits wondered how long they could keep up the pace.

The Giants had staggered through July with an unimpressive record of 15–12 despite playing nearly half their games in the friendly confines of the Polo Grounds. Although they stole a total of sixty-four bases during the month, more than half that number had come in the final two series against the Reds and Cardinals with the rebuilt left side of the infield. Marquard had finally emerged as a genuine star, giving McGraw two aces to throw at enemy teams. Mathewson endured one of the worst months of his career, losing more games than he won and often looking bad in the process, but McGraw did not expect that to continue. Wiltse and Ames showed enough to convince McGraw that they could contribute in the stretch run. Crandall's role had been clarified; in July he started only one game and relieved in six others. Drucke had pitched himself out of McGraw's good graces.

McGraw decided to leave Becker in the outfield in place of Murray. He had been trying to break the tendency of both Murray and Devore to swing at the first pitch. "The result," observed Mathewson, "was that the news of this weakness spread rapidly around the circuit by the underground routes of baseball, and every pitcher in the League was handing Devore and Murray a bad ball on the first one." After one game in which Devore fanned three times, McGraw told them, "If either of you moves his bat off his shoulder at a first ball, even if it cuts the plate, you will be fined $10 and sat down." The very next day Murray forgot the order and swung at the first pitch. McGraw levied the fine and kept him on the bench for nearly a month except to pinch-hit or fill a need. No one outside the clubhouse knew why he wasn't playing and assumed it was because of his slump.[49]

Whether the Giants won this summer or not, concluded the *Sun*, "McGraw now has gathered together a team most of the players of which ought to be good for half a dozen years more of first class playing at the least." It seemed to be a trend in the game. "A majority of the teams in each league are so fixed with young material that they can go on for five or six years with a goodly nucleus of talent such as it is." But none had put their club together so precisely or cultivated it so patiently as McGraw.[50]

The trade had given McGraw exactly the kind of lineup he wanted, one with young legs as well as speed and range in the field. Their mishaps on the bases sometimes made him cringe, but his only major concern was how they would fare as the long haul of August and September approached. While the heat wave reigned during the first half of the month, New York's running game slowed to a crawl. During its eleven days they swiped only seventeen bases, and seven of those came in one game. McGraw could not help but wonder whether his band of thieves would wear down and wilt as the dog days of summer wore on.

On the twenty-eighth, while the Giants were warming up prior to their game with the Cardinals, a gawky individual dressed in his Sunday best ambled onto the field and asked to speak with McGraw. Directed to the manager, he spun out a tale of how he had come from his native Kansas to win the pennant for New York. At the state fair in Kansas a fortune-teller had convinced him that he was destined to pitch for the Giants and help them win the championship. Given the weather and his shortage of pitchers, McGraw figured he had nothing to lose. "Well, that's interesting," he said. "Take off your hat and coat, and here's a glove. I'll get a catcher's mitt and warm you up, and we'll see what you've got."[51]

The stranger gave his name as Charles Victor Faust, food enough for any superstitious person. After flailing both arms in a windmill windup, he let go one pitch after another that looked the same even though McGraw had used Faust's own signals for different ones. "There was no difference in his pitches whatsoever," said Fred Snodgrass. "And there was no speed—probably enough to break a pane of glass, but that was about all. So McGraw finally threw away his glove and caught him bare-handed, thinking to himself that this guy must be a nut and he'd have a little fun with him."

He sent Faust to the plate and told him to hit the ball and run it out. After several vigorous swings, Faust dribbled one toward the shortstop, who juggled it long enough for him to reach first, then threw the ball behind him. To a chorus of laughter the gangly Faust bounced earnestly into a slide into second, then sprawled across third, and finally staggered home, all in his now dusty and tattered Sunday clothes. Even McGraw allowed himself a smile as he sent Faust on his way. The Giants then proceeded to play the miserable game in which they undermined Matty with five errors en route to a 5–2 loss.

During warm-ups the next day Faust showed up again, unfazed by the team's laughter and insistent that he was meant to pitch the club to victory. As poorly as July had gone for the team, the players welcomed his comic relief and even found him a uniform. His expanded repertoire of pranks during practice so amused not only the players but also the fans that McGraw let him sit on the bench for the game. The Giants ran wild that day, winning 8–0 with nine stolen bases. Faust came back on Sunday and, before the huge crowd, repeated his pregame act and watched the game from the bench. It was the laugher in which Wiltse hurled a shutout while the Giants belted fourteen hits and stole five bases. The *St. Louis Post-Dispatch* noted that the Kansas farm boy had "again amused with his awkward batting, fielding, and base running."[52]

Before the start of the game, players from both teams formed a circle near the plate and summoned Faust to their midst. "On behalf of the fans of St. Louis," said Cardinals outfielder Steve Evans, "who thoroughly appreciate your great work since becoming a member of the New York team, I present this slight token to you and hope you will continue to succeed in your chosen profession." He thrust a jewel box toward a delighted Faust, who doffed his cap to the cheering crowd and opened it to find a pocket watch. Encouraged to open it, he did so and was startled when the watch exploded, scattering parts everywhere. Faust stared in bewilderment at the debris as the players and fans collapsed in laughter.

Still Faust was unshaken in his faith, meeting the prank with the same strange, goofy smile he used at every joke played on him. When Wiltse loaded the bases in the first inning, McGraw sent an eager Faust out to warm up just in case. Wiltse proceeded to retire the next twenty-five men in a row. Faust did not show for the Monday game, in which Marquard eked out a 3–2 victory, but when the club reached Union Station en route to Pittsburgh, Faust was waiting for them, ready for the trip. "Did you get your contract and transportation?" asked McGraw. When Faust said no, McGraw told him that he left it with the clerk at the hotel and that Faust should hurry back and get it before the train departed. Faust galloped off in his angular fashion and disappeared into the crowd. "It was the last we saw of 'Charley' Faust for a time," said Mathewson later.[53]

The train went on its way without the strange man from Kansas. "I'm almost sorry we left him," admitted McGraw, who was wise in the ways of good luck charms.[54]

STANDINGS ON JULY 31

	Won	Lost	Pct.		Won	Lost	Pct.
Chicago	56	33	.625	St. Louis	52	40	.565
Philadelphia	56	36	.609	Cincinnati	38	53	.418
New York	55	38	.604	Brooklyn	34	57	.374
Pittsburgh	54	37	.593	Boston	20	72	.217

CHAPTER 13

August: Jinxes and Charms

*"A jinx is the child of superstition, and
ballplayers are among the most superstitious
persons in the world, notwithstanding all this
conversation lately about educated men
breaking into the game and paying no
attention whatever to the good and bad omens.
College men are coming into both the leagues,
more of them each year, and they are doing
their share to make the game better and the
class of men higher, but they fall the hardest for
the jinxes. And I don't know as it is anything
to be ashamed of at that."*

—CHRISTY MATHEWSON

TUESDAY, THE FIRST OF AUGUST, WAS A travel day on which the Giants journeyed to Pittsburgh for a series with the red-hot Pirates. William Russell of the Rustlers was in town trolling the Pirates for players. That night McGraw met with him and closed another deal, selling Mike Donlin to Boston for an undisclosed amount of cash, no other players involved. The longtime fan favorite of the Polo Grounds could still play—he hit .315 for Boston the rest of the season—but he was a relic of past glories without a role in the new machine McGraw had built. His departure confirmed the end of an era in New York baseball. "The Donlin trade caught every one napping," said the *Herald*, "and has caused no little surprise to Pittsburg and Boston fans."[1]

While the Giants traveled to Pittsburgh, the Pirates won their thirteenth straight game. This longest winning streak of the season was tempered by the fact that nine of them had come at the expense of Boston and four from Brooklyn. Before 10,222 fans the Giants put an end to the streak by scoring five runs off Babe Adams in the first two innings on their way to an 8–4 victory. Mathewson, long a Pittsburgh nemesis, pitched a strange game even for him, surrendering fifteen hits, all singles, but never more than one run in any inning. As the *World* noted, "McGraw's men played the hit and run game to death while the very opposite obtained with the enemy." The *Sun* agreed that "the Pirates seemed flatfooted in everything."[2]

That same day the National League's board of directors upheld their president's decision to fine Sherry Magee $200 and suspend him for the rest of the season. Dooin called it "an unjust decision" but Magee conceded that "it's up to the league directors. They run baseball, so what they say goes; but I'm sorry." Magee's apology and the further weakening of the Phillies caused by Dooin's broken leg softened Lynch's stance. "I realize that it was a severe blow to the Philadelphia Club," he said, "but it would have been far better for that club or its officials to have condemned the action . . . than to have it appear that there was justification for his action." On August 11 he reinstated Magee with a warning that he was on probation for good behavior.[3]

After a rainout on the third, Clarke returned to the lineup and helped the Pirates rally for a 5–3 win behind Camnitz as the Giants self-destructed with five errors, two each by Devore and Doyle, undermining solid pitching by Ames, Wiltse, and Crandall. In the final game of the series Marquard matched Lefty Leifield in a pitching duel broken up in the sixth when impressive rookie Max Carey shot a ball past Snodgrass and turned it into a home run. An inning later Marquard hit Leifield in his non-pitching arm with a fastball, forcing him from the game. New York's hopes ended in the ninth when Carey robbed Herzog of extra bases with a sensational one-handed catch. As a reward the Pirates climbed over the Giants into second place. Asked their opinion, the Cubs labeled Pittsburgh as the team to beat for the pennant.[4]

That day in Chicago, Murphy announced that Tinker, the last surviving member of the team's golden-age infield, had been fined $150 and suspended the rest of the season for "listless and indifferent playing in this afternoon's game." Chance was furious that Tinker made little effort to go after a pair of windblown bloops over his head and let the shortstop know it. "I'm damn sick and tired of you letting those flies drop," he raged. "I'm damn sick and tired of you yelling at me," countered Tinker. Chance yanked him from the game and afterward issued a statement saying, "I don't care whether the winning of a pennant depends upon the retention of Tinker or any other player on the Cub line up, but I want to emphasize the fact that while I am manager no player can loaf. Without Tinker I may lose the National League pennant, but I am going to have some discipline in the club."[5]

The Giants used Sunday the sixth to travel to Chicago. A crowd of fourteen thousand graced West End Park in anticipation of another classic pitching duel between Mathewson and Miner Brown. They got nothing of the kind. Brown started the game by hitting Devore in the head, knocking him unconscious. Once revived, he was helped off the field and replaced by Murray. To the surprise of the Giants, Chance and Tinker had made their peace on Sunday and Matty's worst nemesis was in the lineup for the game. All he did was smack two singles, a double, and a triple in four trips to the plate, drive in four runs, score three times, steal home after the triple, and handle nine chances flawlessly in the field, including two double plays. TINKER DEFEATS THE GIANTS WITH SOME ASSISTANCE, blared the World's headline.[6]

Apart from Tinker's exploits, it was an ugly game all around. Matty yielded ten hits and eight runs, Brown thirteen hits and six runs. After replacing Devore, Murray mishandled two balls in left field and was switched to right field with Becker moving over to left. Afterward, when the Cubs were back in their clubhouse, Chance came over to Tinker and said with a big grin, "Damn it, I ought to suspend you every day."[7]

Tinker returned to earth the next day, Devore returned to the lineup, and Evers rejoined the Cubs but did not play. Lew Richie beat the Giants 3–1 in a tight pitcher's duel with Wiltse for his third win over New York, giving Chance hope that he had enough pitching to stay with the Giants. This hope was blasted when New York exploded for eighteen hits off three Cub pitchers and won 16–5 to salvage one game in the series as Marquard coasted to his fourteenth win. "The Giants simply ran riot on the bases and could not be stopped," said the Tribune as the team swiped eight bases, three by Devore, after getting none in the two losses to the Cubs. The victory left them with an unimpressive 2-4 record in the two series against their closest contenders. Pittsburgh edged into first place with Chicago and the Giants close behind.[8]

Thursday the tenth was another travel day as the Giants headed back to the Polo Grounds for a home stand that would last the rest of the month. On the train ride back to New York McGraw had ample time to ponder the feast-or-famine pattern of so many of his team's games. The grind of August and September required some consistency of performance, and so far the Giants had not shown it. *Sporting News* praised the club as "the greatest base running aggregation that has been seen in fast company for years. The Giants have stolen nearly twice as many bases as their nearest rival. With such an advantage as this the club can go along and win regularly, if the pitchers are only half-way effective."[9]

The *Sun* agreed. "The fact remains," it said, "that the Giants since the Herzog-Bridwell deal have been playing a better organized and more aggressive game than at any previous time this year. McGraw has the team department working in effective style."[10]

Mathewson's poor performances in July gave McGraw cause for concern. As in the past when his work slipped, the New York scribes were busy preparing his obituary. The *Herald* mourned, tongue-in-cheek, "Poor old 'Matty'! . . . He was all in, and they were holding dress rehearsals for the funeral and getting ready to hire an orchestra to play Chopin's march." The *Times* agreed that "everything was fixed for 'Matty's' trip to oblivion, except the funeral arrangements. It was whispered that all the steam and fadeaway tricks had left him." The fact that he was only days away from turning thirty-one added fuel to the fear that his time had passed.[11]

The grandstand at the Polo Grounds had a temporary roof over it by the time of their return as work moved forward on the upper deck. The Phillies were the first visitors and Mathewson pressed McGraw to let him start. He had read the papers, and his competitive blood was boiling. McGraw sent him to the mound and was treated to a vintage Mathewson performance in which he allowed Philadelphia eleven hits and a walk but throttled them in the clutch for a 6–0 victory that silenced the critics for a time. He struck out nine, including Fred Luderus four times. "The passing of the great pitcher will be postponed for a while," said the *World*. McGraw put Murray back in the starting lineup for a game and he responded with three hits. Devore continued to run wild, making two of the team's three thefts.[12]

Heywood Broun penned the most captivating reverse obituary for Matty in the *Morning Telegram*. "Every now and then a king is called to show down," he wrote. "Christy Mathewson, who has held his title of premier pitcher in the National League by the divine right of the average, has been compelled to face treason among his subjects this year. More than once the long-drawn cry of 'take him out' has been raised while Mathewson was in the box. The question, 'What is the matter with Matty?' has been freely raised and not a few have deserted him for the cause of the French pretender, Marquard the Rube. Yesterday the King stood before 8,000 of his subjects and answered the question 'What is the matter with Matty?' His answer was, 'Nothing at all,' and his argument was clear and convincing."[13]

These Phillies were far from the energized team that had made life miserable for the Giants early in the season. Dooin was confined to the bench, Magee could not rejoin the team until the sixteenth, and Titus still limped badly even though he had gone back to the outfield. But they had enough fight in them to hand New York a 2–0 loss the next day in a pitching masterpiece marred by four Giants errors. "The Ames jinx was working again," noted the Herald as the redhead renewed his title as the Hard Luck King. "If it rained soup," he said glumly afterward, "I would be caught with a fork. That's the kind of luck I have." The win put the Phillies only two games behind the Giants for third place.[14]

Prior to the warm-ups a familiar figure ambled into the clubhouse "with several inches of dust and mud caked on him," according to Mathewson, "for he had come all the way either by side-door special or blind baggage." A persistent Charlie Faust rode the rails to New York determined to help the Giants win the pennant whether they wanted him or not. What McGraw thought of his presence is not known, but a name like Faust demanded at least a modicum of caution. He let Faust stay, even gave him an old uniform, and brought the Phillies in on the joke. The Phillies players let him bat, steal first, second, third, and score while they laughed themselves silly along with the early arrivals at the ballpark. "Faust has a hallucination that he is a ball player and is sticking to the Giants in the hope of landing a job," reported the Times. Jack Wheeler of the Herald offered his own impression of Faust:

> He looks as much at home in a baseball uniform as Mammoth Minnie, the champion fat woman of the Indiana State fair, would in a cavalry charge. His every move is a picture. He runs like an ice wagon and slides as if he had stepped off a moving trolley car backward. He wears the old Kansas smile that went out of style in this town with side whiskers and affects the brick hair cut—shaved up to his hatline. Besides, he is a charity worker, for he draws no salary. That's what a fortune teller in Marion, Kan. did for New York. He is here uninvited and says that, like the postage stamp, he is going to stick to one thing until he gets there. He plays ball as if he were a mass of mucilage.[15]

It was not unusual for a team to have a live good-luck charm. In his simple-minded way Faust was persistent and persevering but never belligerent. He was as good-natured as he was gullible, almost childlike in his acceptance of what was told him. His behavior, however bizarre, seemed genuine to the core, and he amused the players, most of whom developed a fondness for him. There seemed little harm in giving him a seat on the bench, and the fans adored his antics before a game. Reporters loved the fact that he seemed to have dropped onto the Giants out of nowhere, a synonym for Kansas in New York and other eastern cities. If the team did consider Faust a good-luck charm, he rewarded them at once with a six-game winning streak.

On the fourteenth New York engaged Philadelphia in a doubleheader before a surprisingly huge Monday crowd of more than twenty-five thousand. For the first time the outfield bleachers were packed, giving rise to a host of complaints that the sea of white shirts all but blinded batters. "The white shirts against the broken color scheme of advertisements and dark suits," said the *Herald*, "give a shimmering effect like a moving picture machine and make the ball very hard to see." Poor vision may have influenced the first game in which Marquard and Alexander hooked up in a twelve-inning masterpiece finally won by the Giants 3–2. Marquard never looked better, scattering seven hits and whiffing thirteen batters; Alexander matched him with a six-hitter. In the twelfth inning, with one out, Meyers walked and was replaced at first by Murray. Marquard sacrificed him to second and Devore ended the game with a double down the left-field line.[16]

The game took three hours, pushing the start of the second game to five o'clock. Wiltse was pounded for nine hits, including two home runs, but hung on to win 5–4 in a game called after six innings because of darkness. In the top of the sixth Snodgrass threw out the tying run at the plate, ending the game in controversy. As the Phillies rushed furiously toward Mal Eason, McGraw saw trouble brewing and put himself between the umpire and the Phillies players until the crowd engulfed them all and Eason made his way off the field. The Giants stole four bases in each game, giving them fourteen for the four games. A "black squall" electrical storm with fifty-five-mile-an-hour winds swept the city and canceled the fifth game on the fifteenth, disappointing McGraw because the Phillies had used up their best pitchers and Magee was not due back for another day.[17]

What made Faust's routine so convincing and uproarious to the fans was the utter sincerity of its execution. The finest actor would have struggled to outdo the conviction of his performances. When he pestered McGraw to let him pitch, the manager obliged by sending him behind the bleachers to warm up and then concocting reasons why he wasn't summoned day after day. "He will warm up to-day from 2 o'clock until the end of the second game," reported Sid Mercer of the doubleheader with Philadelphia. "Charlie steamed up on Saturday and would have stepped in at any moment to relieve Ames if his orders had read that way." The orders never came, but day after day Faust dutifully awaited the call to the mound.[18]

Behind the Phillies came the last invasion of western teams, led by Cincinnati. "Fifteen games are to be played in all before the Giants go away again," observed the *Sun*, "and civic pride will be appeased if the Giants can nab ten of those fifteen." On the sixteenth the injury jinx, which had struck all around the Giants but spared them, dealt a crushing blow to the Pirates.[19]

Although nursing a thumb so swollen that it "looked like a rutabaga," Wagner still led the league in hitting at .352. Playing Brooklyn at Washington Park, he singled and went to second on a throw home. His foot hit the bag awkwardly and he went down hard. His teammates helped him to the Superba clubhouse, where the team doctor ordered him to the hospital for X-rays. Afterward, ignoring doctor's orders to rest, he insisted on returning to the ballpark and arrived in time to witness the end of an incredible game in which his pitcher, Elmer Steele, lost a perfect game in the ninth inning to a weak single in a 9–0 victory. The Pirates took little joy in the triumph despite Wagner's upbeat attitude. The ankle was thought at first to be broken but proved to be sprained severely enough to keep him out of the lineup for a month. Also on the sixteenth Roger Bresnahan suffered a severe spike wound on his right hand and was lost to the Cardinals for an indefinite time.[20]

As McGraw well knew from experience, the outcome of every season hinged to a large degree on who received what injuries for how long. A baseball season was a war of attrition. In the past his players had fallen in battle; this year the injury curse had been merciful toward the Giants and unsparing toward all the other contenders. This was a large part of what McGraw and many others in baseball understood as the role of luck. He accepted its benefits even as in past years he had been stoical about its fickleness. The only question for McGraw was whether his team's good fortune would hold through the closing weeks of the season.

Through the years he had pulled several stunts behind the scenes to gratify their superstitions. He recalled with a smirk the time in 1904 when the Giants went into an awful slump. One day Frank Bowerman came into the clubhouse wearing a big smile. "Saw a load of empty barrels on my way to the park today, boys," he said happily. "Watch me pickle that old apple this afternoon." He went out and stroked four hits in five at-bats, giving McGraw a brainstorm. During the next few days other players reported seeing a load of empty barrels and said that if Bowerman could do it, they could too. The Giants won that day, and empty-barrel sightings poured in from other players. As the Giants begin to win again, Billy Gilbert grew suspicious, having seen the empty loads several times. Confronted, McGraw admitted cheerfully that he "hired that teamster by the week to drive around the park and meet you fellows coming in."[21]

No player was immune to superstitions, large or small, not even Mathewson. Over the years McGraw had kept track of the oddities that affected his players and, as with the barrels, tried to turn them to his own and the team's advantage. Faust seemed harmless enough to him. If the Giants won a few games with him on the bench, the players might come to believe that he was indeed not just a comic sideshow but a good-luck charm as well. What mattered in the end, after all, was not whether Faust *was* a charm but whether the players believed he was.

FAUST WAS STILL PRESENT WHEN CINCINNATI arrived at the Polo Grounds to face their worst jinx. On the day that Wagner and Bresnahan fell prey to injuries, Mathewson hurled a record-setting gem, throwing only ninety-two pitches to best the Reds 6–1 for his twenty-second consecutive win against them. The previous record for fewest pitches was thought to be 103. With two out in the ninth, an errant throw by Fletcher enabled speedy Bob Bescher to reach first. He came around to score on a fly ball that Devore lost in the sun for a double. If Fletcher had not erred, Matty would have completed the game in eighty-six pitches. The Giants sent ten men to the plate in the fourth inning to score all six of their runs on the same number of hits. Matty's record improved to 19–9, postponing yet again intimations of his demise.[22]

Everybody got to play in the doubleheader next day as New York pounded out thirty-one hits, good for twenty-five runs, and rolled to 10–4 and 15–2 victories. In the first game Ames did a workmanlike job while Crandall, making his only start of the month in the second, scattered seven hits. Murray, Devlin, and Wilson all got into both games along with a newcomer,

Eugene Paulette. "Dick Hennessey and Rube Faust furnished so much fun between the two games," said the *Times*, "that the crowd almost started a petition to have them perform instead of Cincinnati." Hennessey, the team mascot, had his own warm-up routine that complemented that of Faust. At one point Faust played at warming up Marquard until a pitch slipped through his hands and caught him near the eye, knocking him out briefly. He soon revived enough to lay down a bunt and circle the bases.[23]

In the fifth inning of the first game the teams provide some high comedy of their own. Doyle tripled and tried to score on Snodgrass's grounder to Keefe. The pitcher played it well and threw to catcher Tom Clarke, who dropped the ball. Doyle put on the brakes and scooted back to third; he made it with a leaping slide only to find that Snodgrass was nearly there as well. Snodgrass hurried back to second while the dazed Reds tried to figure where to throw the ball. Seeing their hesitation, Doyle took off again for home. The Reds tried once more to run him down, but first baseman Dick Hoblitzell held the ball too long and Doyle made it back to third. An unhappy Snodgrass had slipped down to the bag and had to beat another hasty retreat while the confused Reds held the ball. The fans roared their approval, especially when word got out that Brooklyn had beaten the Pirates and Boston the Cubs.[24]

Another strong electrical storm gave the Reds a reprieve on the eighteenth but necessitated a doubleheader the next day. Sid Mercer met with Faust over breakfast and arranged a mock ceremony with officials of a fictional license commission that, Faust was assured, had to verify any contract with the Giants, which also had to be signed by McGraw and captain Larry Doyle. Doyle had strained his back in the last game and was still at the hotel but signed readily when Faust presented the document filled with "fearful and wonderful clauses" to him. Mercer had a photographer catch Faust signing the contract "Charles V. Faust." When the mock commissioner asked what the V. stood for, Faust replied, "Victory is my middle name." From then on he became known as Victory Faust.[25]

With Doyle out, Devlin went to third and Herzog moved to second. A record Saturday crowd estimated at thirty-five thousand overflowed the Polo Grounds for what proved to be two tough games. In the first Marquard inexplicably showed nothing and left with two outs in the first inning after walking three and giving up three hits and two runs. The Giants rallied for three runs in the second and two in the fourth while Wiltse held the Reds to a pair of scores until the eighth, when a Fletcher error and single put runners at the corners with no one out. McGraw summoned Mathewson, who pitched deftly out of trouble, and the Giants prevailed, 5–4.[26]

Matty started the second game, but his arm cooled down between games and he found it difficult to get warm again. The Reds jumped on him for nine hits and six runs in five innings before McGraw let Murray bat for him. The fabulous Mathewson jinx over Cincinnati was broken at last. Still, the Giants had taken four of the five games and had Sunday to rest up for the Cubs. By the twentieth Chicago held first place, a game ahead of the Giants and two up on Pittsburgh. Philadelphia had fallen six and a half games off the pace, St. Louis another game beyond that. The pennant race looked once again to be in possession of the three teams that had dominated the National League for the past decade.[27]

"Beginning to-morrow the Giants face the most crucial week they have encountered this season," said the *Press*. "Seven games will be played with the two teams the McGraw troupe must beat out for the flag." In looking over recent performances the writer singled out Fred Snodgrass as "the most improved outfielder in the National League this season . . . 'Snoddy' is not hitting up to his sensational form of last season, but his batting has been hard and timely . . . As a fielder, however, he has improved 100 per cent. He gets everything wafted to his suburb, pulls smoking drives off his shoetops, and his sensational one-hand grabs of apparent triples have featured many recent games. His arm is also strong."[28]

Despite the importance of the forthcoming series, McGraw was in no mood to oblige when Faust persisted in asking him to countersign the contract. When he refused, Faust said he would leave the team and go to Brooklyn. The Cubs were coming to town. "You need me in this Chicago series or you don't need me at all. If I don't sign to-day I leave the team flat on its back, that's all." McGraw told him he could stick around as a free agent, but Faust would not be appeased. They would have to face the Cubs without their newfound charm.[29]

After their strong base running against the Phillies, the Giants stole only a total of eight sacks against the Reds. Backup catcher Tom Clarke surprised them by gunning down several attempts. Running would be even tougher against the Cubs with Archer behind the plate. Once, while playing for Atlanta in the Southern League, he was reputed to have picked men off first, second, and third in the same inning. McGraw decided to leave Becker in the starting lineup, since he was playing well. "No team is better equipped in utility players," said the *Herald*. "When Murray was off form Beals Becker slipped into action without causing the slightest friction. 'Larry' Doyle's injury opened a hole at second base which Herzog promptly plugged up. The versatility of the infielders is one of the strongest bits of insurance against loss of strength through accidents."[30]

The first game with Chicago matched Marquard against Richie, both of whom pitched well enough to last ten innings. "The conflict bore all the trademarks of an old-time New York-Chicago battle," observed the *Times*, "with its tight fielding, tense situations, steady pitches, and a few verbal clashes with the umpires." Marquard bounced back from his last brief outing to hold the Cubs to six hits while fanning ten, but Richie held the Giants to a 2–2 standoff. By the tenth inning the game had gone on for two and a half hours, darkness shrouded the field, and Bill Klem was about to call the affair when, with two out and two strikes on him, Fletcher pushed across a run with a dribbler off Tinker's glove. Along the way Klem banished Evers, who was coaching, for saying some unkind things, then ousted McGraw for the same cardinal sin. McGraw sent Doyle to take his place, but while walking past Klem, Doyle offered a choice opinion as well and joined McGraw in the corner of the dugout.[31]

The *Sun* viewed the game as prime evidence that the starting time should be moved up from four o'clock, especially in August. The *Herald* took notice of a missing person. "Alas!" it reported, "Charles Faust, the comedian of the Giants, jumped the club yesterday because he has not yet been tendered a contract. And a lot of persons went up to the Polo Grounds just to see him run around the bases. Funny if the New York club had to recall him. He certainly draws." The writer took heart when Faust returned to perform his act the next day. "We take back everything we said about Charley Faust being a disloyal subject," said Mercer, who had become the closest student of the weird Kansan. "His pout was short-lived, and he was back on the job yesterday running the bases in his own inimitable style and warming up like an oven before the game."[32]

One interested spectator at the game wrote his novel impressions of the sport. The Marquis of Queensbury chatted first with the scribes from Chicago and New York and admitted to having seen one baseball "match" in Toronto some years earlier. Intrigued but frustrated by not knowing the rules of the game, he observed in the *Chicago Tribune* that "there were times, when, despite the absorbing interest in the game, one had perforce to turn round and listen to the 'patter' of the enthusiastic fans, I believe they are called. Some of them were as funny as a London busman or a cockney comedian." He was impressed that the umpire "does not seem to go about with a bodyguard like an English football referee . . . The manners of baseball must be better." This on a day when three men were ejected during a game in which, declared the *Chicago Tribune,* "there was umpire baiting and trickery on each side, such as is only seen when two worthy clubs are fighting so desperately for the pennant."[33]

Miner Brown took the mound hoping to stop the New York surge and for seven innings did just that as the Cubs marched to a 5–2 lead against an ineffective Ames and Crandall, who relieved him in the fifth. Then the Giants plated three runs in the eighth to tie the game. After Crandall subdued the Cubs in the ninth, Meyers walked and was promptly replaced at first by Murray. Crandall sacrificed him to second, and Devore moved him to third with his fifth single of the day. Doyle, back in the lineup, celebrated his return by torching Brown for a line drive down the right-field line that scored Murray. For the second day in a row the Giants claimed victory in the bottom of the last inning. The effort moved them back into first place by the slimmest of margins. Crandall's steady relief job proved crucial. "When the medals for life savers are being distributed," said the *Times,* "don't overlook Crandall."[34]

"It was a great contest and the Giants played like champions," conceded the *Chicago Tribune.* "The speed that goes with youth was on their side, and it was never a tiring battle that they put up. On the other hand, there was just a hint of fatigue on the part of the Cubs in the closing rounds."[35]

Once again the stay at the top was brief. Back came Richie on one day's rest to oppose Wiltse in Chicago's last game at the Polo Grounds. Before the largest crowd of the week Richie scattered eight hits and five walks as the Cubs touched Wiltse for three runs in the first and three more in the ninth for a 6–2 win. As the *Herald* observed, "He pitched what might be called an alpha and omega game." Although he got none of Chicago's ten hits, Archer squelched two budding Giant rallies by picking Herzog off second in the second inning and Becker off first in the third. During the three games the Giants stole not a single base against Archer's cannon.[36]

"The Chicago club has been working the trick of apparently ignoring opponents on the bases and then picking them off so often that it is astonishing that class athletes fall for the play," scolded the *World.* "Johnny Kling was a master at it and Jimmy Archer is an apt pupil." The Cubs needed a strong catcher. Since parting ways with Jack Pfiester, they did not have a single left-hander on the team, and Chance claimed that he didn't want one even though they were superior at holding runners on first base.[37]

The crippled Pirates arrived in town for a doubleheader on the twenty-fourth and showed they were still full of fight. "Baseball in Manhattan has never reached the feverish heat that is now being shown in the Giants' stubborn fight for the pennant," observed the *Times* ". . . A crowd of 30,000 persons were jammed into the new cement stadium. The main stand and the boxes were crowded, with thousands standing half a dozen deep all the way around the wide promenade. On the second tier were more than 4,000 people and the outfield bleachers were almost filled." They came despite dark, threatening skies and intermittent showers, producing a sea of umbrellas, and they got their money's worth.[38]

In what the *Press* called "one of the most brilliant double-headers ever contested in Manhattan," the teams split a pair of pitching duels. Mathewson lost a heartbreaker to Adams 3–1, thanks in large part to an error by Herzog and a blunder by Doyle, who inexplicably threw out a runner at first instead of nailing Gibson as he lumbered home from third. Adams, who had been struggling, limited New York to six hits and got stellar support, especially from Max Carey, whose sensational catch robbed Herzog of a possible homer. In the second game Camnitz held the Giants to four hits but Marquard was nearly untouchable, allowing only two hits and no walks while striking out eleven Pirates in a 2–1 victory. "Marquard, as has been his habit of late," said the *Herald*, "blotted up most of the spot light, a lot of the cheers and nearly all the glory of the second game. He is as good now as he used to be poor, which is going some."[39]

Brilliance vanished from the park on Friday the twenty-fifth as morning rains turned the field muddy and dark, chilly skies kept the spectators down to a paltry two thousand. The ball gathered goo at every stop, making it hard to see. Doyle endured a personal worst by making four errors. Ames did not make it through the third inning, having issued four walks to go with two hits, but Crandall came on and held the Pirates at bay. The Giants prevailed 3–2 thanks to a Devore triple in the eighth inning that brought home two runs. Latham, who as usual was doing more chattering than coaching, took exception to a call by Hank O'Day, who turned to respond and missed a pitch that would have walked Fletcher. O'Day headed toward third to eject Latham, but a furious McGraw got there first and yelled, "Get off the field!" The *Herald* duly noted that "this is the first time in the history of the game, according to the records, that O'Day and McGraw have agreed on anything." No one mourned when Latham got a three-day suspension.[40]

The win nudged the Giants back into first place because the Cubs, playing across the river in Brooklyn, had their game called on account of rain. For some reason Chicago struggled all summer against the Superbas and had lost the first game of the series. On the twenty-sixth they managed only to split a doubleheader while the Giants waltzed to a 6–2 victory over Pittsburgh. Mathewson and Camnitz, the losers in the doubleheader, both returned on one day's rest—Matty because Wiltse had pulled a muscle in his leg and couldn't go. In typical fashion he yielded nine hits but only once did the Pirates get two of them in the same inning. On a slick, muddy field Pittsburgh also committed seven errors, three of them by Tommy Leach, who had taken Wagner's place at shortstop. Having swiped only three bases in the first three games, New York pilfered four this time, two of them by the battery of Meyers and Mathewson, neither of whom were known as speedsters.[41]

The fans had come to expect some pregame entertainment, and they were not disappointed. While the Catholic Protectory Band played ragtime tunes to the grandstand, Faust did his sliding routine. Afterward he took a turn leading the band, wielding the baton like a baseball bat, while Marquard and Devore, the long and short of it, marched briskly across the field with chests puffed out. As the Pirates limped out of town with three losses in four games, a *Press* columnist thought that "easier sledding is in sight for the Giants than was encountered last week, as McGraw's men draw for their next opponents the two fallen hopes of this year's spirited pennant campaign, the Bresnahan wrecking crew and Dooin's Daisies." They would be followed by ten games with the league doormats, Brooklyn and Boston.[42]

Rain had been a constant presence in New York since the start of the series with Pittsburgh, and two rainouts had occurred in the nine days before that. Despite the weather the crowds had been enormous on most days. Since the Giants' return home on August 11, the Polo Grounds enjoyed more than 250,000 paid admissions, 150,000 of them for the series against the Cubs and Pirates alone. The city had gone baseball mad as never before, not even in the frenzied race of 1908. Then they were considered underdogs to the Chicago juggernaut; now they were regarded as favorites. Kitty Bransfield of the Phillies thought the Giants would take the flag because "the speed limit is ignored by McGraw." He praised McGraw for the way he built the team. "He has been patient with his young players," said Bransfield, "a condition that does not exist everywhere. The reward may have been slow in development but it had paid."[43]

The last of the western visitors, St. Louis, met the Giants on the twenty-eighth and was greeted by McGraw's two lefties. Marquard, unfazed by three errors behind him, continued his run of brilliance by smothering St. Louis 2–0 on one lone single in the eighth inning. Bresnahan, still nursing his spike wound, watched the game from the bench. "With Bresnahan out," said the *Times*, "the team seems as tame as Boston." To the south the Cubs behind Miner Brown manhandled Philadelphia and an overworked Alexander.[44]

Some observers thought the spark had gone out of the Cardinals since their close call on the July 11 train. Club treasurer H. D. Seekamp, who had shared a stateroom with Bresnahan on the ill-fated train, found himself making different travel arrangements. The players insisted on traveling only in steel-reinforced cars like the Pullman they had been in, "one that will stand the knocks and the jars of the average wreck." It had to be lit by electricity because "our experience at Bridgeport taught us that electric-lighted sleepers are the best." They also insisted on being the last car on the train; if it had an observation car, which had to go last, they wanted to be next to it. "Our players still feel the effect of that wreck," Seekamp admitted, "and we are still uncomfortable . . . Since that wreck the St. Louis players have obtained less sleep than any other team in the business. The slightest jar awakens us."[45]

The rains returned Tuesday morning and left the field slick and muddy despite barrels of sawdust dumped on it. "Polo Grounds looked like a shore building lot on Long Island at high tide," said the *Times*. The Cardinals and Bresnahan had another problem as well. Slim Sallee, the cadaverous southpaw who had often done well against New York, fell off the wagon yet again and was suspended after being unable to pitch. Like Raymond he had struggled with his drinking habit for years. At the time he had a 15-9 record, but he did not pitch again that season.[46]

Without Sallee the already thin Cardinal staff was badly overworked. Its weakness showed on the twenty-ninth when three St. Louis pitchers issued twelve walks in a 7–5 loss to the Giants on the sloppy field. Wiltse did not exactly bewitch them, surrendering eight hits in six innings, but Ames and Crandall held the Cardinals in check while New York rallied for six runs in the last three innings. In one of his typical ploys, McGraw sensed the wildness early and ordered his men to wait out the pitchers until the late innings, when he unleashed them. The Giants managed only seven hits and left thirteen men on base; twice Becker fanned with the bases loaded.

The high—or low—light of the game occurred in the sixth when Jim Johnstone, angered by the constant griping and insults of the Cardinals bench, ordered all fourteen men out of the park. Solemnly they formed a single file and marched to the clubhouse. Luckily, Bresnahan had two pitchers warming up behind the outfield or he would have had no relievers.[47]

Two more games were scheduled with St. Louis but on the thirtieth the lingering storm unleashed its full fury, making the field unplayable for both days. In all, this southern storm deluged the city with six-and-a-half inches of rain in seven days. Chicago's entire series with Philadelphia was rained out, meaning that the games would have to be made up in Chicago. Pittsburgh was in Boston and managed to split a doubleheader on the thirtieth. In the first game Clarke finally unveiled his pricey new pitcher, Marty O'Toole. Fans and writers alike had been clamoring for a peek at him but Clarke kept putting off his debut. Dreyfuss went so far as to pay $5,000 to get O'Toole's catcher from St. Paul, making them by far the most costly battery in baseball. Pitching against the worst team in the league, O'Toole struck out nine and walked ten while staggering to a 6–4 victory. He allowed only five hits, two of them by Donlin. In the second game elder statesman Cy Young, recently signed, enjoyed a brief return to his glory days by shutting out the Pirates 6–0.[48]

Clarke had a good reason for keeping O'Toole under wraps. "I had in mind all the time," he said, "what happened to McGraw when he was trying to introduce Marquard into the smart set, and I was afraid the same thing would happen to me." It had taken Marquard nearly three years to master his craft and find his way in the major leagues. On the other hand, the most sensational rookie of 1911, Grover Cleveland Alexander, had no oversized reputation preceding him and slipped into the season with a cluster of early wins before people began taking notice of his talent. What Clarke feared most was a label like "$22,500 lemon" pinned on O'Toole. "I have been told," said Mathewson, "that Clarke was the most relieved man in seven counties when O'Toole came through with that victory in Boston."[49]

In looking at New York's success so far, a St. Louis writer gave most of the credit to the Giants' manager. "Mr. McGraw is one boy who knows something," he observed. Marquard had emerged as a first-rate pitcher because McGraw had the patience and foresight to stay with him through two unimpressive years. About the same time he bought Marquard, he had also paid $4,500 for Bull Durham, who looked to be another top prospect. However, McGraw dispatched him to Toronto within a short time, and he never returned to the majors. "McGraw is one of the best judges of baseball talent, latent or developed, that the game knows," concluded the writer. Another St. Louis writer agreed that "McGraw played the 'waiting game,' developed his men slowly and taught them baseball. Result: They have all come to the fore." Nor did it go unnoticed that the Little Napoleon had seven former players serving as managers, including Bresnahan.[50]

At month's end the Giants sat atop the league by two and a half games over the Cubs and three and a half games over the Pirates. The vagaries of weather had created a marked difference in the number of games played by the three teams. Chicago had completed only 111 games, New York 116, and Pittsburgh 119. The Cubs had won five fewer games than the Giants, while the Pirates had lost five more. As in past years, the disparity in games played meant more doubleheaders toward the end of the season, when players were weary and pitching staffs at their lowest ebb. The Cubs faced the most pressure in that respect. "The Chicago pitching staff is so ragged," said the *Herald*, "that it will probably have a great deal of trouble standing up under a string of double headers on any lot."[51]

But the Giants faced a major difficulty of their own. Since the western clubs had just finished their last eastern swing, all postponed games in the East would have to be played in the home park of the western team. Moreover, the 1911 schedule dictated that the Giants would spend most of the crucial month of September on the road. During this last home stand at the Polo Grounds, New York won fourteen of eighteen games, an almost impossible record to maintain in foreign ballparks. McGraw remembered all too well the nightmare of his club's western swings in 1910.

Sporting News claimed that McGraw "believes that with a lead of four games he can get through the last Western invasion to pennant victory and he has a fine outlook, indeed, to establish that margin before he tackles the Pirates for the last time in the beginning of the final Western tour. Pittsburg seems slipping out of it day by day, and the Cubs have absolutely no chance, unless the pitchers of the Windy City pull themselves together somehow." Clarke and Evers figured that the Giants would need a five-game lead. "Their present success is entirely due to John J. McGraw," Evers added. "I might say that the Giants are a second division team with a first division manager. Without McGraw they wouldn't be heard of."[52]

In all the Giants compiled a record of 16-8 during August but stole only forty-six bases, partly because of an abnormally wet month that turned infields to goo. For the season Brooklyn had lost twelve of thirteen games to their local rivals. Even more, the Giants had managed only a split of eighteen games with the Cubs, while the Superbas had defeated Chicago in eleven of seventeen games. The club had survived the month with no major injuries. Mathewson showed signs of returning to form, but he had been overshadowed by Marquard, who emerged as the league's top pitcher with his brilliant performances. Since a July 18 loss to Cincinnati he had reeled off ten victories, nine of them against teams other than Brooklyn or Boston.[53]

Then there was the matter of Faust. The team had won regularly since he turned up in New York, and the fans enjoyed his antics before games. McGraw had to decide whether to take him along on the last western swing and be charged with making a Faustian bargain. But Faust's newly won fame produced a complication. William Hammerstein offered him a handsome fee to do a vaudeville act. Faust agreed but for one week only, because, he said, the Giants would need him for their coming western tour.[54]

STANDINGS ON AUGUST 31

	Won	Lost	Pct.		Won	Lost	Pct
New York	72	44	.621	St. Louis	61	55	.526
Chicago	67	44	.604	Cincinnati	53	61	.465
Pittsburgh	70	49	.588	Brooklyn	45	69	.395
Philadelphia	64	52	.552	Boston	30	88	.254

CHAPTER 14

September: Road Warriors

*"There is one player on the New York roster
who may be depended on to bear the brunt of
the battle in the enemy's territory. That player
is Rube Marquard. It is one of the oddities of
baseball that a pitcher who at the opening of
the season was considered excess baggage
should become the hope of the team."*

—NEW YORK PRESS

"MANAGER McGRAW . . . HAS ENFORCED discipline this year more than ever," observed a baseball writer. "Two Giants were recently suspended without pay for several days because they talked back, and others were fined because they didn't report for morning practice at 10 o'clock sharp. McGraw insists that the men must earn their salaries, and if they are unfit he makes them sit on the bench with no money. No favorites are played, and there's absolutely no sentiment . . . You've got to hand it to McGraw. He knows how to make the Giants play ball, and that's the secret of their success."[1]

Especially was this true for so young a team. "Some of my friends," said McGraw with a hint of sarcasm, "have repeated again and again the statement that I never had developed a player since I have been a manager, and that the only way in which I could win a championship was by buying seasoned material. Now if this present club doesn't come close to being one which I selected and brought up myself I am willing to get out of base ball. That's one reason why I wish to win. I tried the men out together to play ball in my own way, and I trust that I have got them going right for the championship." If the team could take the pennant, it would be the youngest club ever to do so.[2]

Mathewson confirmed McGraw's complete control over the team. "In 1911 . . . I can safely say that every base which was pilfered by a New York runner was stolen by the direct order of McGraw, except in the few games from which he was absent," he wrote. "Then his lieutenants followed his system as closely as any one can pursue the involved and intricate style that he alone understands." To most observers, the combination of youth and speed accounted for much of the club's success. McGraw reminded them that "it isn't all speed, though. There is some pretty fair batting on the part of the Giants now and then. If you will look over the results of the year you will find that we have been hitting almost all of the pitchers with success."[3]

That the scribes called McGraw "Little Napoleon" was no mystery. The youth of the team had forced McGraw to ride herd on it as never before. "The handicap that McGraw is laboring under," noted *Sporting Life*, "is that he has to work and pull the wires himself. In the entire Giant team he has not a lieutenant who can lend him the assistance that Tinker and Sheckard give Chance of the Cubs, or that Doolin and Knabe can give to the injured Dooin. Fred Clarke has Tommy Leach and Hans Wagner to assist him in the leadership of the Pirates, but McGraw is left to pull all the Giants' wires." One Giant confirmed to the writer that "McGraw is more than 50 per cent to our club."[4]

The September schedule had New York playing a quick set in Philadelphia, coming home for short series against Boston and Brooklyn, and then going to Boston for another series. On the fifteenth the Giants would head west for the final swing that would likely decide their pennant hopes.

The month opened with a doubleheader in Philly for which McGraw had his two aces ready. Since Becker's play had fallen off somewhat, he returned a well-rested Red Murray to the lineup. In the opener Mathewson battled Earl Moore for eleven innings before coming out on top 3–2, spacing ten hits until Fletcher singled, stole second, and rode home on a double by Devore. Matty's fine performance was upstaged by yet another Marquard masterpiece. Rube yielded only a single by Luderus for his second one-hitter in a week in winning 2–0. He walked none, struck out ten, induced fourteen pop ups or fly outs, and allowed only three grounders, two of which he fielded himself. The infield might as well have taken the game off.[5]

"The work of Marquard has long since passed the realm of the spectacular and is rapidly mounting to the marvellous," said the *Tribune*. His recent outings had been the sort of magic usually associated with the likes of Mathewson or Walter Johnson. In his last three games or twenty-seven innings he had permitted only four hits and one run while striking out thirty batters. No one expected him to continued that pace, but neither had anyone expected him to emerge as the top pitcher in the league. Nothing more was heard about the $11,000 lemon. McGraw's patience, ridiculed more than once, had been rewarded beyond even his expectations. Joe Tinker, who had willed himself to be Mathewson's chief tormentor, had no such luck against Marquard. "You can't hit what you don't see," he said. "When he throws his fast one, the only way you know it's past you is because you hear the ball hit the catcher's glove."[6]

Red Dooin returned to the Philadelphia bench for the first time since his injury but could not play. He did not like much of what he saw. The Giants stole six bases in the two games, the Phillies none. They pilfered three more the next day in breezing to a 7–2 lead heading into the eighth inning. Then Crandall, who had been generous with hits, gave up three runs. In the ninth the Phillies got men on first and second with one out and the middle of their order coming to bat when McGraw summoned not Mathewson but Marquard, who had not warmed up. With ten thousand fans "yelling like maniacs," he preserved a 7–6 Giant win.[7]

For two years McGraw had nursed Marquard along after his disastrous first appearance. As Mathewson put it, "Marquard is another man whom McGraw constantly subjects to a conversational massage." On road trips McGraw saw to it from the first that Marquard roomed with Mathewson, a fount of pitching knowledge as well as a splendid influence. Mathewson thought that "the New York newspapers, first by the great amount of publicity given to his old record, and then by criticising him for not making a better showing, had a great deal to do with Marquard failing to make good the first two years he was in New York." McGraw now found himself in the ironic position of having to be careful not to overwork his new star, as he had done with Matty down many a home stretch of the season.[8]

Marquard did not let his newfound fame go to his head, at least for a time. Rather he was grateful for having shed his "lemon" reputation with a vengeance. "Every single day of all the years I spent in the Big Leagues was a thrill for me," he said as an old man. "It was like a dream come true." Unlike some players, he needed no tending or watching. "Myself, I've never smoked or taken a drink in my life," he claimed. "I always said you can't burn the candle at both ends."[9]

On Sunday the third the New York papers reported that Evers had finally returned to the Cub lineup but not in his usual position. Chance had decided to leave Zimmerman at second base and play Evers at third in place of Jimmy Doyle. He smacked a single and a triple to spark Chicago to a 3–1 win over the Reds. The Cubs also acquired veteran first baseman Kitty Bransfield, who had starred on the pennant-winning Pittsburgh teams of 1901–1903. The inability of the Pirates to find a solid first baseman after his departure became known as "the Bransfield curse." Although the Cubs also needed a first sacker, they regarded Bransfield as a pinch hitter.[10]

That day Chicago could do no more than split a doubleheader with the Cardinals, while Pittsburgh lost to Cincinnati. In the American League Connie Mack's Athletics remained comfortably ahead of Detroit, and he was already dispatching a scout to look at potential World Series rivals. A year earlier he had sent men to watch the Cubs and bring back intelligence. This year's scout concluded that the Giants "will be harder to beat than the Cubs ever could be under present conditions. In the first place, the Cubs have lost much of their fire. Frank Chance as a playing manager was without a peer, but he has yet to show his ability as a leader from the bench. McGraw has a splendidly drilled team and fighters. There is not a man on the team who seems to have anything in mind but winning. I went out expecting to see some points of weakness in the Giants, but I could find none that loomed up large."[11]

New York took a seven-game winning streak into the Polo Grounds for a Labor Day doubleheader against lowly Boston. In the morning game the team got six quick runs in the first three innings off Lefty Tyler while swiping six bases off Kling, who was so ineffective that Bill Rariden replaced him and caught the afternoon game as well. Kling's arm, smirked the *Times*, "seemed to be made of crockery." Ames scattered nine hits while waiting for the "Ames hoodoo" that this day never arrived as New York prevailed 6–4 before some ten thousand fans. Three times that number flocked to the ballpark in the afternoon to watch their new favorite hero, Rube Marquard, stifle the cellar dwellers. Once again the southpaw got off to a blazing start, blanking the Rustlers for seven innings.[12]

Then, inexplicably, Marquard lost it in the eighth inning as Boston got five hits, a walk, and a costly error by Fletcher to tie the score at 5–5. McGraw elected not to remove Marquard. After a scoreless ninth the Rustlers reached Rube for a double and two singles in the tenth that, combined with another Fletcher error, produced three runs even as

Marquard struck out two more batters to tie the league record of fourteen. The Giants fought back with two runs in the bottom half but left the tying run on base.

New York's winning streak ended at eight on the eve of a rare luxury, two off days in a row. During that time Chicago took two from St. Louis and closed to within two and a half games off the Giants. Against Brooklyn, their favorite patsy, on the seventh the Giants played poorly enough to lose 4–3 while the Cubs were sweeping two from Cincinnati. Mathewson was again the victim of weak support as the Giants managed only four hits off Cy Barger and made three costly errors. "A muffed throw by Merkle," read the *Sun*'s obituary, "another by Fletcher, a high throw by Herzog and a dropped fly by Snodgrass in their separate costly ways played a part in every Brooklyn run."[13]

By then Faust had opened his little show despite feeling "porely." He told Sid Mercer that "I'll quit any time McGraw gives the word. There is more money in this theatrical game, but I don't want to be an actor. I am keeping in good condition doing my famous windup and slides, but I expect to go west with the Giants next week. McGraw needs all us good pitchers."[14]

The Giants had suffered the indignity of their two ace pitchers losing to the two worst teams in the league, and having their lead cut to one game. The next day Marquard returned to form by stifling the Superbas 3–2. When he weakened in the seventh, giving up five hits and two runs, some in the small crowd on a dark, dismal day yelled, "Take him out!" McGraw ignored their counsel but the *Press* noted that "it was the first time in many moons that the wonderful southpaw has been comforted with those soothing words." The Giants stole six bases compared to only two the day before. "They couldn't help trying to steal bases," suggested the *Herald*. "It was too cold to stand still."[15]

Heywood Broun, who had mostly ignored Faust, abruptly reversed course and wrote a lengthy explanation of the game that declared, "The real reason of the Giants' success, however, lay not in the stanch arm of Marquard, nor the ready bat of Fred Merkle, but in the presence of Charlie Faust. McGraw's dark horse has been absent for the past few days, and it is absolutely certain that the defeats at the hands of Boston and Brooklyn would hardly have happened if he had been within call." Faust's theater manager had brought him to the game, but he had to leave early to do his performance. "No sooner had he left the field," said Broun, "than the tide of battle turned. The Giants made not another run or hit, and Brooklyn came very near victory."[16]

The Saturday game, played in the rain, turned into an exercise in frustration. McGraw desperately wanted to win this last home game against the team the Giants loved to beat. New York started strong with three runs in the first, but Brooklyn battered Crandall and Wiltse for fifteen hits and clawed its way to a 4–3 lead. Since the next day was Sunday, McGraw brought in Mathewson to pitch the last two innings. In the ninth Fred Merkle sparked hope with a single. Although New York had not stolen a base all game on the wet field, McGraw gave Merkle the sign to go on the next pitch. He barely beat the throw to second. Herzog sacrificed him to third and Fletcher brought him home with a sacrifice fly to tie the game. Jim Johnstone then called the game on account of darkness.[17]

"That steal of Merkle's was the critical play of the game," McGraw explained afterward. "I looked to catch them off their guard. No one was out and they would naturally expect me to wait. The chances were one to three against me, but that little bit of ground between first and second base meant the game. If I had lost the crowd would have roasted me for ordering him to steal." That same day Faust wound up his vaudeville week. In his absence the Giants had lost two games and were lucky to tie another. In little more than a month the Kansas farm boy had become a celebrity in the nation's biggest city almost without trying. Well might McGraw have wondered whether the team dared leave Faust behind on the crucial western swing.[18]

On Sunday the tenth the Giants boarded a train for Boston, the first stop on the long trek that would keep them on the road for the rest of the month and the only one in the East. As pitching insurance McGraw had picked up a promising right-hander named Bert Maxwell from Birmingham. He badly wanted these four games against the last-place team to build a bigger lead before facing the western clubs. The Giants' entourage included no less than nine newspapermen and two mascots, young Dick Hennessey and Faust. "I've decided to give up the stage," Faust announced after arriving in Boston. "I thought that the club would need me on this trip, and, besides, I got $150 last week and ain't that enough for any one?"[19]

J. Pluvius Jupiter, the scribes' favorite term for rain, greeted the team on Monday, forcing a doubleheader the next day, their sixth since August 14. "It doesn't help at all, this double header business," growled McGraw, "for the very good reason that it is harder to win two games in one day than two games on two consecutive days." New York now had a total of four doubleheaders on their schedule compared to seven for Chicago, which had more makeup games. A crowd estimated at ten to twelve thousand—mammoth for the Rustlers—turned out to watch the "M & M boys," as the writers called them, subdue Boston. In the first game Marquard did a reprise of his last start against the Rustlers, breezing through six innings with a 5–1 lead before coming unraveled in the seventh as Boston pushed five runs across the plate. Crandall came to the rescue and the Giants retaliated with four runs in the eighth for a 9–6 win.[20]

The second game, billed as a matchup between "Big Six" Mathewson, as the writers liked to call him, and the winningest pitcher in baseball history, proved no contest when forty-four-year-old Cy Young, in the last of his twenty-one seasons, was driven from the mound in the third inning as the Giants piled up nine runs en route to an 11–2 victory. Having swiped only one base in the first game, New York stole six in the second, including one by Mathewson and another of home by Herzog. The onslaught featured four home runs, two by Merkle and one by Doyle. The fourth blast came from Crandall, who entered the game when McGraw decided to rest Mathewson after the second inning.[21]

"Crandall can never tell when he has to work these days," observed the *Times*. "One day he has to relieve a slabster who falls by the wayside and on the next he has to go in because it is too easy for a master twirler like Big Six. Crandall is like a fire horse. He has to be near the harness, ready to gallop out at the first alarm." He would be needed more than ever because McGraw learned that the problem with Marquard was a sore elbow, and it was not clear how long it would bother him.[22]

Ames took the mound in the third game. A few days before the trip, dogged by the constant references in the papers to the "Ames hoodoo" or "Ames jinx," he went to McGraw and said, "I don't see any use in taking me along, Mac. The club can't win with me pitching if the other guys don't even get a foul." McGraw brushed aside his objections and brought Ames to Boston. On the rainy day a package arrived for Ames. Sent by a well-known actress, it contained a necktie and a four-leaf clover along with good-luck wishes. The directions, included in an envelope, stipulated that the clover had to be worn inside both his uniform and street clothes to be effective, while the necktie had to be worn with street clothes and concealed inside his uniform. The necktie was so bright, said Mathewson, "It would have done for a headlight and made Joseph's coat of many colors look like a mourning garment." But Ames decided to try them, saying, "I'd wear you if you were a horseshoe."[23]

Pitching on a cold windy day, his favorite kind of weather, he stifled the Rustlers on three hits and triumphed 4–1, thanks to a few timely hits, steals by Herzog and Fletcher, and five Boston errors. "It was so cold that you could smell moth balls all over the stands," said the shivering *Herald* man. "Everyone had on his winter weights and had put the knee lengths away in the camphor." That night at dinner Ames showed the tie and clover to his teammates and said, "I don't change her until I lose." He also confided to Sid Mercer that he was "glad Faust is going to stick because he certainly has brought good luck to us all." Ames recited game by game how the team had won when Faust was there and lost when he wasn't. "You can say for me," he added, "that I think he is a great man for the team even [if] he never gets a chance to pitch."[24]

"It is amusing to note how the athletes have warmed up to Faust since they have come to regard him as a talisman," said Mercer. "They play pool with him, take him to the theatres, introduce him to everybody, and sympathize deeply with him when he complains of his failure to get in a real game. As for Faust, well, they couldn't lose him if they tried." Faust tried hard to pin McGraw down on when he could pitch, but the manager proved a master of evasion. On September 14 the *Boston Globe* published a team photograph of the Giants that included Faust standing proudly in the last row next to Fred Snodgrass.[25]

The last game in Boston turned into a bizarre hit fest with each team getting sixteen but New York putting theirs to better use for a 13–9 win. Wiltse coasted into the eighth inning with a 7–2 lead, then surrendered four hits and two runs before McGraw sent Mathewson to relieve him. Matty stifled the Rustlers' rally and in the top of the ninth cleared the bases with a double and stole third as the Giants poured six runs across the plate. Feeling secure with a 13–4 lead, McGraw tapped Crandall to replace him and took out two regulars as well. "The day was, to say the least, brisk," said the *Tribune*, "and the Indiana lad had about three minutes in which to limber up." Boston greeted him with a barrage of seven hits augmented by two Giant errors. Five runners scored before Crandall restored McGraw's blood pressure to normal by getting out of the inning. The last two innings took as long as the first seven.[26]

Although New York stole four more bases in the game, McGraw was not pleased with their performance on the base paths. Both Devore and Fletcher managed to get picked off during the game. In the first inning Doyle singled and might have easily taken second but chose not to try. McGraw called time and stalked across the diamond to let Doyle know in clear language what he had failed to do. "When McGraw wanted to chew on someone," Doyle recalled with a smile, "he often took me. I guess it was because I was the captain and made $600 a year extra." The fifteenth was a travel day for the team's last foray into the West, Pittsburgh being the first stop. McGraw signaled his seriousness of purpose by banning card playing on the trip. Players were to pass the time talking baseball with interludes of entertainment provided by Faust, whom McGraw had decided to take along on a swing in which the Giants would need all the luck they could muster.[27]

Twelve writers accompanied the team on its safari. The Giants took with them a four-game lead over the Cubs and six over the Pirates. They had played 127 games, Chicago 124, and Pittsburgh 137. Since Faust joined the team, New York had lost only the one game to Brooklyn; he missed the Boston defeat. The Giants had won nine of eleven with one tie, and boasted a four-game winning streak. "I do not dread this coming trip to the West nearly so much as the fans do," said McGraw. "It's all a question of pitchers, and our twirling staff is going as well as any in the league."[28]

THE TRAIN RATTLED ALONG ITS MONOTONOUS WAY, wreathed in billowing smoke, the wheels singing their clackity tune along the rails. In the stuffy parlor car amid cigar and cigarette smoke the men amused themselves as best they could between meals and before bedtime. McGraw had banned card playing, explained Mathewson, because "he realized that often the stakes ran high, and that the losers brooded over the money which they lost and were thinking of this rather than the game. It hurt their playing, so there were no cards." Faust happily performed his vaudeville act several times with Murray as emcee, adding his own unscripted touches to the performance. At the station in Pittsburgh, Faust complained to Doyle that his suitcase felt heavy. "That's because you've been laying around in the train all day and haven't been working," replied Doyle. He did not bother mentioning the several railroad spikes and pounds of pig iron some of the men had snuck into the suitcase.[29]

The first game at Forbes Field attracted more than twenty thousand fans eager to watch a matchup between the two bonus babies, Marty O'Toole and Marquard. That O'Toole had not yet lost a game added spice to the contest. Marquard declared his elbow to be better and demonstrated it by limiting

Pittsburgh to five hits through seven innings while his mates initiated the rookie with eight hits that scored runs in six different innings for a 6–2 victory. The only runs allowed by Rube came in the first inning when Snodgrass fell down and turned a fly ball into a double and Devore let one roll through him for a cheap home run. Snodgrass atoned for his slip by cutting Tommy Leach down at the plate with a strong throw in the fourth. When Pittsburgh opened the eighth with a walk and single, McGraw did not hesitate to summon Mathewson, who set the Pirates down without a hit.[30]

"This O'Toole is a game bird," conceded the *Times*. "When he gets down to business his red hair sticks up straight like a flame, and his heaves are so swift that they almost bowl the catcher over. No quitting for him." Elsewhere the Cubs, described as "outplayed mentally and physically" by the *Chicago Tribune*, lost to Brooklyn 4–2 and also lost Evers to a three-day suspension.[31]

Clarke was frustrated, not only because the Pirates had dropped so far back but also because a charley horse kept him out of the lineup at a time when he was having one of his best seasons at the plate. Wagner had willed himself back into the lineup by playing first base, but his bad ankle hampered his hitting. Even so, he willingly joined in the pregame fun by standing in against Faust's windmill windup with three mighty swings that found nothing but air. Faust strutted to the bench in a cloud of applause from the crowd. Dick Hennessey performed his act as well, taking a turn at first base and catching every ball hurled at him by the Giants infielders. None of this bothered McGraw, who realized that it kept everyone loose without distracting them from the business at hand.[32]

Sporting News climbed aboard the Victory Faust bandwagon by stressing that "this peculiar character has worked wonders as a mascoter in McGraw's camp. It is a strange superstition that has overcome the Giants, but they believe his presence spells luck . . . Giant athletes state that on the bench Faust calls the turn on nearly every man, predicting base hits or runs with rarely a miss. Upon looking back into the records again they find that he has been on the bench 26 days, and that in that time they have won 26 games . . . The Giants have taken his presence as a winning hunch, and even as business-like as John McGraw is, the Giant chief says that he would rather lose any one man on the club." Connie Mack, most likely with tongue firmly in cheek, said publicly that Faust would bring the Giants enough luck to win the pennant.[33]

McGraw used Mathewson because the next day was Sunday. On their day off some of the players strolled through Schenley Park after breakfast while others were content to sit around the lobby and talk. Wiltse, bothered by a lame hip, went over to Youngstown, Ohio, to see the famed healer John "Bonesetter" Reese, who manipulated the pain out of him. Although Reese had no medical credentials and saw patients as a sideline to his job with a steel company, he had an uncanny gift for fixing or alleviating sore limbs. Dozens of major leaguers swore by him. Drucke went with Wiltse to have Reese look at the problem in his shoulder caused by the lurching elevated.[34]

That evening after dinner some of the players followed Mathewson to the checker club at the YMCA, where he took on eight challengers and lost only one game. They seemed a confident bunch to the scribes, only one of whom noticed that the club had won nine straight road games dating back to August. However, Chicago swept a doubleheader from Brooklyn that day to cut New York's lead to four games. Herzog grew upset when word came that his mother had been stricken with paralysis, and he expected to be called home.[35]

On Monday the eighteenth Matty returned to the mound and stifled Pittsburgh 7–2 on four hits to run his record to 24–12. The Giants scored all their runs in the first two innings, but this time McGraw let his ace go the route even though he had pitched in five of the last nine games. New York ran the Pirates and catcher Mike Simon dizzy, stealing eight bases, five in the first two innings, and goading Simon into two errant throws. One hit Snodgrass in the back of the head at second base. He got up, stole third, and then left the game in favor of Becker. So completely did the Giants dominate, noted the *Herald*, that "most of the crowd stopped watching the game and gave attention to 'Charley' Faust warming up. That was lots more interesting."[36]

Tuesday broke cool and wet with a morning shower, but the tarpaulin at Forbes Field kept the diamond dry. The *Tribune* called it "a regular Ames day." Clad in his special tie and clover leaf, Red took the mound and limited Pittsburgh to five hits as the Giants won 3–1 to sweep the series. Doyle doubled in the first inning, stole third, and came home on a grounder. The Giants scored single runs in the next two innings, played solid defense behind Ames, and stole four bases, making fifteen for the series. The *Herald*'s man got wind of the special necktie and asked Ames about it. "It's lucky," he replied, "and I'm going to wear it until I lose." The victory increased New York's lead to six games over Chicago, which got only one hit and lost to the Phillies.[37]

McGraw was growing more confident of the team's chances every day, his enthusiasm held in check only by fear of jinxing the outcome, as seemed to have happened in 1908. The *Sun* reported that McGraw "now admits that the Giants will win the pennant. 'But,' he adds, 'I want to win it as soon as possible.'" The *Times* agreed that the Little Napoleon, "invariably conservative in his predictions, has caught the spirit of unbridled confidence of the players and says he can't see where the Giants can lost [*sic*] now."[38]

BRIMMING WITH CONFIDENCE, THE GIANTS RODE into St. Louis with a seven-game winning streak to play back-to-back doubleheaders. They found a team gasping for air from a schedule that forced them to play seven doubleheaders in eight days. The Cardinals had been a nemesis to New York this season and last, but Bresnahan's team was having troubles of its own, not the least of which was his absence from the lineup. St. Louis still hovered above the .500 mark but struggled to nudge Philadelphia from fourth place. Club owner Helene Britton watched only the first game. The *Times* suggested that she "didn't have the heart to stay and see her team get it twice in the same place, on the same day, by the same Giants."[39]

In the first game Marquard demonstrated his return to form by blanking St. Louis 4–0 on four hits. While Faust regaled the St. Louis fans with his act, McGraw told Doc Crandall to pitch the second game. The Giants staked him to two runs in the first inning but St. Louis drove him from the hill in the sixth. Tied 4–4 in the eighth with a thunderstorm threatening, the Giants scored three runs and then obeyed McGraw's dictum to make outs while the fans cried for umpire Cy Rigler to call the game. Rigler let the Cardinals bat in the gloom, then called a halt with the Giants ahead 7–4.

Unable to play himself, Bresnahan ordered his catchers Jack Bliss and young Ivey Wingo to stop the Giants' running game at all costs. In the early innings of the first game Bliss did just that, throwing out five men trying to steal. McGraw then told his batters to sacrifice runners to second until the fifth when Meyers on first and Merkle on third caught the Cardinals by surprise with a double steal. Altogether New York stole four bases off Bliss and three more in the second game off Wingo. However, both Herzog and Snodgrass were picked off first.[40]

Their "rampant, unrestrained sprinting on the bases," as the *Times* called it, proved but a prelude to the next day's doubleheader in which the Giants stole seven bases in each game. While piling up thefts, they also worried opposing players and managers to distraction with the threat of doing so every time any one of them got on base. But McGraw's tactic of constant running also backfired. Seven times during the second twin bill Giants runners were gunned down on the bases. Doyle blasted a triple but was caught trying to steal home. Snodgrass was picked cleanly off first base but stole second because no one was there to take the throw. Murray almost fell for the old hidden-ball trick before McGraw yelled a warning just in time.[41]

In the first game Wiltse, still bothered by his ailing hip, managed to gut his way to the ninth inning with a 3–1 lead despite four errors behind him, gave up a run, and needed Mathewson's help in getting the last two outs. Having won ten straight games, McGraw decided to spare the other pitchers by giving Bert Maxwell his first start. The Cardinals jumped on him for five runs in the first two innings and twelve hits in all as they stopped New York's winning streak 8–7. A relaxed McGraw let the rookie go the distance. After he walked to the dugout and slumped down on the bench steeped in gloom over his performance, Marquard went to console him. "I know just how you feel," he sympathized. "You ought to see what they did to me at first."[42]

Faust also needed consoling. He had received a "black hand letter" from Chicago accusing him of being a jinx for other teams in the league and warning that something would happen to him if he didn't go back to Kansas at once. Already the scribes had accepted his middle name as "Victory" and dubbed him the team's charm. "Faust is now considered the official 'jinx' for the other teams," said the *Times*, "and Manager McGraw wouldn't release him for money."[43]

By the fifth game of the series the Giants had run themselves ragged, physically and literally. More than once during the season the constant running and sliding had taken a toll on their uniforms, and new ones had to be sent for to preserve decency. "Nearly every man on the club had slid the seat out of his uniform pants," said McGraw. "We had patched and patched until the principal feature of our pants was safety pins." In one game Devore tore the bottom out of his pants and had to be escorted off the field by a shield of teammates covering his rear. Nor was he alone in this problem. "Shins have been barked, uniforms and stockings ripped beyond repair, and shoes spiked and tattered," noted the *Times*. "When the Giants get back to Coogan's Hollow they will be battle scarred, sure enough." After purloining twenty-one bases in four games against St. Louis, the Giants let the last contest go by without a single theft. "The fallaway slide has proved so disastrous on the team's uniforms," explained the *Tribune*, "that McGraw refused to run the risk of having any one arrested for indecent exposure."[44]

Ames again showed his newfound mettle by taking a 3–0 lead into the eighth inning. After yielding a run in the eighth, he loaded the bases with one out in the ninth. McGraw called on Marquard, who gave up a two-run double to Ed Konetchy, tying the score. In the tenth Meyers reached on an error and with two out scurried home on a double by Devore, a lead and victory that Marquard barely preserved. Three years after his infamous boner, Merkle still had to endure the old taunts. "The rooters here yell 'Bonehead' at Merkle no matter who makes the error that is on a play at first base," said the *Sun*. "If Merkle doesn't stop throws impossible to stop he is a 'bonehead.' More boneheads like him would strengthen any team."[45]

Sid Mercer attributed the victory to Faust, and Mathewson agreed with him. According to Mercer, Faust was warming up with Mathewson behind the stands when Marquard got into trouble. Matty told him to get to the bench, adding, "You know you were not there the other day when we almost lost in the ninth inning." Faust lit out for the bench in his loping fashion, halting the game briefly while he crossed the infield and planted himself conspicuously on the bench. The Giants on the bench cheered his return. "We can't lose now," cried Becker, "look, here comes Charley." At that point Marquard settled down and retired the next two batters for the win. "Then," said Mercer, "the Giants decamped a triumphal procession with Faust proudly marching in the lead."[46]

Earlier in the day Mathewson paid a visit to the St. Louis Stock Exchange to look over the quotations. Some of his teammates thought him as much a whiz at finance as at checkers. "It was sort of a hobby with Christy," recalled his wife Jane. "He was wonderful at it, and he constantly read books on finance. But he never accepted financial favors from anyone. He could have made thousands of dollars. He was offered many products wholesale, but he always refused to accept anything on the basis of what he was as a ball player." At the exchange he was mobbed by messenger boys, who persuaded him to wad some paper into a ball and demonstrate how he threw the fadeaway.[47]

By this time Faust had unveiled some of his pet eccentricities. He was especially fond of manicures and massages. "He would go into the barber shop with any member of the team who happened to be getting a shave," said an amused Mathewson, "and take a massage and manicure for the purposes of sociability as a man takes a drink." During the stay in St. Louis, Faust achieved a personal best by getting five manicures in one day. He also had a passion for pie, eating some at every meal along with a small half before bedtime. To humor him, McGraw continued sending him behind the stands to warm up. Faust did so eagerly, awaiting the day that he would be summoned to the mound.[48]

On September 24, after the Giants had left town, S. Carlisle Martin favored Faust with a lengthy interview in the Sunday *St. Louis Post-Dispatch*. His portrait introduced some new details—real or invented—to the public, including the fact that Faust spoke with a German accent that the New York writers apparently ignored, pronouncing his middle name as "Wictor." Asked about his family, he said, "Vell . . . I've god a brudder who can pitch. I've caught him and he's got more breaks dan Wiltse or Mathewson, I t'ink." With his gap-toothed smile he told the story of the fortune-teller who said he was destined to pitch the Giants to the pennant and also to marry a girl named Lulu. He did not know Lulu but was going to San Francisco to find her after the season. His three goals in life were to pitch for the Giants, marry Lulu, and stop only at hotels that served apple pie. Martin could not help but be impressed with how earnest Faust was in everything he said.[49]

Cincinnati was the next stop on the road show that was fast turning into a triumphal procession. "It's all over but the shouting," shouted the *Press*, "and the best team triumphed . . . All hail to the Giant Champions of 1911." Mathewson, who had not lost to the Reds in Cincinnati since mid-1908, greeted his favorite patsies in customary fashion, allowing ten hits and three walks but only two runs while the Giants collected ten hits of their own and romped to a 6–2 win. "The Giants went on the field in patched uniforms and refrained from running the bases in order to comply with the laws of decency," reported the *Press*. On the anniversary of his 1908 blunder, Merkle smacked a single and double while handling ten chances flawlessly. Prior to the game Faust moved his act to the outfield but had to cut it short when a fly ball conked him in the head.[50]

That same day lowly Boston torched four Chicago pitchers for thirteen hits to smite the Cubs 14–6, putting the losers a full eight games behind the Giants. The bandwagon was fast gaining momentum. From Brush came a telegram to McGraw saying, "May good luck and Charley Faust stay with you." Treasurer John Whalen came out from New York to see for himself the brand of ball that was captivating the league. The ever politic Garry Herrmann hosted a dinner for the New York writers traveling with the team. McGraw was the guest of honor and received a toast as "manager of the pennant winning team of the National League and the next World's Champions." At Herrmann's request Faust delivered a rendition of a piece called "For the Good of the Game" and was rewarded with a bouquet of roses borrowed from the premises.[51]

The *Press* emphasized the patience McGraw had shown in building a winning team. Doyle was the only starter who had played regularly on the near-miss team of 1908. "The wonderful team of speed merchants has been built up entirely by McGraw's patience and his ability to judge young talent. Many of McGraw's present stars sat on the bench from one to three seasons before they had a chance to display their wares. This list includes Merkle, Marquard, Devore, Snodgrass and Fletcher, all of them important cogs in the Little Napoleon's speed machine . . . The Giants, man for man, are the fastest team that has been welded together in the history of modern baseball."[52]

A St. Louis writer saw McGraw as a brilliant teacher, one of whose star pupils was the Cardinals' own Bresnahan. "McGraw is an adapter . . . Whatever the character of the available material, McGraw molds his team to it and its policy is governed thereby," he noted. "This year the keynote of McGraw's success is speed . . . It was McGraw that developed this speed and adapted it to his uses. McGraw is essentially a developer—a TEACHER." If the Giants clashed with the Athletics in the World Series, he added, "it will not be a battle of Napoleons, as suggested, but of school teachers. For Mack is, to even a greater degree than McGraw, a molder of his own men."[53]

While Cincinnati had always been helpless against Mathewson, they also acted as chief nemesis for Marquard and beat him 6–5 on Sunday. The loss especially bothered Marquard because the large crowd of about 15,000 included some 1,100 of his friends and admirers who came over in two special trains from Indianapolis. The *Herald* observed that it was the first time the Giants had lost when Faust was on the bench. Faust insisted the fault was not his because he did not believe in playing ball on Sunday.[54]

"Marquard is the puzzle just now," suggested *Sporting News*. "Without doubt he is the best left-hander in either league, but he is suffering from a kink in his pitching elbow. He has been bothered in his last five starts. The trouble appears to be overwork. He will now be able to rest up and if he is in shape for the Athletics McGraw will face Philadelphia stronger than his club has ever been before." On Monday the twenty-fifth Crandall restored order by blanking the Reds 2–0 on four hits, but the Giants stole no bases and seemed lethargic. "They ran the bases with lead in their shoes," sniffed the *Times*.[55]

That day the Philadelphia Athletics clinched the American League pennant by walloping Detroit, their nearest competitor, 11–5. Earlier a reporter had asked McGraw if he had someone scouting the Athletics. "No," he said flatly. "I don't want to know anything about the way they play, till we meet them on the field. That is, if we do." A short time later he said the papers had told him Connie Mack had spies watching New York games. "I don't know whether that is so or not," he added, "but certainly we have none on his trail. I believe in snap judgments on the field when the battle is on to figure out moves, not in prearranged judgments."[56]

Tuesday was an off day on which the Giants took the train to their last western adversary, the Cubs. In recent years, especially 1910, New York had fared poorly at West End Park. This year the Giants still had done no better than split sixteen games with Chicago. McGraw wanted very much to clinch the pennant in the four games with the Cubs, but he sensed that the strain was starting to tell, that the players were tired and growing stale. Their high level of play, especially on the bases, had spoiled the writers into expecting it every day and commenting sourly when it did not happen. To help restore their energy he asked Wilbert Robinson to come out from Baltimore and join the team for awhile. When Robinson did not appear in Cincinnati, McGraw repeated the request in more urgent terms.[57]

Damon Runyon added his own piquant twist by claiming that "rumors seeped into the Giant camp this morning that a foul plot is on foot among Chicago fans to kidnap Charles Victory Faust, court jester and official jinx of the big town team." To foil the plot, said Runyon, a Pinkerton guard had been assigned him and all strangers nudged aside who tried to approach him at the Auditorium Annex hotel. A large crowd arrived early to watch "Charles Victory Faust, Dick Hennessey, and all the other circus features of Manager McGraw's spectacular production entitled, 'Winning the Baseball Quilt of 1911.'" A bemused Sam Weller of the *Chicago Tribune* noted that "C. 'Simp' Faust, official jinx for the Giants, introduced some novel base running during his practice session ... Today he will exhibit the latest thing in wind-ups. He claims a base runner can't tell whether he's about to pitch the ball or whether he's waving at friends in the grandstand."[58]

The crowd then delighted in an 8–0 rout of the Giants as Lew Richie, fast earning status as a Giant killer, bested Marquard. Murray got three hits but infuriated McGraw by getting picked off second base. Mathewson took the hill next day determined to even the series but reckoned without his personal nemesis. On a dark, oppressive day with drizzle falling, he waged a pitching duel with King Cole, the brilliant young pitcher who would finish 18–7 in 1911. The Giants scratched out a run in the first and would have had one more if Devore, who had walked to start the game, had not tried to steal. "He ran as if he was dragging an anchor," sneered the *Times*, and catcher Jimmy Archer easily threw him out. The *Press* observed that it was New York's first attempt to steal on Archer in five games, and the team did not try again. In the third inning the Cubs put two men on base and Tinker promptly lofted a double over Devore's head, scoring both runners, giving Chicago the second game 2–1.[59]

The loss cut New York's lead to five and a half games. The Giants had fourteen games left to play, Chicago nine. If the Cubs swept the series, as they had done the previous year, they would be in striking distance of first place. Fortunately, the twenty-ninth was an off day, giving everyone time to catch their breath. Wilbert Robinson had arrived the night before and was quick to say, "The men look stale to me. I can tell because I haven't seen them every day." McGraw agreed completely and decided on a remedy wholly out of character. "The players were going around with a haggard look in their eyes and heavy lines in their faces," he said later. The jovial Robinson lightened the mood at once. "Who's dead around here?" he brayed. "What's the matter?" At McGraw's suggestion he not only slapped backs and joked around but took some of the men out for a few glasses of ale to relax them. "That was an abstemious club," McGraw stressed. "We had no difficulty about rules of conduct."[60]

To the scribes McGraw put on a stolid face, saying that the law of averages had finally caught up with his club. "I don't see anything to fret about," he told the *Herald*. "Of course . . . I am disappointed at losing these two games, because the sooner the thing is decided the sooner I can begin to rest my men, and that is what they need, especially Mathewson and Marquard. If I can give my regular players a week's rest it will greatly increase our chances in the world's series." The *Times* thought the Giants were "tired, not physically but mentally. The nervous strain of the last few weeks' fight has kept them under a high tension, and it is beginning to worry them." The team had "lost its dash and vim and slowed up on the bases. It was the daring base running that had taken the other teams unawares, but the players are so fagged out now that no base stealing has been attempted . . . Devore has slowed up noticeably and has not been running the bases at his normal speed for more than a week."[61]

Chance was under no illusions as to his club's chances. "I don't see any hope for the Cubs," he admitted. "New York has too big a lead for us for this time in the race . . . Of course we are going to keep on fighting, because baseball is one of those things that you never can tell about." He mused that "it's the hardest thing in the world to clinch a title. A team that is under a strain often slumps, while a nine that has no worries will breeze along and win games. The best thing that could happen to the Giants is the hard fight that we are giving them here. It gets the team accustomed to fighting and puts the players on edge for the world's series." He recalled how his famed 1906 team cruised so easily to the pennant "and simply could not hustle toward the end of the season." The result was a shocking loss in the World Series to a White Sox team that did not clinch first place until the last week of the season.[62]

On a cold, damp last day of September, McGraw sent Ames out against Miner Brown. In the first inning Devore beat out a grounder that rolled up Tinker's arm, then watched Doyle unload a towering home run into the right-field bleachers. Taking no chances with a 2–0 lead, McGraw sent Matty, Marquard, Wiltse, Crandall, and Faust back of the stands to warm up, but Ames needed no help. Still under the spell of his charms, he scattered six hits and survived four Giant errors in a 3–1 victory. The *Press* conceded that "the Giants did not play like champions," but the victory closed out the most successful month of their season.[63]

Unlike the two previous seasons, when the club slumped badly on its last western swing, the Giants played at a blistering pace on their way to a 19-6 record with one tie in September. In those twenty-six games the team stole an amazing eighty-two bases before their energy flagged. No one kept count of how many uniforms they shredded in the process. With thirteen games left to play, the flag seemed tantalizingly close to their grasp. Ahead lay a final game with the Cubs and makeup games with Pittsburgh, Philadelphia, and Brooklyn before the team finally came home to the Polo Grounds.

STANDINGS ON SEPTEMBER 30

Team	Won	Lost	Pct.	Team	Won	Lost	Pct.
New York	90	50	.643	St. Louis	73	70	.511
Chicago	87	58	.600	Cincinnati	67	80	.456
Pittsburgh	82	66	.554	Brooklyn	60	82	.428
Philadelphia	78	64	.549	Boston	37	104	.262

CHAPTER 15

October: Sweet Victory

*"The Giants constitute a combination of old
and young men who work together with
harmony and smoothness. How in the world
Manager McGraw trained this collection of
players into such a compact, effective playing
machine will always be one of the mysteries of
baseball. The little manager doesn't say what
intuitive knowledge he has which would enable
him to know that men who were incompetent a
few seasons ago would gradually develope [sic]
into flag champions."*
    —THE NEW YORK TIMES

*"If a pitcher needed nothing but a wind-up I'll
back Charley Faust against the world."*
    —JOHN McGRAW

THE FINAL GAME AGAINST CHICAGO mattered because McGraw wanted to deflate any lingering hope the Cubs might have, and because he needed to see if Marquard could bounce back from his last two ugly starts. Morning rains turned the field into a sea of mud only slightly leavened by loads of sawdust, and a howling crowd did what it could to rattle Marquard. For seven innings he engaged in a taut, scoreless duel with Richie. Then the Giants came alive with two runs in the eighth and three more in the ninth for a 5–0 victory, sealing Chicago's doom.[1]

The team needed three more wins to clinch the flag and had next to play three games in three different cities. That night the club left for Pittsburgh to close down Forbes Field for the season with a makeup game. In raw, chilly weather McGraw decided to give Wiltse, sore hip and all, the honors, and he thanked the manager by blanking the Pirates 3–0 on two meek singles. While the Giants had scrambled to gain an even split in their season's games with Chicago, they captured sixteen wins in twenty-two games with Pittsburgh.[2]

The next stop on the road trip was Philadelphia, where the audience included Connie Mack and several of his players who wanted to see the Giants for themselves. The team gave them some food for thought. Through five innings Crandall waged an even 3–3 battle with Alexander; in the sixth New York exploded for nine runs, driving Alexander to cover in a 12–3 rout. After the big inning the team did what it could to hurry the game along. In the eighth they managed to go down on three pitches. Afterward they trooped happily to the station to catch the train that would take them to a pair of games in Brooklyn.[3]

"Johnny came marching home again last night," brayed the *Press*. "What Johnny? Why, Johnny McGraw and his band of Conquering Giants. They came home in style, too, pulling into the Pennsylvania station on the Pennant special . . . twenty-nine of them in the party, counting the scribes and Wilbur [sic] Robinson, Arlie Latham, Dick Hennessey, the mascot, and Charles Victory Faust. Every man jack of them had a smile on his face a yard wide and confidence supreme was writ on his features."[4]

Having added two more wins, the Giants stood at the brink, needing one more to cop the pennant. McGraw had no doubt as to who should have the honors. It was only fitting that the man who had last carried the team to the world championship try to lock down their quest for another one. Matty was pitted against Brooklyn's finest, lefty Nap Rucker, a matchup McGraw welcomed because he wanted to give his men practice for their encounter against the veteran Eddie Plank of the Athletics. Before a surprisingly sparse crowd of about 4,500, many of them Giant fans who took the subway to Brooklyn, Mathewson won a sparkling pitcher's duel 2–0, ending five long seasons of frustration for McGraw and his club. Still the *Tribune* commented that "the Giants looked battle-scarred, haggard and worn after their hard campaign in the West."[5]

McGraw could not say enough about the team that had just given him his first pennant since 1905. "I may have managed ball clubs which I thought were better machines than the present one," he said, "but none of which I am more proud. Taking every point into consideration, we have just concluded the greatest trip I have ever known. I have been connected with nothing like it. Here was a young team, a team that had been in and out through the greater part of the year, game enough to rally quickly in the face of defeat and make its winning fight on the road. I have never driven a team harder." He also lavished praise on one player in particular. "I am not given to promiscuous praise," he said, "but I want to say right here that I regard Merkle as the greatest first baseman in the profession, and I have seen all the great ones in action."[6]

Sporting Life reflected on yet another example of the strange vagaries of baseball. "In the Fall of 1908," it noted, "when Johnny Evers, by his quick thinking, won a pennant for the Cubs, which would have belonged to the Giants but for the oversight of Fred Merkle ... Who would have thought that today Evers is practically down and out, a sick man, in no shape to play, while Merkle has become the best first baseman in the National League and one of the most valuable players in the business."[7]

HAVING GAINED THE PRIZE, McGRAW could now concentrate on preparing the team for meeting the Athletics. There remained another week of meaningless games to be played, posing the dilemma of how to rest his players without causing them to lose their edge. Meyers especially needed time off; despite being banged up from the inevitable injuries catchers accumulated, he appeared in 133 games in 1911 and still managed to lead the team in hitting. During the stretch run he had put together a seventeen-game hitting streak. Those who had earlier scorned the Chief as not being up to the job once held by Bresnahan had to eat their words.[8]

Meyers played with a chip on his shoulder, using the endless stream of racial barbs as fuel for his drive to succeed. "When I first started every one was out to get me," he told a reporter, "and all the crabs playing ball would come into me spikes first and call me all the names that they had been accustomed to apply to the umpires. I couldn't get back, for what chance has an Indian? What chance has he ever had?" The scribes too often echoed the witless slurs hurled by fans and players alike, but many of the New York writers had come to appreciate his talent, especially as he challenged Honus Wagner and Fred Clarke for the batting title. "Meyers has become the deepest student of batting on the team," observed the *Times*. "His work with the stick has shown that there is not a pitcher on the circuit that he isn't familiar with." Devore thought that if the Chief had batted cleanup instead of eighth, he would have scored twice as many runs as anyone in the league.

The *Tribune* agreed that "in his quiet, unassuming way he has done as much, if not more than any other player in bringing the pennant to the Polo Grounds." *Sporting Life* listed the three M's of the Giants as "Mathewson, Marquard, Myers."[9]

On a chilly October 5, as Maxwell defeated the Superbas, the National Commission announced the details of the World Series. All games would begin at two P.M. They would alternate from one city to the other with a seventh game, if needed, decided by lot; New York won the coin toss and would host the first game on October 14. The Giants set their official prices for tickets at a steep $25 for boxes, $3 for reserved upper grandstand, $2 for reserved lower grandstand, and $1 for general admission. Philadelphia charged only $3 for boxes but the same amount for reserved lower and the first twelve rows of reserved upper grandstand, $2 for the remaining upper grandstand, and $1 for general admission. Solemnly the commission cautioned the public against "paying higher prices than those fixed in this bulletin."[10]

Unseasonable cold and the threat of rain held the crowd under 2,500 as New York returned to the Polo Grounds on the sixth for a doubleheader against the Phillies. Meyers and Merkle sat out both games, while Devore and several others played in only one, but the winning continued. Ames continued his streak in a 10–5 first game rout. In the second session the Giants put up four runs in the first inning and Crandall held on for a 5–4 victory, their eighth straight. McGraw was not about to let them stop running; New York stole two bases in the first game and four more in the second. Nor did he ease up on his dictum that players had to report to the field at ten A.M. for practice when at home.[11]

Boston came to town on the seventh to make up a game before a sparse crowd on a muddy field beneath glowering skies in windy weather the *Sun* described as "cold enough for football." Only three Giants regulars played the whole game. Marquard pitched five innings as warm-up for the Series, then gave way to Drucke, whose wildness led to a 5–2 Rustler victory and the end of New York's winning streak. Ex-Giants star Mike Donlin pleased the spectators with a home run, but this treat paled before one offered up by McGraw. In the ninth inning he sent in the pitcher who had warmed up more in recent weeks than any other, but always without seeing action. Charlie Faust's moment had come at last.[12]

Entering to a groundswell of cheers usually reserved for Mathewson or Marquard, Faust faced four Boston batters, yielding a double, a sacrifice,

and a sacrifice fly before getting Donlin to ground out. Although Grover
Hartley made New York's final out in the ninth, the Rustlers obligingly
stayed on the field to let Faust bat. He nubbed a roller back to pitcher Lefty
Tyler, who pegged it over Tenney's head at first. Faust commenced his
ritualistic journey around the bases as one wild throw followed another
until the last one nailed him at the plate. The fans bellowed their approval.
"It was the proudest moment of Faust's life, however," said the *Sun*, "for
he had pitched in a Giant uniform—a reward for his hypnotic influence
over the New Yorks' rivals." By the strangest concatenation of events
the obscure Kansas farm boy had worked his way into the major-league
record books.[13]

Philadelphia, which had finished its season, stayed active with a series of
games against a collection of American League all-stars headed by Ty Cobb,
who had batted a sensational .420 that summer. The A's had done the same
thing in 1910 before beating the Cubs in the World Series. After Sunday the
eighth, however, the Giants still had four games to play against Brooklyn.
New York romped 10–4 in the first contest, marred only by Doyle turning
an ankle while rounding first. He was found to have no torn ligaments or
broken bones, but it was just the sort of thing McGraw feared most in these
last games.[14]

Having swept sixteen of nineteen games from the Superbas with one tie,
New York dropped the last three with little resistance. Maxwell lost a 2–1
heartbreaker in ten innings. Rain the next day forced a doubleheader on
Columbus Day. In the first game Ames, hitherto invincible with his charms,
pitched well but finally met his match, losing 3–0 in what proved to be the
fastest game of the season, played in only sixty-four minutes. The final
game treated some eight thousand spectators to another Faustian vignette
on the way to a 5–2 loss. After Drucke and Maxwell failed to contain the
enemy, Faust entered in the ninth. Already he had tried three times to take
the mound only to be persuaded by fast-talking Larry Doyle that he was not
sufficiently warmed up. This time McGraw let him stay as the crowd
bellowed its approval.

Using his windmill warm-up, Faust managed to retire the side except for
a single and an error by Gene Paulette. "His posture just before his windup,"
said the *Sun*, "followed by sweeping convulsions of his arms, tearing the air
into geometric tatters, so dismayed the Brooklyn batters that they failed to
score in the inning in which they faced the sunflower phenom. Faust's
elbow ball, a forearm floater which came up airily as a soap bubble, so

deceived Daley of Brooklyn that that player fell flat when he missed it with a mighty lunge. The spectators were convulsed . . . Umpire Brennan was so agitated that he covered his face with his hand and his chest pad shook violently."[15]

This time Faust got a legitimate time at bat. Brooklyn's Eddie Dent nicked him in the wrist with a pitch, sending him to first base. He summoned the next batter, Herzog, and told him, "I am going to steal second and third, and I want you to squeeze me home." True to his word, he "waddled to second and rolled to third," as the *Times* saw it. From there he flew home with a spread-eagle landing as Herzog dutifully laid down a bunt in a play that was, said the *Sun*, "a cross between a squeeze and a joke." Thus did one of the most dramatic seasons in National League history come to a close, and thus did Charlie Faust enter the record books as both pitcher and batter with two steals to his credit. He had also pitched the last regular-season inning for the Giants.[16]

Finally the overlong season reached its end. "The prolonged season of the National League has been productive of nothing excepting an unnecessarily late season for starting the world series," complained the *Times*, among others. "Messrs. Ebbets and Murphy of the Brooklyn and Chicago Clubs, respectively, believed that fandom wanted to see baseball on Columbus Day . . . hence the schedule was drawn to cover this holiday."[17]

The twin loss kept the Giants from finishing the season with a hundred wins, but they dominated the league in several categories. The pitching that seemed so dubious in the spring came into its own despite the failure of Raymond. Mathewson finished with a 26-13 record and led the league in earned run average with 1.99, the only hurler under the 2.00 mark. Marquard compiled a sparkling 24-7 record and topped the league in strikeouts with 237. Only Alexander, who completed a record season for a rookie at 28-13, had more wins. Crandall closed the season at 15-5, Wiltse at 12-9, and the rejuvenated Ames at 11-10. As a staff the Giants led the National League in earned run average at 2.69 and in complete games with 95. They struck out the most batters, 771, and issued the fewest walks, 369.

On the other side of the ledger, New York easily took the team batting title with an average of .279, twelve points higher than second-place Boston. Meyers finished third in batting at .332 and Fletcher fifth with .319. Doyle trailed only Schulte of Chicago in total bases and slugging percentage, and topped everyone in triples with 25. Most impressive of all, the team set a record that has never been equaled with 347 stolen bases, 57 more than Cincinnati and 133 more than Chicago, their nearest competitors. While Bob Bescher of the Reds won the individual title going away with 81 steals, the next five leaders were all Giants: Devore with 61, Snodgrass with 51, Merkle with 49, Herzog and Murray with 48 apiece. Doyle had 38, Fletcher 22, and Becker 20.

As the pundits and fans alike realized, McGraw's emphasis on and faith in the speed game had been vindicated. His young, eager, obedient players made more than their share of mistakes on the bases and in the field, but they played with a passion the way McGraw had instructed them. The only two position players over thirty were Meyers, who was that age, and Devlin, the old man of the team at only thirty-one. Mathewson at thirty and Wiltse, a year older, were the only pitchers in their thirties. Marquard was only twenty-four, Crandall a year younger. Merkle was still only twenty-two, Devore and Snodgrass twenty-three, Doyle twenty-four, Becker twenty-five, and Murray twenty-seven.

Having proven themselves worthy of enduring the long haul, the next challenge was to see how well they handled the short schedule and cruel, unpredictable vagaries and pressures of a World Series. As for McGraw himself, the experts tumbled over each other in heaping praise on his performance. He was, said the *Tribune*, "the man who by his shrewdness, keenness and force proved himself once more one of the greatest managers in the game . . . Many a man would have hesitated to make a radical change in his infield while in the very midst of a grueling struggle, but not so McGraw . . . That his judgment has been justified no one will question; that he made the move at just the right time no one can doubt."[18]

Better than most pundits, *Sporting Life* appreciated in detail what McGraw had accomplished. "Like his great rival, Connie Mack," it said, "Manager McGraw labored assiduously for five years to reconstruct his team after his own ideas with material of his own selection, and undeterred by criticism, abuse and ridicule he persevered in his self set task until he reached the desired goal with the machine he had built slowly year by year around the one conspicuous survivor of the old machine, Christy Mathewson, who is today the only member of the team who was on the team when McGraw assumed charge of it a decade ago. The radical nature of McGraw's reconstruction is illustrated by the fact that the present team contains but four members of the 1905 World's Championship team, and three of these are pitchers, while Devlin is now only a substitute."[19]

FINAL STANDINGS OCTOBER 12

Team	Won	Lost	Pct.	Team	Won	Lost	Pct.
New York	99	54	.647	St. Louis	75	74	.503
Chicago	92	62	.597	Cincinnati	70	83	.458
Pittsburgh	85	69	.552	Brooklyn	64	86	.427
Philadelphia	79	73	.520	Boston	44	107	.291

CHAPTER 16

World Series: The Long and Short of It

*"After the World Series last year, Joe Tinker, the
Cub shortstop, remarked that the Athletic [sic]
constituted the greatest baseball machine he
had ever seen. He said there wasn't a weak spot
in it. This is the same combination that has
swept through the American League this
season . . . The Athletic infield is a bunch of
youngsters—McInnes [sic], Collins, Barry, and
Baker—players whom no one dreamed would
ever become stars. Connie Mack's acute
judgment of ball players is not surpassed by any
manager in the game."*

—THE NEW YORK TIMES

"NEW YORK HAS BEEN THINKING OF NOTHING except the big event
for a week," enthused the *Press*, "and nothing has been talked
about except the World Series . . . The series is talked about in
London, Paris and Yokohama just the same as it is talked about in the land
of Uncle Sam. One enterprising Yokohama newspaper will get 600 wires
by cable each day of the games."[1]

By 1911 the World Series had become a major event not only nationally
but in several foreign countries as well. That year's series was the first to be
played entirely in modern, steel-and-concrete stadiums, and the National
Commission decreed for the first time that no spectators would be allowed
on the playing field. An army of journalists clamored for the right to cover
the games, and fifty telegraphers stood ready to transmit every play to cities
around the country as well as baseball-mad Havana. One steamship line
arranged to get details of the games by wireless for passengers heading
out to sea. For the first time, too, journalists struck deals with leading

participants to ghostwrite daily accounts for syndication in their paper. Mathewson made such an arrangement with John Wheeler of the *Herald* that paid him $500; Marquard had his own arrangement with Frank G. Menke.[2]

Participants were not the only ballplayers enlisted to lend their expertise in the press box. Ty Cobb, Hughie Jennings, Red Dooin, Pop Anson, George Mullin, and Hal Chase all served as special writers for the series. Another interested spectator was Blanche McGraw. In 1905 she had watched the games at the Polo Grounds but not in Philadelphia. "Going to another city with my husband was a snare and delusion," she admitted. "I never saw him, and I doubt that he knew I existed. He remained close to the players." This time, however, McGraw took her to all the games in both cities.[3]

The spectacle was expected to set another, less welcome record as well. The *Sun* predicted that "more money will be wagered on the result of the world's series . . . than on any sporting event ever held in this country." The odds hovered around even money. *Sporting News* agreed that "there is betting in spite of all the laws which have been trained to curb the gambling predilection in the breast of man." Some New Yorkers were reportedly going to Philadelphia in hopes of finding better odds there. The experts, fans, and rival players were as evenly divided as the oddsmakers as to who would win.[4]

Enthusiasm in Manhattan had already reached fever pitch when the season ended. The Giants led the league in another category especially pleasing to Brush: attendance. An estimated 675,000 fans had pushed through the turnstiles in 1911. Arrangements were made to erect an electrified board at the Polo Grounds so that fans could follow the games played in Philadelphia. The board, representing a baseball diamond, stood twenty-five feet high and thirty-five feet wide, with three hundred electric lights to flash the action. Brush had allocated all four hundred boxes, many of them to mail orders, before tickets went on sale at nine A.M. on the morning of the twelfth. Despite some rain, a line of eager fans began forming well before midnight, ready to storm the second floor of the St. James Building in hopes of getting tickets.[5]

The line included representatives of virtually every ticket agency and speculator in the city. Billy Gray arrived at seven A.M. and went down the line pulling out known speculators and some fifty messenger boys he suspected of working for them. Despite the presence of detectives who tried to weed out hired thugs and maintain order, large numbers of tickets fell into their hands. By ten A.M. Broadway ticket agencies were already offering tickets for sale and scalpers hawked them on the streets for double their official price. One speculator somehow got his hands on a block of nine hundred tickets. Some fifteen thousand general admission tickets were held back for sale at the ballpark the next day for their official price of one dollar. In Philadelphia only a third of the applications could be filled; one of those failing to get a ticket was James S. Sherman, vice president of the United States. In both cities the police were already mobilizing to protect the public from both scalpers and pickpockets.[6]

SHIBE PARK IN PHILADELPHIA WAS THE FIRST modern ballpark when it opened on April 12, 1909. The creation of owner Ben Shibe, it held about twenty-five thousand, not including an enclosure that could hold some ten thousand standees. The team it housed was the most formidable one Connie Mack had yet put together. Like McGraw, he had watched his winning team of 1905 gradually decline and, in his shrewd, patient manner, set about constructing a new blend of players even more capable than the last. After finishing second twice, fourth, and sixth, the Athletics cruised to the pennant in 1910 by fourteen and a half games and crushed the Cubs in five games in the World Series.[7]

The jewel of the team was its so-called "$100,000 infield" composed of outstanding rookie John "Stuffy" McInnis at first, the incomparable Eddie Collins at second, John Barry at short, and Frank Baker, who led the American League in home runs in 1911 with eleven, at third. The outfield featured Briscoe Lord in left, Rube Oldring in center, and in right the veteran Danny Murphy, who had played second for many years until Collins arrived. For catching duties Mack relied on the veteran Ira Thomas for his fielding expertise and Jack Lapp for his bat. The pitching staff was excellent and deep. Jack Coombs was the workhorse, compiling a record of 31-9 in 1910 and "slumping" to 28-12 this past season. Two old warriors, Chief Bender (17-5) and lefty Eddie Plank (23-8) formed the nucleus with Coombs with support from Cy Morgan (15-7) and Harry Krause (11-8). Many of the pundits regarded Bender as the ace of the staff, arguing that Coombs had not pitched that well in 1911 despite his record.

What this team could do above all else was hit. It led the league in batting with a .296 average, and individual averages were even more impressive: Collins .365, Lapp .353, Baker .334, Murphy .329, McInnis .321, Lord .310,

Oldring .297, Thomas .273, and Barry .265. Even Coombs wielded a mean stick, batting .319. As for New York's vaunted speed game, Mack professed not to be worried. "All this talk about the base running of the Giants makes me laugh," he said in an interview. "The Giants' stolen bases are not worrying us a bit. When was a World Series won by base running? Never. World's championships are won in the pitcher's box and that is where we are going to show the advantage. Base running? It makes me laugh."[8]

Mack was entirely right in his emphasis on pitching. Every World Series since 1905 had been dominated by pitching, none more so than the 1905 classic between these same two teams, in which every one of the five games was a shutout. Mathewson and Bender had been the chief antagonists in that series, and both were likely to play key roles in 1911. However, Jack Coombs had won three games in the 1910 World Series, and the Giants had Rube Marquard, ready to make his debut on the game's largest stage. Thomas and Meyers were considered among the best at throwing out runners, and the speed game mattered little if a team could not get men on base. Philadelphia was deemed to have one other advantage: It led the American League in fielding average as well. The infield in particular was regarded as one of the smoothest performing groups ever assembled, while the Giants infield was notoriously inconsistent. "There is no doubt," said the *Sun*, "that the Philadelphia infield in its entirety is the best in the game to-day."[9]

Some American Leaguers worried that McGraw's infamous baiting of players from the coaching box would unsettle the Athletics and give the Giants an unfair advantage. Mack instructed his men to pay no heed to anything said to them during the game, and to do no kicking over any decision by the umpires. "He has made it plain," noted the *Sun*, "that he wants nothing but clean ball playing and he is going to insist on it." This had always been his practice. In contrast to McGraw he seemed utterly calm, even phlegmatic, but his self-control had always worked for him. "When we played the Cubs last fall," he said, "an attempt was made to rattle some of our best men, but it was a dismal failure. My players know that the Giants' coaches will try to rattle them, but it will be a waste of time. It's all in the game, however, and we are not going to protest or find fault. If McGraw can rattle us he will be entitled to whatever can be gained."[10]

Sporting News thought otherwise. "Even if the rules issued to the umpires did not provide a curb," it observed, "it might be said in Mr. McGraw's behalf that he has ceased to play the game that way. Even in his coarsest moments in the past McGraw was only showing that he was a master at what was at the time an understood part of the game. But the game has advanced and John McGraw has advanced with it. He has only recently said that he would be willing to give anything—a pennant almost—if he could live down the nickname indicative of methods long since abandoned."[11]

On the eve of the first game yet another ticket scandal threatened to upstage the game itself. With scalpers offering boxes for $450 and grandstand seats at $8 and $10, Billy Gray issued a statement adamantly denying that the club had allowed speculators to get their hands on them. He offered to pay $5,000 to anyone providing proof that the Giants had done so. Even worse, it was discovered that someone had printed thousands of counterfeit tickets that were being grabbed up by an unsuspecting public. The bogus versions were crude in that the signatures of Brush and John Whalen were printed at the bottom rather than signed, as they were on the real items. The genuine article had heavier print and different type in certain areas, but the presence of the fakes promised mass confusion when the Polo Grounds opened its gates for the first game.[12]

Connie Mack brought his team to New York by train on the night before the first game and installed them in the Hotel Somerset. The National Commission set up shop in the Waldorf and the Baseball Writers' Association of America in the Martinique, while Ban Johnson favored the Wolcott. "The whole hotel section was like various parts of a camp on the night before a battle," reported the Sun. In their usual fashion neither manager would divulge his choice of pitchers for the opener. Mack did reveal what had been suspected: that Stuffy McInnis would not play because of a wrist injury. First base would be manned by Harry Davis, longtime captain of the A's, who had begun his career in 1895 with none other than the Giants. Now thirty-seven, he was in the twilight of a distinguished career and had batted only .197 during the season in which he yielded his position to McInnis.[13]

Mack took this loss with his usual equanimity. Others considered it a major factor. If McInnis could not start, said the Press, the Athletics would "be under a big handicap. This youngster is one of the greatest players developed in recent years and some of his playing this season was phenomenal . . . Harry Davis, at one time the greatest first sacker in the American League, and also one of the greatest batsmen that ever wore the spangles, is only a shadow of the Harry of old . . . Davis has slowed up in his fielding and gets around the bases like an ice wagon."[14]

Around two P.M. the first hopefuls began gathering outside the Polo Grounds, prepared to endure a chilly night to land one of the fifteen thousand bleacher tickets to be sold on the morning of the first game. At ten that night a saloon at the corner of Eighth Avenue and 155th Street displayed a large sign advertising tickets for sale at double or triple their face price. By midnight the line on Coogan's Bluff had hundreds of people, many of them boys, who had brought stools, food, and other necessities for an overnight wait in hopes of selling their place in line. The crowd was a sociological stew of classes and remained well-behaved through the night. Bonfires dotted the bluff until the grounds looked like a regimental encampment. An occasional automobile party with hampers of food prepared by chefs mingled with brown bags from tenements. Men and boys alike ate, drank coffee or something stronger, and sometimes slept; some hired a boy to hold their place and wandered off to one of the saloons in the neighborhood.[15]

Sportswriter Fred Lieb and his wife lived in an apartment house on West 145th Street. When he awoke on the morning of October 14, he saw an endless line of people stretching across the street. Most of them stood reading newspapers; some had packages containing their breakfast or lunch. After breakfast Lieb wandered down to the street and asked a policeman what was going on. "Don't you know what is going on in this city today?" the cop replied with a surprised look. They're lined up to see the first game of the World Series at the Polo Grounds."

"Good God," murmured Lieb. "The Polo Grounds is a mile from here!"

"Yea," answered the policeman. "For those at the end of the line, more than that. And half of this crowd never will get in."[16]

He was right. Large numbers were turned away once the bleacher admissions ran out. Squads of police had been mobilized to keep order outside the park and to ensure reasonably calm entry once the gates opened. None were stationed inside the park, where a force of 350 special police and detectives recruited from the Pinkerton and three other agencies had been hired to police the crowd.[17]

Before the first game the National Commission handed out a statement from the manufacturer of the balls assuring the public that, contrary to widespread belief, there was no difference in those used in the two leagues. "The balls that will be used in the World's Series . . . will be the exact duplicates of the balls that were used in the World's Championship Series of 1910 and the same as have been used by both major leagues in all championship games during the entire season of 1911," it concluded.[18]

Game 1

As the sun rose on a mercifully clear if cool day, preparations inside the stadium were well under way. Before seven A.M., when the street lamps were extinguished, Billy Gray arrived to supervise the five hundred ushers admitted through a small gate at the main entrance. The ushers all wore red hats so as to be easily spotted once the crowd descended. Behind them came the army of special policemen and detectives. Harry Stevens was already there, giving directions to his 350 vendors, seventeen bartenders, 150 scorecard boys, and 50 cooks and bottle washers. Down in the caterer's lair sat twenty-five thousand sandwiches and a mountain of peanuts in small brown bags. On every side soft drinks packed in ice were piled high, yet still Stevens complained that he could not satisfy demand. Ten building inspectors arrived to examine the new parts of the ballpark as well as the older wooden ones and pronounced them safe. The fire commissioner informed everyone that under no circumstances could the aisles be used for anything other than passage.[19]

Management had hoped to use empty space in the big structure for as many as five thousand standees, but the building inspectors refused to issue a permit for it. After the telegraph operators and linemen were admitted, the box office and turnstile operators took their places, each one protected by one of the special policemen. At nine-oh-two A.M. the blowing of a shrill whistle signaled time to open the gates and allow admission into the park under police supervision. Few ticket holders arrived that early to claim their reserved seats, but the gates leading to the bleachers had lines waiting eagerly to fill the fifteen thousand seats across the outfield. The first person to enter was a middle-aged woman clutching a black leather bag stuffed with food. She scurried quickly to the long rows of seats and settled into one directly behind center field.

Some speculators managed to buy dollar tickets but were herded inside by special policemen. A few managed to squeeze their way outside to look for buyers. Instead most found waiting detectives, who whisked them to the station. As the spectators filed in, a man stood quietly nearby watching them. John B. Day had owned the Giants in their glory days of the late 1880s when the team twice won the championship, but he was ruined when the Players' National League was organized in 1890 and the players deserted him. Asked where he was sitting, he said, "Oh, I have no seat. I don't care for any. I'd rather stand up. You see I like to walk around. Sometimes I become so enthusiastic that I can't keep my seat." He heaped praise on the current team and its achievement before strolling up the runway into the grandstand, shaking hands with people who recognized him.

Shortly after his departure an elderly man using a cane limped through the gate. "Smiling Jim" Mutrie had managed those Giants from 1883 to 1891, and he gazed in wonderment at the spectacle before him. "This makes me feel like a kid," he said. "The Giants were champions in my day and here they are champions again." He recalled playing in the old Brotherhood Park on the field then called the Polo Grounds. Behind him came Mike Tiernan, the star right fielder of the 1889 team, his once lean body now generously expanded. "I'm a big fellow nowadays," he chuckled. "Good living and easy business—that is, the gin mill business—have put on the weight and I couldn't run around the bases in less than five minutes without dropping dead from heart disease." He ambled off in search of Day and Mutrie for a little pregame reminiscing.

As the bleachers filled, clouds of blue cigar and cigarette smoke wafted upward. When several women appeared, the crowd treated them to the tradition of tossing newspapers, peanut bags, and other missiles at their bonnets. Some grew indignant and ordered their escorts to find other seats. "A man who takes a woman into that stand is either a piker or an idiot," opined a grizzled Pinkerton. "Timid persons have no business here." As the grandstand began filling up, the first wave of notables arrived, including Ban Johnson, Garry Herrmann, A. G. Spalding, Adrian "Cap" Anson, Tom Lynch, John Heydler, John M. Ward, and former National League presidents Nick Young and A. C. Mills, and Harry Payne Whitney. "Here comes Brush!" rose the cry as a gate in centerfield opened to admit the owner's limousine, which moved to its place in right field.

At a quarter to one the Athletics started walking slowly across the field to their bench accompanied by a generous round of applause, especially from the Philly rooters who had come over for the game. Dressed in blue sweaters over their gray uniforms, they were led by Harry Davis and Eddie Collins. Connie Mack, dressed as always in his dark suit, towered above them in the middle of the pack. Then the cordial applause turned into a roar as the Giants, led by Matty, made their appearance. McGraw sprang a surprise on the crowd: The team wore new black uniforms with white belts, a white "NY" logo intertwined on the left sleeve, white stockings, and black caps with white visors, a throwback to those worn by the 1905 and also the 1889 champions. Everyone had on the new outfit except Faust, who made do with his old uniform.

As the teams warmed up, the players intermingled. Doyle shook hands with Chief Bender and Ira Thomas. Meyers spotted Bender and rushed over to exchange greetings while fans howled the inevitable war whoops. Photographers were everywhere taking pictures, and captured McGraw shaking hands with Mack as well as Doyle and Davis, the two captains, doing the same. Shortly before two o'clock the four umpires strolled onto the field: Bill Klem and Bill Brennan from the National League, Tom Connolly and Bill Dineen of the American League. The two extras would be stationed on the foul lines and were there primarily in case something happened to Klem behind the plate or to Dineen, who had the field. Mack sent Davis to meet with McGraw as the umpires went over the ground rules. More pictures, including McGraw and Davis shaking hands.

This done, a one-armed man named E. Lawrence Phillips, summoned from Washington as official announcer for the National Commission, announced the batteries from the pitcher's mound. His eagerly-awaited news produced no surprises: Bender and Thomas for Philadelphia, Mathewson and Meyers for New York. The first game would be a rematch of the first game in 1905 but with an added twist. The date, October 14, was exactly the one on which the same two pitchers had met in game five of that series, and Matty had walked away with a 2–0 victory to clinch the series. History hung over the game like a guardian angel or a devilish imp, depending on the outcome. Just before the game started, McGraw hurried over to the As' bench and again shook hands with Mack.

With the ceremonies done and the photographers chased off the field, Matty took the mound and Klem settled in behind the plate. The crowd waited anxiously to see whether he still had the magic of old. They were not disappointed. He struck out Lord and Oldring before Collins lined to Devore on the first pitch. With one out in the bottom half Doyle reached on an infield hit and promptly stole second. However, Bender fanned both Snodgrass and Murray to end the threat. Baker opened the second inning with a single, was sacrificed to second, and took third on a passed ball. Harry Davis then confounded the experts by rapping a single through the hole, scoring Baker with the first run scored by the A's off Mathewson in twenty-nine innings. In the third Oldring ripped a double to left with two out and Collins worked a walk, but Matty struck out Baker to end the threat.[20]

"Bender talked to the Giant players all through that first game," Matty recalled. "The one in which he wore the smile, probably because he was a pitcher old in the game and several of the younger men on the New York team acted as if they were nervous. Snodgrass and the Indian kept up a running fire of small talk every time that the Giants' center-fielder came to the plate." None of the other Athletics talked to the Giants or responded to attempts to bait them.[21]

Bender looked unbeatable until the fourth inning, when Snodgrass managed to get hit by a pitch and took second when Murray grounded out. Merkle struck out, and Herzog stroked a slow roller to Collins, who inexplicably muffed it. Snodgrass read the error and hustled around third to the plate, just beating a good throw from Collins as the crowd roared its approval. Herzog took second on the play but died there as Fletcher fanned for the second time. With the score tied, Mathewson bore down and matched Bender inning after inning until the seventh. The A's went down in order. Fletcher opened the Giants' half by rolling out to first. Meyers stepped in, having done nothing against his fellow Chief. "Perhaps," waxed the Times, "the mind of these two Redmen went far back to the barren, arid plains . . . Maybe they wished they had tomahawks in their hands instead of a bat and baseball."

Meyers hammered a shot over Lord's head that hit the cigarette sign in left only a foot below the top of the wall and contented himself with a double. Matty fanned for the second out but Devore, having already robbed Thomas of a triple with a brilliant catch, sliced one to left for a double that scored Meyers. Given a lead, Mathewson mowed down the Athletics in order the next two innings to give the Giants a 2–1 victory, allowing only six hits and the lone walk. He threw only 94 pitches compared to 140 for Bender. But the Chief had been equally effective, yielding only five hits and striking out eleven. Six years earlier the two pitchers had given up exactly the same number of hits. The Giants scored the same number of runs, the A's one more but still not enough. Only three Athletics—Davis, Lord, and Murphy—played in that game, and Matty was the lone Giants participant. In one crucial category, however, the modern figures dwarfed those of 1905. The gate receipts of $77,359 for game one totaled $8,924 more than the take for all five games of the 1905 series.[22]

The New York fans bubbled over with enthusiasm, while the two managers were predictably more cautious. Mack observed that it was just one game and his team would surely bounce back. Collins admitted freely that his error cost the game for the A's and predicted they would still win the series. An old adage said that "as goes the first game, so goes the series," but McGraw was not convinced. Like Mack, he realized that it was only one game. He surprised the experts by pointing out what he deemed the turning point of the game in the fourth inning. With Snodgrass on first, Bender got two quick strikes on Murray. Fearing a double play, McGraw signaled for a hit-and-run. Snodgrass bolted early for second as Murray hit the hard grounder to Collins. "Had Snodgrass not got the good start to second," he stressed, "there would have been a certain double play, or at least Snodgrass would have been retired." No one would have been in position to score on the Collins fumble. "I consider that this play won the game."[23]

That evening the Giants, looking awkward in dress clothes, were guests of honor at the New York Theatre for a testimonial in their honor given by the Citizens' Committee of the City of New York, of which Big Tim Sullivan was chairman. Before a packed audience that included many performers, twenty-five acts by George M. Cohan and others entertained before each player and Charlie Faust were introduced and presented with a handsome trophy. McGraw received a gold watch with a diamond fob and a framed and wreathed set of resolutions praising him and the team. McGraw gave a short speech of thanks, after which Faust offered some remarks and sang a tune. Former heavyweight champion James J. Corbett had the honor of pulling a rope that raised the National League pennant on a flagstaff. After their night of celebration the Giants caught the nine A.M. train next morning for Philadelphia, where they checked into the Hotel Majestic.[24]

Game 2

The rain that fell through the night gave way to a warm and sunny day for the game. Shibe Park was no less packed with people, including a generous contingent of New York fans, than the Polo Grounds had been. With the bleachers filled, thousands more crowded into the space behind a temporary fence in the outfield. The roofs and windows of houses surrounding the park were jammed with people who had paid for the privilege of watching the game from afar. As in New York, hundreds of police kept order in the park and outside it. "While Shibe Park seems small as compared with the Polo Grounds," sniffed author Rex Beach, writing for the *Times*, "it is agreeably free from glaring advertising signs—a testimonial to the good sense of the management—and one does not come away with that unpleasant taste of ketchup, beer, Turkish cigarettes, baked beans, and cheese, which remains after a visit to the home of the Giants."[25]

Although McGraw said nothing until game time, it was a foregone conclusion that Marquard would pitch the second game. Mack was expected to counter with Coombs, but the "Tall Tactician," as the scribes had dubbed him, surprised everyone by naming Eddie Plank as his starter, thereby setting up a duel between two premier left-handers. At thirty-six Plank had lost some durability but little of his skill and speed. Having been in two series games but never won, he showed his mettle by fanning Devore to open the game and three more times afterward. After Doyle flied out, Snodgrass again got nicked by a pitch, but Murray lined out to Collins.

Those who wondered how Marquard would fare under the pressure of a series game had reason for concern. His first pitch bounced up to Meyers, and the crowd began to taunt him because his windup took so long. Lord greeted him with a single, took second when Murray fumbled the ball, and advanced to third on Oldring's sacrifice. With Collins at bat, Marquard uncorked a wild pitch that allowed Lord to score easily. In his column he claimed that "the Athletics had discovered our battery signals on Saturday, and the Chief and I had framed up a set on Sunday, which we had not had much chance to rehearse." As Meyers and the infielders hurried to calm Marquard, McGraw sent Crandall to warm up. Collins smacked a single, but Marquard regained his poise enough to fan Baker and get Murphy on a fly to Devore. The Giants retaliated in the second when Herzog doubled to center and went to third on Fletcher's grounder. The Chief brought him home with a ringing single to center.

At that point the game settled into another tense pitching duel. Plank was magnificent, allowing only five hits and whiffing eight. Marquard, too, found his groove and yielded a mere four hits, but one of them proved fatal. In the sixth inning both Lord and Oldring hit hard drives to the outfield that were caught. Collins then stroked a curveball down the left-field line for a double, the first hit Marquard had surrendered since the first inning. Up stepped Baker, who had struck out on three pitches and grounded weakly to Doyle. "Baker is a bad man," said Marquard the next day in his ghostwritten column for the *Times*, "and I had been warned against him, and I had the right dope, too." Baker had gone down on curveballs and was known to murder fastballs. With the count one and one, Meyers signaled for another curveball, but for some reason Marquard decided to slip a high fastball by him. Baker was not fooled and lofted the pitch over the right-field fence for a two-run homer, circling the bases to a wildly cheering crowd.

The infielders were furious with Marquard; Meyers alone tried to console him. "I will bear the blame, for the fault was mine," Rube said afterward in his column. "I gave him just what he was looking for, though he had bitten on two curves already." Crandall shut the Athletics down for the last two innings but the Giants could do nothing with Plank. Merkle alone got on base but Plank picked him off. No one stole a base in the game. Neither pitcher walked a man. Philadelphia left only two men on base and the Giants three as the A's waltzed away with a 3–1 triumph. While horns, bells, whistles, and cheers engulfed the field, the Giants changed hurriedly and headed for the train back to New York.

"The Giants didn't practise with their usual pepper," noted the *Sun* of the team's pregame warm-up. "The weather was of the midsummer sort in which ballplayers revel, but the Giants were listless in practice." During the game they committed three errors, two by outfielders Murray and Devore, and they showed nothing of their running game. In the sixth inning Snodgrass hit a shot to left field and tried to stretch it into a double only to find the ball waiting for him in Barry's glove. So effectively did Plank stifle the Giants' bats that the team never came close to mounting any kind of serious threat.

"Well, it's a tie now," said McGraw, "but we are going to win two with Matty. Then we'll send Marquard right back again, and with the experience he got to-day he will prove much better. It was a trying test for him with such a big crowd to deal with, and under the circumstances he should not be censured. He pitched a good game . . . I'll admit that Plank pitched better than I expected, but he can't do it every day." In his column Marquard noted that "the sun is in the pitcher's eyes all the time at Shibe Park, and I was not used to it," but he added that "Plank did not seem to mind it, and he pitched a wonderful game."[26]

Game 3

During warm-ups Chief Bender agreed to participate in a small slice of history. He had always refused to pose for pictures before an important game, but on this occasion he was induced to stand with Meyers while the swarm of photographers clicked madly away. Bender, who had a German father and a Chippewa mother, detested the bigotry toward his people as much as Meyers, but he chose to mask it with a smile and keep his resentment inside. More than Meyers he tried to distance himself from his tribal heritage. Meyers called him "one of the nicest people you'd ever meet." Rube Bressler, who roomed with Bender, described him as "one of the kindest and finest men who ever lived." Mack said of him, "If I had all the men I've ever handled, and they were in their prime, and there was one game I wanted to win above all others, Albert would be my man."[27]

The sun that basked so cheerfully on game two gave way the next day to dark, glowering skies and the threat of rain for what proved to be a momentous game. Back in their home park, McGraw hesitated not at all in bringing back Mathewson on one day's rest, while Mack went to his third ace, Coombs, with Lapp as his catcher. Both pitchers got off to a fast start; fourteen strikes were thrown before a ball was called. In his usual fashion Matty was generous with hits, allowing nine with no walks, but kept the Athletics from scoring. Coombs was even more effective, walking four while limiting the Giants to three hits. The Athletics stole two bases out of three attempts. The Giants figured they could run on Lapp as they had not against Thomas; they made five attempts and were gunned down every time. In the field Doyle played a brilliant game but the rest of the infield compiled a total of six errors, three by Herzog, two by Fletcher, and one by Merkle.[28]

Still Mathewson kept the Giants in the game. With one out in the third, Meyers slapped a shot that bounded over Baker's head for a single. Mathewson followed with a single to right that moved the Chief to third base. Devore then dribbled one to Barry, who hesitated when Meyers rumbled home and had to take the force at second base. Devore tried to steal second but was thrown out, leaving the Giants with the one run and a lead that Mathewson protected tenaciously. Barry opened the eighth inning with a double to left. Lapp managed to beat out a slow roller to Fletcher, moving Barry to third with none out. Coombs, a dangerous hitter, hit a grounder to Doyle, who fired the ball home in time to nail Barry. Lord smacked another grounder at Doyle, who flipped it to Fletcher for the force, but Fletcher dropped the ball.

That would have loaded the bases with only one out, but on the play Lapp thought he might be able to score and rounded third too far. Doyle alertly threw the ball to Meyers, who relayed it to Herzog, who ran down Lapp. Mathewson bore down and fanned Oldring to get out of a tight jam.

Heading into the ninth with a 1–0 lead, he induced Collins to bounce to
Herzog, who threw him out. That brought up Baker. In his column for
the *Herald* ghosted by Wheeler, Marquard had been chastised for throwing
the fatal fastball to Baker. Matty got two quick strikes on Baker with curveballs and seemed poised to offer him another one. Ever the thinking pitcher,
he reasoned that Baker would be sitting on the curveball. Instead he fired a
fastball and watched Baker pile into it for another rainbow into the right-
field stands. Thanks to his performance during these two days, he would
always be known thereafter as Homerun Baker.[29]

Or so said the *Times*. The *Tribune* said the count was one and one but did
not identify the pitch, saying only that "Matty, remembering Marquard's
experience of the day before, passed up one of his famous 'fadeaways' or so
it looked, for the third." According to the *Sun*, "As Matty had been fooling
Baker with curve balls he naturally stuck to that kind of action." With the
count two and one, "the fourth was a curve with medium speed that came
in over the corner of the plate just below Baker's waist." The *Press* did not
mention the count but agreed that "King Christy, instead of falling into
Rube's mistake and putting over a straight one, sent a beautiful curve."[30]

Years later Fred Lieb still remembered "the awesome silence that followed
the crash of Baker's bat." As Baker circled the bases, the crestfallen
Mathewson realized that the game still could be won, but the life seemed to
go out of the Giants. Murphy hit a grounder to Herzog, who threw the ball
well past Merkle for a two-base error, but Matty got the next two men to end
the inning. Coombs retired the Giants in order, sending the game into extra
innings. In the tenth one play ignited what proved to be a lasting controversy. In the first game Snodgrass had given Baker a slight spike wound on
a hard slide. This time, trying without success to get hit by a pitch, he
walked and was sacrificed to second by Murray. With Merkle at bat, Lapp
fumbled a pitch and Snodgrass unwisely took off for third. Lapp recovered
the ball quickly and hurled it to Baker. Seeing that he was dead on arrival,
Snodgrass slid into the bag with spikes high, ripping Baker's uniform from
groin to knee and giving him a much nastier wound than the first one. Even
the New York fans booed and hissed at what looked like an obvious attempt
to hurt the man who had hit the two home runs. Despite the wound, Baker
stayed in the game.[31]

Merkle then worked a walk and tried to steal; Connolly called him out on
a play that sent the Giants players howling in protest. One of several close
calls that had not gone their way, it unsettled them. McGraw berated

Connolly for several minutes and barely avoided being tossed. On his way back to the bench he caught the eye of his old adversary, Ban Johnson, in the National Commission box and barked, "This is a sure-thing game. Old American League methods . . . You've got it all framed up to rob us." No one agreed with him. Connolly had six close plays to judge in the game. "From the press stand," wrote Francis Richter, "Connolly's decisions appeared to be fair and correct in every case." Afterward Tom Lynch complimented Connolly on handling a tough situation admirably.[32]

With one out in the eleventh, Collins whacked a single. Baker hit a hot shot to Herzog, who again threw the ball past Merkle, sending Collins to third and Baker to second. Murphy then hit an easy grounder to Fletcher, who fumbled it, allowing Collins to score. Davis jumped on Mathewson's first pitch for a single to right, plating Baker, but a strong throw by Murray nailed Baker at third. Davis tried to steal second but Meyers got him so easily that Doyle stood with the ball waiting for him. But the damage had been done. In their half of the eleventh Herzog led off with a double, the first Giants hit since the third inning. Fletcher lined out to Lord and Meyers grounded out to Collins, Herzog scooting to third. Becker pinch-hit for Mathewson and hit a roller to Collins, who muffed it for his second error of the game, allowing Herzog to score. Becker then tried to steal second but was out by a wide margin, a fitting end to a frustrating game for Mathewson and the Giants.

Stone-faced Jack Coombs pitched a superb game, retiring New York in order in seven of the eleven innings. So did Mathewson, who was undone by one bad pitch and some poor fielding behind him. "It was the hardest game to lose I ever saw," said Marquard's column afterward, "and Matty lost it the same way I lost the second game in Philadelphia. After the ninth inning Marquard asked Matty what had happened. "The same thing you did, Rube," he replied. "I gave Baker a high, fast one. I have been in the business for a long time and have no excuse." Even more than Marquard he was aware of Philadelphia's ability to steal signals. "The Athletics have a great reputation as being a club able to get the other team's signs if they are obtainable," he wrote afterward. "This is their record all around the American League circuit. Personally I do not believe that Connie Mack's players steal as much information as they get the credit for, but the reputation itself, if they never get a sign, is invaluable."[33]

The mild-mannered Baker took some exception to the exchange of opinions by the ghostwriters. "If you believe what Marquard and Mathewson say," he told a Philadelphia reporter wryly, "I can't hit a ball only in one spot. Taking it all in all, I'm a lucky guy to be in the league at all, after they get done telling where I hit 'em and where I miss 'em. Want to know the kind of balls I hit for those two homers? Marquard gave me a fast one on the inside. Matty handed me a curve about knee-high. It didn't look a bit different than the other curves he handed me all through the series . . . All of us have our groove, all of us are suckers for certain kinds of ball. But when you're feeling in the mood, you can hit almost any thing, especially when you are wise that they are trying to cross you up."[34]

During the game Mathewson didn't think the A's had the signs because the Giants thought they had discovered how they got them. The culprit was their small, hunchbacked, white-haired batboy and mascot, who snuck a peek at the catcher's sign every time he went out to pick up a bat. Matty arranged with Meyers that he would give the signs instead of vice versa. Meyers put down bogus signs to keep the operation secret. "That home run beat the Giants yesterday," said Marquard's ghostwriter. "They were a beaten team and they knew it when the score was tied." The attempt to stir up a controversy between the pitchers went nowhere, but one harsh fact could not be ignored. Not only did the Athletics lead the series, they had finally beaten Mathewson for the first time.

After the game Mathewson admitted that he had pitched himself out in trying to win, throwing more curveballs than usual, which made it more difficult to recover from the game in a short time. That fact did not bode well for the Giants.

Strange Interlude

On the spiking of Baker, the *Tribune* noted that his "awkward manner in tagging out runners has frequently got him into trouble." As the Athletics left their train in Philadelphia at ten thirty that night, Baker was seen walking with a slight limp. He told reporters that he was not bitter toward Snodgrass. "I will not say that he did it intentionally," he added. "I have no hard feelings against Snodgrass. I am not seriously hurt, anyhow, and you may say that I will play in to-morrow's game." Asked his views on the contest, Coombs said tersely, "I won my game. I do not think comment is necessary."[35]

The concern about Baker being able to play proved irrelevant, for on Tuesday night the eighteenth Jupiter Pluvius paid Philadelphia a visit. So hard did the rain fall that the four umpires visited Shibe Park and at eleven forty A.M. called off the game. The weather system that brought the rain proceeded to camp off the Jersey coast, bringing more rain and another postponement on Thursday. A third day of hard rain on Friday deferred the game yet again and turned the field into such a quagmire that even if the weather cleared a game on Saturday was unlikely. Since a game could not be played on Sunday, the teams would go at least five days without playing, something that had never happened in the World Series. The National Commission, already under fire for creating a schedule that went so deeply into October, faced the prospect of a series that might extend into November. On Saturday the twenty-first more rain fell than during the previous days. The umpires took some soundings around the field and, according to the *Tribune*, "were unanimous in the opinion that conditions were ideal for water polo, but that a baseball game had better be omitted." That night it poured even harder, ensuring that no game would be played on Monday.[36]

The long delay posed complications for both teams. The rules laid down by the National Commission stipulated that the game had to be played in Philadelphia, which lacked a gymnasium large enough for the teams to practice. The players got little exercise and no batting practice except for one brief afternoon, which concerned McGraw, given the poor performance of his team at the plate in the first three games. On the plus side it gave Mathewson enough rest time to pitch again without strain, although all the pitchers ran the risk of losing their sharpness. Baker's wounds on his wrist and thigh proved somewhat more serious than originally thought, but the delay gave him some healing time. He laughed off the injury and told reporters, "I'll be in the game if I have to sport a wooden leg."[37]

The long hiatus also spawned a lot of nonsense to fill the vacuum of inactivity. Wild rumors surfaced: Baker seriously ill with blood poisoning! Snodgrass shot by deranged fan! In fact Baker was fine and McGraw had sent Snodgrass back to New York to escape the abuse being heaped on him by fans in Philadelphia. Rube Oldring of the Athletics had a real problem: the death of his sister, who had been ill with tuberculosis for months. "I'll play the series out," he told Mack. "I'll play it out . . . She suffered for a long time and her death was not unexpected. But I loved Lillian—nobody knows how much." Fortunately for him, the continued downpours enabled him to go to Mount Vernon, New York, for the funeral on Sunday the twenty-second. McGraw, too, had a problem in the form of a sharp rebuke from the National Commission for "unwarranted conduct and language" in his dispute with Tom Connolly. The commission warned that another such incident would result in banishment from the game and all future games of the series. Fred Merkle got slapped with a one-hundred-dollar fine for his part in the protest and a similar threat of banishment for any repetition of the behavior.[38]

Excited comments by fans and baseball people alike on the spiking lingered in the papers for days. Snodgrass gave his version in an interview. "The runner has the right of way," he said, "and Baker, instead of taking a safe position straddled the bag and dropped on his knees, holding the ball in two hands. Had I wanted to I could not have checked my speed . . . He dropped down on the cushion directly in my path and waited for me in such a position that he could not help getting hurt. Photographs of the play will prove my statement correct. There is no ball player living for whom I have greater respect than Frank Baker. We are friends and I would not cripple him for the world. I feel the criticism that has been directed toward me keenly."[39]

Asked his opinion, McGraw dismissed the incident as one of the "fortunes of war." He chafed at his team doing nothing but hanging around the Hotel Majestic, waiting for the weather to clear. Mathewson dug out an old checkerboard and took on all comers until, tired of winning, he amused himself with billiards. An overwrought Philadelphia fan accosted Fletcher outside the hotel and the two nearly came to blows before other players stepped in and sent the man on his way. The Giants players extended their sympathy to Oldring after his return from the funeral.[40]

The most pressing problem involved finding ways to get Shibe Park in shape once the monsoon finally ended. "I have never seen the grounds in worse shape," said Mack. "The drainage arrangements are sufficient to handle the average heavy rain that lasts two or three days, but this steady downpour has been too much for them, and the grass has held the water like a sponge." Liberal amounts of sand and sawdust were poured over the infield, but the rain simply overwhelmed them and the outfield was saturated and badly puddled. The National Commission suggested burning oil on the field to dry it, but Mack was adamant that doing so would ruin the outfield grass and cost the club several thousand dollars. On the twentieth Klem declared that even a day of sunshine would not render the field fit for play.[41]

After four days of lounging about Philadelphia, McGraw took his troops home to New York once the Saturday game was called. He hoped to get in a practice at the Polo Grounds on Sunday if the weather permitted. Mack declared otherwise for his team. "We have never practised on Sunday," he said, "and I will not permit it to be done at this time." That day the drizzle in Philadelphia finally stopped and the sun popped out, but at six that evening a steady downpour blasted any hope of a game on Monday. "Shibe Park is now a misnomer," quipped the *Tribune*. "It should be called Shibe Pond." That night the Giants returned to Philadelphia intent on practicing if no game was played. Red Dooin invited them to use the Phillies' park at Broad and Huntington Streets. When the game was canceled early Monday morning, both teams slogged onto muddy fields to get in as much work as they could.[42]

Game 4

On Tuesday the twenty-fourth the sun finally returned to Philadelphia along with a brisk northwest wind that helped dry the field enough to play ball. On Monday the field had been worked over feverishly with huge sponges to dry the outfield and loads of sawdust dumped on the infield. Despite all efforts, the ground remained soft and spongy, a harsh blow to any attempt by the Giants to ignite their running game. In both cities fans waited breathlessly to learn who would do the pitching. The answer, when it was finally divulged at game time, came as no surprise: a rematch between Mathewson and Bender. After an unprecedented delay of six days, the World Series resumed.

The pundits assumed that the long layoff would benefit the Giants pitchers most, especially the overworked Mathewson. However, in the past he had often pitched better on short notice than on extended rest. For the crucial playoff game in 1908 he had enjoyed five days off and yet thought he had nothing on the ball. By contrast Bender, although only twenty-seven, did not do well without sufficient rest between starts. The Giants jumped on him right away as Devore tapped a bouncer that Bender deflected to Barry and beat the throw to first. Doyle walloped one into the gap in right and made it to third when Oldring slipped on the wet grass going after it. Snodgrass waited out a chorus of boos before lofting a fly to deep left that enabled Doyle to score easily. Murray and Merkle went down quietly but the Giants had two quick runs.[43]

Mathewson looked like his masterful self when his turn came, throwing hard and on target. Lord and Oldring fanned, Collins bounced a single through the hole, and Baker went down on strikes. Bender regained his touch and the two adversaries looked unhittable until the fourth inning, when nothing went right for Mathewson. Baker tormented him again with a double into the left-field gap. Murphy followed with a shot almost to the same place for another double, and Harry Davis whistled one down the right-field line for a third straight double. Barry bounced to Herzog for the first out, moving Davis to third. Thomas then managed a fly to right, scoring Davis when Murray's throw was wide. Bender grounded out but three runs were in, giving Philadelphia the lead. In the fifth Matty got two quick outs before Collins stroked a single to right and Baker chased him home with another double, this one to right.

With a 4–2 lead Bender breezed along, yielding seven hits but nothing more on the scoreboard. Matty surrendered ten hits, six of them doubles, before Becker pinch-hit for him in the eighth, and Wiltse finished up. The crowd heaped raucous jeers on Mathewson, the first time they had had the privilege of abusing the man who had throttled them in 1905. He had now lost two World Series games, and the Giants faced the three-to-one deficit from which escape rarely occurred. "Matty did not derive as much benefit from the period of inactivity as McGraw and he himself had hoped," suggested Marquard's column. "He was feeling well in the morning, but when he got up to the grounds he complained to me that he did not feel in his best form by any means."[44]

"Well, I got him at last," Bender told a reporter. "By winning that game to-day I have fulfilled one of the biggest ambitions I ever had in baseball. I got Matty finally." Connie Mack had a different reaction, telling American League umpire Billy Evans that his only regret after the third game was that it came at the expense of Mathewson. Frederick Courtenay Barber, writing for the *Press*, delivered a telling summary of the day's events. "McGraw's men," he said, "were outpitched, outbatted, outfielded and generally outplayed. They also were outwitted, for in the sixth round Captain Doyle ran into a transparent trap that retired him on a double play."[45]

As for Bender's performance, one reporter paid him high if racist praise. "When the Pilgrims landed on Plymouth Rock," he wrote, "they first fell upon their knees, and then fell upon the aborigines. Things have changed. The aborigines now fall upon the whites and make short work of them."[46]

Game 5

With their backs to the wall, the Giants arrived back in New York to prepare for game five the next afternoon, October twenty-fifth. Despite all of John Murphy's ministrations, the Polo Grounds was still soggy in spots, especially in the outfield. Another enormous crowd descended on the park to help the Giants stave off final defeat. McGraw tapped Marquard to pitch, while Mack chose Coombs over Plank. Both hurlers sailed through the first two innings with little trouble. "The third stanza," said the *Times*, "ought to be accompanied by the soft creepy music which prepares one for something sad." Fletcher threw out Barry, but Lapp lined a single to left. Coombs rolled what looked an easy double-play ball to Doyle, who tried to rush his motion and dropped the ball. Lord popped out to Doyle, and Marquard seemed on his way out of trouble. Oldring had broken his bat in the first inning and had to borrow Baker's club. He used it to belt a long drive into the left-field stands for a three-run homer. Collins followed with a single and stole second, but Baker hit a grounder to Merkle, who dove into first to beat him for the final out.[47]

The New York rooters sank into despair. Meyers led off the third with a single, and McGraw sent Becker to bat for Marquard, telling him that he would pitch again in Philadelphia. Barry made an acrobatic grab of Becker's liner and would have doubled Meyers had Davis not dropped his throw. But Devore struck out and Lapp cut Meyers down trying to steal. The burden then fell to Ames, who had yet to pitch in the series. With great poise he limited the Athletics to two hits over the next four innings but the Giants could not break through against Coombs until the bottom of the seventh. Merkle walked and was safe at second when Collins dropped Barry's throw on Herzog's grounder. Fletcher bounced one to Davis, who forced Herzog at second while Merkle hustled to third. Meyers plated him with a long fly to right that also moved Fletcher to second. Ames being a poor hitter, McGraw sent Crandall to bat for him. Doc worked a walk but Devore rolled one to Davis, who flipped to Coombs covering.

The Giants had narrowed the gap to 3–1 but were running out of time. In the eighth Doyle singled and was sacrificed to second. Coombs stepped out of the box and began rubbing his leg. It appeared as if he had pulled something in his thigh, and the infielders gathered around him. He threw a practice pitch to Lapp and determined to keep going. Murray, still looking for his first hit in the series, struck out for the third time and Merkle grounded to Baker. Coombs seemed to be home free as he started the ninth, and spectators began streaming toward the exits. Herzog went down on a grounder to Barry, but Fletcher blooped one into short left field for a double. Loud cheers greeted Meyers, who hit another roller to Barry for the second out. McGraw decided to let Doc Crandall hit for himself, and he responded with a shot into the right-field gap for a double, scoring Fletcher.

With Crandall, breathing hard, on second as the tying run, the crowd stopped its exodus and turned into a howling, pleading mob. Josh Devore, who had gone hitless in four trips, ripped a single to left field and, with McGraw frantically waving him onward, Crandall barreled all the way home. Devore then tried to steal second and was erased, sending the game into extra innings. Crandall had to catch his breath enough to pitch. He got Lapp on a comebacker, and Coombs, batting for himself, hit a dribbler and made it to first when Meyers's throw pulled Merkle off the bag. The effort did Coombs in, and he gave way to pinch runner Amos Strunk. Lord lofted a fly to Devore and Oldring hit a roller that Meyers pounced on and threw him out. Thus did Crandall avoid having to face Collins and Baker in the tenth.

Mack sent Plank to the mound, probably wishing he had done so an inning earlier. Doyle greeted him with his fourth hit and second double of the game, a shot to left field. Snodgrass dropped a bunt that Plank grabbed and tried to get Doyle but failed, putting runners at the corners with no one out. The crowd had worked itself into a frenzy by this time, but Murray hit a weak fly to Murphy that was too shallow for Doyle to come home. Then came the most bizarre play of an already strange game. Merkle smacked a high fly down the right-field line that almost reached the fence. Murphy faced a dilemma: If he caught the ball, Doyle would likely score the winning run; but if he let it drop and it fell in fair ground, the run would also score. Murphy decided to catch it and heave a desperate throw to the plate, but Doyle beat it home to score the winning run.

Or did he? While the Giants celebrated and the crowd rained cheers on them, plate umpire Bill Klem stood silently and said nothing. As Mack and his players headed toward the clubhouse, the umpires followed and changed clothes to catch the train for Philadelphia. Before leaving, however, Klem told reporters that Doyle never touched home plate and had missed it by six inches. He waited in silence for the Athletics to protest, but Lapp, waiting for Murphy's throw, never saw it and neither did any of his teammates. Afterward Doyle insisted that he had touched the plate, but both official scorers, J. Taylor Spink of *Sporting News* and Francis C. Richter of *Sporting*

Life, corroborated Klem's version. McGraw, coaching third, saw the play and asked Klem, "Did you see it, Bill?" Klem said he had. What would he have done if they appealed? asked McGraw.[48]

"I would have given my decision as I saw it," replied Klem, "but you see what a mess I would have got myself into."

"Well, I would have protected you," said McGraw as he walked away.

Informed of Klem's statement, Connie Mack said, "I will make no protest. The Giants won the game and are entitled to the victory. Doyle was safe at the plate by fifteen feet, and the question of whether he slid over the plate or alongside of it is a matter of minor importance. I never have bickered and never will bicker over decisions of umpires or try to win games on technicalities."[49]

"As the Athletics harbor no Johnny Evers in their number," said the *Tribune*, "this technicality was overlooked, no protest was made, and the game was declared a victory for the Giants." The *Sun* marveled that "many exciting ball games have been witnessed in this city, but this one was the limit. Suddenly raised from the depths of despair, the crowd went into paroxysms of boundless joy and for fully ten minutes after the winning run had been scored men and women rushed about the stands and went over the field as if they had lost their senses."[50]

The *Press* saw in the game something even larger. "It was more than the triumph of the Giants; it was more than the triumph of the remarkable McGraw," it editorialized. "It was the superb vindication of baseball— the unexcelled American game, without anything in the range of athletic sports to challenge it for unfailing interest, unexpected accident, repeated excitement and marvelous sensation."[51]

John T. Brush was not there to witness the victory. The lateness of the season and urgent advice of his physician had compelled him to head for Chicago to see his specialist prior to beginning his winter sojourn in Texas. He was greatly pleased when the results reached him. "His condition is much better than yesterday," said his doctor, "and he seemed to improve visibly after the game ended."[52]

Game 6

The most tantalizing question prior to game time was who would pitch for each team in this critical contest. As the smallest crowd of the series—only about twenty thousand—filed into Shibe Park, McGraw had all of his pitchers warming up while Mack confined his choice to Bender, Plank, and Cy Morgan. No one expected Mathewson to go after his eleven-inning effort; the most likely choice during warm-ups seemed to be Marquard. Pundits figured that Mack would go with Plank because Bender was not a pitcher to come back on one day's rest. Both managers sprang surprises. McGraw decided to start Ames, and Mack stunned everyone by selecting Bender rather than saving him for a possible game seven.[53]

Neither did anyone expect the kind of game that unfolded. After several classic struggles culminating in the fabulous comeback by the Giants in game five, the fans were treated this day to a comedy of errors on the part of both teams. McGraw had brought his team to town early to ensure a good night's rest for them, and in pregame practice they looked sharp and more eager to play than the somewhat listless Athletics. The first inning set the tone when, after Devore grounded out, Doyle whaled one over Murphy's head that hit the fence a foot shy of going over, forcing him to settle for a double. Snodgrass could not advance him with a fly to left, but Murray lined one to right that Murphy simply dropped, giving the Giants a gift run. In his eagerness to get a good lead, Murray was picked off by Bender to end the inning.

Ames started with three straight balls to Lord but got him to ground out to Doyle, whereupon he fanned Oldring and Collins. With one out in the second, Herzog lived on an error by the usually sure-handed Barry—one of three he made that day—and stole second but died there. Ames also allowed a runner to reach second but go no farther. To open the third he actually managed a single, only his seventh hit of the season, but the Giants came away with nothing. The Athletics tied the score in their half when Thomas walked, moved to second on Bender's bunt, and scored on Lord's double into the right-field crowd. Just when the game seemed to be settling into a taut duel, the deciding break, as McGraw liked to call it, arrived unexpectedly.

After New York went out quickly in the fourth, Baker launched a single to center. Murphy did likewise, sending Baker to third. Davis rammed a grounder at Doyle, who tried to get Baker at home, but Tom Connolly called him safe on a close play. With runners on first and second, Barry dropped a bunt down the first base line. Ames fielded it cleanly but hit Barry in the head with his throw, and the ball rolled into right field. Murray hurried to pick it up and tried to get Barry at second base only to throw it over Doyle's head. Before Devore could retrieve the elusive ball, three more runs had scored. The Giants had converted a bunt into a home run of sorts and found themselves down 5–1.

Having found his rhythm, Bender mowed down the Giants. In the fifth, New York got two men on base with two out, but Devore struck out. Although Ames surrendered only four hits in four innings, McGraw sent Wiltse out for the fifth. He retired Philadelphia in short order, and so were the Giants in the sixth, thanks in large measure to splendid catches by Baker and Oldring. In their half the A's picked up another run as Snodgrass misjudged a fly ball by Murphy and turned it into a double. Murphy took third on a grounder and scored on a double by Barry. Herzog opened the seventh by living on another Barry error and stayed there as Davis made a great catch of a foul by Fletcher, and both Meyers and Wiltse struck out.

In the bottom of the seventh, the Giants saw their hopes vanish in a spectacle of humiliation. After Bender flied out, a barrage of six hits abetted by a Merkle error and a successful squeeze play let five runners cross the plate before McGraw mercifully removed Wiltse in favor of Marquard. With two men on base the Rube let loose with a wild pitch that cleared the bases, giving the Athletics seven runs for the inning and a 13–1 lead. A disgusted McGraw did not return to the coaching box in the eighth. Bender allowed the Giants a meaningless run in the ninth, but the rout was complete; he had held them to 4 hits while throwing only 101 pitches.

The Giants had lost the series in convincing fashion. It was the worst beatdown yet inflicted on any team in a World Series, one that would not be topped until 1936, when the Yankees pounded another Giants team 18–4. After the final out McGraw walked over to the Philadelphia bench to congratulate Mack. "You have the best team, Connie," he said. "You beat us squarely, and we have no excuse to offer. I take off my hat to your grand team." Later, while Mack was being showered with congratulations by club officials, Mathewson walked through the door with a smile and extended his hand. "I congratulate you and your team," he said. "You beat us fairly and squarely." Touched by the sentiment, Mack gave the pitcher's hand a warm squeeze. "His reply was unheard," noted a reporter. Bill Klem offered a different compliment, calling the Athletics "as a whole the finest team" he had ever umpired for.[54]

"They were a great team," said Meyers late in life, "there's no doubt about that. Especially that '$100,000 infield' . . . But I still think we were the better club. They had our signs or could read our pitchers, or something. They knew what Marquard was pitching, Matty, too." Later in life McGraw observed, "Our club was pretty well worn out and shot to pieces when we faced the Athletics . . . in 1911. I do not give that as a reason for our defeat, but it was a contributing cause." Paddy Livingston, the As' third-string catcher, said harshly, "It makes me laugh when they compare the New York base runners with Ty Cobb. All they know is when to make fake starts. They don't know how to get a lead on our pitchers. Devore is almost as fast a man as Cobb, but he lacks 10 or 12 feet of getting Ty's read. And you always know which one of their starts is a fake. They are too easy."[55]

After the series Ira Thomas claimed that the Athletics feared Mathewson the most and had studied him in detail. They noticed "a certain little step he made that he would pitch this famous ball," said Thomas. "That movement was almost minute, and I daresay even 'Matty' did not know he made it, but every time he pitched his 'fadeaway' he made that one little step that warned us of what was coming . . . Every player of our team who stepped to the plate faced 'Matty' with the one idea in his head—to take the 'fadeaway.' We knew every ball 'Matty' would pitch. We learned that from his motions. We knew when the 'fadeaway' was coming, and I can safely say that 'Matty' never saw an Athletic bat swing at his 'fadeaway.'" Their hope had been to "kill 'Matty' off in the first game," Thomas added, and they succeeded. "'Matty' pitched himself out in that game and we all felt that he could never beat us again. Which he did not."[56]

Whether it was the prowess of the Athletics or their own fatigue or a combination of both, the Giants did not play their game. In six games they batted a pitiful .175 and stole only four bases. Doyle and Meyers alone had any success, hitting .304 and .300 respectively. No other regular hit even .200. Red Murray emerged as the ultimate goat, going hitless in twenty-one appearances. Snodgrass managed a feeble .105, Fletcher .130, Merkle .150, Devore .167 with eight whiffs, and Herzog .190. They committed sixteen errors to eleven for the A's, who also got most of the timely hits. However, Meyers, the man supposedly still learning his trade, set a record for a six-game series that still stands by throwing out a dozen runners.[57]

Mathewson thought the Athletics had discussed and practiced ways to thwart the Giants' running game. "Mack had been watching the Giants for weeks previous to the series," he wrote, "and had had his spies taking notes . . . Mack's pitchers cut their motions down to nothing with men on the bases, microscopic motions, and they watched the runners like hawks.

Thomas had been practicing to get the men." The first time Devore tried to steal second he was caught several feet from the bag. "And you call yourself fast," said Collins in a rare comment from one of the Athletics.[58]

The series rewarded both players and owners by setting new records in attendance, receipts, and worldwide attention. Attendance totaled 179,891 for the six games with receipts of $342,365. The victorious Athletics each took home $3,654.59, the losing Giants $2,436.39; the two owners each collected $90,108.72, and the National Commission added $34,236.45 to its treasury. New York did not forget its heroes even in defeat. On the evening of October 28 a large audience cheered and entertained them at a special dinner at the Imperial Hotel. All eyes looked to next season and the hope of a return engagement against Philadelphia. Meanwhile, there was some more ball to be played for most of the team.[59]

On Saturday, November 11, they joined McGraw on a ship bound for Havana to make a few dollars playing a dozen games against Cuba's best players while enjoying themselves in the bargain. Marquard stayed home to do a vaudeville routine, and Chief Meyers declared himself exhausted and wanted only to go home to California and rest. Merkle, Murray, Snodgrass, and Ames also declined to go, but McGraw added Mike Donlin to the roster for the trip. Blanche McGraw, Jane Mathewson, and five other wives also went along, as did several writers and umpire Cy Rigler. Each player was guaranteed $500 and an experience they would not soon forget, a useful antidote for the sour ending to such a sweet season.[60]

CHAPTER 17

The McGraw Dynasties

*"What a great man he was! Oh, we held him
in high esteem. We respected him in every way.
According to Mr. McGraw, his ball team never
lost a game; he lost it, not his players. He
fought for his players, and protected them."*
— JOHN "CHIEF" MEYERS

*"The best times we have are when we are
thinking about the good times we are going to
have."*
— JOHN McGRAW

TIME PROVED McGRAW RIGHT IN BELIEVING that he had forged a dynasty. The Giants went on to cop the pennant in both 1912 and 1913 but, to his chagrin, lost the World Series both years, first to the Boston Red Sox and then to the Athletics. By then the team, like all dynasties, had run its course and the players began to disperse in trades and retirements. In 1914 the Giants lost out to the so-called Miracle Braves that surged back from last place on July 4 to win the flag by ten and a half games and stun the Athletics in the World Series. Members of that team included pitcher Dick Rudolph, who went 27-10; John Evers at second; Hank Gowdy catching; and Josh Devore as one of several platooning outfielders.

In 1912, McGraw lost his most important and reliable supporter when a truck struck John Brush's automobile in Harlem, causing two broken ribs and a serious hip injury. After treatment he boarded a train that would take him to a sanitarium in southern California to recuperate. On November 26, while traveling through Missouri, Brush died. His body was returned to Indianapolis, where McGraw served as one of the honorary pallbearers and delivered one of the eulogies. "He was as tender as a dear girl," he said with obvious emotion, "as resourceful as a man in the fullest of grand health . . . What a wonderful—what a beautiful character was John T. Brush." In 1913 the Giants unveiled a new stairway leading to the Polo Grounds and named it after Brush. His son-in-law, Harry Hempstead, then managing the department store in Indianapolis, succeeded him as president of the Giants. One of his first steps was to give McGraw a new contract for five years at $30,000 a year.[1]

In 1915 McGraw suffered the ignominy of finishing in last place for the first time since his initial season with the Giants. Undaunted, he managed to win the pennant two years later only to lose the World Series yet again. The game was changing in ways not to McGraw's liking, moving steadily away from the heady, running, scratch-for-a-run-any-way-you-can game toward one built around the long ball. McGraw adjusted but not all the way; he still favored brains, speed, and hustle over slugging. Putting together a new dynasty, he finished second for three straight years and then won four pennants in a row. In 1921 and 1922 he finally had the satisfaction of reclaiming the World Series as well. Victory was made even sweeter by beating the new hometown favorites, the Yankees, twice in a row before losing to them in 1923 and then to the Washington Senators in 1924.[2]

In the seven remaining years of his career, McGraw's Giants finished second and third three times each and fifth once. By 1930 his health had begun to deteriorate. The broken nose suffered in 1903 continued to give him trouble despite an operation in 1922. He developed a prostate condition that by 1932 had worsened to the point that he knew something was very wrong after returning from the first road trip of the season. His doctor advised him to make no more road trips but only manage the team at the Polo Grounds, an idea that McGraw naturally found repugnant.[3]

The man widely considered to be the best and best-known manager in baseball—his only challenger being his old adversary, the ageless Connie Mack—was deeply tired and discouraged. In thirty-one years he had won ten pennants and three World Series, but none since 1924. Like the country, he was worn down and beaten by depression. Like the country, too, he sensed bitterly that his best days had come and gone. The game he loved, that America loved, had passed him by, left him enamored more of its past than of its present or future. It had grown younger as he grew older, discarding speed and finesse for raw power. If he had any doubts about the change, a perfect example came on June 2, 1932, when the uptown Yankees whipped the Philadelphia Athletics 20–13 in a wild game that featured ten home runs. The Yankees hit seven of the homers, with Lou Gehrig personally accounting for four of them to set a modern record.[4]

The team that McGraw had transformed into the toast of New York had become a pale shadow of its past glory. The Yankees were the toast of the city now, drawing big crowds to watch Babe Ruth, Gehrig, and others bludgeon the ball into submission. The time was drawing near when he would have to surrender the thing he had loved most, that had always been at the core of his existence: the game. He had played it brilliantly and managed it even more brilliantly, but those glories had long since passed. He was only fifty-nine years old, but in baseball years it felt more like a century.

All his life McGraw had been a battler. As a boy he had fought to survive and to play ball at whatever cost. As both a player and a manager he had fought to win games any way he could, with no regard for the toll exacted on himself or others. To that end he had bought, sold, and traded more players than any other manager. For thirty years, too, he had struggled with poor health, the fight made worse by his fondness for food and drink. Neither the fight nor the will to win had left McGraw, but the strength to do so had faded badly.

"Defeat was his mortal enemy," Blanche observed later. "He was a force that knew only one compromise: victory. All else was of minor importance, for without victory baseball had no meaning for him. By the same token, life without baseball also had little meaning for him. It was his meat, his drink, his dream, his blood and breath, his reason for existence." Nevertheless, he decided, it was time to let go, to stop trying to keep up with a game and a regimen made for younger, healthier men.[5]

One thing was clear to him: Blanche would accept whatever decision he made. For thirty years she had dutifully organized her life around the rhythms and vagaries of the baseball season without uttering a complaint that anyone heard. In the old days, before they had a settled home, she would pack a bag and go visit her mother in Baltimore whenever John left on a road trip. When he was at home they managed to have a life together away from the ballpark despite the demands of his job and the pressure he put on himself. She understood him better than anyone, knew he was sick, and was fearful of what another road trip might do to him.[6]

On that June 2, 1932, with the Giants idled by rain, McGraw summoned his star first baseman, Bill Terry, with whom he had not spoken since February, and asked him if he wanted to become manager. A stunned Terry said later that he had never played harder than during the period he and McGraw were not speaking because he wanted to show that he was the bigger person. "But at that moment," he admitted, "I never felt smaller, and he showed me in ten seconds what a really big and genuine man he was. I was overcome, but not completely, because I had sense enough to draw in a deep breath and say, "I'll take it!" When McGraw went home to his house in Pelham Manor, Blanche asked why he was home so early. "I quit," he said.[7]

The next day McGraw stayed at home while club secretary Jim Tierney summoned reporters to the office of owner Charles Stoneham, who had bought control of the team in 1919, and handed out a typed statement McGraw had signed. "For over two years," it began, "I have been contemplating the necessity of turning over the management of the Giants to some one else. My doctor advises me, because of my sinus condition, that it would be inadvisable to attempt any road trips with the club this season, so I suggested to Mr. Stoneham that another manager be appointed . . . to which Mr. Stoneham agreed."[8]

He wanted a man who was "thoroughly familiar with my methods and who had learned his baseball under me." That man was Bill Terry, who would have "full and complete charge and control of the team." McGraw would not retire entirely from baseball but serve as vice president and adviser in the office. "During my thirty years with the Giants," he concluded, "the fans have been extremely loyal to me, for which they have my heartfelt thanks, and hope they will give Terry the same loyalty and support."[9]

Once the news broke, the tributes poured in from all sides. "John J. McGraw has been a great character in the development of baseball," said Commissioner Kenesaw Mountain Landis, "and I am very sorry to see him go." Emil Fuchs, president of the Boston Braves, called McGraw "one of my best friends . . . I consider him the greatest manager in the game." Braves manager Bill McKechnie agreed that McGraw was "the greatest of managers. I've played with him and fought with him and I can say only what everybody else will agree to, that his connection with baseball has been one of its greatest assets." Dan Howley, manager of the Reds, thought that "the greatest figure in baseball stepped off the diamond . . . The game won't look the same with McGraw out of the picture."[10]

Refreshed by a good night's sleep, McGraw seemed surprised the next day when reporters called at his home in Pelham. They found him more like the McGraw they knew as he reminded them with a twinkle in his eye, "They haven't buried me yet." Pressed for more details on his resignation, he answered reluctantly, "There was really no other logical step I could have taken. When my doctor told me I could do no more traveling this Summer and that I could not even sit on the bench, both Mr. Stoneham and I agreed that some drastic action was required if ever we were to get our team going as it should."[11]

Gradually the team lost the distinctive imprint McGraw had given it and came more and more to resemble other teams. Fred Snodgrass later described the change:

> Players in my day played baseball with their brains as much as their brawn. They were intelligent, smart ballplayers. Why, you *had* to be! You didn't stay in the Big Leagues very long in those days unless you used your head every second of every game . . . Now they're all trying to hit the ball over the fence. It's mostly brute strength . . . In my day a home run was a rarity. You *couldn't* hit the ball over the fence in most parks in those days, because the ball was too dead! So we were always playing for small scores, for one run or two. As a result, there was a premium on intelligence . . . the ability to outwit and outthink the other team. And on speed and strategy.[12]

Only once did McGraw return to the diamond. In 1933 he and his old adversary Connie Mack were asked to manage in the first All-Star Game at Comiskey Park in Chicago. The yin and yang of baseball posed one last time together for pictures in the ninety-degree heat before the game, but once in the dugout McGraw let Terry and St. Louis second baseman Frankie Frisch handle the decisions. Afterward he went into the American League dressing room to congratulate all the players. He and Mack were surrounded by players from both teams asking them to autograph balls for them. When the Giants won the pennant that year, he followed the team happily, attended the World Series games against the Washington Senators, and was genuinely pleased when they won.[13]

By the fall McGraw's prostate cancer had spread alarmingly. On Sunday, February 25, 1934, forty-one days shy of his sixty-first birthday, he died. Tributes poured in from across the nation, and an estimated 3,500 people braved bitter cold to attend his funeral at St. Patrick's Cathedral in Manhattan. The body was then taken to Baltimore for burial. Blanche, who had been devoted to him for so long, knew McGraw best. "John," she told a reporter, "had the mind of a man and the heart of a boy." On opening day at the Polo Grounds in April 1934 she was present to hear a bugler play taps in her husband's honor prior to the game.[14]

McGraw's longtime adversary, the Tall Tactician, who experienced more baseball from the inside than anyone over the course of his lengthy career, deserves the last word. In 1943, Connie Mack told former Giants outfielder Red Murray, "John McGraw in my opinion was the outstanding manager of all time. Have made many talks about baseball and I always say the same thing about John."[15]

Epilogue: The Parade Passing

"It's great to be young and a Giant!"
— LARRY DOYLE

REGARDLESS OF HOW THEIR CAREERS TURNED out, most of the 1911 Giants enjoyed long if not always satisfactory lives. The three who died at an early age could not have been more different from each other. For Bugs Raymond the addiction to alcohol seemed to curse everything else he did. While playing some semipro baseball, he returned to work as a pressman. Separated from his wife, he also lost his five-year-old daughter to the flu. In September 1912, while watching a local baseball game, he got into an argument with a man named Fred Cigranz, who hit him in the head with a baseball bat. Three weeks earlier he had been in a brawl and received several hard blows to the head. On this September day he returned to his shabby room at the Hotel Veley and died of a cerebral hemorrhage alone and friendless. He was thirty years old.[1]

The fate of Charlie Faust was as sorrowful as that of Raymond. Having failed to work his magic in the World Series, he dangled in a sort of limbo with the team. A return to vaudeville that fall turned into a fiasco. In the spring of 1912 he turned up in Hot Springs, Arkansas, where he "trained" with the several teams in camp there before trying to foist himself on a reluctant McGraw. The Giants got off to a blazing start without Faust, standing 50-11 at the end of June. Faust announced that he would join the Cubs. "I've been patient with Mr. McGraw," he told a Giant, "but I don't think he likes me anymore. They made me pay 75 cents to get into the park Monday." But he kept trying to rejoin the Giants, showing up in Chicago in July and again in St. Louis only to be rebuffed.[2]

By then McGraw had grown not only tired of but alarmed by Faust's behavior. Although New York's record tailed off after McGraw sent Faust packing, none of the players wanted him back. Finally Faust returned to his Kansas farm exactly a year after he first introduced himself to the Giants.

Little is known of his life after July 1912. Still restless, he left the farm for California, worked a variety of jobs, and moved to Seattle, where his brother George lived, in November 1913. The following February he was arrested for insanity in Portland, Oregon, and committed to the state asylum at Salem. He was released in July to the custody of his brother, who in December had him committed to the Western Washington Hospital at Steilacoom, Washington. He was found to have tuberculosis and died from the disease on June 18, 1915, a sad figure who never stopped believing that he was destined to pitch in the major leagues.[3]

By contrast, the life of Christy Mathewson continued to be a parade of triumphs for several more years. For three seasons he remained one of the league's best pitchers, averaging twenty-four wins. In the World Series of 1912 and 1913 he went a combined 1-3 despite allowing less than one earned run per game. In 1915, a season in which both the Giants and Athletics crashed to last place, Mathewson slipped to 8-14, and it became obvious that his glory days were over. Still eager to manage, McGraw granted his wish in July 1916 by trading him to Cincinnati along with Edd Roush and Bill McKechnie for, of all people, Buck Herzog, then managing the Reds, and outfielder Red Killefer.

Never one to fool himself, Matty knew he could no longer pitch. Under his guidance the Reds had a lackluster season, but on Labor Day he came out of retirement to pitch one last game against the Cubs. His opponent for this special matchup would be Mordecai Brown, like Matty making his last appearance on the mound. He was a month shy of forty, Matty was thirty-six, and neither had his former skills, but a large crowd turned out to bathe in the nostalgia. The game wasn't much: Matty allowed fifteen hits and got three himself, while Brown surrendered nineteen safeties and made two of his own. The Reds staggered to a 10–8 win. "Both of these great pitchers were finished," recalled Chicago writer James T. Farrell, who was twelve at the time, "and about all Matty had left was his wonderful sense of motion." Farrell called it "the most sentimental game I ever attended."[4]

In 1917, Mathewson piloted the Reds to fourth place, but the following year he quit in August of a war-shortened season to become a captain in the Army's Chemical Warfare Division, joining fellow captain Ty Cobb. Both were involved in training men to withstand the release of poison gas. On the way to France, Matty managed to survive the flu that had begun to ravage the globe in the worst pandemic in history, but it weakened his lungs. During a test exercise in France he and Cobb both received an accidental dose of mustard gas. Matty remained hospitalized until after the Armistice and did not return home until the spring of 1919. Garry Herrmann had not heard from him during that time and reluctantly hired Pat Moran to manage the Reds. Finding his old friend without a job, McGraw offered him one as a coach for the Giants but he had to give it up in June 1920.[5]

Bothered by a persistent cough through 1919, Mathewson consulted a doctor the following spring and was told in June that he had tuberculosis, the same disease that had killed his younger brother Henry and other members of his family. He and Jane moved to the nation's best-known treatment center for the disease, Lake Saranac in the Adirondack Mountains. There he suffered a collapsed lung and bouts of depression eased by news in 1921 that the Giants had won the pennant. Not until 1923 did he recover enough to venture back into baseball as president of the Boston Braves on a light schedule. The effort proved too much for him. In the spring of 1925 he suffered a relapse and returned to Saranac Lake, aware that he could never leave there again.[6]

On the morning of October 7, 1925, he told his wife, "Now, Jane, I suppose you will have to go out and have a good cry. Don't make it a long one. This cannot be helped." He died quietly that afternoon at the age of forty-five and was buried near the campus of Bucknell University with McGraw and Larry Doyle among the pallbearers. Tributes poured in from across the nation. Eleven years later the National Baseball Hall of Fame was founded in Cooperstown, New York, and the first five immortals of the game voted into it were Ty Cobb, Babe Ruth, Honus Wagner, Walter Johnson, and Christy Mathewson, who for a generation of Americans represented their ideal of a player and a gentleman.

THE LIFE OF THAT OTHER OLDER GIANTS hero, Mike Donlin, never escaped its pattern of constant ups and downs. He returned to baseball in 1911 because his *Stealing Home* show with Mabel had played itself out and her career in vaudeville had gone stale. After being traded to Boston he hit a solid .315 in fifty-six games, but Boston didn't care to meet his salary demands and traded him to Pittsburgh in February 1912. That year he played seventy-seven games and compiled a .316 average for the Pirates, who responded by putting him on waivers in December. That same month Mabel died from cancer that had been diagnosed only that fall. The Phillies claimed him off waivers but Donlin chose to retire. Later in 1913 he changed his mind and played thirty-six games with Jersey City of the International League. McGraw invited him to join his postseason barnstorming tour around the world and gave him another shot with the Giants in 1914.[7]

"The Apollo of the whackstick is back with the Giants," trumpeted the *World.* However, Donlin managed to hit only .161 in thirty-five games, all as a pinch hitter. His major-league career was finished, but in 1917 Donlin managed Memphis of the Southern Association and appeared in sixteen games but left in midseason. Four years later, at the age of forty-three, he played one last game with the Kalamazoo Celery Pickers of the Central League. He had married Rita Ross of the musical-comedy team Ross & Fenton in October 1914 and tried to revive his career in show business. After a vaudeville venture flopped, he moved to motion pictures, starting with one about his own life, *Right off the Bat,* in 1915. In between these activities he managed a semipro team in New Jersey, ran a baseball clinic and boxing tournament in Cuba, and taught baseball to American soldiers in France. In 1918 he went to California as a scout for the Braves.[8]

While there his old friend John Barrymore helped get him into some films, and he served as consultant for movies involving baseball. But his old pattern of being constantly short of money persisted as he scrounged for jobs in baseball and acting. In 1927 a number of film stars staged a minstrel show to raise funds for Donlin to get a major operation at the Mayo Clinic. In 1933 he landed a part in one last film, and in the spring asked a friend if he could get a coaching job with the Giants. Nothing came of it. On September 24, 1933, a heart attack ended the life of the once fabled Turkey Mike. In November 1908, *Baseball* magazine had published an article called "On Just Being a Fan" by Mabel Hite. "I used to think that an actress' life very nearly tested human endurance," she wrote, "but now I believe that a baseball player has more tiffs by far with unkind fate . . . Every day a man plays baseball it takes just so many hours off his final days. The work is very exacting. It uses up the best of a man's life, and then leaves him high and dry."[9]

Red Ames, he of the bad luck, remained a solid member of the pitching staff in 1912 with an 11-5 record. However, the following May he was traded to Cincinnati; in July 1915 he moved to the Cardinals and pitched well for them until 1919, when he finished his career with the Phillies. Like so many other players at the end of their careers, Ames spent a few years in the minors before retiring in 1923 to his hometown of Warren, Ohio. His son, Leon Junior, pitched in the minors until 1929. Red found work at a Warren dairy company where he accidentally inhaled ammonia fumes from a defective drum that seriously damaged his lungs. Hard luck, it seemed, pursued him even after his playing days. He was only fifty-four when he died on October 8, 1936. Along with Raymond, Mathewson, and Beals Becker, Ames was the only other member of the team who failed to live at least into his sixties.[10]

After 1911 Becker enjoyed a brief but productive career. A native of El Dorado, Kansas, he remained with the Giants through 1912. The following year he went to Cincinnati but was traded in June to the Phillies. He hit .324 for them in 1913 and .325 in 1914 but fell off to .246 in 1915, his last year in the majors even though he was only twenty-nine. In 1913 he set a record by hitting two inside-the-park homers in one season. He played in three World Series, two with the Giants and one with the Phillies, but went hitless in nine at-bats. For another decade he bounced around the minor leagues before retiring in 1925. In 1935 he was living in Porterville, California, and worked in the fruit-packing business. He died on August 16, 1943, at the home of his sister in Huntington Park, California, at the age of fifty-seven.[11]

Art Devlin had little to celebrate after the World Series. In December he and his wife separated and later divorced, her father saying, "I have heard stories that Devlin has not been doing the right thing by her." That month the Giants sold him to the Boston Rustlers, for whom he had a decent season in 1912 and a mediocre one the next year, when the team sent him to Rochester of the International League. After a few years in the minors he worked as a coach for three National League teams, including the Giants, from 1919 through 1935. In 1921 he tried vainly to get McGraw to sign a Columbia University student by the name of Louis Gehrig. Later he coached at Fordham while scouting for the Giants and Braves, and persuaded McGraw to sign one of his finds, second baseman Frankie Frisch.[12]

After baseball Devlin went through a number of jobs. During the 1930s he directed the sandlot baseball program in Bayonne, New Jersey. In 1941 he became an attendant at the Hudson County Hospital for Contagious Diseases in Laurel Hill, New Jersey, where one of his fellow workers was Danny Murphy of the Athletics. During the war he worked in Washington for the Home Owners' Loan Corporation. In the summer of 1948 he fell ill with a heart ailment. The death of his second wife on August 16 left him despondent as well as weak, and he died on September 18. To many veterans of his time he remained the outstanding third baseman of that generation.

Art Fletcher enjoyed a longer career in baseball than any of the other members of the 1911 Giants. He played on four pennant-winning teams with New York and served as team captain in 1917. Although he never again hit .300, he remained a solid performer at the plate and in the field, except during the World Series, where he batted only .191 and committed a dozen errors in twenty-five games. In June 1920, McGraw traded him to the Phillies for Davy Bancroft, an excellent shortstop. After a strong season with a weak team, Fletcher sat out the 1921 campaign after both his father and brother passed away that spring. He played one more year, then agreed to retire and manage the Phillies. His fiery leadership improved the team's play but failed to push the team higher than sixth place. In October 1926 the Phillies let him go.[13]

The Philadelphia experience drained any desire Fletcher had for managing, but the following season Miller Huggins persuaded him to join the Yankees as a coach. He found this job to his liking and remained with the Yankees until 1945, when heart problems forced him to retire. During that time he turned down several opportunities to manage again. The most impressive came in 1929 when Miller Huggins died and Colonel Jake Ruppert, owner of the Yankees, offered the position to Fletcher. Dumbfounded when Fletcher declined, Rupert said, "I never heard of such a thing, a man not wanting to manage my club." To his wife, Irene, Fletcher said, "I just refused to take the best job in baseball."

"I'm glad," she replied.

"So am I," he said.

When Joe McCarthy took charge of the Yankees in 1931, Fletcher became his right-hand man. "I am going to miss Fletcher," said a crestfallen McCarthy when Fletcher retired. "There never was a fellow like him." During his career with the Yankees he happily collected eleven more World Series checks to go with his four for the Giants. He and Irene lived in what a reporter called "a hideaway apartment in New York. They can be reached only by telegram." With their daughters grown, they spent much of their time driving around the country, sightseeing. After retiring, they continued to live comfortably in Fletcher's hometown, Collinsville, Illinois, until his death from a heart attack in Los Angeles on February 6, 1950.

DOC CRANDALL NEVER AGAIN EQUALED HIS stellar 1911 season, but he remained a solid performer during the next two pennant-winning campaigns, becoming the first pitcher to make over thirty relief appearances in 1913. On August 6 of that year McGraw surprised everyone by sending him to St. Louis for catcher Larry McLean only to buy him back twelve days later. The following year Crandall and catcher Grover Hartley jumped to the Federal League St. Louis team for two years until the league folded. After brief appearances with the St. Louis Browns in 1916 and Boston Braves in 1918, he spent the next eleven years in the minor leagues, most of it with Los Angeles in the Pacific Coast League. He tried owning the Wichita team of the Western League for two years, then retired until 1930, when he became pitching coach for the Pirates for four years. After managing a Des Moines team that included his son Jim as a catcher, he coached for two more years before leaving baseball in 1938. For a time he worked as a guard in an aircraft plant. Sometime around 1936 he was diagnosed with arteriosclerosis that eventually led to a series of strokes. He died of a cerebral hemorrhage on August 17, 1951, in the Mission Hospital in Bell, California.[14]

No one had a more intense love-hate relationship with McGraw than Buck Herzog. "I cannot stand having him on my ball club telling me what to do much of the time instead of taking orders from me," said McGraw, "but I need him on the club if I am to win pennants." For his part Herzog admitted that "the old man and I had our arguments. I guess we both liked to win so well. But, when he got into a pinch and needed some one to put fire into his team, I am glad to remember he always was calling back Buck Herzog." He remained a mainstay on the 1912 pennant winner, and in the World Series set a record that endured for half a century by collecting twelve hits. In 1913, however, an injury cost him his job as a regular. He got into only ninety-six games and had a nightmare series in which he got only one hit in nineteen at-bats.[15]

In December 1913, while McGraw was absent on a world tour, Harry Hempstead traded Herzog and Grover Hartley to Cincinnati for speedster Bob Bescher. Hartley promptly fled to the Federal League, but Garry Herrmann named Herzog playing manager of the Reds. McGraw was furious at the news, and Herzog brought the Reds in last. A year later Herzog's team climbed to seventh, ahead only of the Giants. In typical fashion Herzog battled with umpires, his own underachieving players, and the front office. In 1916 a rebuilding McGraw brought Herzog back in the trade that sent Mathewson to Cincinnati as manager. Playing second base in 1917, Herzog hit only .235 but the Giants won the pennant in an acrimonious season that, among other things, saw Herzog get suspended for failing to make the final road trip because of a back injury, and make a critical error in the World Series won by the White Sox.[16]

In January 1918 McGraw dispatched Herzog for the final time to the Braves, where he played a season and a half before being shipped to the Cubs. After a poor 1920 season with Chicago, ending with the suspicion that he was one of several Cubs who had thrown a game to Philadelphia (nothing against him was proven), he was released and lingered a year in the minors with a record $20,000 contract before quitting the game when it wasn't renewed. In 1924 he managed Newark of the International League briefly and moved on to coach the U.S. Naval Academy's team. With a wife and three children to support, he became athletic director for the Second Army Corps until the post was abolished, then persuaded the president of the Baltimore & Ohio Railroad to make him the "athletic passenger agent" drumming up sports business for the line. Later he worked at a Maryland racetrack.[17]

Although Herzog had always done well and lived comfortably, at some point he lost or sold his farm in Maryland and found it difficult to keep a job or maintain the standard of living he had always enjoyed. During the winter of 1952–53 the police found him in the lobby of a Baltimore hotel destitute, in rags, and seriously ill. They took him to City Hospital, where he was found to have advanced tuberculosis. He died on September 4, 1953, and was buried in Denton, Maryland. No mention was made of his family or their whereabouts.[18]

Few players could rival Josh Devore's record of being on four pennant winners in four years, yet those were also his last years in the major leagues. He played in 106 games for the 1912 Giants, batting .275, and made one of the greatest catches of all time in the third game of the World Series. After a slow start in 1913, however, he was traded in May to Cincinnati along with Red Ames and third baseman Heinie Groh for pitcher Art Fromme. Three months later the Reds sold him to the Phils, for whom he played until July 3, 1914, when he was traded to the Boston Braves and reunited with his former Newark Indians manager, George Stallings. The next day the last-place Braves began their miraculous run to the pennant and World Series triumph over the Athletics. Stallings platooned his outfielders, which limited Devore's playing time. In the series he struck out in his only plate appearance; it proved to be his last major league at-bat when the Braves released him before the start of the next season.[19]

Devore bought stock in a minor-league team in Chillicothe, Ohio, near his hometown and acted as player-manager. After a failed tryout with the Phillies, he embarked on a minor-league career that lasted through 1924, interrupted only in 1918 when he enlisted in the Army. Afterward he settled in Chillicothe with his wife, Catherine, and daughter, Patricia, who became a national swimming champion. He managed restaurants and worked as a grocer. Always known as easygoing and affable, he had a weakness for gambling and, some said, for drink. Late in life he developed lung cancer and died on October 6, 1954, just a month before turning sixty-seven.[20]

The man hailed by several writers as the "second Mathewson" never came even close to his idol. The promise shown by Louis Drucke vanished as quickly as it had arisen. After his disappointing 1911 season he appeared in only one game the following year before being sent to Toronto of the International League. For a few years he lingered in the minors before calling it quits. He joined the Army during World War I and then returned to his hometown of Waco and life as a cotton farmer. Drucke claimed, possibly with justification, that he was never the same after the arm injury suffered on the elevated train in 1911. Certainly he never pitched as well after it. On September 22, 1955, he died of a cerebral thrombosis at his home in Waco. He was sixty-six.[21]

As his teammates well knew, Fred Merkle was always smarter than most people gave him credit for, but bad luck seemed to dog him throughout life. He enjoyed a career year for the Giants in 1912 only to be involved in another controversial play that revived the label of "bonehead." He did good service for the Giants until 1916, when McGraw concluded that his level of play had declined even though he was only twenty-seven. In August the Giants traded him to Brooklyn, which won the pennant and enabled Merkle to play in a fourth losing World Series. Early in the 1917 season the Cubs, having lost first baseman Vic Saier to a broken leg, bought Merkle from Brooklyn. He remained a starter for three years with Chicago and in 1918 played in his fifth World Series for yet another losing team.[22]

Released after the 1920 season, Merkle spent four years putting up big numbers for Rochester of the International League. In June 1925 the Yankees hired him as coach and pinch hitter. In 1926 he endured his sixth losing World Series, this one with the Yankees. A year later the Yankees let him go to make room for a more fiery coach, his old teammate Art Fletcher. Merkle signed on to manage Reading of the International League but was fired in June. He moved to Daytona Beach, Florida, and bought a farm on which he raised fruit crops. For a brief time he managed a team in that town, but one day a player called him a bonehead. Merkle left the field and never returned. The Depression so reduced his finances that he was obliged to work on a WPA project to make ends meet. During these years he shunned his old baseball mates and rebuffed any newspapermen who tried to contact him, blaming them for perpetuating the "bonehead" myth of 1908.

Merkle's fortunes improved after World War II. He became a partner in a small company that manufactured fishing tackle. His attitude toward the past softened enough for him to take part in an Old-Timers' Day at the Polo Grounds and don the uniform he had worn for a decade. For twenty years Merkle suffered from hypothyroidism that by 1954 aggravated a heart condition. On March 2, 1956, he died of a coronary occlusion at the age of sixty-seven and was buried in Daytona Beach, the most misunderstood Giant of them all.[23]

Following his horrible 1911 World Series, Red Murray had the satisfaction of redemption, batting .323 in the 1912 Series and making two catches described as "spectacular" in the sixth game. He remained a steady performer for the Giants until 1914, when he slumped and lost his full-time job. In 1915 the Giants traded him to the Cubs, but he stayed only for the rest of the season. He planned to retire but was persuaded to play for Toronto of the International League by a childhood friend who managed the team. In 1917 Murray had a few at-bats for the Giants before quitting the game for good. He returned to his hometown, Elmira, New York, married Beatrice Riley in 1920, and ran his own tire and battery store for two decades. He also served as the town's recreation director for eighteen years and for three years as a Democratic alderman.[24]

Through the years he and Beatrice kept in touch with several of his old teammates, especially Larry Doyle. In 1943, at age fifty-nine, he lobbied many of his baseball acquaintances, including Connie Mack, for letters of recommendation in his efforts to join the Navy as a recreation director. Mack sent along three letters and noted that "those World Series games you mentioned were the highlights of my baseball career." He enjoyed a pleasant and active life until the fall of 1958, when he was diagnosed with acute stem cell leukemia. The disease advanced rapidly, and he died on December 4 of that year.[25]

Except for eighteen appearances with Brooklyn of the Federal League in 1915, Hooks Wiltse spent his entire career with the Giants. His two appearances in the 1911 World Series marked the only time he pitched in the classic, but in the 1913 Series he took over first base when injuries benched both Merkle and Snodgrass and threw out two runners at the plate in the bottom of the ninth inning. After the Giants released him on August 29, 1914, he managed, pitched, and played first base mostly for Buffalo of the International League through 1924. He spent the next year as pitching coach for the Yankees, played for Reading of the International League in 1926, then left the game. He went back home to Syracuse, where he sold real estate and involved himself in local politics during the 1930s, first as an alderman and then as deputy assessor.[26]

In 1904 Wiltse had married Della Audrey Schaffer, to whom he remained devoted for the rest of his life. "I came home and got married," he claimed, "because there were too many pretty girls in New York." Della went to all the Giant games and often to spring training as well. They were part of the world tour of 1914 along with the McGraws and Mathewsons, returning home on the *Lusitania* a year before a German submarine sank it. In 1953 the New York Association of Base Ball Players started to tout Wiltse for the Hall of Fame, but he knew better. "I haven't a chance," he observed, "for newspaper men of to-day don't even know who I am." That same summer a physical examination revealed that he had emphysema caused by chronic bronchitis. He fought it for several years before losing the battle on January 21, 1959.[27]

Fifteen years after Wiltse left the Giants a reporter asked McGraw about Wiltse's ability as a fielder. "You can take Brown, Matty . . . and all the rest of the great fielding pitchers," replied McGraw, "and none was better than Wiltse with those long arms, hands which became talons spindling legs thin face and shark nose he was indeed a ball hawk. If every boy in America held this man up as his idol and if honest effort and decency, willingness gameness, and loyalty were counted he would be among the greatest of baseball forever."[28]

Although Art Wilson spent fourteen years in the major leagues, he never achieved the level of play expected of him when he first came up with the Giants. He continued to back up Chief Meyers through the pennant years of 1912 and 1913, then jumped to Chicago of the Federal League for two seasons. His first season there was the only time he appeared in more than a hundred games. In February 1916 the Pirates signed him but traded him in July to the Cubs. After a disappointing season and a half he was shipped to the Boston Braves along with old teammate Larry Doyle in January 1918. He played part-time there through 1920 and was let go. His career ended the following year with two appearances and one at-bat with the Cleveland Indians. After leaving baseball, Wilson settled in Chicago. What he did for a living over the years remains a mystery. He had a wife and daughter, who married and lived in Scottsbluff, Nebraska. She was his only known survivor when he died from a heart attack on June 12, 1960, in the Chicago hotel room where he lived.[29]

Bert Maxwell, the pitcher brought up late in 1911, did not stick with the team and had only a brief fling with Brooklyn of the Federal League in 1914. He died in Brady, Texas, on December 10, 1961. Grover Hartley, the promising catcher, stayed with the Giants until traded to the Reds with Herzog in December 1913. Falling into a dispute with his new manager, he defected to St. Louis of the Federal League in 1914, then moved to the St. Louis Browns in 1917 after the new league ceased operations. He appeared in only nineteen games before being sent to Columbus of the American Association as catcher and manager.[30]

The move triggered a curious odyssey for Hartley. After several years in the minors, he was acquired in 1927 by the Boston Red Sox at age thirty-eight and appeared in 103 games, batting .275. Boston let him go and Cleveland picked him as a coach. By 1934 he had served as coach for the Pirates and Browns as well. That year a bizarre situation left the Browns short a catcher, forcing the manager to activate Hartley. At age forty-six, the oldest man ever to start a major-league game at the time, he played in five games and hit a double in his three times at bat.[31]

After 1936, Hartley involved himself as manager and sometimes owner of several minor-league teams in Ohio. During World War II he served two years as recreation director in Columbus, Ohio, where he lived. In 1946 he had one last fling in the majors as a coach for the Giants, after which he and his wife, Marie, moved to Daytona Beach, Florida. He served as field and business manager for the local club and had Fred Merkle as a coach for a short time. Back to Ohio he went in 1948 to manage a Lima team before returning to Florida. Except for a stint as coach of a Georgia State League team in 1950, he remained in Daytona Beach until his death on October 19, 1964, closing out an amazingly diverse and nomadic career in baseball.[32]

Where Hartley became a baseball nomad, another little-used Giant, Gene Paulette, wound up as a baseball pariah. Paulette did not stick with the Giants in 1912 and bounced around the minors until 1916, when the St. Louis Browns picked him up. The Browns placed him on waivers in June 1917, and he was claimed by the Cardinals. He played well for the last-place Redbirds in

1918 but got off to a slow start the following year and was shipped to the Phillies in July 1919. A year later he had his best year, hitting .288 as Philadelphia's regular first baseman. During his stay in St. Louis, however, he had consorted with some notorious gamblers and came under suspicion for attempting to throw games. On March 24, 1921, amid the notorious Black Sox scandal, Judge Landis, the new commissioner of baseball, made Paulette the first player to be permanently banned from the game. Ongoing news about the larger scandal buried the action in obscurity.[33]

Not yet thirty, Paulette found himself with a wife and two children to support and no job. He returned to his home town of Little Rock, Arkansas, and followed his father and a slew of uncles in working for the Missouri Pacific Railroad. He began as a yard worker and worked his way up to the position of yardmaster. On February 8, 1966, he died of a massive heart attack, never having lived down the taint of scandal that ended his career.[34]

John McGraw called Al Bridwell "one of the gamest players I ever knew," but he never qualified as one of the luckiest. In coming to the Giants in 1908, he joined a contender only to be traded away in the middle of the team's first pennant-winning season. As a result he never got into a World Series. After playing sparingly for Boston in 1912 he was sold in November to Chicago, where he replaced Joe Tinker, who had left to manage Cincinnati. In 1914 he joined the exodus to the Federal League and spent two years with the St. Louis club. After World War I, Bridwell managed a succession of minor-league teams until 1925, when he went to work for a steel company. For two years he managed a strong amateur team. In 1930 he became sheriff of Scioto County, Ohio, and held the position until 1935, when he took a job as police lieutenant in the security department of the Wheeling Steel Corporation and remained there until his retirement.[35]

Bridwell continued to follow baseball, especially the Reds, on both radio and television. In 1966, replying to a letter from Larry Doyle, he wrote, "Yes, Pete Rose reminds me most of Old Times. He is a hustler every minute of game and that is what it takes." He enjoyed being interviewed by Lawrence S. Ritter for his book, *The Glory of Their Times: The Story of the Early Days of Baseball Told by the Men Who Played It,* and told him, "I've got regrets about certain things since I left baseball . . . But in baseball—I don't know—I don't really think I'd change a thing. Not a thing. It was fun all the way through. A privilege, that's what it was, a privilege, to have been there." He thought a moment, then made one correction. "I wish I'd never gotten that hit that set off the whole Merkle incident," he said. "I wish I'd struck out instead. If I'd done that, then it would have spared Fred a lot of unfair humiliation." He died on January 23, 1969, at the age of eighty-five.[36]

The 1911 season elevated the image of Chief Meyers from that of a piece of cultural exotica with inadequate catching skills to one of the most capable backstops and talented hitters in the National League. Having set a long-standing World Series record with twelve assists in six games, he enhanced that image with a career year in 1912, batting .358, second only to Heinie Zimmerman's .372. In the losing World Series against the Red Sox he hit .357. The following year Meyers "slumped" to .312 and played in only one Series game because of injuries to his throwing hand while warming up for the second one. His performance tailed off during the next two years, and in February 1916 the Giants sold him to the Brooklyn Robins, a team of veterans that included Rube Marquard, former A's pitcher Jack Coombs, Jake Daubert, Zack Wheat (whose mother was a full-blooded Cherokee), and a spare outfielder named Casey Stengel. The manager was McGraw's old partner, Wilbert Robinson.[37]

Meyers jokingly called the team "an old crippled-up club," but it edged out the Phillies for the pennant in 1916. Meyers hit only .247 but did well in the clutch and was a steady influence in the field. He caught three games in a losing World Series effort against the Red Sox, but the season proved to be his last hurrah: At thirty-seven he had slowed considerably. He split the 1917 season between Brooklyn and the Boston Braves and in October was released. The following year he played for Buffalo of the International League, managed by his old teammate Hooks Wiltse, then joined the Marines at season's end less than a month before the war's end. Discharged in March 1919, he started that season managing and playing for New Haven of the Eastern League but was replaced in midseason by Danny Murphy, the former Athletic. It was his last fling at professional baseball.[38]

Having lost his mother four years earlier, Meyers sold his farm in New Canaan, Connecticut in 1920 and, with his wife, Anna, returned to his roots in southern California. He went to work as a construction foreman for the San Diego Consolidated Gas & Electric Company. Reporters and others who talked to him found Meyers to be an intelligent, well-spoken, and cultured man far removed from the crude stereotype of his people. Irvin Cobb once asked him what his two favorite paintings were. Meyers replied, "The Quest for the Holy Grail" in the Boston Public Library and "Custer's Last Stand." Why the latter, asked Cobb. "Well," replied Meyers, "it's no Rembrandt, but it tells a beautiful story. It's the only picture done by a white man that I ever saw where my crowd is getting as good as an even break."[39]

The Chief had prepared himself well for life after baseball. He owned a house in San Diego and a farm near Riverside, and he had saved money from his baseball years. However, he reckoned without the worst depression in American history, which cost him his properties and much of his savings along with his livelihood. He took what jobs he could find, including a stint as part-time scout for the Reds thanks to McGraw's influence, but his hard times grew even harder. Much later he told a reporter, "I went back to the reservation and slept under a big tree. It was a far different life than I had known . . . On the third morning, I woke up and told myself . . . 'You're not the only Indian that went broke . . . Get up and go out and get to work.'"[40]

He went to the Mission Indian Agency in Riverside and found a job as head of law enforcement for the Indian reservations of southern California. The Chief became an actual chief of police for thirty reservations and held the post from 1933 to 1945, when, having repaired his fortunes, he retired. An interviewer in 1945 described him as "a cultured man, who spends his spare time reading poetry and philosophy." Another said he "has the vocabulary of a college prof." He renewed his contact with baseball and became something of a celebrity. Before a game of the 1949 World Series at Ebbets Field, Yankees manager Casey Stengel brought together members of the 1916 Brooklyn Robins, including Meyers and Wheat. Though still living on a meager income, he strengthened his ties to his heritage by working to restore the old mission chapel on the Santa Rosa Indian Reservation.[41]

Like Bridwell and others, Meyers consented to being interviewed by Lawrence Ritter, who found it hard going at first. "The Chief resented white society," Ritter recalled, "but once he accepted you, he was as warm and open an individual as you're ever likely to meet. He never forgot he was an Indian, and he made no bones about his resentment, but he wouldn't let that come between you." Publication of the best-selling book in 1966 brought renewed fame to the interviewees, and Meyers became friends with Ritter, whose day job was chairman of the finance department at NYU's Graduate School of Business Administration. Meyers received invitations to appear on television and at other events as well as requests for autographs. In his final years he lived in a mobile home in Rialto, between Riverside and San Bernardino. After several months' illness he died on July 25, 1971, just four days shy of his ninety-first birthday.[42]

Informed of his death, Ritter recalled something Meyers had told him at their first meeting seven years earlier. "I am like an old hemlock," he said. "My head is still high but the winds of close to a hundred winters have whistled through my branches, and I have been witness to many wondrous and many tragic things. My eyes perceive the present, but my roots are imbedded [sic] deeply in the grandeur of the past."[43]

CONTROVERSY FOLLOWED FRED SNODGRASS throughout his baseball career, but he weathered it better than most. Although his numbers declined over the next four years, he remained a steady performer for the Giants during their pennant years, batting .269 in 1912 and .291 in 1913. However, he hit only .212 in the 1912 series, and in the deciding game dropped an easy fly ball at a crucial moment. That he made a spectacular catch of a drive by the next batter got buried in the ongoing legend of Snodgrass's muff. After a walk, Tris Speaker hit a towering foul toward first that should have been the final out. Merkle could have reached it easily, but for some reason Mathewson, who was pitching, called for Meyers to take it. Meyers couldn't reach it, and Speaker promptly singled in the winning run. Both Snodgrass and Merkle had to endure decades of taunts for their failure. Merkle wasn't to blame for not getting the foul ball, but Snodgrass admitted that "because of over-eagerness, or over-confidence, or carelessness, I dropped it. It's something that I'll never forget."[44]

In August 1915, Snodgrass was hitting only .194 after 103 games when the Giants sold him to Boston. After a mediocre 1916 season with the Braves he went home to California, played one year in the Pacific Coast League, and retired from the game. "I was tired of baseball when I did quit," he admitted in 1942. He went into the home appliance business in Oxnard and did very well. In 1930 he was elected to the city council and served three terms before being elected mayor in 1937. He stayed in office only eleven months before resigning, then moved to Ventura, where he lived with his wife, Josephine, and their two daughters. Snodgrass bought two ranches in Ventura County, growing lemons on one and walnuts on the other. "California is my home state," he told a reporter, "and I adore it." However, when he died on April 5, 1974, after a long and prosperous life, the headline of his obituary in the *New York Times* read, "Fred Snodgrass, 86, Dead; Ball Player Muffed 1912 Fly."[45]

Laughing Larry Doyle continued to spark the Giants through the pennant years and beyond. Even in 1915, when the team finished last, he led the league in hitting with a .320 average. In the fall of 1913 he got married and turned down a lucrative two-year contract from the Federal League. In 1914 he fell off to .260, supporting McGraw's belief that a player needed a year to adjust to marriage. When he slumped again in 1916, the Giants traded him on August 28 to the Cubs, where he reunited with Fred Merkle. He hit only .254 in 1917 and was shipped to the Braves in January 1918 only to be sent back to the Giants four days later. A broken leg cost him most of the 1918 season, but the next year he played in 113 games and hit .289. He was thirty-seven when in 1920 he wound up his major-league career by batting .285 in 137 games.[46]

The mystery surrounding Doyle is what he did to earn a living after his playing days. For two years he managed different minor-league clubs, and he was said to have worked at various jobs for the Giants over the next two decades. What is known is that he and his wife, Gertrude, had three children. Even before the Depression, Doyle had fallen on hard times financially and emotionally. One Thanksgiving Day McGraw received a phone call from Doyle. "I hate to bother you, Mac," he said hesitantly, "but I don't know what to do. It's not me so much as the children. I just can't let them go hungry . . . and there's nothing more . . . to sell." Both the McGraws got the picture. "Mismanagement of salaries and savings and an unfortunate domestic situation had victimized one of the happiest of ballplayers," Blanche surmised.[47]

McGraw sent for Doyle at once. He arrived with the three children and was put to work "as a sort of trunk supervisor for the Giants, and part-time chauffeur." Gertrude died in 1937, and five years later Laughing Larry's good nature took a major blow when he was diagnosed with tuberculosis. As a young man he had worked in the mines in Illinois, and he was a smoker. Blanche McGraw and Jane Mathewson, with help from National League president Ford Frick, joined forces to raise enough money to send Doyle to the Trudeau Sanitarium at Saranac Lake, where Matty had gone to recuperate.[48]

Doyle spent the rest of his days in Saranac, with rare trips to New York for medical attention or special occasions, and was happy to remain there. "New York, you can keep it," he said. "Too much smell, too many people." Fittingly, he came to occupy the bed endowed in the name of Christy Mathewson. So successful was the fight against tuberculosis, long the nation's number one killer, that in 1954 the Trudeau Sanitarium closed its doors after seventy years. Its last patient was Larry Doyle.[49]

The doctors had predicted he would not last more than four or five months, but Doyle survived for thirty-two years. The disease's hold on him weakened but did not leave entirely. After Trudeau closed, he continued to live in Saranac for the rest of his life, sitting on the porch of his little place at 9 Church Street and sharing memories of old-time baseball. He kept in touch with old teammates such as Meyers, and mourned their passing. In Saranac village he became one of the most admired and popular residents; a youth baseball league was named after him. Even when his eyes failed, his memory remained sharp and clear. He lived to the ripe old age of eighty-six, dying on March 1, 1974, just as elsewhere spring training camps for a game far different from the one he had played were moving into high gear.[50]

IF THE GIANTS HAD FORMED A TONTINE in 1911, Rube Marquard would have come out the winner as the last man standing. After his slow start he enjoyed a long and mostly successful career. In 1912 he started the season with an incredible nineteen-game winning streak, beating every team in the league at least twice, finished at 26-11, and went 2-0 in the World Series with an earned run average of only 0.50. A year later he recorded a 23-10 season but lost his only World Series decision. In 1914 he slumped to a horrendous 12-22, had a record of 9-8 the following year, and got the Giants to send him to Brooklyn and its manager, his old mentor Wilbert Robinson. He stayed with the Robins for five years, interrupted in 1918 by a stint in the Navy, and got into two more World Series with them in 1916 and 1920, having missed most of the 1919 season with a broken leg.[51]

Before game four of the 1920 World Series, a Cleveland undercover policeman arrested Marquard for scalping his box-seat tickets. Although the judge let him off gently, an irate Charlie Ebbets sent him to Cincinnati for pitcher Dutch Reuther. He posted a 17-14 record for the Reds in 1921 but was traded to Boston the following February. After four seasons of losing records with the Braves, he retired after the 1925 season. Between 1926 and 1933 he knocked around the minor leagues as both player and manager, finally retiring from the game altogether after the 1933 season.[52]

During his glory days in New York, Marquard stepped willingly into the spotlight as a celebrity, much as Mike Donlin had done. He wrote a newspaper column; advertised products; appeared in a silent movie, *Rube Marquard Wins*, in 1912; and made it to the Broadway stage singing, dancing, and telling jokes. He met Blossom Seeley, a gorgeous actress and successful performer. She and Marquard put together a popular act that earned them $1,000 a week each in performances across the country. Although Blossom was married, they fell in love. Blossom shed her husband in January 1913 and, three months pregnant, married Marquard. Despite the scandal, or because of it, their act remained popular. As biographer Larry Mansch observed, "They were in love with each other, and in love with the lives they led."[53]

"We're a great battery, this little girl and I," Marquard told a reporter. For a time they were, but by 1920 both the marriage and Rube's celebrity status had faded. They divorced, and Marquard found solace in a stunning beauty named Naomi Malone, whom he married just before the 1921 season. Where Blossom had refused to give up her career even after the arrival of Richard Jr., Naomi became the devoted wife who went to every home game and was there to greet him at home afterward. Once Marquard ceased to be a hot property, he pursued the grind of baseball until he finally tired of it. After leaving the game, Marquard lived for another fifty-five years, mostly in comfort with pride and without bitterness toward his former career.[54]

He and Naomi traveled and lived quietly in Baltimore with winters spent in Coral Gables, Florida, where they bought a house. A second career engaged Marquard because, he told a reporter, "it keeps one out of doors." He worked the betting windows at Pimlico, Belmont, and other racetracks. Larry Doyle once found him behind the $50 window at one track. In 1963 the *Daily News* printed a photograph of him behind the window with the caption, "Rube Marquard: He stays with the action." Over the years he endured the loss of his former teammates; the deaths of McGraw and Mathewson affected him especially deeply. He never forgot how McGraw had stuck with him through the "lemon" years before 1911.[55]

Rube and Naomi remained a devoted couple until her death on July 21, 1954. Marquard stayed single until October 1955, when he married a wealthy widow named Jane Hecht Guggenheimer, whom he had met on a cruise only three weeks earlier. She shared Rube's energy and love of sports like golf, tennis, and bowling while introducing him to ballroom dancing. They became a popular couple at the exclusive Suburban Country Club in Pikesville, a Baltimore suburb. Marquard enjoyed going to ball games and attending old-timer celebrations. Like Bridwell, Meyers, and Snodgrass, he fell under the spell of Larry Ritter and contributed an interview that became the first chapter in the book. In 1971, Marquard earned the distinction of being elected to the Hall of Fame. He enjoyed life to the ripe old age of ninety-three, dying in his sleep at his Pikesville apartment on June 1, 1980.[56]

With the passing of its last marcher, Rube Marquard, the parade vanished into the mists of time, leaving in its wake only memories of the men and deeds gone by.

Appendix A: The 1908 Brush Committee Report

Later accounts of the attempted bribery episode have not gone far beyond echoing earlier criticisms. David Anderson called the investigation "a farce. It was a successful cover-up . . . the investigation sent a clear message that preserving the status quo was more important than getting to the truth or confronting the gambling issue." He also asserted that Klem's 1908 affidavit "says the money came from Giants players." It says no such thing. In fact, Klem quotes Creamer as assuring him that "McGraw or the players don't know anything about it." In making this error Anderson assumed too much from Woodruff's exposé of April 24, 1909, which said, *"Those who profess to know say* that the affidavit of Umpire Klem stated that the man who approached the umpire said he was acting on behalf of three New York players." Not only was this hearsay evidence twice removed, but those who professed to know did not in fact know at all. Late in life Klem wrote, "I will go to my grave wondering where the money he offered me came from."[1]

Historian Harold Seymour called the attempt "another example of the owners' policy of concealment or at best grudging disclosure, which foreshadowed their handling of the 1919 World Series scandal." After the latter gained headlines, none other than Horace Fogel stepped forth with a story that someone from the Giants had attempted to fix some of the late-season games with the Phillies. However, Fogel was hardly a credible source, having himself been banished from baseball in 1912 for charging that Roger Bresnahan, as manager of the Cardinals, helped the Giants win the pennant that year by fielding a weak team against them. More serious charges came from Phillies catcher Red Dooin and several of his players, who claimed in 1924 that they had been offered $40,000 to throw a three-game series against the Giants in 1908. Dooin added that the money had been put in his lap "by a noted catcher of the New York Giants while I was in a railroad station."[2]

Dooin and his teammates refused the offer but decided not to report it, saying, "The other players and myself believed it would be in the best interest of baseball not to say anything, as none of us accepted the bribes." The catcher in question is surely Roger Bresnahan, but by 1924 no one showed interest in following up the allegation and proof of it has never been established. What is clear is that gambling was a way of life in the nation, in every big city, and in baseball. "There is more gambling on baseball about local parks now than at any time in history," declared the *New York Tribune* in August 1908. "It hasn't become an open proposition yet, but it is drifting that way. New York bettors are not educated to the game yet. Over in Chicago, St. Louis, and Cincinnati, the gambling element has been well schooled. But it will not take New Yorkers long to get wise if the thing is permitted."[3]

In lambasting or lampooning the magnates, critics have largely overlooked the handicaps under which the Brush Committee operated. They persist in ignoring the obvious problem at the heart of their dilemma: no corroborating evidence and no way to get it. The committee had no authority to compel anyone to do anything, and could not even approach Creamer without revealing his identity. Even if it chose to do so, nothing required Creamer to speak to the members or respond to their questions. As a first step Brush and Ebbets went to see DeLancey Nicoll, a prominent attorney and former district attorney for New York City, to get his opinion on whether Creamer had committed a crime punishable under New York law. Nicoll told them that the acts as described in the umpire's letters did not constitute a crime under New York law, and that the district attorney would not attempt a prosecution. However unsavory the incident, the key fact was that it had absolutely no effect on the outcome of the game. So much, then, for the Dreyfuss argument.[4]

The magnates have been accused repeatedly of trying to soften or hide the incident, their main concern being to protect their teams. Anyone reading chapter seven of this book should see that their concern was genuine, sincere, and powerful. They agonized over finding a useful path to follow in dealing with the issue, the more so since they also had to cope with a president whose behavior was embarrassing the league at every turn. Of course they wanted to protect their clubs; it would be naïve to think otherwise. They were, after all, businessmen and baseball was their business. Whatever their individual reasons for owning a club, no one wanted to lose money in the process. But that does not mean they ignored or downplayed the broader issues at stake, which were present often in their discussions.

No aspect of the episode received more censure than the decision to put John Brush at the head of the committee, yet he was in some respects the logical choice. If you start with the assumption that he was innocent, which all of the other owners did, who had more at stake in unearthing the guilty parties? Who had more political clout in New York? Herrmann might have been a more logical choice, but in the end he went carefully over the final report as drafted by Brush, and both men signed it, as did Ebbets and Pulliam. Those who criticized the committee's work and its report as something between superficial and a cover-up have offered no suggestions as to what else the committee could or should have done. In practical terms, digging deeper into who was behind Creamer would have gained nothing other than a libel suit if Creamer's name had been mentioned before completing the process.[5]

The report offered little or any new information because the committee had none beyond the names it withheld. "There is no doubt but that a great many wagers in New York and other cities had been made contingent upon the Championship race of 1908," it said. Betting was endemic not only in baseball but in all sports. "It is a condition that has always existed and always will," said the report. It concluded that "attempts may again be made to influence umpire or player (it is impossible to guard against it since it is no crime) but they will no more affect or destroy the integrity of the game than the decry by the anarchist against law and order affects or destroys the justice of it."[6]

Writer Cait Murphy said of this statement, "The conclusion bespeaks a blindness so willful that it would take tragedy to penetrate the fog. And that tragedy comes in 1919, when the Black Sox of Chicago take up with gamblers and deliberately lose the World Series. That is the price baseball pays for its complacency. In 1908, baseball blossoms. But it also buries deeper the seed of its darkest hour." Other writers point ominously to the 1908 bribery attempt as the prelude to the scandal of 1919.[7]

Linking these two events as if the one were a prelude to the other is absurd and a serious misreading of history. For one thing, it reads history backward. For another, it suggests that some firm or strong action in 1908 might have prevented the scandal of 1919. What possible action in 1908 could have even remotely influenced the later event? Murphy, like other writers, flogs the committee for its inaction but stops short of saying what it should have done. Nor does she or anyone else spell out the link between 1908 and 1919 other than that they both involved gambling in baseball. But so did dozens of other episodes going back to the 1870s, including some major ones that involved players throwing games.

First, the facts: 1908 was a bribe offered to umpires and refused; 1919 involved bribes offered to several players and accepted, thereby creating an actual crime. A grand jury indicted the players, who were found not guilty in the trial that followed. Organized baseball then flexed its newly created muscle in the form of Commissioner Kenesaw Mountain Landis, a former federal judge, who banned the players from the game for life regardless of the verdict or their actual role in the scandal. He had the authority to do so. In 1908 the National Commission, consisting of Herrmann, Pulliam, and Ban Johnson, presided over organized baseball with similar power. Even if it wanted to ban someone from the game for life, who would it have been? No player was involved, and all sides agreed that the umpires had done the right thing, not only in refusing the bribes, but in reporting them. The commission had only Creamer, no longer even connected to a team, and it banned him from every park in organized baseball.

The only way to get at the source of the bribe was through Creamer, who stonewalled the question until his death during the flu epidemic of 1918. If he was as innocent as he claimed, why did he not pursue steps to establish that fact? The awkward fact for those seeking the truth was that Creamer could not at the same time proclaim his innocence and name the parties behind the bribe attempt he said did not happen. The most likely scenario is that gambling interests orchestrated the attempt, but which interests? New York in 1909 was full of likely suspects, including but not limited to the names that surfaced during the owners' meetings. Such was their influence in the city and its politics that no one cared to run afoul of them, especially the owners.

Baseball, like the rest of America, moved on to new and fast-changing times, but gambling never went away. It is worth remembering that the Black Sox scandal occurred eleven years later. Many of the critics write as if it marked a decisive turning point in how the sport handled its gambling problem. But the basic issue is still with baseball as it is with the larger nation. There may have been fewer attempts to fix games by bribing players, but betting still surrounds the sport in one form or another, Pete Rose being only the most conspicuous example. Nearly every major daily newspaper carries the point spread on professional games of every type and college games as well. Offices have their betting pools, states have their lotteries, and many cities and states depend heavily on the proceeds from the proliferating network of casinos to balance their budgets. And one need only look at the enormous sums involved in online fantasy leagues such as DraftKings and FanDuel.

Gambling in all its many forms is far more conspicuous, pervasive, and influential today than ever before, and in most cases it has been legitimized as well. Baseball will continue to be one of its primary targets, if only because it plays many more games than any other professional sport. Seen in this broader context, the 1908 episode seems more like a positive outcome and a nonevent than the prelude that opened the door to larger scandals.

Appendix B: Statistics of the 1911 New York Giants

Player	Games	AB	R	H	BA	2B	3B	HR	SB
Meyers	133	391	48	130	.332	18	9	1	7
Fletcher	112	326	73	104	.319	17	8	1	20
Doyle	143	526	102	163	.310	25	25	13	38
Wilson	66	109	17	33	.303	9	1	1	6
Snodgrass	151	534	83	157	.294	27	10	1	51
Murray	140	488	70	142	.291	27	15	3	48
Merkle	149	541	80	153	.283	24	10	12	49
Devore	149	565	96	158	.280	19	10	3	61
Devlin	95	260	42	71	.273	16	2	0	9
Bridwell	76	263	28	71	.270	10	1	0	8
Herzog	69	247	37	66	.267	14	4	1	22

Pitcher	Games	GS	CG	Won	Lost	SHO	SVS	SO	BB	IP
Mathewson	45	37	29	26	13	5	3	141	38	307
Marquard	45	33	22	24	7	5	3	237	106	272.2
Ames	34	23	13	11	10	1	2	118	54	205
Wiltse	30	24	11	12	9	4	0	92	39	187.1
Crandall	41	15	9	15	5	2	5	94	51	198.2
Drucke	15	10	4	4	4	0	0	42	41	75.2
Raymond	17	9	4	6	4	1	0	39	33	81.2
Maxwell	4	3	3	1	2	0	0	8	7	31

Abbreviations

CT	*Chicago Tribune*
HOF	Hall of Fame
NYH	*New York Herald*
NYP	*New York Press*
NYS	*New York Sun*
NYT	*New York Times*
NYTR	*New-York Tribune*
NYW	*New York World*
SLPD	*St. Louis Post-Dispatch*
SL	*Sporting Life*
SN	*Sporting News*

Notes

PROLOGUE: THE RITE OF SPRING

1. *SL*, Jan. 5, 1911; *NYH*, March 19, 1911.
2. Peter Morris, *Level Playing Fields: How the Groundskeeping Murphy Brothers Shaped Baseball* (Lincoln, NE, 2007), 101–102.
3. G. H. Fleming, *The Unforgettable Season* (New York, 1981), 19; Mrs. John J. [Blanche] McGraw, *The Real McGraw* (New York, 1953), 231.
4. Morris, *Level Playing Fields*, 48–49, 77. The Giants and Orioles groundskeepers are often confused; they were in fact brothers in the same business. Tom Murphy started as the Orioles groundskeeper but got into some personal trouble and was replaced by his brother John, who later went to the Giants to work for McGraw. See the splendid and very helpful study by Morris.
5. Fleming, *Unforgettable Season*, 19; McGraw, *The Real McGraw*, 231; *NYW*, Feb. 11 and 12, 1911; *SL*, Nov. 26, Dec. 3 and 10, 1910, Jan. 14 and 21, Feb. 18, 1911.
6. *SL*, April 8, 1905, and Dec. 31, 1910; *NYP*, Jan. 8, 1911; John J. Evers, *Touching Second* (Mattituck, NY, 1910), 54.
7. Lawrence Ritter, *The Glory of Their Times* (New York, 1966), 211–12.
8. Christy Mathewson, *Pitching in a Pinch* (New York, 1912), 209–10.
9. *NYP*, Jan. 8, 1911.
10. Ibid., Jan. 11 and Feb. 20, 1911; *NYW*, March 19, 1911.
11. Fred Lieb, *Baseball as I Have Known It* (New York, 1977), 18, 24, 255; McGraw, *The Real McGraw*, 276.
12. *NYP*, Feb. 21, 1911; *NYW*, Feb. 21, 1911; Ritter, *Glory of Their Times*, 86.
13. *NYP*, Feb. 22, 1911; *NYW*, Feb. 22, 1911; *SL*, Feb. 25, 1911.
14. Ritter, *Glory of Their Times*, 86; *SL*, Dec. 31, 1910.
15. *NYP*, Feb. 24, 1911; John J. McGraw, *My Thirty Years in Baseball* (Lincoln, NE, 1995 [1923]), 99.
16. *NYP*, Feb. 24 and 25, 1911; *NYW*, Feb. 24–27, 1911; *SL*, Feb. 25, 1911; Morris, *Level Playing Fields*, 102.
17. McGraw, *Thirty Years*, 100; Mathewson, *Pitching in a Pinch*, 214–18.
18. McGraw, *Thirty Years*, 20–21.
19. *NYT*, March 1, 1911; *NYTR*, March 1, 1911; *NYH*, March 1, 1911; *NYP*, March 1, 1911; Unidentified clippings, June 12 and Sept. 15, 1910, and undated, Louis Drucke scrapbook, HOF.
20. *NYTR*, March 1, 1911; *NYP*, March 1, 1911, *NYW*, March 1, 1911; *NYT*, March 2, 1911.
21. *NYW*, March 1, 1911; Fleming, *Unforgettable Season*, 24. Marquard is usually listed as six–three or –four.

22. Larry D. Mansch, *Rube Marquard: The Life and Times of a Baseball Hall of Famer* (Jefferson, NC, 1998), 70–72.
23. *SL*, Dec. 31, 1910, Jan. 14, Feb. 18, and March 4, 1911.
24. Ritter, *Glory of Their Times*, 86; Tom Simon, ed., *Deadball Stars of the National League* (Washington, DC, 2004), 51; Unidentified clipping, Sept. 29, 1948, Arthur Devlin file, HOF; *SN*, March 2, 1911; *SL*, March 4, 1911.
25. Mathewson, *Pitching in a Pinch*, 213–14; *SN*, March 2, 1911.
26. *NYH*, March 2 and 3, 1911; *NYTR*, March 2 and 3, 1911; Mathewson, *Pitching in a Pinch*, 211; *NYT*, March 3, 1911; *NYW*, March 3, 1911; *NYS*, March 3, 1911.
27. *NYW*, March 3, 1911; *NYTR*, March 3, 1911; Mathewson, *Pitching in a Pinch*, 225; McGraw, *The Real McGraw*, 233.
28. *NYW*, March 4–7, 1911; *NYTR*, March 5–7, 1911; *NYS*, March 5–7, 1911; *NYH*, March 5–7, 1911; *NYT*, March 5–7, 1911.
29. *NYS*, March 8, 1911; *NYT*, March 8, 1911; *NYW*, March 8, 1911; *NYTR*, March 8, 1911; *NYH*, March 8, 1911; *NYP*, March 8, 1911; *SL*, Jan. 21, March 18, 1911.
30. *SL*, Jan. 21, Feb. 25, March 18, 1911.
31. *NYTR*, March 9, 1911; *NYP*, March 9, 1911; *NYS*, March 9, 1911; *NYW*, March 9, 1911.
32. *SN*, March 9, 1911; *NYP*, March 9, 1911; *NYS*, March 9, 1911; *NYW*, March 9, 1911; *NYH*, March 9, 1911; *NYT*, March 9, 1911; *SL*, March 11, 1911; Mathewson, *Pitching in a Pinch*, 209.
33. *NYT*, March 10, 1911; *NYTR*, March 10, 1911; *NYS*, March 10, 1911; *NYW*, March 10, 1911.
34. *NYP*, March 11, 1911; *NYT*, March 11, 1911; *NYH*, March 11, 1911; *NYS*, March 11, 1911; *NYTR*, March 11, 1911; *NYW*, March 11 and 14, 1911.
35. *NYW*, March 12 and 13, 1911; *NYTR*, March 12 and 13, 1911; *NYS*, March 12 and 13, 1911; *NYH*, March 12 and 13, 1911.
36. *NYT*, March 14 and 15, 1911; *NYS*, March 14 and 15, 1911; *NYTR*, March 14 and 15, 1911; *NYW*, March 14 and 15, 1911; *NYH*, March 15, 1911.
37. *NYT*, March 16–18, 1911; *NYH*, March 16–18, 1911, *NYS*, March 16 and 18, 1911; *NYW*, March 16–18, 1911; *NYTR*, March 17 and 18, 1911; *NYP*, March 17 and 18, 1911.
38. *NYH*, March 8, 13, and 16, 1911; *NYW*, March 8, 19, and 24, 1911; *NYT*, March 19, 1911; *NYP*, March 19, 1911.
39. *NYW*, March 20 and 21, 1911; *NYTR*, March 20 and 21, 1911; *NYS*, March 20 and 21, 1911; *NYH*, March 20, 1911; *NYT*, March 20 and 21, 1911.
40. *NYTR*, March 22, 1911; *NYS*, March 22, 1911; *NYT*, March 22, 1911, *NYH*, March 22, 1911.
41. *NYW*, March 22, 1911; Evers, *Touching Second*, 232.
42. Evers, *Touching Second*, 240–42.
43. *NYTR*, March 23, 1911; *NYS*, March 23, 1911; *NYW*, March 23, 1911; *NYP*, March 23, 1911. The gaspergou is a southern version of the freshwater drum.
44. *NYW*, March 24, 1911; *NYTR*, March 24, 1911; *NYH*, March 24, 1911; *NYT*, March 24, 1911; *NYS*, March 24, 1911.
45. *NYP*, March 25, 1911; *NYS*, March 25, 1911; *NYT*, March 25, 1911; *NYTR*, March 25, 1911; *NYH*, March 25, 1911; *NYW*, March 25, 1911; *CT*, March 25, 1911.
46. *NYW*, March 25, 1911; *NYT*, March 25, 1911; *NYTR*, March 25, 1911; *NYP*, March 25, 1911; *NYS*, March 25, 1911.
47. *SL*, March 25, 1911.
48. McGraw, *The Real McGraw*, 45.
49. *NYT*, March 26–29 and April 6, 1911; *NYTR*, March 26–29 and April 6, 1911; *NYS*, March 26–29, 1911; *NYH*, March 27–29, 1911; *NYW*, March 27–29 and April 6, 1911.

50. *NYS*, March 30 and 31, 1911; *NYTR*, March 30 and 31, 1911; *NYW*, March 30 and 31, 1911; *NYT*, March 30 and 31, 1911; *NYH*, March 30 and 31, 1911; *NYP*, March 31, 1911. The quotation is from the *NYW*, March 31.

51. *NYT*, March 31, 1911; *NYW*, March 31, 1911; *NYP*, March 31, and April 1, 1911; *NYTR*, March 31, 1911; *NYS*, March 31, 1911, *NYH*, March 31, 1911.

52. *NYP*, April 1, 1911; *NYH*, April 1, 1911; *NYS*, April 1, 1911; *NYW*, April 1, 1911; *NYT*, April 1, 1911.

53. *NYH*, April 2 and 3, 1911; *NYS*, April 2 and 3, 1911; *NYT*, April 2 and 3, 1911; *NYW*, April 2 and 3, 1911; *NYTR*, April 3, 1911.

54. *NYT*, April 6–8, 1911; *NYS*, April 6–8, 1911; *NYW*, April 6–8, 1911; *NYTR*, April 6–8, 1911; *NYH*, April 6–8, 1911.

55. *NYP*, March 19, 1911; *NYW*, April 8, 1911; *NYH*, April 8, 1911.

56. *NYS*, April 9 and 10, 1911; *NYTR*, April 9 and 10, 1911; *NYT*, April 9 and 10, 1911; *NYH*, April 9 and 10, 1911; *NYW*, April 9 and 10, 1911.

57. *NYH*, April 11, 1911; *NYW*, April 11, 1911; *NYTR*, April 11, 1911; *NYS*, April 11, 1911; *NYT*, April 11, 1911; *NYP*, April 11, 1911.

58. *NYT*, April 10, 1911; *NYTR*, April 9 and 12, 1911; *NYS*, April 12, 1911; *NYH*, April 12, 1911.

59. *NYTR*, April 9, 1911. Forsythe is not mentioned in the article but he was the only rookie first baseman in camp and was the first to be let go.

60. Ibid.

61. *SL*, April 15, 1911.

1: THE MASTERMIND

1. Unless otherwise indicated, this discussion is drawn largely from Charles C. Alexander, *John McGraw* (Lincoln, NE, 1995 [1988]), 9–81, and McGraw, *The Real McGraw*, 23–152.

2. McGraw, *The Real McGraw*, 24.

3. Ibid., 55; McGraw, *Thirty Years*, 47–48.

4. Unless otherwise indicated, all team and individual statistics in this book are drawn from *The Baseball Encyclopedia* (New York, 1980) and from Baseball-Reference.com.

5. *Baseball Encyclopedia*, 590, 988.

6. McGraw, *Thirty Years*, 57; McGraw, *The Real McGraw*, 77–78.

7. McGraw, *Thirty Years*, 56–58, 67.

8. *Baseball Encyclopedia*, 121, 124, 128. No one knows why the figure of sixty feet six inches was chosen.

9. Quoted in Alexander, *McGraw*, 38–39. Prior to 1901 the umpire could call a foul ball a strike if he thought the batter was fouling it off on purpose.

10. McGraw, *Thirty Years*, 67; McGraw, *The Real McGraw*, 72–73.

11. McGraw, *The Real McGraw*, 73.

12. Glenn Dickey, *The History of National League Baseball Since 1876* (New York, 1979), 19–21.

13. Morris, *Level Playing Fields*, 34–35.

14. McGraw, *Thirty Years*, 64–65, 68–69; McGraw, *The Real McGraw*, 78–79.

15. Alexander, *McGraw*, 54; *Baseball Encyclopedia*, 1087.

16. Dickey, *National League*, 16–18; McGraw, *Thirty Years*, 217–18.

17. Alexander, *McGraw*, 58, 62–63; David Quentin Voigt, *American Baseball: From the Gentleman's Sport to Commissioner System* (University Park, PA, 1983), 229–30, 255, 266–67.

18. McGraw, *The Real McGraw*, 115–20.

19. Alexander, *McGraw*, 66–67.

20. Ibid., 68–69; McGraw, *The Real McGraw*, 128–35.

21. Bozeman Bulger, "Genius of the Game," *Saturday Evening Post* (July 9, 1932), 24.

22. Eugene C. Murdock, *Ban Johnson: Czar of Baseball* (Westport, CT, 1982), 39.

23. Ibid., 45; Harold Seymour, *Baseball: The Early Years* (New York, 1960), 307–309.

24. Seymour, *Early Years*, 310–13.

25. Ibid., 314; Alexander, *McGraw*, 76–77; McGraw, *The Real McGraw*, 138–39.

26. Alexander, *McGraw*, 78–80; McGraw, *The Real McGraw*, 151–58.

27. McGraw, *The Real McGraw*, 1–5; Alexander, *McGraw*, 82–83. Alexander says Blanche was the oldest child but Blanche herself refers to Jeannette as her older sister.

28. McGraw, *The Real McGraw*, 1–22. The remainder of this section is drawn from this source.

2: The Business of Baseball

1. Seymour, *Early Years*, 75–110.

2. Ibid., 265–69; Robert F. Burk, *Never Just a Game: Players, Owners, & American Baseball to 1920* (Chapel Hill, NC, 1994), 123–26; James D. Hardy, *The New York Giants Base Ball Club: The Growth of a Team and a Sport, 1870–1900* (Jefferson, NC, 1996), 136, 141–45.

3. Seymour, *Early Years*, 293–94; Burk, *Never Just a Game*, 135; Voigt, *American Baseball*, 230–31.

4. Burk, *Never Just a Game*, 136; Seymour, *Early Years*, 299–300.

5. Seymour, *Early Years*, 303–304; Burk, *Never Just a Game*, 137.

6. Seymour, *Early Years*, 304; *Baseball*, Sept. 1911, 19.

7. Seymour, *Early Years*, 296–97; Voigt, *American Baseball*, 227–28; Hardy, *New York Giants*, 154–55; Steven A. Riess, *Touching Base: Professional Baseball and American Culture in the Progressive Era* (Urbana, IL, 1999), 72.

8. Voigt, *American Baseball*, 227–31; Seymour, *Early Years*, 296–97.

9. Seymour, *Early Years*, 299–305; Voigt, *American Baseball*, 238–40, 268–70; Hardy, *New York Giants*, 166–68.

10. Hardy, *New York Giants*, 166–68; Seymour, *Early Years*, 305–314; Voigt, *American Baseball*, 271; Burk, *Never Just a Game*, 142–51.

11. Hardy, *New York Giants*, 171–74; Seymour, *Early Years*, 317; Riess, *Touching Base*, 73.

12. Seymour, *Early Years*, 316–17; Riess, *Touching Base*, 73–74; Voigt, *American Baseball*, 304; Burk, *Never Just a Game*, 152.

13. Hardy, *New York Giants*, 174–77.

14. Seymour, *Early Years*, 318–21; Voigt, *American Baseball*, 304–305; Burk, *Never Just a Game*, 152–53; Hardy, *New York Giants*, 177–91; Arthur Bartlett, *Baseball and Mr. Spalding* (New York, 1951), 267–84.

15. Seymour, *Early Years*, 322; Burk, *Never Just a Game*, 153–55; Murdock, *Ban Johnson*, 53–54.

16. McGraw, *The Real McGraw*, 158–60; Alexander, *McGraw*, 85; McGraw, *Thirty Years*, 130–31; Bulger, "Genius of the Game," 24, 26.

17. McGraw, *The Real McGraw*, 161–62; Alexander, *McGraw*, 85.

18. McGraw, *The Real McGraw*, 174.

19. Ibid., 162–63; Alexander, *McGraw*, 85–88.

20. McGraw, *The Real McGraw*, 19–20.

21. Ibid., 155–57.

22. Joseph Durso, *The Days of Mr. McGraw* (Englewood Cliffs, NJ, 1969), 44–45.

23. McGraw, *The Real McGraw*, 164; McGraw, *Thirty Years*, 124–25. Blanche excused her husband's gambling by saying, "It was part of his life and times. It was being one of the grown-up group, and matching wits with the bet-holders." McGraw, *The Real McGraw*, 140.

24. McGraw, *The Real McGraw*, 162–63.

25. Ibid., 164–65; Alexander, *McGraw*, 90–91; McGraw, *Thirty Years*, 131–32. McGraw's own version is slim and highly selective. Kelley was reinstated in less than a week.

26. McGraw, *Thirty Years*, 132; *NYT*, July 10, 1902.

27. McGraw, *Thirty Years*, 109; Alexander, *McGraw*, 90–92; *NYT*, July 9 and 17, 1902; Noel Hynd, *Giants of the Polo Grounds: The Glorious Times of Baseball's New York Giants* (New York, 1988), 110; Murdock, *Ban Johnson*, 56; McGraw, *The Real McGraw*, 166; Bulger, "Genius of the Game," 26.

28. Alexander, *McGraw*, 92–93; McGraw, *The Real McGraw*, 165–68, 179–80; Hardy, *New York Giants*, 194–95; Riess, *Touching Base*, 75; *NYT*, July 17, 1902. By scrounging players from other teams, the Orioles managed to limp through the season but finished in last place.

29. Simon, *Deadball Stars*, 50; Alexander, *McGraw*, 98–99; Hynd, *Giants of the Polo Grounds*, 117–18; McGraw, *The Real McGraw*, 188.

30. McGraw, *The Real McGraw*, 164–65; Hynd, *Giants of the Polo Grounds*, 118–19. Murdock, *Ban Johnson*, 63, 76; Riess, *Touching Base*, 79–82; Ronald M. Selter, *Ballparks of the Deadball Era* (Jefferson, NC, 2008), 113–15.

31. Seymour, *Early Years*, 322–23; Harold Seymour, *Baseball: The Golden Age* (New York, 1989 [1971]), 8–9; Simon, *Deadball Stars*, 235–36; Burk, *Never Just a Game*, 156–57; Murdock, *Ban Johnson*, 61–63.

32. Seymour, *Early Years*, 299, 321–24; Lee Allen, *The Cincinnati Reds* (Kent, OH, 2006 [1948]), 74–77.

33. Bill Lamberty, "Harry Pulliam," SABR Biography Project; Arthur D. Hittner, *Honus Wagner: The Life of Baseball's "Flying Dutchman"* (Jefferson, NC., 1996), 43–48.

34. Burk, *Never Just a Game*, 159.

3: THE MASTER BUILDER

1. McGraw, *The Real McGraw*, 134, 182, 187–88; Bulger, "Genius of the Game," 26; *NYT*, July 18, 1902.

2. *NYT*, July 18 and 20, 1902.

3. Ibid., January 9 and July 18, 1902. For more on Fogel, see Frederick G. Lieb and Stan Baumgartner, *The Philadelphia Phillies* (Kent, Ohio, 2009 [1948]), 84–87.

4. McGraw, *The Real McGraw*, 184–87; McGraw, *Thirty Years*, 134–35; Alexander, *McGraw*, 96–97; Ray Robinson, *Matty: An American Hero* (New York, 1993), 32–37.

5. McGraw, *The Real McGraw*, 183.

6. Ibid., 22, 155, 183, 186; *NYT*, July 17, 1902.

7. McGraw, *The Real McGraw*, 192.

8. McGraw, *Thirty Years*, 118.

9. Ibid., 98; McGraw, *The Real McGraw*, 215.

10. *SL*, Sept. 3, 1910.

11. McGraw, *The Real McGraw*, 5, 197, 228–29.

12. Ibid., 228; McGraw, *Thirty Years*, 11; Ritter, *Glory of Their Times*, 14–15.

13. McGraw, *The Real McGraw*, 194; Ritter, *Glory of Their Times*, 83–84.

14. Ritter, *Glory of Their Times*, 123, 208.

15. McGraw, *Thirty Years*, 1–2.

16. Ronald A. Mayer, *Christy Mathewson: A Game-by-Game Profile of a Legendary Pitcher* (Jefferson, NC, 1993), 42–48, 139–41; McGraw, *Thirty Years*, 192.

17. Robinson, *Mathewson*, 3–25.

18. Ibid., 26–30.

19. Ibid., 31–35; McGraw, *The Real McGraw*, 184–85; *NYT*, July 1, 1902.

20. Robinson, *Mathewson*, 37; Mayer, *Christy Mathewson*, 43; McGraw, *The Real McGraw*, 216. Fogel claimed that he put Mathewson there because his regular first baseman was hurt and Matty hit better than any of the other pitchers. See Lieb and Baumgartner, *Philadelphia Phillies*, 85. Five years later Fogel, still smarting, gave his version of events. See *SN*, June 8, 1907.

21. McGraw, *Thirty Years*, 142.

22. Robinson, *Mathewson*, 44; McGraw, *Thirty Years*, 139–42; Bulger, "Genius of the Game III," 26, 59–60.

23. Robinson, *Mathewson*, 42–43.

24. McGraw, *The Real McGraw*, 190–91.

25. Ibid., 192–93.

26. Ibid., 187; Morris, *Level Playing Fields*, 71–74.

27. McGraw, *The Real McGraw*, 193, 324; Ritter, *Glory of Their Times*, 92–93; Alexander, *McGraw*, 102–103.

28. Alexander, *McGraw*, 103–104; Simon, *Deadball Stars*, 42–43.

29. Alexander, *McGraw*, 99; McGraw, *The Real McGraw*, 201; Simon, *Deadball Stars*, 49.

30. McGraw, *The Real McGraw*, 201–202; Simon, *Deadball Stars*, 49; *Literary Digest*, July 20, 1912, 119; *SL*, Sept. 2, 1911; *Baseball*, Sept. 1911, 17–20.

31. McGraw, *The Real McGraw*, 202; Simon, *Deadball Stars*, 49; Durso, *Days of McGraw*, 81; *SL*, Jan. 9, 1909.

32. Seymour, *Golden Age*, 5; Alexander, *McGraw*, 106–107; Mayer, *Christy Mathewson*, 69.

33. *Baseball*, Sept. 1911, 18; Simon, *Deadball Stars*, 49; Hynd, *Giants of the Polo Grounds*, 178; McGraw, *Thirty Years*, 138.

34. *Baseball*, Sept. 1911, 18; Simon, *Deadball Stars*, 113.

35. Frank Graham, *McGraw of the Giants* (New York, 1944), 26.

36. Ibid., 26–27; McGraw, *Thirty Years*, 135–36; Simon, *Deadball Stars*, 51; Durso, *Days of McGraw*, 52.

37. Simon, *Deadball Stars*, 37–38, 42; Unidentified clipping, Sept. 29, 1948, Arthur Devlin file, HOF; McGraw, *Thirty Years*, 151; Alexander, *McGraw*, 108; Mathewson, *Pitching in a Pinch*, 115. The other deaf-mute was William "Dummy" Hoy, who played in the majors from 1888 to 1902.

38. Simon, *Deadball Stars*, 47–48, 53–54.

39. *SL*, April 2 and 16, 1904.

40. Hynd, *Giants of the Polo Grounds*, 123–24; Alexander, *McGraw*, 106–107; Mayer, *Christy Mathewson*, 67.

41. Mayer, *Christy Mathewson*, 69–70.

42. McGraw, *The Real McGraw*, 18; Simon, *Deadball Stars*, 55.

43. Simon, *Deadball Stars*, 55–56.

44. Ibid., 56.

45. Mathewson, *Pitching in a Pinch*, 121; Ritter, *Glory of Their Times*, 167; Hynd, *Giants of the Polo Grounds*, 127.

46. Mathewson, *Pitching in a Pinch*, 97, 118; *Literary Digest*, June 20, 1914, 1501.

47. *Literary Digest*, June 20, 1914, 1500–1501; Mathewson, *Pitching in a Pinch*, 99, 103; McGraw, *Thirty Years*, 32.

48. *SL*, Sept. 3 and 10, 1904.

49. Ibid., Aug. 13, 1904.

50. Ibid., July 30, 1904.

51. Ibid., Oct. 1, 8, and 15, 1904; McGraw, *Thirty Years*, 155–56.

52. *SL*, Oct. 1 and 8, 1904.

53. Ibid., Oct. 1 and 29, Nov. 19, 1904. Hynd, *Giants of the Polo Grounds*, 128–29; Alexander, *McGraw*, 109.

4: RIVALS

1. For these figures and more detail, see Maury Klein and Harvey A. Kantor, *Prisoners of Progress: American Industrial Cities 1850–1920* (New York, 1976), 68–114.
2. McGraw, *Thirty Years*, 159–60; Simon, *Deadball Stars*, 348.
3. McGraw, *Thirty Years*, 40–41; Morris, *Level Playing Fields*, 88. Apparently sportswriters coined the term from McGraw's use of Strang "in a pinch." See Alexander, *McGraw*, 111–12.
4. Simon, *Deadball Stars*, 149; Frederick G. Lieb, *The Pittsburgh Pirates* (New York, 1948), 44–47, 75–76.
5. Lieb, *Pittsburgh Pirates*, 42–43, 46; Simon, *Deadball Stars*, 149–50.
6. Lieb, *Pittsburgh Pirates*, 41–43; *Baseball Encyclopedia*, 2528; *Literary Digest*, July 20, 1912, 122. The *Baseball Encyclopedia* list of those traded differs slightly from that of Lieb; I have used its version.
7. McGraw, *Thirty Years*, 201. For details on Wagner see Hittner, *Honus Wagner*, passim.
8. Lieb, *Pittsburgh Pirates*, 64–67.
9. Simon, *Deadball Stars*, 145–46, 159.
10. Ibid., 151–52; Lieb, *Pittsburgh Pirates*, 60–64.
11. Hittner, *Honus Wagner*, 131–34, 137.
12. McGraw, *Thirty Years*, 161.
13. *SL*, May 27, 1905.
14. Ibid., April 22, 1905; Alexander, *McGraw*, 111.
15. McGraw, *Thirty Years*, 159.
16. *SL*, April 8, 1905.
17. Mathewson, *Pitching in a Pinch*, 97, 104–105; *Literary Digest*, June 20, 1914, 1500.
18. Alexander, *McGraw*, 112; McGraw, *The Real McGraw*, 204–205.
19. William J. Klem and William J. Slocum, "Jousting with McGraw," *Collier's* (April 7, 1951), 50.
20. Ibid., 31, 50.
21. Ibid., 50.
22. McGraw, *The Real McGraw*, 204–205.
23. Ibid.; McGraw, *Thirty Years*, 161.
24. Mathewson, *Pitching in a Pinch*, 98–99.
25. McGraw, *Thirty Years*, 161–63.
26. *SL*, June 24, 1905.
27. Ibid., May 27, 1905.
28. Ibid., June 3, 1905; Klem, "Jousting with McGraw," 50; Graham, *McGraw of the Giants*, 28–31; Alexander, *McGraw*, 113. In his memoir McGraw said he would tell about the "Hey, Barney!" incident, but he never did. McGraw, *Thirty Years*, 163.
29. *SL*, June 3, 1905; Graham, *McGraw of the Giants*, 30–31; Alexander, *McGraw*, 113–14.
30. *SL*, June 3, 1905.
31. Ibid., June 10, 1905; Unidentified clippings, June 3 and 10, 1905, McGraw File, HOF; Graham, *McGraw of the Giants*, 31–32; Alexander, *McGraw*, 114–15; Seymour, *Golden Age*, 25–27; *SN*, July 7, 1906.
32. Graham, *McGraw of the Giants*, 33.
33. *SL*, June 10 and 17, 1905.
34. Ibid., June 17, Aug. 12 and 19, 1905; Graham, *McGraw of the Giants*, 31; McGraw, *Thirty Years*, 163; Alexander, *McGraw*, 115–16. In those days Pittsburgh was usually spelled without the "h."

35. *SL*, Sept. 30, 1905.

36. Ibid., June 24 and July 22, 1905; Graham, *McGraw of the Giants*, 31; Robinson, *Mathewson*, 66.

37. *SL*, Aug. 26, Sept. 2 and 14, Oct. 7, 1905; McGraw, *Thirty Years*, 157–58.

38. Seymour, *Golden Age*, 137.

39. Connie Mack, *My 66 Years in the Big Leagues* (Mineola, NY, 2009 [1950]), 92–96; Hynd, *Giants of the Polo Grounds*, 133–34.

40. Hynd, *Giants of the Polo Grounds*, 135; *SL*, Oct. 14 and 21, 1905.

41. *SL*, Oct. 21, 1905; Robinson, *Mathewson*, 75–76; McGraw, *Thirty Years*, 142.

42. Hynd, *Giants of the Polo Grounds*, 137; Alexander, *McGraw*, 117–18; McGraw, *The Real McGraw*, 211; *SL*, May 6, Oct. 21, Nov. 4 and 18, 1905. The losing share was $382.

43. *SL*, Dec. 23, 1905.

44. Ibid., Oct. 28, 1905; Graham, *McGraw of the Giants*, 34.

5: FRESH BLOOD

1. McGraw, *The Real McGraw*, 252–53; Bulger, "Genius of the Game," 60.

2. Graham, *McGraw of the Giants*, 35–36; Mathewson, *Pitching in a Pinch*, 139. For more detail on the lobster palaces, see the splendid account in Lewis A. Erenberg, *Steppin' Out: New York Nightlife and the Transformation of American Culture, 1890–1930* (Westport, CT, 1981), 33–59.

3. Luc Sante, *Low Life: Lures and Snares of Old New York* (New York, 1991), 171–72.

4. McGraw, *The Real McGraw*, 212; Alexander, *McGraw*, 119; Durso, *Days of McGraw*, 67–69.

5. Graham, *McGraw of the Giants*, 35–36.

6. Ibid., 36–37.

7. Simon, *Deadball Stars*, 87; *Baseball*, Aug. 1909, 59–60.

8. *Baseball*, Oct. 1911, 18; Simon, *Deadball Stars*, 91; Mathewson, *Pitching in a Pinch*, 297; Evers, *Touching Second*, 60.

9. Simon, *Deadball Stars*, 95; Evers, *Touching Second*, 60–61.

10. Evers, *Touching Second*, 61–62, 65; Simon, *Deadball Stars*, 97.

11. Evers, *Touching Second*, 62–63; Simon, *Deadball Stars*, 97.

12. Evers, *Touching Second*, 64; Simon, *Deadball Stars*, 99; Voigt, *American Baseball*, 33.

13. Evers, *Touching Second*, 63–64; Simon, *Deadball Stars*, 103–104.

14. Cindy Thomson and Scott Brown, *Three Finger: The Mordecai Brown Story* (Lincoln, NE, 2006), 6–22.

15. Frank Deford, *The Old Ball Game* (New York, 2005), 138; Seymour, *Golden Age*, 149; Mathewson, *Pitching in a Pinch*, 82–83; Hynd, *Giants of the Polo Grounds*, 150; Ritter, *Glory of Their Times*, 123–24.

16. Simon, *Deadball Stars*, 107; Evers, *Touching Second*, 68–69.

17. Simon, *Deadball Stars*, 107–108; Ritter, *Glory of Their Times*, 91; Evers, *Touching Second*, 158.

18. Simon, *Deadball Stars*, 109; Evers, *Touching Second*, 67–68.

19. Simon, *Deadball Stars*, 91; Evers, *Touching Second*, 65; *Baseball*, May 1911, 4–5.

20. Evers, *Touching Second*, 69; *Baseball*, May 1911, 5; *SL*, April 8, 105. Selee lived only until July 1909, dying in Denver at the age of forty–nine.

21. Evers, *Touching Second*, 66–67; Simon, *Deadball Stars*, 111–12.

22. *SL*, July 29, Aug. 5, 12, and 14, Sept. 9, Oct. 7, Nov. 11, 1905; *SN*, July 8, 1909.

23. *Baseball*, April 1909, 21–22.

24. Evers, *Touching Second*, 69–71; Simon, *Deadball Stars*, 113, 116, 123–24.

25. Simon, *Deadball Stars*, 121; Evers, *Touching Second*, 71.

26. Simon, *Deadball Stars*, 119; Evers, *Touching Second*, 71–72.

27. McGraw, *The Real McGraw*, 213–14.

28. Unidentified clipping, Feb. 17, 1906, Donlin File, HOF; Alexander, *McGraw*, 119–120; Simon, *Deadball Stars*, 56.

29. Alexander, *McGraw*, 120; Robinson, *Mathewson*, 79; Mayer, *Christy Mathewson*, 108–10.

30. Alexander, *McGraw*, 120; McGraw, *Thirty Years*, 185–86; McGraw, *The Real McGraw*, 214–15; Mayer, *Christy Mathewson*, 109–10; *SN*, July 21, 1906.

31. For details on Seymour see Bill Kirwan, "Cy Seymour," SABR Biography Project, SABR.org and Seymour's file and scrapbooks, HOF.

32. *SN*, Nov. 3, 1906; *NYT*, Aug. 25, 1906; Alexander, *McGraw*, 123.

33. *SN*, July 7, Aug. 18, Nov. 10, 1906.

34. McGraw, *Thirty Years*, 185–86.

35. Alexander, *McGraw*, 123–24; *SN*, Oct. 6 and 20, Nov. 10, Dec. 8, 1906.

36. Alexander, *McGraw*, 124–25; McGraw, *The Real McGraw*, 212; Simon, *Deadball Stars*, 56; *SN*, Feb. 2, 1907.

37. *SN*, Dec. 29, 1906.

38. Ibid., April 6, Nov. 21, 1907; Alexander, *McGraw*, 124–25; Simon, *Deadball Stars*, 56.

39. McGraw, *Thirty Years*, 189; Simon, *Deadball Stars*, 58.

40. Simon, *Deadball Stars*, 58; Fleming, *Unforgettable Season*, 171; Unidentified clipping, Larry Doyle file, HOF.

41. Simon, *Deadball Stars*, 58–59; *Daily News*, Sept. 23, 1963; Unidentified clipping, Doyle file, HOF; McGraw, *Thirty Years*, 189.

42. Simon, *Deadball Stars*, 58–59; Fleming, *Unforgettable Season*, 17.

43. Alexander, *McGraw*, 125–26.

44. *SN*, July 4 and 11, Aug. 29, 1907.

45. Ibid., July 25, 1907.

46. Ibid., May 25, 1907; Frank Graham, *The New York Giants: An Informal History* (New York, 1952).

47. *SN*, July 25, Aug. 29, 1907; Graham, *New York Giants*, 126–27.

48. McGraw, *Thirty Years*, 185.

6: STARTING OVER

1. *SL*, April 8, 1905.

2. *SN*, July 25, Aug. 29, Sept. 19, Nov. 28, 1907; *New York American*, Nov. 10, 1907; Fleming, *Unforgettable Season*, 1–3.

3. Fleming, *Unforgettable Season*, 7; *SN*, Jan. 2, 1908.

4. Fleming, *Unforgettable Season*, 4–5; *SN*, Nov. 28, Dec. 5, 1907, Jan. 6, 1908; Alexander, *McGraw*, 129; Simon, *Deadball Stars*, 61.

5. Fleming, *Unforgettable Season*, 9–10, 22, 146; Simon, *Deadball Stars*, 309–10; McGraw, *The Real McGraw*, 216.

6. Ritter, *Glory of Their Times*, 117–22; Unidentified career list, Al Bridwell file, HOF.

7. Fleming, *Unforgettable Season*, 16, 18; *SN*, Dec. 19 and 26, 1907; Mathewson, *Pitching in a Pinch*, 302; McGraw, *The Real McGraw*, 216.

8. McGraw, *Thirty Years*, 187.

9. Ibid., 16; Ritter, *Glory of Their Times*, 84–86; Simon, *Deadball Stars*, 65; Fleming, *Unforgettable Season*, 13. These sources contradict each other on one detail. Snodgrass, in his interview with

Ritter, says he was aboard a train to spring training four days after McGraw offered him a contract. But spring training didn't begin until late February, and the *NYS*, cited by Fleming in note 12, reports McGraw leaving for Los Angeles in early January. To confuse the matter further, the profile in Simon says that Snodgrass joined the Giants after his school year ended in June.

10. Ritter, *Glory of Their Times*, 86–87.

11. Simon, *Deadball Stars*, 69; Hynd, *Giants of the Polo Grounds*, 143; Fleming, *Unforgettable Season*, 33; Unidentified clipping, April 16, 1936, Charles Herzog file, HOF.

12. McGraw, *Thirty Years*, 40; Bozeman Bulger article, unidentified clipping, James Otis Crandall file, HOF.

13. Simon, *Deadball Stars*, 67; Mathewson, *Pitching in a Pinch*, 57–58.

14. Two unidentified clippings, Crandall file, HOF.

15. Fleming, *Unforgettable Season*, 18–24, 33.

16. Ibid., 34–36, 58, 64–66; *NYT*, Aug. 12, 1907; Simon, *Deadball Stars*, 349; Alexander, *McGraw*, 130. Alexander says that McGinnity did not return until May 30, but Fleming's record shows him pitching on May 11.

17. Fleming, *Unforgettable Season*, 10–11, 15, 29–31, 34–35, 37, 43–44; Hittner, *Honus Wagner*, 164–66; *SN*, March 12, 1908.

18. Fleming, *Unforgettable Season*, 38.

19. Ibid., 40–42, 50–53, 62, 75, 80–81, 83; Unidentified clipping, May 7, 1908, McGraw file, HOF.

20. Simon, *Deadball Stars*, 59; Fleming, *Unforgettable Season*, 99–104, 106, 114–15, 120, 127, 133, 139.

21. Ralph Berger, "Moose McCormick," SABR Biography Project, SABR.org; Fleming, *Unforgettable Season*, 115–16, 132–33; *NYT*, July 5, 1908.

22. Mansch, *Rube Marquard*, 5–14. Mansch has done a fine job of clarifying some of the obfuscations about Marquard, many of them derived from the pitcher himself, such as the wrong birth date.

23. Ritter, *Glory of Their Times*, 1–12, 15; Mansch, *Rube Marquard*, 10–17; Simon, *Deadball Stars*, 63; Biographical form, Rube Marquard folder, HOF. The form, filled out by Marquard himself, lists his schooling as five years and his birth date at 1889.

24. Mansch, *Rube Marquard*, 18–39; Ritter, *Glory of Their Times*, 12–13; Fleming, *Unforgettable Season*, 111–12, 177.

25. Unless otherwise indicated, this section on Meyers is drawn from William A. Young's careful biography, *John Tortes Meyers: A Baseball Biography* (Jefferson, NC, 2012), 9–77.

26. Ibid., 14.

27. Ibid., 43, 48; Fleming, *Unforgettable Season*, 112. Young says that Meyers was sold to the Giants on July 20. That may be the official date of sale, but papers for the transaction were filed with the National Commission on June 29 according to the *Globe* article.

28. Alexander, *McGraw*, 129, said that "McGraw never had a long-range plan for the Giants. For him rebuilding was always a matter of building for the present, putting together a winner for next season." The pattern of McGraw's acquisitions in 1907–1908 indicates otherwise.

29. Fleming, *Unforgettable Season*, 114–40, 150–52, 159.

30. Ibid., 158.

31. Ibid., 188–200; David W. Anderson, *More Than Merkle* (Lincoln, NE, 2000), 156.

32. Fleming, *Unforgettable Season*, 206–208, 213, 224. According to Fleming, the *Globe* was the only New York paper to report the incident.

33. Ibid., 212–27; *NYT*, Sept. 9–12 and Sept. 18, 1908.

34. Fleming, *Unforgettable Season*, 228–38; *NYT*, Sept. 18–20 and 22, 1908; *SL*, Sept. 19 and 24, 1908.
35. *NYT*, Sept. 23, 1908; Fleming, *Unforgettable Season*, 239–43.
36. For different versions of the game see Fleming, *Unforgettable Season*, 243–51; Cait Murphy, *Crazy '08* (New York, 2007), 177–98; Lowell Reidenbaugh, *100 Years of National League Baseball 1876–1976* (St. Louis, 1976), 60–62; Alexander, *McGraw*, 133–34; Mathewson, *Pitching in a Pinch*, 188–89; McGraw, *Thirty Years*, 180–83; McGraw, *The Real McGraw*, 217–19; Graham, *McGraw of the Giants*, 46–49; Hynd, *Giants of the Polo Grounds*, 145–49; Seymour, *Golden Age*, 149–54; Robinson, *Mathewson*, 97–102; John P. Carmichael, *My Greatest Day in Baseball* (New York, 1945), 37–41; Deford, *Old Ball Game*, 139–43; *NYT*, Sept. 24, 1908; *SN*, Oct. 1, 1908; *SL*, Oct. 3, 1908. My account borrows from several of them.
37. *SL*, Unknown October 1914 date, clipping in Fred Merkle file, HOF.
38. Fleming, *Unforgettable Season*, 248. For differing versions of what happened after Bridwell's hit see the sources in note 36 and the following: Charles Murphy to Harry Pulliam, Sept. 23, 1908, Merkle file, HOF; Henry O'Day to Pulliam, Sept. 23, 1908, Merkle file, HOF; Cyrus C. Miller to Pulliam, Sept. 25, 1908, Merkle file, HOF; John T. Brush to the President and Board of Directors of the National League, Sept. 28, 1908, Merkle file, HOF; Affidavit by Fred Merkle, Oct. 3, 1908, Merkle file, HOF; P. T. Powers to Brush, Sept. 29, 1908, Merkle file, HOF; *SL*, unknown Oct. 1914, clipping in Merkle file, HOF; Unidentified clipping, February 6, 1930, Merkle file, HOF. The 1914 clipping gives O'Day's later version, the 1930 clipping that of Hofman. Murphy's version names some of the reporters who heard O'Day declare the game a tie.
39. Robinson, *Mathewson*, 101; Klem, "Jousting with McGraw," 51. The Robinson source is somewhat suspect in that he includes no source references in his book and I have not found this incident elsewhere. However, it does fit McGraw's personality, and he was notorious for unleashing a stream of obscenities when agitated.
40. Fleming, *Unforgettable Season*, 248; Hynd, *Giants of the Polo Grounds*, 149; McGraw, *The Real McGraw*, 218–19.
41. *NYT*, Sept. 24 and 25, 1908; *SL*, Oct. 3, 1908; *SN*, Oct. 8, 1908.
42. Pulliam statements, Sept. 24 and 25, 1908, Merkle file, HOF; Murphy to Pulliam, Sept. 25, 1908, Merkle file, HOF; Brush to Pulliam, Sept. 25, 1908, Merkle file, HOF; Pulliam to Brush, Sept. 25, 1908, Merkle file, HOF; Pulliam to August Herrmann, Oct. 3, 1908, Merkle file, HOF; *SN*, Oct. 8, 1908; *SL*, Oct. 10, 1908; Fleming, *Unforgettable Season*, 251–54; Murphy, *Crazy '08*, 195–96.
43. Pulliam statements, Sept. 26 and 30, 1908, Merkle file, HOF; Murphy to John A. Heydler, Sept. 30, 1908, Merkle file, HOF; Herrmann to Pulliam, Oct. 3, 1908, Merkle file, HOF; *NYT*, Sept. 25, 1908; Fleming, *Unforgettable Season*, 251–54.
44. *SN*, Oct. 8, 1908; Mathewson, *Pitching in a Pinch*, 190–91; Simon, *Deadball Stars*, 47; Fleming, *Unforgettable Season*, 255, 265; McGraw, *The Real McGraw*, 219.
45. Paul Dickson, *Baseball's Greatest Quotations* (New York, 2008), 146; Fleming, *Unforgettable Season*, 255–57.
46. Simon, *Deadball Stars*, 63; Fleming, *Unforgettable Season*, 255–57.
47. *NYT*, Sept. 27 and 28, 1908; *SN*, Sept. 17, 1908; Fleming, *Unforgettable Season*, 258–59, 264; Mayer, *Christy Mathewson*, 166.
48. *NYT*, Sept. 29 and 30, 1908; Fleming, *Unforgettable Season*, 268–71; Mayer, *Christy Mathewson*, 166; Lieb and Baumgartner, *Philadelphia Phillies*, 79.
49. Fleming, *Unforgettable Season*, 272–76, 279–80; Mayer, *Christy Mathewson*, 166–67; *NYT*, Oct. 1–3, 1908.
50. Fleming, *Unforgettable Season*, 281–84; Mayer, *Christy Mathewson*, 167.

51. Pulliam to Brush, Oct. 2, 1908, Merkle file, HOF; Pulliam to Murphy, Oct. 2, 1908, Merkle file, HOF; *NYT*, Oct. 3–6, 1908; Fleming, *Unforgettable Season*, 273–79, 288–99. The first pages cited have the full text of Pulliam's announcement.

52. Anderson, *More Than Merkle*, 169–70; *SL*, Oct. 10, 1908.

53. "In Re – Appeal of the New York and Chicago Clubs Pertaining to the Finding Made by President Harry C. Pulliam," Oct. 6, 1908, Merkle file, HOF; Pulliam to Brush, Oct. 7, 1908, Merkle file, HOF; *NYT*, Oct. 7, 1908; *SL*, Oct. 17, 1908; Fleming, *Unforgettable Season*, 288–96.

54. Mathewson, *Pitching in a Pinch*, 195–97.

55. Fleming, *Unforgettable Season*, 300–305; *NYT*, Oct. 8 and 9, 1908. The *Times* featured its account of the game on the front page for the first time.

56. Carmichael, *My Greatest Day in Baseball*, 173–75.

57. Fleming, *Unforgettable Season*, 302; Mathewson, *Pitching in a Pinch*, 197, 199; Mayer, *Christy Mathewson*, 167; Robinson, *Mathewson*, 107.

58. Fleming, *Unforgettable Season*, 310, 312; Mathewson, *Pitching in a Pinch*, 198; Murphy, *Crazy '08*, 259; Carmichael, *My Greatest Day in Baseball*, 175–76.

59. Carmichael, *My Greatest Day in Baseball*, 135, 176.

60. *NYT*, Oct. 9, 1908; *NYTR*, Oct. 9, 1908.

61. Ibid.; Mathewson, *Pitching in a Pinch*, 186–88, 202. One writer said that Mathewson had motioned Seymour to play deeper on Tinker and was ignored, but Mathewson wrote that "I don't recall giving any advice to 'Cy,' as he knew the Chicago batters as well as I did and how to play for them."

62. *NYT*, Oct. 9, 1908; *NYTR*, Oct. 9, 1908; Mathewson, *Pitching in a Pinch*, 204.

63. Fleming, *Unforgettable Season*, 309, 314–15; *NYT*, Oct. 9, 1908; Evers, *Touching Second*, 79.

64. Mathewson, *Pitching in a Pinch*, 205.

7: Bitter Aftertastes

1. "Proceedings of the National League Adjourned Annual Meeting," Feb. 16, 1909, 83–97, 210, HOF; hereafter cited as Adjourned Meeting Proceedings; Anderson, *More Than Merkle*, 225.

2. National League Board Meeting Minutes, 24–32, hereafter cited as Board Meeting; *SL*, Jan. 23, 1909; *SN*, Dec. 10, 1908.

3. Board Meeting, 10–12, 160–61; *NYT*, June 15, 1908.

4. Board Meeting, 193–96, 269–70.

5. Ibid., 273–74. For other versions of this incident see Klem, "Jousting with McGraw," 54; Seymour, *Golden Age*, 283; Anderson, *More Than Merkle*, 210–22; Murphy, *Crazy '08*, 261; Alexander, *McGraw*, 136–37. The rumors about Boston gained traction from the fact that Joe Kelley, the team's manager, was McGraw's old Oriole teammate and longtime friend.

6. Ibid., 273–75, 287–88, 346.

7. Ibid., 275–76.

8. Ibid., 270–71, 277–78.

9. Ibid., 277–79.

10. Ibid., 271–72, 279–82.

11. Ibid., 283–94, 313; *SN*, Oct. 1, 1908.

12. Board Meeting, 294–301, 303, 392; Adjourned Meeting Proceedings, 177.

13. Board Meeting, 302–14.

14. Ibid., 304–19, 325–50. Although the dates of the sessions differ, the minutes are paged continuously and are treated as one document here. It is not clear why they waited an extra day to meet again; possibly Brush could not come on the 10th.

15. Ibid., 350–57.
16. Ibid., 357–61.
17. Ibid., 362–68.
18. Ibid., 368–78.
19. Ibid., 379–85.
20. Ibid., 386–89.
21. Ibid., 390–416. These pages include the complete statement.
22. Ibid., 416–19.
23. *SL*, Dec. 19, 1908.
24. Anderson, *More Than Merkle*, 117; Sante, *Low Life*, 268–69.
25. David Von Drehle, *Triangle: The Fire That Changed America* (New York, 2003), 191; Sante, *Low Life*, 270–72.
26. Adjourned Meeting Proceedings, 169.
27. *SN*, Dec. 17, 1908, Jan. 28, Feb. 11 and 18, 1909; *SL*, Jan. 30, Feb. 6, 1909.
28. Adjourned Meeting Proceedings, 80–83.
29. Ibid., 39–45, Feb. 11, 18, 26, 1909; *SL*, Feb. 27, 1909.
30. Adjourned Meeting Proceedings, 40–41.
31. Ibid., 101–102.
32. Ibid., 101–106, 11.
33. Ibid., 113–18.
34. Ibid., 131–39.
35. The full report is in ibid., 146–52.
36. Ibid., 153–54, 163–92, 205, 222–29, 314–19. The names in this document were not cut out but covered over by heavy lead pencil. Some of them can still be made out under the right light.
37. *SL*, Feb. 13 and 27, March 6, 1909; *SN*, Feb. 25, March 4, 1909.
38. *CT*, April 20, 1909. The article contains the text of the decision.
39. Ibid., April 24 and 25, 1909.
40. Ibid., April 25, 1909; *SN*, June 3, 1909; *SL*, May 8, 1909; Alexander, *McGraw*, 140.
41. Murphy, *Crazy '08*, 286; *SN*, June 3, 1909.
42. *NYT*, July 29, 1909; *SN*, Feb. 25, April 1 and 8, June 3, Aug. 5, 1909; *SL*, May 29, June 5, 12, and 17, Aug. 7, 1909.
43. *NYT*, July 29, 1909; *SL*, June 26, July 31, 1909; Simon, *Deadball Stars*, 23; Harold Kaese, *The Boston Braves* (New York, 1948), 119; Lieb and Baumgartner, *Philadelphia Phillies*, 82. Durham was a Philadelphia politico and one of the team's owners.
44. *Baseball*, Nov. 1908, 8–9; Ralph Berger, "Moose McCormick," SABR Baseball Biography Project, SABR.org.
45. *Baseball*, March 1909, 7–8.
46. Robinson, *Mathewson*, 112–14; Mathewson to Herrmann, Jan. 2, 1913, Christy Mathewson File, HOF; *SL*, Jan. 23, 1909. Robinson said that Nick competed in no sports while at Lafayette, but *Sporting Life* quotes the college paper as describing his performance in pitching for the freshman team. *SL*, Oct. 17, 1908, Jan. 23, 1909.
47. Robinson, *Mathewson*, 114.

8: Coming Together

1. *SL*, Oct. 17 and 24, 1908.
2. Mathewson, *Pitching in a Pinch*, 185–86. Saves were not recorded in those days and were computed much later.

3. *SL*, Oct. 24, 1908.

4. Simon, *Deadball Stars*, 61.

5. McGraw, *The Real McGraw*, 221; Alexander, *McGraw*, 139; *SN*, Jan. 28, 1909; *SL*, Nov. 21, 1908. Alexander says the raise was only $300 but does not cite a source.

6. Simon, *Deadball Stars*, 56; Alexander, *McGraw*, 143; *SN*, Feb. 18, July 22, 1909; *SL*, Oct. 24, Dec. 5, 1908, Jan. 30, July 24, 1909. Donlin and Hite previewed their show in Albany on Oct. 19. A copy of Chicago's Majestic Theatre program for Jan. 11, 1909, which includes Hite and Donlin in *Stealing Home*, is in the Donlin File, HOF.

7. Graham, *McGraw of the Giants*, 50–51; *SN*, Dec. 17 and 24, 1908; *SL*, Nov. 14 and 28, Dec. 5, 12, and 19, 1908. Garry Herrmann of the Reds was also rumored to want Bresnahan.

8. Graham, *McGraw of the Giants*, 50–51; *SN*, Dec. 17 and 24, 1908; *SL*, Nov. 14 and 28, Dec. 5, 12, and 19, 1908, Jan. 9, 1909.

9. Simon, *Deadball Stars*, 73.

10. McGraw, *Thirty Years*, 19.

11. Simon, *Deadball Stars*, 342; Graham, *McGraw of the Giants*, 51. For some of Raymond's antics see *SL*, Nov. 21, 1908.

12. Simon, *Deadball Stars*, 75; *SN*, Feb. 15, 1950, clipping in Art Fletcher file, HOF; Fred Lieb column, March 8, 1933, unidentified clipping, Fletcher file, HOF.

13. Simon, *Deadball Stars*, 75; McGraw, *The Real McGraw*, 227.

14. *NYT*, April 27, 1909; *SN*, March 25, 1909; *SL*, Feb.13, March 20 and 27, April 3, May 15, June 26, 1909. Several writers persisted in misspelling Meyers's name.

15. *NYT*, April 10, 1909.

16. Kirwin, "Cy Seymour," SABR Baseball Biography Project; Mathewson, *Pitching in a Pinch*, 135–36; *SL*, Feb. 20, 1909.

17. Alexander, *McGraw*, 145; *SL*, June 26, July 3, 10, 17, and 24, Aug. 14 and 28, Sept. 4, 1909.

18. *SL*, Sept. 4 and 25, Oct. 9, 16, and 23, Nov. 13, 1909; Mayer, *Christy Mathewson*, 184.

19. *SL*, July 3, 10, and 24, Nov. 20, 1909.

20. McGraw, *Thirty Years*, 104; Mayer, *Christy Mathewson*, 172; *SL*, July 24, 1909.

21. Unidentified clippings, Joshua Devore file, HOF. The Meridian club claimed that the Giants did not make the second $375 payment. See Allen McCants to John E. Bruce, no date, McCants to August Herrmann, May 9, May 13, and May 15, 1908, all in Devore file, HOF.

22. Mathewson, *Pitching in a Pinch*, 43–44; *Literary Digest*, June 20, 1914, 1504.

23. Unless otherwise indicated, this section is drawn from McGraw, *The Real McGraw*, 246–53.

24. Ibid., 325.

25. Fleming, *Unforgettable Season*, 201.

26. *SL*, June 26, July 3, Nov. 20 and 27, Dec. 4 and 25, 1909; Kaese, *Boston Braves*, 119; Seymour, *Golden Age*, 28–29; *SN*, June 24, Aug. 19, Nov. 4 and 11, Dec. 23, 1909; Jon Daly, "Tom Lynch," SABR Baseball Biography Project, sabr.org.

27. Seymour, *Golden Age*, 30–31; Lieb and Baumgartner, *Philadelphia Phillies*, 84–86; *SN*, Dec. 2, 1909; *SL*, Dec. 4, 1909.

28. *SL*, Nov. 6, 1909, Jan. 15 and 29, Feb. 5, April 9, May 7, 1910. Gray had been in the theatrical business for thirty years.

29. *SL*, June 26, 1909, May 28, 1910.

30. Ibid., June 5, 1909, Feb. 12, April 9, 1910; *SN*, March 11, April 29, 1909; Mathewson, *Pitching in a Pinch*, 41–42; McGraw, *Thirty Years*, 160; Evers, *Touching Second*, 97.

31. *SL*, Nov. 20, Dec. 4, 1909, Feb. 19 and 26, May 14, 1910.

32. Ibid., Jan. 22, April 9, and 16, 1910.

33. Ibid., March 29, April 23, May 14, 1910; Simon, *Deadball Stars*, 310.

34. *SL*, June 4 and 11, 1910; Ritter, *Glory of Their Times*, 87.

35. Ritter, *Glory of Their Times*, 87; *SL*, June 18, Aug. 13, 20, and 27, 1910.

36. Simon, *Deadball Stars*, 47, 54; Mathewson, *Pitching in a Pinch*, 58–59; McGraw to Crandall, Aug. 23, 1909, Crandall file, HOF.

37. Unidentified clippings, Louis Drucke file, HOF; *SL*, June 4, July 30, 1910.

38. Mansch, *Rube Marquard*, 65–68; *SL*, May 14, June 4, 11, and 25, 1910; Alexander, *McGraw*, 148–49; Mansch, *Rube* Marquard, 65–68.

39. *SL*, June 25, July 9, 23, and 30, Aug. 6, Sept. 3 and 10, 1910; Alexander, *McGraw*, 149.

40. *SL*, March 26, June 4 and 11, Aug. 6, Sept. 10, 1910, March 11, 1911.

41. Ibid., April 9, May 28, June 18 and 25, Aug. 6, 13, and 20, Sept. 3, Oct. 22, 1910.

42. Ibid., June 4, July 2 and 23, Aug. 6, 20, and 27, 1910; *Baseball*, May 1911, 27–31; Evers, *Touching Second*, 93–94; *CT*, Feb. 5, 1911.

43. *SL*, April 9, May 21, June 18 and 25, July 2, 9, and 30, Aug. 6 and 20, Sept. 3, Oct. 22, 1910.

44. Ibid., Oct. 22, 1910; Lieb, *Pittsburgh Pirates*, 157; Hittner, *Honus Wagner*, 198.

45. *SL*, June 4 and 25, Sept. 3, 10, and 24, Oct. 22, 1910.

46. Ibid., June 4 and 25, July 9, Aug. 20, Oct. 8, 1910.

47. Ibid., Oct. 29, Nov. 5 and 12, 1910; Hynd, *Giants of the Polo Grounds*, 159–61; Mayer, *Christy Mathewson*, 199–200; Robinson, *Mathewson*, 118–20; Simon, *Deadball Stars*, 72.

48. *SL*, Oct. 8, Nov. 5, 12, and 19, Dec. 3 and 24, 1910, Jan. 7, 1911; Kaese, *Boston Braves*, 122–23.

49. *SL*, Nov. 12 and 26, Dec. 3, 1910; Alexander, *McGraw*, 150. Murphy told McGraw he could have Kling once he was reinstated, but the National Commission ruled that Kling had to play at least one year with the Cubs.

50. *SL*, Nov. 26, Dec. 24, 1910.

51. Ibid., Dec. 3 and 24, 1910.

52. Ibid., Oct. 15, Nov. 26, Dec. 3, 17, and 24, 1910, Jan. 28, Feb. 11, 1911.

53. Ibid., Jan. 21, Feb. 18, 1911.

54. Ibid., Feb. 11 and 18, 1911.

9: April: All Fired Up

1. *SL*, April 15, 1911.

2. Bureau of the Census, *Historical Statistics of the United States: Colonial Times to 1970* (Washington, DC, 1975), 1:9, 11, 14–19, 32, 55, 379.

3. Ibid., 1:164, 166, 168, 213; *NYH*, April 9, 1911.

4. *NYH*, April 16, 1911.

5. *NYP*, July 30, 1911.

6. Ibid., March 18, 1911; *SL*, April 15, May 13, 20, and 27, 1911.

7. *SL*, April 15 and 22, 1911.

8. *NYP*, July 30, 1911; Ritter, *Glory of Their Times*, 274; Fleming, *Unforgettable Season*, 15.

9. *NYP*, April 13, 1911; *NYW*, April 13, 1911.

10. *NYTR*, April 1, 1911; Lieb, *Baseball as I Have Known It*, 21; *NYT*, March 18 and 31, 1911. For opening day see *NYH*, April 13, 1911; *NYTR*, April 13, 1911; *NYT*, April 13, 1911; *NYP*, April 13, 1911; *NYW*, April 13, 1911; *NYS*, April 13 and 14, 1911. For pictures of the day see *NYT*, April 23, 1911.

11. *NYP*, April 14, 1911; *NYW*, April 14, 1911; *SL*, Jan. 29, 1910.

12. McGraw, *The Real McGraw*, 186.

13. *NYH*, April 9, 1911; *SL*, June 4, 1910.

14. *CT*, April 21, 1911.

15. Lieb, *Baseball as I Have Known It*, 16, 23–26, 243–48.

16. Ibid., 30, 243, 246–48. Runyon also indulged in verse. For a sample see *SL*, April 1, 1911.

17. Ibid., 23–26, 252–53.

18. *NYH*, April 14, 1911; *NYP*, April 14, 1911; *NYW*, April 14, 1911; *NYTR*, April 14, 1911; *NYT*, April 14, 1911; *NYS*, April 14, 1911.

19. The list of fires is in *NYH*, March 26, 1911. For the Triangle Shirtwaist Factory fire, see all major New York newspapers, March 26, 1911, and the week following. See also the full and fascinating account of the fire and its context in Drehle, *Triangle*.

20. Selter, *Ballparks of the Deadball Era*, 152, 171, 175–76; *CT*, March 18, 1911.

21. *NYP*, April 14, 1911; *NYW*, April 14, 1911; *NYH*, April 14, 1911; *NYT*, April 14, 1911; *NYS*, April 14, 1911; *NYTR*, April 14, 1911. Unless otherwise indicated, the story of the fire is drawn from these sources.

22. *NYH*, April 15, 1911.

23. *NYTR*, April 15, 1911.

24. Ibid.; *NYS*, April 15, 1911; *NYH*, April 15, 1911; *NYT*, April 15, 1911; *NYP*, April 15, 1911. These same sources cover the next paragraph as well.

25. *SL*, March 5, 1910; *SN*, May 13, 1909.

26. *SN*, April 20, 1911; *SL*, April 22, 1911.

27. Durso, *Days of McGraw*, 81.

28. *NYTR*, April 23, 1911; *NYP*, April 23, May 4, 1911; *NYT*, April 23, 1911; *NYS*, April 24, 1911; *SL*, April 29, May 13, 1911; *NYH*, May 4, 1911.

29. Selter, *Ballparks of the Deadball Era*, 113–20. Selter includes a photo of the park taken in 1910.

30. *NYW*, April 16, 1911; *NYS*, April 16, 1911; *NYH*, April 16, 1911; *NYT*, April 16, 1911; *NYTR*, April 16, 1911; *NYP*, April 16, 1911.

31. *NYW*, April 17 and 18, 1911; *NYT*, April 17 and 18, 1911; *NYTR*, April 17 and 18, 1911; *NYH*, April 17 and 18, 1911; *NYS*, April 17 and 18, 1911.

32. *NYW*, April 18, 1911; *NYH*, April 18, 1911; *NYTR*, April 18, 1911; *NYS*, April 18, 1911; *CT*, April 15, 1911; Alex Semchuck, "Addie Joss," SABR Baseball Biography Project.

33. *NYTR*, April 19, 1911; *NYT*, April 19, 1911; *NYW*, April 19, 1911; *NYP*, April 19, 1911; *NYH*, April 19, 1911; *NYS*, April 19, 1911.

34. *NYTR*, April 20, 1911; *NYS*, April 20, 1911; *NYH*, April 20, 1911; *NYP*, April 20, 1911; *NYT*, April 20, 1911.

35. Ibid., April 24, 1911.

36. Mansch, *Rube Marquard*, 68–69.

37. *NYT*, April 21–25, 1911; *NYH*, April 21–25, 1911; *NYW*, April 22–25, 1911; *NYTR*, April 22–25, 1911; *NYS*, April 22–25, 1911.

38. *NYS*, April 26 and 27, 1911; *NYW*, April 26 and 27, 1911; *NYP*, April 26 and 27, 1911; *NYTR*, April 26 and 27, 1911; *NYT*, April 26 and 27, 1911; *NYH*, April 26 and 27, 1911; *SL*, April 29, 1911.

39. *NYP*, April 28 and 29, 1911; *NYW*, April 28 and 29, 1911; *NYTR*, April 28 and 29, 1911; *NYH*, April 28 and 29, 1911; *NYS*, April 28 and 29, 1911; *NYT*, April 28 and 29, 1911.

40. *NYTR*, April 30, 1911; *NYT*, April 30, 1911; *NYH*, April 30, 1911; *NYW*, April 30, 1911; *NYS*, April 30, 1911.

10: MAY: HOME AWAY FROM HOME

1. John M. Burns, *Thunder at Sunrise: A History of the Vanderbilt Cup, the Grand Prize and the Indianapolis 500* (Jefferson, NC, 2006), 1–117.

2. Ibid., 118–27.

3. *NYH*, Sept. 17, 1911.

4. *NYS*, May 2, 1911.

5. *SL*, June 3, 1911.

6. *NYH*, May 3, 1911; *NYTR*, May 2 and 3, 1911; *NYT*, May 2 and 3, 1911; *NYS*, May 3, 1911; *NYW*, May 3, 1911.

7. *NYW*, May 4–6, 1911; *NYT*, May 4–6, 1911; *NYP*, May 4–6, 1911; *NYTR*, May 4–6, 1911; *NYS*, May 4–6, 1911; *NYH*, May 5 and 6, 1911.

8. *NYS*, May 7, 1911; *NYW*, May 7, 1911; *NYH*, May 7, 1911; *NYT*, May 7, 1911; *NYTR*, May 7, 1911; *NYP*, May 7, 1911.

9. *SN*, May 11, 1911.

10. *CT*, March 5–9, 14, and 19, April 6, 1911; Simon, *Deadball Stars*, 96, 117, 124–25.

11. Simon, *Deadball Stars*, 91–92, 131; *SL*, June 3 and 24, 1911; *Baseball*, Oct. 1911, 10.

12. *CT*, May 6 and 9, 1911; *NYH*, May 15, 1911; *SN*, May 18, 1911; Simon, *Deadball Stars*, 96, 124.

13. *CT*, March 3, 11, and 12, April 9 and 13, 1911; Simon, *Deadball Stars*, 120, 122.

14. *NYH*, May 10, 1911; *NYT*, May 10, 1911; *NYP*, May 10, 1911, *NYTR*, May 10, 1911; *NYS*, May 10, 1911; *NYW*, May 10, 1911.

15. *NYW*, May 11–13, 1911; *NYTR*, May 11–13, 1911; *NYS*, May 11–13, 1911; *NYT*, May 11–13, 1911; *NYH*, May 11–13, 1911.

16. Simon, *Deadball Stars*, 339–41, 344–57.

17. Ibid., 361; *CT*, March 30, 1911; *SL*, June 24, 1911.

18. *NYT*, May 14 and 16, 1911; *NYTR*, May 14 and 16, 1911; *NYS*, May 14 and 16, 1911; *NYW*, May 16, 1911; *NYH*, May 14 and 16, 1911; *NYP*, May 14, 1911; *SN*, May 18, 1911.

19. *SL*, May 20, 1911; *NYT*, May 16, 1911.

20. *SN*, May 18, 1911.

21. *CT*, May 17, 1911.

22. *NYH*, May 17 and 18, 1911; *NYW*, May 17 and 18, 1911; *NYP*, May 18, 1911; *NYTR*, May 17 and 18, 1911; *NYS*, May 18, 1911; *NYT*, May 17 and 18, 1911; *SL*, May 27, 1911.

23. Lieb, *Pittsburgh Pirates*, 157–58; Simon, *Deadball Stars*, 164, 168; *CT*, March 3, 1911.

24. Lieb, *Pittsburgh Pirates*, 156–60; Simon, *Deadball Stars*, 165–66, 169–78.

25. *NYS*, May 19, 1911; *NYW*, May 19, 1911; *NYT*, May 19, 1911; *NYH*, May 19, 1911; *NYTR*, May 19, 1911.

26. *NYS*, May 20 and 21, 1911; *NYTR*, May 20 and 21, 1911; *NYT*, May 20 and 21, 1911; *NYW*, May 20 and 21, 1911; *NYH*, May 20 and 21, 1911; *NYP*, May 21, 1911.

27. *SL*, June 24, 1911; *NYT*, May 23–25, 1911; *NYW*, May 23–25, 1911; *NYH*, May 23–25, 1911; *NYTR*, May 23–25, 1911; *NYS*, May 23–25, 1911; *NYP*, May 25, 1911; Mayer, Christy *Mathewson*, 206.

28. *NYT*, May 26, 1911; *NYTR*, May 26, 1911; *NYW*, May 26, 1911; *NYS*, May 26, 1911; *NYH*, May 26, 1911.

29. *NYH*, May 1 and 14, 1911; *NYS*, May 1, 1911; *NYTR*, May 1 and 4, 1911; *NYT*, May 1, 4, and 14, 1911.

30. *NYP*, May 28, 1911.

31. Ibid.; *NYTR*, May 28, 1911; *NYT*, May 28 and 29, 1911; *NYS*, May 28, 1911; *NYW*, May 28, 1911. Unless otherwise indicated, the story of the fire is pieced together from these sources.

32. The fullest account of the animal house tragedy is *NYTR*, June 4, 1911. Bonavita's own version is in *NYW*, May 28, 1911. Not surprisingly, all of the accounts contradict one another in some details.

33. *NYT*, May 29, 1911.

34. *NYTR*, May 28, 1911; *NYW*, May 28, 1911.

35. Lieb and Baumgartner, *Philadelphia Phillies*, 89–94.

36. Simon, *Deadball Stars*, 191–95, 205.

37. Ibid., 209; *SL*, May 20, 1911; Lieb and Baumgartner, *Philadelphia Phillies*, 91–92.

38. *NYT*, May 27, 1911; *NYH*, May 27, 1911; *NYS*, May 27, 1911; *NYW*, May 27, 1911; *NYTR*, May 27, 1911.

39. *NYT*, May 28, 1911; *NYH*, May 28, 1911; *NYTR*, May 28, 1911; *NYS*, May 28, 1911; *NYW*, May 28, 1911; Mathewson, *Pitching in a Pinch*, 18–19.

40. *NYT*, May 30, 1911; *NYH*, May 30, 1911; *NYTR*, May 30, 1911; *NYS*, May 30, 1911; *NYW*, May 30, 1911.

41. *NYT*, May 31 and June 1, 1911; *NYW*, May 31 and June 1, 1911; *NYH*, May 31 and June 1, 1911; *NYS*, May 31 and June 1, 1911.

11: JUNE: DOGFIGHT

1. *SN*, June 1, 1911.

2. *NYP*, June 3, 1911; *NYTR*, June 3, 1911; *NYW*, June 3, 1911; *NYP*, June 3, 1911; *NYT*; *CT*, June 2 and 3, 1911.

3. *NYP*, June 4, 1911; *NYTR*, June 4, 1911; *NYW*, June 4, 1911; *NYT*, June 4, 1911; *CT*, June 2–6, 1911.

4. *NYP*, June 5 and 6, 1911; *NYTR*, June 5 and 6, 1911; *NYS*, June 5 and 6, 1911; *NYW*, June 5 and 6, 1911; *NYT*, June 5 and 6, 1911.

5. *NYT*, June 4, 8, and 12, 1911; *NYP*, June 4, 1911; *NYW*, June 4 and 8, 1911; *NYTR*, June 12, 1911; *SL*, June 10 and 17, 1911.

6. *SL*, June 17, 1911.

7. *NYP*, June 7, 1911; *NYT*, June 7, 1911; *NYTR*, June 7, 1911; *NYS*, June 7, 1911; *NYW*, June 7, 1911.

8. *NYW*, June 7 and 8, 1911; *NYTR*, June 8, 1911; *NYP*, June 8, 1911; *NYT*, June 8, 1911; *SL*, June 17, 1911; *CT*, June 8, 1911. On that same June 7 the Cubs made six errors.

9. *NYP*, June 9 and 10, 1911; *NYTR*, June 9 and 10, 1911; *NYW*, June 9 and 10, 1911; *NYT*, June 9 and 10, 1911.

10. *NYP*, July 16, 1911; *NYH*, May 16, 1911; *NYT*, July 12, 1911.

11. Voigt, *American Baseball*, 2:52; Ritter, *Glory of Their Times*, 91.

12. Mathewson, *Pitching in a Pinch*, 96–97, 127; Evers, *Touching Second*, 168–69.

13. Evers, *Touching Second*, 171.

14. *NYW*, June 11, 1911; *NYP*, June 11, 1911; *NYTR*, June 11, 1911; *NYT*, June 11, 1911; *SL*, June 24, 1911; *CT*, June 11–14, 1911.

15. *NYT*, June 12–15, 1911; *NYP*, June 12–15, 1911; *NYW*, June 12–15, 1911; *NYTR*, June 12–15, 1911; *SL*, June 17, 1911.

16. *NYW*, June 15 and 16, 1911; *NYTR*, June 16, 1911; *NYT*, June 16, 1911; *NYP*, June 16, 1911.

17. *NYP*, June 17, 1911.

18. Ibid.; *NYW*, June 17 and 18, 1911; *NYTR*, June 17, 1911. Various sources have differing versions of when and how Raymond was suspended. Several say it occurred during the series with the Pirates, but Raymond started that game and pitched again in both Cincinnati and St. Louis.

19. McGraw, *Thirty Years*, 20; McGraw, *The Real McGraw*, 226.

20. McGraw, *Thirty Years*, 21–24. For a slightly different version see the January 1912 column by Sid Mercer in Arthur Raymond file, HOF.

21. This episode is taken from Ibid., 22–24.
22. Ibid., 19–20.
23. *NYW*, June 18, 1911; *NYT*, June 18, 1911; *NYTR*, June 18, 1911; *NYP*, June 18, 1911; *SL*, July 1, 1911.
24. *NYTR*, June 19, 1911; *NYP*, June 19, 1911; *NYT*, June 19 and 20, 1911; *NYW*, June 19, 1911.
25. *SL*, June 24, 1911.
26. *NYW*, June 21–23, 1911; *NYTR*, June 21–23, 1911; *NYT*, June 21–23, 1911; *NYP*, June 22 and 23, 1911.
27. *CT*, June 20, 1911.
28. *NYTR*, Jun 24, 1911; *NYW*, June 24, 1911; *NYP*, June 24, 1911; *NYT*, June 24, 1911.
29. *NYP*, June 24, 1911; *NYW*, June 24, 1911; *NYTR*, June 28, 1911.
30. *NYW*, June 25, 1911; *NYT*, June 25, 1911; *NYP*, June 25, 1911.
31. *NYT*, June 25, 1911; *SL*, July 1, 1911; *CT*, June 21 and 22, 1911.
32. *NYT*, June 26–28, 1911; *NYTR*, June 28, 1911; *NYW*, June 28, 1911; *NYP*, June 28, 1911. The writers occasionally referred to Brooklyn as the Dodgers in 1911 but much more often as the Superbas.
33. *NYTR*, June 28, 1911; *NYP*, June 25, 1911; *NYW*, June 28, 1911.
34. *NYP*, June 25, 1911.
35. Ibid., June 29, 1911; *NYT*, June 29, 1911; *NYW*, June 29, 1911.
36. *NYT*, June 29, 1911; *NYP*, June 29, 1911; *NYW*, June 29, 1911.
37. *NYTR*, June 30, 1911; *NYT*, June 30, 1911; *NYP*, June 30, 1911.
38. *NYP*, July 1, 1911; *NYT*, July 1, 1911; *NYTR*, July 1, 1911; *NYW*, July 1, 1911.
39. *NYT*, July 1, 1911.
40. Ibid., July 2, 1911; *NYTR*, July 1; *CT*, July 1, 1911.
41. *NYT*, July 2, 1911; *CT*, July 2 and 3, 1911.
42. *SL*, July 8, 1911.

12: July: Dog Days

1. *NYT*, July 3 and 4, 1911; *CT*, July 3–7, 1911; *SLPD*, July 2–7, 1911.
2. Unless otherwise indicated, this account of the heat wave is drawn from *NYT*, July 3–13; *NYTR*, July 3–13, 1911; *NYW*, July 3–13, 1911.
3. Drehle, *Triangle*, 12–13; *SLPD*, July 5, 1911.
4. Drehle, *Triangle*, 14–15.
5. *NYW*, July 13, 1911.
6. Ibid., July 2 and 3, 1911; *NYTR*, July 2 and 3, 1911; *NYT*, July 2 and 3, 1911; *NYS*, July 2, 1911; *CT*, July 2–6, 1911; *SLPD*, July 3, 1911.
7. *NYT*, July 4 and 5, 1911; *NYW*, July 4 and 5, 1911; *NYTR*, July 4 and 5, 1911; *NYP*, July 4 and 5, 1911.
8. *NYT*, July 5, 1911; *NYW*, July 5, 1911; *NYTR*, July 5, 1911; *NYS*, July 5, 1911.
9. *NYTR*, July 6, 1911; *NYW*, July 6, 1911; *NYS*, July 6, 1911; *NYT*, July 6, 1911.
10. Mathewson, *Pitching in a Pinch*, 29–30, 220–21.
11. Gabriel Schechter, *Victory Faust: The Rube Who Saved McGraw's Giants* (Los Gatos, CA, 2004), 52.
12. *NYP*, July 7, 1911; *NYTR*, July 7, 1911; *NYW*, July 7, 1911; *NYS*, July 7, 1911; *NYT*, July 7, 1911; *CT*, July 7, 1911; *SLPD*, July 6, 1911.
13. *NYW*, July 8 and 9, 1911; *NYT*, July 8 and 9, 1911; *NYTR*, July 8 and 9, 1911; *NYS*, July 8 and 9, 1911; *NYP*, July 8 and 9, 1911; *CT*, July 8 and 9, 1911.

14. *NYT*, July 11, 1911; *NYTR*, July 11, 1911; *NYP*, July 9 and 11, 1911; *NYS*, July 11, 1911; *NYW*, July 11, 1911; *CT*, July 11, 1911.
15. *NYP*, July 13, 1911; *SN*, July 13, 1911.
16. *NYTR*, July 10, 1911.
17. *NYW*, July 9, 1911.
18. Ibid.
19. *NYTR*, July 10, 1911; *SLPD*, July 21, 1911.
20. *NYTR*, July 11, 1911; *NYP*, July 11, 1911; *NYT*, July 11, 1911; *NYW*, July 11, 1911; *CT*, July 11, 1911.
21. *NYW*, July 11, 1911; *NYT*, July 11, 1911.
22. *NYT*, July 11, 1911; *NYW*, July 11 and 14, 1911; *NYP*, July 11, 1911; Mathewson, *Pitching in a Pinch*, 18.
23. This account is drawn from the *SLPD*, July 11, 1911.
24. *NYP*, July 12, 1911; *NYT*, July 12, 1911; *NYTR*, July 12, 1911; *NYW*, July 12, 1911; *NYS*, July 12, 1911.
25. *NYTR*, July 13, 1911; *NYT*, July 13, 1911, *NYW*, July 13, 1911; *NYS*, July 13, 1911.
26. *NYT*, July 14, 1911; *NYS*, July 14, 1911; *NYTR*, July 14, 1911; *NYW*, July 14, 1911; *CT*, July 14, 1911. This game offers a good example of the inconsistencies in scorekeeping mentioned earlier. The *Times* credited the Giants with four stolen bases, Clarke with five hits, and the Pirates with twelve hits. Other papers and *Sporting Life* recorded only two stolen bases for New York, ten hits for Pittsburgh, and gave Drucke an error on one of Clarke's at bats.
27. *NYS*, July 15, 1911; *NYT*, July 16, 1911.
28. *NYTR*, July 15 and 16, 1911; *NYT*, July 15 and 16, 1911; *NYS*, July 15 and 16, 1911; *NYW*, July 16, 1911; *CT*, July 16, 1911. The Chicago paper gave the Cubs nine errors; most New York papers and *Sporting Life* gave them eight.
29. Kaese, *Boston Braves*, 122–24; *NYT*, July 17, 1911; *CT*, July 17 and 18, 1911. Miller complained that he had not received a promised pay raise.
30. *NYT*, July 18 and 19, 1911; *CT*, July 20, 1911.
31. *NYT*, July 19, 1911; *NYTR*, July 19, 1911; *NYW*, July 19, 1911.
32. *NYT*, July 20, 1911; *NYTR*, July 20, 1911; *NYW*, July 20, 1911; *NYS*, July 20, 1911.
33. *NYT*, July 20 and 22, 1911; *NYTR*, July 22, 1911; *NYW*, July 22, 1911; *CT*, July 22, 1911.
34. *NYTR*, July 22 and 24, 1911; *NYS*, July 23, 1911; *SLPD*, July 22, 1911.
35. *NYTR*, July 22, 1911; *NYT*, July 22, 1911; *NYS*, July 23, 1911.
36. Ibid., July 29, 1911.
37. *SL*, July 15, 1911.
38. *NYW*, July 22–24, 1911; *NYT*, July 22, 1911; *NYTR*, July 22, 1911; *NYP*, July 23 and 24, 1911; *SLPD*, July 23, 1911. O'Toole had pitched in three games with the Reds in 1908 but did not stick with the team.
39. *NYP*, July 9, 1911; *NYS*, July 21, 1911; *NYTR*, July 21, 1911; *NYT*, July 21, 1911; *NYW*, July 21, 1911; *SLPD*, July 11, 12, and 21, 1911.
40. Quoted in *SLPD*, July 21, 1911.
41. *NYT*, July 22, 1911; *NYTR*, July 22, 1911; *NYP*, July 22, 1911; *NYS*, July 22, 1911; *NYW*, July 22, 1911.
42. *NYT*, July 23, 1911; *NYTR*, July 23, 1911; *NYP*, July 23, 1911; *NYS*, July 23, 1911; *NYW*, July 23, 1911.
43. *NYTR*, July 24, 1911.
44. Ibid., July 24–26, 1911; *NYT*, July 24–26, 1911; *NYW*, July 25 and 26, 1911; *NYS*, July 25 and 26, 1911.
45. *NYT*, July 26 and 27, 1911; *NYW*, July 26 and 27, 1911; *NYS*, July 26 and 27, 1911; *NYTR*, July 26 and 27, 1911; *NYP*, July 27, 1911; *CT*, July 27, 1911; *SLPD*, July 27, 1911.

46. *NYTR*, July 28 and 29, 1911; *NYT*, July 28 and 29, 1911; *NYS*, July 28 and 29, 1911; *NYW*, July 28 and 29, 1911; *SLPD*, July 29, 1911.

47. *NYW*, July 30 and 31, 1911; *NYS*, July 30 and 31, 1911; *NYT*, July 30 and 31, 1911; *NYTR*, July 30 and 31, 1911.

48. *NYTR*, Aug. 1, 1911; *NYT*, Aug. 1, 1911; *NYW*, Aug. 1, 1911; *NYH*, Aug. 1, 1911; *NYS*, Aug. 1, 1911.

49. Mathewson, *Pitching in a Pinch*, 127–28; *SL*, Aug. 19, 1911.

50. *NYS*, July 30, 1911.

51. This section is drawn from Schechter, *Victory Faust*, 4–9; Ritter, *Glory of Their Times*, 93–95; John J. McGraw, "Big League Stuff," *Liberty* magazine (date unknown), 20. I have been unable to find the dates for the three-part Liberty articles. McGraw's version of his experience with Faust in *Liberty* is unreliable because it simply does not fit the facts of the games and dates. He does not even mention Faust in his book on baseball. Snodgrass's version in Ritter has several errors, and the version in Alexander, *McGraw*, 155, has some inaccuracies as well. Schechter has the fullest account but no documentation. See his book, pp. 60–62, for the four different versions of how and where Faust connected with the Giants in St. Louis.

52. Schechter, *Victory Faust*, 7; *SLPD*, July 30, 1911.

53. Mathewson, *Pitching in a Pinch*, 248–49. Schechter, *Victory Faust*, 8, notes that the *SLPD* said Faust was not present, while the *New York Globe* said he was present every day but refused to put on a uniform for the game. The local version seems more convincing. None of the New York papers I consulted mentioned him.

54. Mathewson, *Pitching in a Pinch*, 236.

13: JINXES AND CHARMS

1. *NYH*, Aug. 2, 1911; *NYTR*, Aug. 2, 1911; *SLPD*, Aug. 7, 1911.

2. *NYT*, Aug. 3 and 12, 1911; *NYH*, Aug. 3 and 12, 1911; *NYTR*, Aug. 3, 1911; *NYW*, Aug. 3, 1911; *NYP*, Aug. 3, 1911; *NYS*, Aug. 3, 1911.

3. *NYT*, Aug. 3, 5, and 17, 1911; *NYH*, Aug. 3 and 5, 1911; *NYTR*, Aug. 3, 1911; *NYW*, Aug. 3, 5, and 17, 1911; *NYP*, Aug. 3 and 5, 1911; *NYS*, Aug. 3 and 5, 1911; *SN*, Aug. 10, 1911.

4. *NYS*, Aug. 5 and 6, 1911; *NYT*, Aug. 5 and 6, 1911; *NYH*, Aug. 5 and 6, 1911; *NYTR*, Aug. 5 and 6, 1911; *NYW*, Aug. 5 and 6, 1911; *CT*, Aug. 5, 1911.

5. *NYS*, Aug. 6, 1911; *NYT*, Aug. 6, 1911; *SN*, Aug. 10, 1911; *CT*, Aug. 6 and 7, 1911; Carmichael, *My Greatest Day*, 136.

6. *NYW*, Aug. 8, 1911; *NYH*, Aug. 8, 1911; *NYT*, Aug. 8, 1911; *NYTR*, Aug. 8, 1911; *NYS*, Aug. 8, 1911; *NYP*, Aug. 8, 1911; *CT*, Aug. 8, 1911; Carmichael, *My Greatest Day*, 137–38.

7. Carmichael, *My Greatest Day*, 138.

8. *NYW*, Aug. 9 and 10, 1911; *NYTR*, Aug. 9 and 10, 1911; *NYH*, Aug. 9 and 10, 1911; *NYT*, Aug. 9 and 10, 1911; *NYS*, Aug. 9 and 10, 1911; *CT*, Aug. 9 and 10, 1911.

9. *SN*, Aug. 10, 1911; *SLPD*, Aug. 11, 1911.

10. *NYS*, Aug. 6, 1911.

11. *NYH*, Aug. 12, 1911; *NYT*, Aug. 12, 1911.

12. *NYW*, Aug. 12, 1911; *NYT*, Aug. 12, 1911; *NYH*, Aug. 12, 1911; *NYTR*, Aug. 12, 1911; *NYS*, Aug. 12, 1911.

13. Schechter, *Victory Faust*, 65–66.

14. *NYH*, Aug. 13, 1911; *NYW*, Aug. 13, 1911; *NYT*, Aug. 13, 1911; *NYP*, Aug. 13, 1911; *NYTR*, Aug. 13, 1911; *NYS*, Aug. 13, 1911.

15. *NYT*, Aug. 13, 1911; *NYH*, Aug. 13, 1911; Mathewson, *Pitching in a Pinch*, 249.

16. *NYT*, Aug. 15, 1911; *NYP*, Aug. 15, 1911; *NYW*, Aug. 15, 1911; *NYH*, Aug. 15, 1911; *NYS*, Aug. 15, 1911; *NYTR*, Aug. 15, 1911.

17. *NYT*, Aug. 15 and 16, 1911; *NYH*, Aug. 15 and 16, 1911; CT, Aug. 12, 1911; *NYW*, Aug. 16, 1911; *SLPD*, July 12, 1911.

18. Schechter, *Victory Faust*, 72.

19. *NYS*, Aug. 16, 1911.

20. *NYH*, Aug. 17, 1911; *NYT*, Aug. 17, 1911; Hittner, *Honus Wagner*, 205–206.

21. Mathewson, *Pitching in a Pinch*, 245–47; McGraw, "Big League Stuff," 20.

22. *NYT*, Aug. 17, 1911; *NYH*, Aug. 17, 1911; *NYTR*, Aug. 17, 1911; *NYW*, Aug. 17, 1911; *NYS*, Aug. 17, 1911; *SN*, Aug. 24, 1911.

23. *NYT*, Aug. 18, 1911; *NYW*, Aug. 18, 1911; *NYH*, Aug. 18, 1911; *NYTR*, Aug. 18, 1911; *NYS*, Aug. 18, 1911; *NYP*, Aug. 18, 1911.

24. *NYS*, Aug. 18, 1911; CT, Aug. 18, 1911.

25. *NYTR*, Aug. 19, 1911; Schechter, *Victory Faust*, 78–79.

26. *NYS*, Aug. 20, 1911; *NYT*, Aug. 19 and 20, 1911; *NYW*, Aug. 19 and 20, 1911; *NYH*, Aug. 20, 1911; *NYTR*, Aug. 20, 1911.

27. *NYT*, Aug. 20, 1911; *NYH*, Aug. 20, 1911; *NYTR*, Aug. 20, 1911; *NYW*, Aug. 20, 1911; *NYS*, Aug. 20, 1911.

28. *NYP*, Aug. 20, 1911.

29. Schechter, *Victory Faust*, 81.

30. *NYH*, Aug. 21 and 28, 1911; *SN*, Aug. 24, 1911.

31. *NYT*, Aug. 22, 1911; *NYH*, Aug. 22, 1911; *NYTR*, Aug. 22, 1911; *NYW*, Aug. 22, 1911; *NYS*, Aug. 22, 1911.

32. *NYS*, Aug. 22, 1911; *NYH*, Aug. 22 and 23, 1911; Schechter, *Victory Faust*, 83.

33. CT, Aug. 22, 1911.

34. *NYT*, Aug. 23, 1911; *NYH*, Aug. 23, 1911; *NYP*, Aug. 23, 1911; *NYS*, Aug. 23, 1911; *NYW*, Aug. 23, 1911; *NYTR*, Aug. 23, 1911.

35. CT, Aug. 23, 1911.

36. Ibid., Aug. 24, 1911; *NYT*, Aug. 24, 1911; *NYTR*, Aug. 24, 1911; *NYH*, Aug. 24, 1911; *NYS*, Aug. 24, 1911; *NYW*, Aug. 24, 1911.

37. *NYW*, Aug. 24, 1911; *NYT*, Aug. 24, 1911.

38. *NYT*, Aug. 25, 1911.

39. Ibid.; *NYP*, Aug. 25, 1911; *NYTR*, Aug. 25, 1911; *NYH*, Aug. 25, 1911; *NYS*, Aug. 25, 1911; *NYW*, Aug. 25, 1911.

40. *NYH*, Aug. 26, 1911; *NYT*, Aug. 26, 1911; *NYTR*, Aug. 26, 1911; *NYS*, Aug. 26, 1911; *NYP*, Aug. 26, 1911.

41. *NYT*, Aug. 27, 1911; *NYTR*, Aug. 27, 1911; *NYP*, Aug. 27, 1911; *NYS*, Aug. 27, 1911; CT, Aug. 25 and 26, 1911.

42. *NYP*, Aug. 27, 1911; *NYT*, Aug. 27, 1911.

43. *NYH*, Aug. 28, 1911.

44. Ibid., Aug. 29, 1911; *NYT*, Aug. 29, 1911; *NYTR*, Aug. 29, 1911; *NYP*, Aug. 29, 1911; *NYS*, Aug. 29, 1911; *SLPD*, Aug. 29 and 30, 1911.

45. *SLPD*, Aug. 12, 1911.

46. Ibid., Aug. 28, 1911; *NYT*, Aug. 30, 1911; Simon, *Deadball Stars*, 346; *NYP*, Oct. 22, 1911. Unlike Raymond, however, Sallee showed up for spring training in 1912 a changed man and revived his career.

47. *NYT*, Aug. 30, 1911; *NYS*, Aug. 30, 1911; *NYH*, Aug. 30, 1911; *NYTR*, Aug. 30, 1911.

48. *NYTR*, Aug. 31, 1911; *NYT*, Aug. 31 and Sept. 1, 1911; *NYS*, Sept. 1, 1911; *NYH*, Sept. 1, 1911.

49. Mathewson, *Pitching in a Pinch*, 32–35.
50. *SLPD*, Aug. 13, 24, and 25, 1911.
51. *NYH*, Sept. 1, 1911; *CT*, Sept. 1, 1911.
52. *SN*, Aug. 31, Sept. 7, 1911; *SL*, Sept. 2, 1911.
53. *NYH*, Aug. 28, 1911; *NYS*, Sept. 1, 1911.
54. Schechter, *Victory Faust*, 92–94.

14: September: Road Warriors

1. *SL*, Sept. 23, 1911.
2. Ibid., Sept. 30, 1911.
3. Mathewson, *Pitching in a Pinch*, 126–27; *SL*, Sept. 30, 1911; *SN*, Sept. 7, 1911.
4. *SL*, August 26, Sept. 2, 1911.
5. *NYTR*, Sept. 2, 1911; *SN*, Sept. 2, 1911; *NYP*, Sept. 2, 1911; *NYS*, Sept. 2, 1911; *SL*, Sept. 9, 1911.
6. *NYTR*, Sept. 2, 1911; Mathewson, *Pitching in a Pinch*, 30.
7. *NYS*, Sept. 3, 1911; *NYP*, Sept. 3, 1911; *NYT*, Sept. 3, 1911; *SN*, Sept. 3, 1911; *NYTR*, Sept. 3, 1911.
8. Mathewson, *Pitching in a Pinch*, 50–51, 113; McGraw, *Thirty Years*, 103–104; Ritter, *Glory of Their Times*, 16.
9. Ritter, *Glory of Their Times*, 13–16.
10. *CT*, Sept. 2 and 3, 1911; David W. Anderson, "Kitty Bransfield," SABR Baseball Biography Project.
11. *CT*, Sept. 18, 1911; *NYT*, Sept. 4, 1911; *NYTR*, Sept. 4, 1911.
12. *NYT*, Sept. 5, 1911; *SN*, Sept. 5, 1911; *NYTR*, Sept. 5, 1911; *NYP*, Sept. 5, 1911; *NYS*, Sept. 5, 1911.
13. *NYS*, Sept. 8, 1911; *SN*, Sept. 8, 1911; *NYT*, Sept. 8, 1911; *NYTR*, Sept. 8, 1911; *CT*, Sept. 7, 1911.
14. Schechter, *Victory Faust*, 97–98.
15. *NYP*, Sept. 9, 1911; *NYTR*, Sept. 9, 1911; *SN*, Sept. 9, 1911; *NYT*, Sept. 9, 1911.
16. Schechter, *Victory Faust*, 99–100.
17. *NYTR*, Sept. 10, 1911; *NYT*, Sept. 10, 1911; *SN*, Sept. 10, 1911; *NYS*, Sept. 10, 1911; *SL*, Sept. 16, 1911.
18. *NYTR*, Sept. 10, 1911.
19. Ibid., Sept. 12, 1911; *NYS*, Sept. 12, 1911; *SN*, Aug. 31 and Sept. 7, 1911. The *Times* of Sept. 12 says that Faust "dropped in suddenly from New York."
20. *SN*, Sept. 13, 1911; *NYS*, Sept. 13, 1911; *NYP*, Sept. 13, 1911; *NYTR*, Sept. 13, 1911; *NYT*, Sept. 13, 1911.
21. *SN*, Sept. 13, 1911; *NYS*, Sept. 13, 1911; *NYP*, Sept. 13, 1911; *NYTR*, Sept. 13, 1911; *NYT*, Sept. 13, 1911.
22. *SN*, Sept. 13 and 14, 1911; *NYS*, Sept. 14, 1911.
23. Mathewson, *Pitching in a Pinch*, 235–36.
24. Ibid., 236; *NYTR*, Sept. 14, 1911; *NYS*, Sept. 14, 1911; *SN*, Sept. 14, 1911; *NYT*, Sept. 14, 1911; Schechter, *Victory Faust*, 108.
25. Schechter, *Victory Faust*, 108–110.
26. *NYS*, Sept. 15, 1911; *SN*, Sept. 15, 1911; *NYTR*, Sept. 15, 1911; *NYT*, Sept. 15, 1911.
27. *NYTR*, Sept. 15, 1911; *NYS*, Sept. 15, 1911; *SN*, Sept. 15 and 16, 1911; *SN* clipping, Doyle file, HOF.
28. *CT*, Sept. 16, 1911; *SN*, Sept. 15, 1911; *SL*, Sept. 9, 1911.
29. *NYTR*, Sept. 15, 1911; Mathewson, *Pitching in a Pinch*, 51.

30. *NYTR*, Sept. 17, 1911; *SN*, Sept. 17, 1911; *NYS*, Sept. 17, 1911; *NYT*, Sept. 17, 1911; *NYP*, Sept. 17, 1911; *SN*, Sept. 21, 1911.

31. *SN*, Sept. 17, 1911; *CT*, Sept. 17, 1911.

32. *SN*, Sept. 17 and 20, 1911.

33. Ibid., Sept. 21, 1911.

34. Ibid., Sept. 20, 1911; *SL*, Oct. 10, 1908.

35. *SN*, Sept. 18 and 20, 1911; *NYS*, Sept. 20, 1911.

36. *NYTR*, Sept. 19, 1911; *SN*, Sept. 19, 1911; *NYT*, Sept. 19, 1911; *NYS*, Sept. 19, 1911; *NYP*, Sept. 19, 1911.

37. *NYTR*, Sept. 20, 1911; *NYS*, Sept. 20, 1911; *SN*, Sept. 20, 1911; *NYP*, Sept. 20, 1911; *NYT*, Sept. 20, 1911; *CT*, Sept. 20, 1911.

38. *NYS*, Sept. 20, 1911; *SN*, Sept. 20, 1911.

39. *SN*, Sept. 21, 1911; *NYP*, Sept. 18, 1911; *SLPD*, Sept. 11, 1911.

40. *SN*, Sept. 21, 1911; *NYP*, Sept. 21, 1911; *NYTR*, Sept. 21, 1911; *NYT*, Sept. 21, 1911; *NYS*, Sept. 21, 1911.

41. *SN*, Sept. 22, 1911; *NYS*, Sept. 22, 1911.

42. *NYP*, Sept. 22, 1911; *SN*, Sept. 22, 1911; *NYS*, Sept. 22, 1911; *NYTR*, Sept. 22, 1911; *NYT*, Sept. 22, 1911.

43. *NYTR*, Sept. 22, 1911; *SN*, Sept. 22, 1911.

44. *SN*, Sept. 23, 1911; McGraw, *Thirty Years*, 197–98; *NYTR*, Sept. 23, 1911.

45. *SN*, Sept. 23, 1911; *NYTR*, Sept. 23, 1911; *NYS*, Sept. 23, 1911; *NYP*, Sept. 23, 1911.

46. Schechter, *Victory Faust*, 124–25; Mathewson, *Pitching in a Pinch*, 251. Mathewson said it was the eleventh inning, not the tenth, and that he was in the dugout when McGraw sent him out to fetch Faust.

47. *SN*, Sept. 23, 1911; Mayer, *Christy Mathewson*, 216.

48. Mathewson, *Pitching in a Pinch*, 252.

49. *SLPD*, Sept. 24, 1911. Schechter, *Victory Faust*, 126–30 reproduces the entire article.

50. *NYTR*, Sept. 24, 1911; *NYT*, Sept. 24, 1911; *NYP*, Sept. 24, 1911; *NYS*, Sept. 24, 1911; *SN*, Sept. 24, 1911.

51. *NYTR*, Sept. 24, 1911; *NYT*, Sept. 24, 1911; *SN*, Sept. 24 and 25, 1911; *NYP*, Sept. 25, 1911; *CT*, Sept. 24, 1911; Schechter, *Victory Faust*, 133–35.

52. *NYP*, Sept. 24, 1911.

53. *SLPD*, Sept. 21, 1911.

54. Ibid., Sept. 25, 1911; *NYTR*, Sept. 25, 1911; *NYT*, Sept. 25, 1911; *NYS*, Sept. 25, 1911; *SN*, Sept. 25, 1911; Schechter, *Victory Faust*, 137.

55. *NYTR*, Sept. 26, 1911; *NYT*, Sept. 26, 1911; *NYS*, Sept. 26, 1911; *SN*, Sept. 26 and 28, 1911; *NYP*, Sept. 26, 1911.

56. *SN*, Sept. 23, 1911; *NYS*, Sept. 25, 1911.

57. *NYTR*, Sept. 25 and 27, 1911; Unidentified clipping, Sept. 27, 1911, Charles Faust folder, HOF.

58. Unidentified clipping, Sept. 27, 1911, Faust folder, HOF; Schechter, *Victory Faust*, 142–43; *CT*, Sept. 27 and 28, 1911.

59. *NYT*, Sept. 28, 1911; *NYP*, Sept. 28 and 29, 1911; *NYTR*, Sept. 28 and 29, 1911; *SN*, Sept. 28 and 29, 1911; *NYS*, Sept. 28 and 29, 1911; *CT*, Sept. 29, 1911. Cole's promising career was cut short in 1915 when he was diagnosed with tuberculosis; he died the following year.

60. *NYTR*, Sept. 29, 1911; *CT*, Sept. 29, 1911; McGraw, *Thirty Years*, 198–99.

61. *NYTR*, Sept. 30, 1911; *SN*, Sept. 29 and 30, 1911.

62. *NYTR*, Sept. 30, 1911; *NYT*, Sept. 30, 1911.

63. *NYP*, Oct. 1, 1911; *NYT*, Oct. 1, 1911; *SN*, Oct. 1, 1911; *NYS*, Oct. 1, 1911; *NYTR*, Oct. 1, 1911.

15: October: Sweet Victory

1. *NYT*, Oct. 2, 1911; *NYP*, Oct. 2, 1911; *NYS*, Oct. 2, 1911; *NYTR*, Oct. 2, 1911.
2. *NYP*, Oct. 3, 1911; *NYTR*, Oct. 3, 1911; *NYT*, Oct. 3, 1911; *NYS*, Oct. 3, 1911. Some scorers labeled Carey's single an error by Herzog, which gave Wiltse a one-hitter.
3. *NYT*, Oct. 4, 1911; *NYS*, Oct. 4, 1911; *NYP*, Oct. 4, 1911; *NYTR*, Oct. 4, 1911.
4. *NYP*, Oct. 4, 1911.
5. Ibid., Oct. 5, 1911; *NYTR*, Oct. 5, 1911; *NYT*, Oct. 5, 1911; *NYS*, Oct. 5, 1911.
6. Schechter, *Victory Faust*, 159; *SL*, Oct. 14, 1911.
7. *SL*, Oct. 14, 1911.
8. Young, *John Tortes "Chief" Meyers*, 85.
9. Ibid., 86–87; *NYT*, Sept. 18, 1911; *NYTR*, Oct. 9, 1911.
10. *NYT*, Oct. 6, 1911; *NYS*, Oct. 6, 1911; *NYTR*, Oct. 6, 1911; *SL*, Oct. 14, 1911.
11. *NYT*, Oct. 7, 1911; *NYS*, Oct. 7 and 8, 1911; *NYTR*, Oct. 7, 1911.
12. *NYT*, Oct. 8, 1911; *NYS*, Oct. 8, 1911; *NYTR*, Oct. 8, 1911.
13. *NYT*, Oct. 8, 1911; *NYTR*, Oct. 8, 1911; *NYS*, Oct. 8, 1911.
14. *NYT*, Oct. 10, 1911; *NYP*, Oct. 10, 1911; *NYS*, Oct. 10, 1911; *NYTR*, Oct. 10, 1911; *SL*, Sept. 16 and 30, Oct. 21, 1911. The *Press*, the *Times*, and *Sporting Life* listed one stolen base, the *Sun* and *Tribune* four. While such discrepancies were common, rarely was the spread this dramatic.
15. *NYS*, Oct. 13, 1911; *NYTR*, Oct. 13, 1911.
16. *NYS*, Oct. 13, 1911; *NYTR*, Oct. 13, 1911; *NYT*, Oct. 13, 1911.
17. *NYT*, Oct. 12, 1911.
18. *NYTR*, Oct. 9, 1911.
19. *SL*, Oct. 21, 1911.

16: World Series: The Long and Short of It

1. *NYP*, Oct. 14, 1911.
2. Alexander, *McGraw*, 156–57; *SN*, Oct. 12, 1911.
3. McGraw, *The Real McGraw*, 235.
4. *NYS*, Oct. 6, 1911; *SN*, Oct. 12, 1911. For a variety of predictions on the outcome see *SN*, Oct. 12, 1911.
5. *NYS*, Oct. 9, 1911; *NYT*, Oct. 12, 1911.
6. *NYT*, Oct. 13, 1911; *NYTR*, Oct. 13, 1911.
7. *NYT*, Oct. 9, 1911; Selter, *Ballparks of the Deadball Era*, 135–37.
8. *SL*, Sept. 30, 1911.
9. *NYT*, Oct. 8, 1911; *NYS*, Oct. 8, 1911.
10. *SL*, Oct. 7, 1911; *NYS*, Oct. 12, 1911.
11. *SN*, Oct. 12, 1911.
12. *NYT*, Oct. 14, 1911; *NYP*, Oct. 14, 1911; *NYS*, Oct. 14, 1911; *NYTR*, Oct. 14, 1911. The *Press* and *Tribune* have photos of the real and bogus tickets.
13. *NYS*, Oct. 14, 1911.
14. *NYP*, Oct. 14, 1911.
15. Ibid.; *NYT*, Oct. 14, 1911; *NYTR*, Oct. 14, 1911; *NYS*, Oct. 14, 1911.
16. Lieb, *Baseball as I Have Known It*, 33–34.
17. *NYS*, Oct. 15, 1911.
18. *SL*, Oct. 28, 1911.
19. *NYS*, Oct. 15, 1911; *NYTR*, Oct. 15, 1911. Unless otherwise indicated, the pregame description is drawn from these sources.

20. Game details are drawn from *NYTR*, Oct. 15, 1911; *NYT*, Oct. 15, 1911; *NYS*, Oct. 15, 1911; *SL*, Oct. 28, 1911.

21. Mathewson, *Pitching in a Pinch*, 16.

22. *NYT*, Oct. 15 and 16, 1911.

23. Ibid., Oct. 16, 1911; *NYP*, Oct. 16, 1911; *NYS*, Oct. 16, 1911; *NYTR*, Oct. 16, 1911.

24. *NYT*, Oct. 16, 1911; *NYS*, Oct. 16, 1911; *NYTR*, Oct. 16, 1911.

25. *NYTR*, Oct. 17, 1911; *NYT*, Oct. 17, 1911; *NYS*, Oct. 17, 1911; *NYP*, Oct. 17, 1911; *SL*, Oct. 28, 1911. The account of game two is drawn from these sources.

26. *NYS*, Oct. 17, 1911; *NYT*, Oct. 17, 1911.

27. *NYS*, Oct. 18, 1911; *NYTR*, Oct. 18, 1911; Young, *John Tortes "Chief" Meyers*, 89–94. Young says the photos of the two men were taken before the first game, but both papers cited here mention it being done prior to the third game.

28. *NYT*, Oct. 18, 1911; *NYS*, Oct. 18, 1911; *NYP*, Oct. 18, 1911; *NYTR*, Oct. 18, 1911; *SL*, Oct. 28, 1911. The account of the game is drawn from these sources.

29. *NYT*, Oct. 18, 1911.

30. *NYTR*, Oct. 18, 1911; *NYS*, Oct. 18, 1911; *NYP*, Oct. 18, 1911. Blanche McGraw offered yet another version of what happened: "A third strike came over and down. Baker swung and missed. The ball hit the heel of Chief Meyers' glove, bounced away and to the dugout, exactly like the Mickey Owen passed ball thirty years later. The umpire ruled that Baker had ticked the ball. . . . Baker hit the next pitch out of the park." McGraw, *The Real McGraw*, 235–36.

31. Lieb, *Baseball as I Have Known It*, 82.

32. *SL*, Oct. 28, 1911.

33. *NYT*, Oct. 18, 1911; Mathewson, *Pitching in a Pinch*, 149–50.

34. *SL*, Oct. 28, 1911.

35. *NYTR*, Oct. 18, 1911.

36. Ibid., Oct. 19–24, 1911; *NYT*, Oct. 19–24, 1911; *NYS*, Oct. 19–24, 1911; *NYP*, Oct. 19–24, 1911; *SL*, Oct. 28, 1911. This section is drawn from these sources.

37. *NYP*, Oct. 19, 1911.

38. *SL*, Oct. 28, 1911.

39. *NYS*, Oct. 19, 1911.

40. *NYT*, Oct. 19, 1911.

41. *NYS*, Oct. 22, 1911.

42. *NYTR*, Oct. 23, 1911.

43. Ibid., Oct. 25, 1911; *NYT*, Oct. 25, 1911; *NYS*, Oct. 25, 1911; *NYP*, Oct. 25, 1911. The account of this game is drawn from these sources.

44. *NYT*, Oct. 25, 1911.

45. *NYTR*, Oct. 25, 1911.

46. Young, *John Tortes "Chief" Meyers*, 94.

47. *NYTR*, Oct. 26, 1911; *NYT*, Oct. 26, 1911; *NYS*, Oct. 26, 1911; *NYP*, Oct. 26, 1911. The account of this game is drawn from these sources.

48. *NYTR*, Oct. 26, 1911; *NYP*, Oct. 26, 1911; *NYT*, Oct. 26, 1911; *NYS*, Oct. 26, 1911.

49. *NYTR*, Oct. 27, 1911.

50. Ibid., Oct. 26, 1911.

51. *NYP*, Oct. 26, 1911.

52. *NYTR*, Oct. 26 and 27, 1911; *SL*, Nov. 4, 1911.

53. *NYTR*, Oct. 27, 1911; *NYT*, Oct. 27, 1911; *NYP*, Oct. 27, 1911; *NYS*, Oct. 27, 1911. The account of this game is drawn from these sources.

54. *NYP*, Oct. 27, 1911; *NYTR*, Oct. 27, 1911.

55. Ritter, *Glory of Their Times*, 172–73; McGraw, *Thirty Years*, 199; *NYT*, Oct. 27, 1911; *SL*, Oct. 28, 1911.
56. *NYH*, Nov. 5, 1911.
57. Young, *John Tortes "Chief" Meyers*, 102.
58. Mathewson, *Pitching in a Pinch*, 278–79.
59. *NYT*, Oct. 27, 1911.
60. Alexander, *McGraw*, 158–59.

17: THE McGRAW DYNASTIES

1. Alexander, *McGraw*, 166–67; Simon, *Deadball Stars*, 50; *SL*, Dec. 7, 1912. The stairway still exists even though the Polo Grounds does not, and was rededicated in 2014.
2. For McGraw's later career see Alexander, *McGraw*, 158–324.
3. McGraw, *The Real McGraw*, 324–26.
4. *NYT*, June 3, 1932.
5. McGraw, *The Real McGraw*, 190.
6. Ibid., 214, 325.
7. Ibid.; Alexander, *McGraw*, 307; *NYT*, June 4, 1932; Durso, *Days of McGraw*, 215; Graham, *McGraw of the Giants*, 260–61.
8. *NYT*, June 4, 1932.
9. Ibid.
10. Ibid.
11. Ibid., June 5, 1932.
12. Ritter, *Glory of Their Times*, 90–91.
13. Alexander, *McGraw*, 310–14.
14. *St. Louis Star-Times*, Feb. 27, 1934, clipping in McGraw file, HOF.
15. Mack to Murray, Feb. 25, 1943, Red Murray file, HOF.

EPILOGUE: THE PARADE PASSING

1. *NYT*, Sept. 10, 1912; *NYW*, Sept. 10, 1912, clippings in Raymond file, HOF; Simon, *Deadball Stars*, 343.
2. Schechter, *Victory Faust*, 184–234.
3. Ibid., 235–55; Charles Faust death certificate, Faust file, HOF.
4. Robinson, *Mathewson*, 178–79; Thomson and Brown, *Three Finger*, 153–54; Mayer, *Christy Mathewson*, 302–304.
5. Robinson, *Mathewson*, 190–95; Mayer, *Christy Mathewson*, 304–305.
6. Robinson, *Mathewson*, 203–215; Mayer, *Christy Mathewson*, 306–307.
7. Simon, *Deadball Stars*, 56–57.
8. Ibid.
9. Ibid.; *Baseball*, Nov. 1908, 24.
10. Simon, *Deadball Stars*, 48.
11. Unidentified clippings, Beals Becker folder, HOF.
12. Ibid., 52; *SN*, Sept. 29, 1948, clipping in Devlin file, HOF. Fred Lieb wrote the obituary for *SN*.
13. Simon, *Deadball Stars*, 76; McGraw, *The Real McGraw*, 275; *SN*, Feb. 15, 1950; Undated *Saturday Evening Post* clipping in Fletcher file, HOF; Unidentified clipping, Jan. 8, 1946, Fletcher file, HOF.

14. Simon, *Deadball Stars*, 68; Four unidentified clippings, Crandall file, HOF; James Crandall death certificate, Crandall file, HOF.
15. Simon, *Deadball Stars*, 69–70; Unidentified clipping, Jan. 22, 1953, Herzog file, HOF; Unidentified clipping, April 16, 1936, Herzog file, HOF.
16. Simon, *Deadball Stars*, 69–70; Alexander, *McGraw*, 196–204.
17. Simon, *Deadball Stars*, 70; Unidentified clippings, Herzog file, HOF.
18. Unidentified clipping, Herzog file, HOF; Charles Herzog death certificate, Herzog file, HOF.
19. Bill Nowlin (ed.), *The Miracle Braves of 1914: Boston's Original Worst-to-First World Series Champions* (SABR Digital Library, February 17, 2014), 46–47.
20. Ibid., 47; Joshua Devore death certificate, Devore file, HOF; Unidentified clippings, Devore file, HOF.
21. "Louis Drucke," Baseball-Reference.com; Unidentified clippings, Drucke file, HOF.
22. *SN*, March 14, 1956, clipping in Merkle file, HOF; Simon, *Deadball Stars*, 62. Fred Lieb wrote the obituary in *SN*.
23. Frederick Merkle death certificate, Merkle file, HOF; *SN*, March 14, 1956.
24. Simon, *Deadball Stars*, 74.
25. Ibid.; John J. Murray death certificate, Murray file, HOF.
26. Simon, *Deadball Stars*, 54; Hooks Wiltse to Ernest Lanigan, Nov. 25, 1953, Wiltse file, HOF.
27. *Syracuse Herald-Journal*, July 26, 1954, clipping in Wiltse file, HOF; Wiltse to Lanigan, Nov. 25, 1953; George LeRoy Wiltse death certificate, Wiltse file, HOF.
28. George Wiltse, "Memory Lane," Wiltse file, HOF.
29. Unidentified clippings, Wilson file, HOF; Charles Smutny to Joseph E. Simenic, Dec. 11, 1962, Wilson file, HOF; Arthur Wilson death certificate, Wilson file, HOF. Wilson's daughter signed the death certificate.
30. Mike Cooney, "Grover Hartley," SABR Biography Project.
31. Cooney, "Grover Hartley."
32. Ibid.
33. Bill Lamb, "Gene Paulette," SABR Biography Project.
34. Ibid.; Eugene Edward Paulette death certificate, Paulette file, HOF.
35. McGraw, *Thirty Years*, 180–81; Unidentified list of Bridwell's career, Bridwell file, HOF.
36. Bridwell to Doyle, Nov. 23, 1966, Bridwell file, HOF; Ritter, *Glory of Their Times*, 124; Albert H. Bridwell death certificate, Bridwell file, HOF.
37. Young, *John Tortes "Chief" Meyers*, 104–67.
38. Ibid., 167–87.
39. Ibid., 187–90.
40. Ibid., 190–93.
41. Ibid., 193–99.
42. Ibid., 199–205; *Riverside, California, Press*, July 27, 1971, clipping in Meyers file, HOF.
43. Young, *John Tortes "Chief" Meyers*, 204.
44. Ward Morehouse column, unidentified clipping, Snodgrass file, HOF.
45. Ibid.; Simon, *Deadball Stars*, 66.
46. Simon, *Deadball Stars*, 60.
47. McGraw, *The Real McGraw*, 318.
48. Ibid., 318–19; Simon, *Deadball Stars*, 60; *Daily News* clipping, Larry Doyle file, HOF.
49. *New York Journal-American*, Dec. 21, 1964, clipping in Doyle file, HOF; *New York Herald-Tribune*, Dec. 4, 1954, clipping in Doyle file, HOF.

50. Unidentified clipping, March 16, 1974, Doyle file, HOF; Unidentified clipping, undated, Doyle file, HOF.
51. Mansch, *Rube Marquard*, 102–185; Richard W. Marquard form, Rube Marquard file, HOF. This form was apparently sent to many old-time players by the Hall of Fame to collect basic information on them.
52. Mansch, *Rube Marquard*, 183–200.
53. Ibid., 121–27.
54. Ibid., 127, 133, 141–42, 148–51, 171–72, 178, 181, 188–90.
55. Ibid., 200; *Daily News*, Sept. 23, 1963, clipping in Doyle file, HOF.
56. Mansch, *Rube Marquard*, 204–221.

APPENDIX A: THE 1908 BRUSH COMMITTEE REPORT

1. Anderson, *More Than Merkle*, 210, 215, 220; Board Meeting, 334; Klem, "Jousting with McGraw," 54. The emphasis is mine. Although Anderson did research at the Hall of Fame, he evidently did not run across the minutes of the board meetings. Instead he relied on Klem's article in Collier's, written some four decades later.
2. Seymour, *Golden Age*, 283–85; Alexander, *McGraw*, 135.
3. Alexander, *McGraw*, 135; Fleming, *Unforgettable Season*, 156–57.
4. For discussions of this episode see Seymour, *Golden Age*, 283–84; Alexander, *McGraw*, 139–40; Anderson, *More Than Merkle*, 210–23; Murphy, *Crazy '08*, 284–87.
5. Adjourned Meeting Proceedings, 145–46. Anderson, *More Than Merkle*, 213, called the appointment of Brush "outrageous in view of the facts of the case." What he calls facts were in fact allegations.
6. The full report is in ibid., 146–52.
7. Murphy, *Crazy '08*, 286–87.

Bibliography

GENERAL

Allen, Lee. *The American League Story* (New York, 1962).

——. *The Cincinnati Reds* (Kent, Ohio, 2006 [1948]).

——. *The National League Story* (New York, 1965 [1961]).

Alexander, Charles C. *Our Game* (New York, 1991).

Anderson, David. *More than Merkle* (Lincoln, Neb., 2000).

Baldassaro, Lawrence and Richard Johnson. *The American Game: Baseball and Ethnicity* (Carbondale, Ill., 2002).

Bartlett, Arthur. *Baseball and Mr. Spalding* (New York, 1951).

Bell, Christopher. *Scapegoats: Baseballers Whose Careers Are Marked by One Fateful Play* (Jefferson, N.C., 2002).

Benson, Michael. *Ballparks of North America* (Jefferson, N.C., 1989).

Bevis, Charlie. *Sunday Baseball: The Major Leagues' Struggle to Play Baseball on the Lord's Day, 1876–1934* (Jefferson, N.C., 2003).

Brown, Warren. *The Chicago Cubs* (New York, 1946).

Burk, Robert F. *Never Just a Game: Players, Owners, & American Baseball to 1920* (Chapel Hill, 1994).

Burns, John M. *Thunder at Sunrise: A History of the Vanderbilt Cup, the Grand Prize and the Indianapolis 500, 1904–1916* (Jefferson, N.C., 2006).

Carmichael, John P. *My Greatest Day in Baseball* (New York, 1945).

Cash, Jon David. *Before They Were the Cardinals* (St. Louis, 2002).

Chadwick, Bruce and David Spindel. *The Chicago Cubs: Memories and Memorabilia of the Wrigley Wonders* (New York, 1994).

——. *The Giants: Memories and Memorabilia from a Century of Baseball* (New York, 1993).

Cooper, John Milton Jr. *Pivotal Decades: The United States, 1900–1920* (New York, 1990).

Deford, Frank. *The Old Ball Game* (New York, 2005).

Dewey, Donald. *The Tenth Man: The Fan in Baseball History* (New York, 2004).

Dickey, Glenn. *The History of National League Baseball since 1876* (New York, 1982).

Dickson, Paul. *Baseball's Greatest Quotations* (New York, 1992).

Durso, Joseph. *The Days of Mr. McGraw* (Englewood Cliffs, N.J., 1969).

Dworkin, James B. *Owners Versus Players: Baseball and Collective Bargaining* (Boston, 1981).

Ehrenberg, Lewis. *Steppin' Out: New York Nightlife and the Transformation of American Culture, 1890–1930* (Chicago, 1981).

Enright, Jim. *Baseball's Great Teams: The Chicago Cubs* (New York, 1975).

Evers, John J. and Hugh S. Fullerton. *Touching Second: The Science of Baseball* (Chicago, 1910).

Fleming, G. H. ed. *The Unforgettable Season* (New York, 1982).

Foster, John B. *Spalding's Official Base Ball Record* (New York, 1907–1932).

Frommer, Harvey. *New York City Baseball* (New York, 1980).

Gentile, Derek. *The Complete Chicago Cubs* (New York, 2002).

Gershman, Michael. *The Evolution of the Ballpark* (New York, 1993).

Gilbert, Thomas. *Dead Ball* (New York, 1996).

Gold, Eddie and Art Ahrens. *The Golden Era Cubs* (Chicago, 1985).

Graham, Frank. *The Brooklyn Dodgers: An Informal History* (New York, 1945).

——. *McGraw of the Giants* (New York, 1944).

——. *The New York Giants* (New York, 1952).

Hardy, James D. Jr. *The New York Giants Base Ball Club: The Growth of a Team and a Sport, 1870 to 1900* (Jefferson, N.C., 1996).

Haywood, Charles. *General Alarm: A Dramatic Account of Fires and Firefighting in America* (New York, 1967).

Honig, Donald. *The Chicago Cubs* (New York, 1991).

Hynd, Noel. *The Giants of the Polo Grounds* (New York, 1988).

Jordan, David. *The Athletics of Philadelphia* (Jefferson, N.C., 1999).

Kaese, Harold. *The Boston Braves* (New York, 1948).

Kahn, James M. *The Umpire Story* (New York, 1953).

Kuklick, Bruce. *To Everything a Season: Shibe Park and Urban Philadelphia* (Princeton, 1991).

Liberman, Noah. *Glove Affairs: The Romance, History, and Tradition of the Baseball Glove* (New York, 2003).

Lieb, Fred. *The Baltimore Orioles* (New York, 1955).

——. *Baseball as I Have Known It* (New York, 1977).

——. *The Pittsburgh Pirates* (1948).

Lieb, Fred and Stan Baumgartner. *The Philadelphia Phillies* (Kent, Ohio, 2009 [1948]).

Lowry, Philip. *Green Cathedrals* (Cooperstown, N.Y., 1986).

Major League Baseball. *The Baseball Encyclopedia* (New York, 1980).

Morris, Lloyd. *Incredible New York* (New York, 1951).

Morris, Peter. *Level Playing Fields: How the Groundskeeping Murphy Brothers Shaped Baseball* (Lincoln, Neb., 2007).

Murphy, Cait. *Crazy '08: How a Cast of Cranks, Rogues, Boneheads, and Magnates Created the Greatest Year in Baseball History* (New York, 2008).

Powers, Albert Theodore. *The Business of Baseball* (Jefferson, N.C., 2003).

Rader, Benjamin. *Baseball: A History of America's Game* (Urbana, Ill., 1993).

Reidenbaugh, Lowell. *100 Years of National League Baseball 1876–1976* (St. Louis, 1976).

Riess, Steven A. *Touching Base: Professional Baseball and American Culture in the Progressive Era* (Urbana, Ill., 1999).

Ritter, Lawrence S. *The Glory of Their Times* (New York, 1966).

——. *Lost Ballparks: A Celebration of Baseball's Legendary Fields* (New York, 1992).

Sante, Luc. *Low Life: Lures and Snares of Old New York* (New York, 1991).

Selter, Ronald M. *Ballparks of the Deadball Era* (Jefferson, N.C., 2008).

Seymour, Harold. *Baseball: The Early Years* (New York, 1960).

——. *Baseball: The Golden Age* (New York, 1989 [1971]).

Shannon, Bill and George Kalinsky. *The Ballparks* (New York, 1975).

Simon, Tom (ed.). *Deadball Stars of the National League* (Washington, 2004).

Smizik, Bob. *The Pirates* (New York, 1991).

Snyder, John. *Cubs Journal: Year by Year and Day by Day with the Chicago Cubs Since 1876* (Cincinnati, 2005).

Spink, Alfred. *The National Game* (St. Louis, 1910).

Stein, Leon. *The Triangle Fire* (Ithaca, 2001 [1962]).

Sullivan, Mark. *Our Times: The War Begins, 1909–1914* (New York, 1932).

Thornley, Stew. *Land of the Giants: New York's Polo Grounds* (Philadelphia, 2000).

Voigt, David Quentin. *American Baseball: From the Gentleman's Sport to the Commissioner System* (University Park, 1983).

Von Drehle, David. *Triangle: The Fire That Changed America* (New York, 2003).

——. *American Baseball: From the Commissioners to Continental Expansion* (University Park, 1983).

White, G. Edward. *Creating the National Pastime: Baseball Transforms Itself* (Princeton, 1998).

Biographies and Memoirs

Alexander, Charles C. *John McGraw* (Lincoln, 1988).

Anson, Adrian. *A Ball Player's Career* (New York, 1900).

Bartlett, Arthur. *Baseball and Mr. Spalding* (New York, 1951).

Bogen, Gil. *Johnny Kling: A Baseball Biography* (Jefferson, N.C., 2006).

——. *Tinker, Evers and Chance: A Triple Biography* (Jefferson, N.C., 2003).

Browning, Reed. *Cy Young* (Amherst, Mass., 2000).

DeValeria, Dennis and Jeanne Burke DeValeria. *Honus Wagner: A Biography* (Pittsburgh, 1995).

Graham, Frank. *McGraw of the Giants: An Informal Biography* (New York, 1944).

Hageman, William. *Honus: The Life and Times of a Baseball Hero* (Champaign, Ill., 1996).

Hartley, Michael. *Christy Mathewson* (Jefferson, N.C., 2004).

Hittner, Arthur D. *Honus Wagner: The Life of Baseball's "Flying Dutchman"* (Jefferson, N.C., 1996).

Mack, Connie. *My Sixty-six Years in the Big Leagues* (Philadelphia, 1950).

Mansch, Larry D. *Rube Marquard: The Life and Times of a Baseball Hall of Famer* (Jefferson, N.C., 1998).

Mathewson, Christy. *Pitching in a Pinch* (New York, 1912).

Mayer, Ronald A. *Christy Mathewson: A Game-by-Game Profile of a Legendary Pitcher* (Jefferson, N.C., 1993).

McGraw, Blanche. *The Real McGraw* (New York, 1953).

McGraw, John J. *How to Play Baseball* (New York, 1914).

——. *My Thirty Years in Baseball* (New York, 1923).

Murdock, Eugene C. *Ban Johnson: Czar of Baseball* (Westport, Conn., 1982).

Rice, Grantland. *The Tumult and the Shouting: My Life in Sport* (New York, 1954).

Robinson, Ray. *Matty: An American Hero* (New York, 1993).

Schechter, Gabriel. *Victory Faust: The Rube Who Saved McGraw's Giants* (Los Gatos, Cal., 2000).

Seib, Philip. *The Player: Christy Mathewson, Baseball and the American Century* (New York, 2003).

Smiles, Jack. *Ee-Yah: The Life and Times of Hughie Jennings* (Jefferson, N.C., 2005).

Thomson, Cindy, and Scott Brown. *Three Finger: The Mordecai Brown Story* (Lincoln, Neb., 2006).

Young, William A. *John Tortes "Chief" Meyers: A Baseball Biography* (Jefferson, N.C., 2012).

ARTICLES

Ahrens, Arthur. "Tinker v. Matty: A Study in Rivalry," *Baseball Research Journal* (1974), 14–19.

"Baseball Has Changed Some in Thirty Years, Says John J. McGraw," *Literary Digest*, LXI (May 10, 1919), 96–101.

Bradley, Hugh. "McGraw," *American Mercury*, XXVI (August 1932), 461–69.

Bulger, Bozeman. "Genius of the Game III," *Saturday Evening Post*, CCIV (July 7, 1932), 24, 26, 59–62.

Burkholder, Edwin V. "How Charley Faust Won a Pennant for the Giants," *Reader's Digest*, LVII (October 1950), 79–82.

Busch, Thomas S. "Searching for Victory: The Story of Charles Victor[y] Faust," *Baseball Research Journal* (1983), 82–85.

Creamer, Robert. "John McGraw, Manager," *Sports Illustrated*, LIV (April 13, 1981), 61.

"Czar McGraw," *Literary Digest*, XLVIII (June 20, 1914), 1499–1502.

Dubbs, Greg. "Jim Sheckard: A Live Wire in the Dead-Ball Era," *Baseball Research Journal* (1980), 134–39.

Edelman, Rob. "Mike Donlin, Movie Actor," *Baseball Research Journal* (2001), 73–75.

Evans, Billy. "Why the Giants Win," *Harper's Weekly*, LIX (July 25, 1914), 82.

"The Exciting Close of the Baseball Season," *Current Literature*, LI (November 1911), 468–70.

"Fortunes Made in Baseball," *Literary Digest*, XLV (July 20, 1912), 119–25.

Foster, John B. "John T. Brush: A Power in Baseball," *Baseball Magazine*, III (May 1909), 17–20.

———. "The Magnificent New Polo Grounds," *Baseball Magazine*, VII (October 1911), no pagination.

Fox, Edward Lyell. "Baseball as the Players See It," *Outing*, LVIII (May 1911), 143–53.

———. "What is Inside Baseball?" *Outing*, LVIII (July 1911), 488–97.

Fullerton, Hugh S. "How the Ball Players of the Big Leagues Live and Act When Off the Diamond," *American Magazine* (June 1911), 321–29.

———. "Watch His Arm! The Science of Coaching," *American Magazine* (August 1911), 463–72.

———. "The Right and Wrong of Baseball," *American Magazine* (October 1911), 724–30.

———. "Freak Plays that Decide Baseball Championships," *American Magazine*, LXXIV (May 1912), 114–21.

Hopper, James. "Training with the Giants," *Everybody's Magazine* (June 1909), 743–49.

Kavanaugh, Jack. "Bugs Raymond," *Baseball Research Journal* (1996), 125–27.

Klem, William J. with William J. Slocum. "Jousting with McGraw," *Colliers* (April 7, 1951), 30–31, 50–51, 54.

Koerper, Henry C. "The Catcher was a Cahuilla: A Remembrance of John Tortes Meyers (1880–1971)," *Journal of California and Great Basin Anthropology*, vol. 24, no. 1 (2004), 21–40.

Lane, F. C. "The Greatest Problem in the National Game: The Critical Situation in Sunday Baseball," *Baseball Magazine*, VII (October 1911), 21–28.

"The Manager's Part in Making a Ball Team," *Literary Digest*, XLVI (March 29, 1913), 731–34.

"Marquard and His Predecessors," *Literary Digest*, XLV (July 6, 1912), 36–38.

Mathewson, Christy. "Why We Lost Three World's Championships," *Everybody's*, XXXI (October 1914), 537–47.

McGraw, John. "Baseball Changes of Thirty Years," *Baseball Magazine*, XXII (May 1919), 11–14.

——. "Big League Stuff: A Series of Final Revelations," *Liberty Magazine* (date unknown), part 1, 7–11; part 2, 18–22; part 3, 28–31, 34.

——. "Rooting to Victory," *Collier's*, XLVII (July 15, 1911), 18.

"McGraw Collects," *Literary Digest*, LIV (May 5, 1917), 1358.

McNeill, Don. "That Man McGraw," *Coronet*, XXXVI (June 1954), 77.

"Matty," *Literary Digest*, XLV (November 16, 1912), 932–33.

Morse, J. D. "Changes in the World of Baseball," *Baseball Magazine*, VII (September 1911), 39–42.

Sangree, Allan. "No More War in Baseball," *Baseball Magazine*, VII (August 1911), 21–28, and (September 1911), 21–29.

Schwartz, John. "From One Ump to Two," *Baseball Research Journal* (2001), 85–86.

Thompson, Dick. "Matty and His Fadeaway," *Baseball Research Journal* (1996), 93–96.

"Why Matty Lasts," *Literary Digest*, XLVII (August 1913), 299–300.

NEWSPAPERS

Chicago Tribune
New York American
New York Evening Journal
New York Herald
New York Press
New York Sun
New York Times
New-York Tribune
New York World
St. Louis Post-Dispatch
Sporting Life
Sporting News

WEBSITES

Baseball-Reference.com
SABR.org

MANUSCRIPT MATERIALS

Giamatti Research Center, National Baseball Hall of Fame. Cooperstown, NY.

Index

A Note on the Author

Maury Klein is renowned as one of the finest historians of American business and economy. He is the author of many books, including *A Call to Arms: Mobilizing America for World War II*; *The Power Makers: Steam, Electricity, and the Men Who Invented Modern America*; and *Rainbow's End: The Crash of 1929*. He is professor emeritus of history at the University of Rhode Island. Klein lives in Saunderstown, Rhode Island.